ORIGINS

CANADIAN HISTORY TO CONFEDERATION

ORIGINS

CANADIAN HISTORY TO CONFEDERATION

R. DOUGLAS FRANCIS/RICHARD JONES/DONALD B. SMITH

SECOND EDITION

Holt, Rinehart and Winston of Canada, Limited
Toronto   Montreal   Orlando   Fort Worth   San Diego
Philadelphia   London   Sydney   Tokyo

Canadian Cataloguing in Publication Data

Francis, R.D. (R. Douglas), 1944-
   Origins: Canadian history to Confederation

2nd ed.
Companion volume to: Destinies: Canadian history since Confederation.
Includes bibliographical references.
ISBN 0-03-922862-2

1. Canada – History – To 1763 (New France).
2. Canada – History – 1763-1867.　　I. Jones,
Richard, 1943-　　.　　II. Smith, Donald B., 1946-
III. Title.

FC161.F73 1992　　　971.06　　　　C91-094405-9
FC1026.F73 1992

Editorial Director: Heather McWhinney
Acquisitions Editor: Sheila Malloch
Developmental Editor: Irene Cox
Editorial Assistant: Deborah Jarret-Chase
Director of Publishing Services: Steve Lau
Editorial Manager: Liz Radojkovic
Editorial Co-ordinator: Marcel Chiera
Production Manager: Sue-Ann Becker
Production Assistant: Denise Wake
Copy Editor: Darlene Zeleney
Cover and Interior Design: John Zehethofer
Typesetting and Assembly: Compeer Typographic Services Ltd.
Printing and Binding: John Deyell Company

Cover: *Mekinac River and Lake, C.E.,* by Alfred Worsley Holstock. Courtesy of the Royal Ontario Museum, Toronto, Canada.

♾ This book was printed in Canada on acid-free paper.

1 2 3 4 5　　　96 95 94 93 92

For our children:
Marc, Myla, and Michael Francis
Marie-Noëlle, Stéphanie, Serge-André, and Charles-Denis Jones
David and Peter Smith

A small part of Canada's future

Preface

Origins and *Destinies* sketch the history of Canada from the beginning of human occupation to the present. The purpose of both volumes is to outline how this immense country (the second largest in the world) came to be, to explain how its regions developed, and to relate the common history of its diverse population. Throughout the two volumes, we have reviewed regional developments while keeping Canada as a whole the focal point of the study.

This project began in 1983, when we, as professors of Canadian history, felt the need to synthesize and supplement the older texts, most of which were conceived and written in the 1940s and 1950s, and many of which were still in use. We wanted an up-to-date history for first-year university and college students, one that would incorporate the new historical research of the last quarter-century — the social as well as the political and economic accounts of our past.

Origins, the first volume, tells the history of pre-Confederation Canada — of the Native people and of the coming of the Norse, the Portuguese, the Spanish, the Basques, and particularly the French and the British, who eventually established permanent European settlements. Anyone seeking to understand our diversity today must first examine the pre-Confederation era, when our present regional personalities were first formed in Atlantic Canada, in the St. Lawrence River Valley, on the Great Lakes, on the Red River, and on the Pacific Coast.

Destinies, our second volume, takes Canada's story from 1867 to the present day. Unlike the United States, our country did not experience a uniform wave of expansion westward from the Atlantic seaboard. In many cases, the European communities in Canada began as pockets of settlement, independent of one another, at different times, and with people of different European backgrounds. In *Destinies*, we show how Canada came to take the transcontinental form it did, and how the various groups within its boundaries came together to create one country. We point out the various regional, ethnic, and social tensions that have shaped our nation's history, as well as the means by which these differences were resolved.

The text is designed with the student of introductory Canadian history in mind. Each chapter treats a major topic, theme, or period, and includes subsections to aid students in organizing the material. Through the use of fully documented quotations from works by Canadian historians and of up-to-date annotated bibliographical references at the end of each chapter, we identify the major historical writings on the events covered. We provide a "Related Readings" section at the end of each chapter. This section identifies useful articles in the third edition of R. Douglas Francis and Donald B. Smith, eds., *Readings in Canadian History*, Volume 1, *Pre-Confederation*, and Volume 2, *Post-Confederation*.

Because historians are not impartial observers, but themselves participants in the world around them, their work necessarily mirrors their own time. Current concerns, conventions, and perceptions are reflected in the very issues that historians select for study. In this second edition of *Origins* and *Destinies*, we have included a series of boxed inserts that highlight some of the debates and differences of opinion that have arisen among historians over such questions. In addition, we have added "time lines" to help students follow the chronological sequence of events. Finally, all of the chapters, as well as the bibliographical sections at the end of each, have been updated for this edition.

viii

Students seeking more extensive bibliographical information are directed to the following works. Important annotated bibliographical guides to the study of Canadian history include D.A. Muise, ed., *A Reader's Guide to Canadian History*, vol. 1, *Beginnings to Confederation* (Toronto, 1982); J.L. Granatstein and Paul Stevens, eds., *A Reader's Guide to Canadian History*, vol. 2, *Confederation to the Present* (Toronto, 1982); Carl Berger, ed., *Contemporary Approaches to Canadian History* (Toronto, 1987); and John Schultz, ed., *Writing about Canada: A Handbook for Modern Canadian History* (Scarborough, Ontario, 1990). An invaluable bibliography (without annotation) is Paul Aubin and Louis-Marie Côté's *Bibliographie de l'histoire du Québec et du Canada/Bibliography of the History of Quebec and Canada*, published (in several volumes) by the Institut québécois de recherche sur la culture in Quebec City. Easy to use, it contains more than 100 000 titles, all published between 1946 and 1985. Current bibliographies of the most recent publications are published in each issue of the *Canadian Historial Review* and the *Revue d'histoire de l'Amérique française*.

Acknowledgements

In preparing the first edition of *Origins*, we benefited enormously from the advice and suggestions of many Canadian historians. We would like to thank Gratien Allaire of the Faculté Saint-Jean, University of Alberta; Phillip Buckner of the University of New Brunswick; Jean Daigle of the Université de Moncton; Olive Dickason of the University of Alberta; John Dickinson of the Université de Montréal; Robin Fisher of Simon Fraser University; Gerald Friesen of the University of Manitoba; James Hiller of Memorial University of Newfoundland; Douglas Leighton of the University of Western Ontario; Ken Munro of the University of Alberta; Colin Read of the University of Western Ontario; and Phyllis Senese of the University of Victoria, who each read and provided us with criticisms of individual chapters within their respective research areas. On several specific issues we benefited from the comments of Michel Granger of Brooks, Alberta (on the Acadians); James Helmer of the University of Calgary (on recent archaeological findings); Ingeborg Marshall of Portugal Cove, Newfoundland (on the Beothuk); Bea Medicine of the University of Calgary (on the Native peoples' view of their origins); Dale Miquelon of the University of Saskatchewan (on recent historical writing on the economic impact of the conquest of New France); Keith Regular of Elkford, B.C. (on Newfoundland); Daniel Richter of Dickinson College, Carlisle, Pennsylvania (on the Iroquois Confederacy).

With regard to the first edition of *Destinies*, we thank the following people, who read chapters of the manuscript and offered valuable criticism and advice: Douglas Baldwin of Acadia University; Gail Cuthbert-Brandt of Glendon College, York University; John English of the University of Waterloo; Gerald Friesen of the University of Manitoba; Jim Miller of the University of Saskatchewan; William Morrison of Brandon University; Howard Palmer of the University of Calgary; Margaret Prang of the University of British Columbia; John Thompson of McGill University; Keith Walden of Trent University; and William Westfall of York University.

The following historians read the manuscripts in their entirety for Holt, Rinehart and Winston. Although they did not always agree with our approach and interpretation, they offered very valuable suggestions for improving the final manuscripts. For *Origins*, we wish to thank Joseph Cherwinski of Memorial University of Newfoundland, Douglas Leighton of the University of Western Ontario, Olive Dickason of the University of Alberta, and Phyllis Senese of the University of Victoria. For *Destinies*, we thank William Acheson of the University of New Brunswick, Thomas Socknat of the University of Toronto, Donald Swainson of Queen's University, and Eric Sager of the University of Victoria.

For making the volumes of the first edition possible, we warmly thank Tony Luengo, formerly of Holt, Rinehart and Winston, who first accepted the proposal, and Tessa McWatt, for seeing it to completion. We are also indebted to Edie Franks, Editorial Co-ordinator, and to Wendy Jacobs, our copy-editor, as well as the others at Holt, Rinehart and Winston who were involved in the production of the original *Origins* and *Destinies*.

The office staff of the Department of History at the University of Calgary performed the heroic task of typing up many of the numerous drafts of the original manuscripts. Our thanks to Liesbeth von Wolzogen, Olga Leskiw, Marjory McLean, Jodi Steeves, and Joyce Woods, and to Barbara Nair for preparing the index for the first edition of *Origins*.

Douglas Francis wishes to thank Pat Kates and her staff in Secretarial Services at York University for typing drafts of his chapters of the original manuscripts during his sabbatical year, and the staff at McLaughlin College, York University, for providing him with office space and a pleasant atmosphere during that year.

With regard to the preparation of the second edition of *Origins* and *Destinies*, we thank Elizabeth Abbott and Laurel Sherrer of Chronicle Publications in Montreal for allowing us to look through illustrations collected for the *Chronicle of Canada* project. We thank the following individuals for their remarks on *Origins* and *Destinies*: Doug Baldwin at Acadia University; Sarah Carter at the University of Winnipeg; Olive Dickason at the University of Alberta; A. Ernest Epp at Lakehead University; R.H. Roy and Phyllis Senese, at the University of Victoria; and M. Brook Taylor at Mount Saint Vincent University. We are also grateful to Bob Beal for his notes on *Origins* and the first half of *Destinies*. Richard Jones wishes to thank Dr. E. Royle, head of the history department at the University of York in Heslington, England, for providing him with office space and tranquillity during a sabbatical year devoted largely to this project. John David Hamilton of Keswick, Ontario, and Mark Dickerson of the University of Calgary provided help specifically with Chapter 16, "Aboriginal Canada and the North since 1945," in *Destinies*. With regard to the preparation of *Origins*, we are very grateful to Jean Barman, University of British Columbia, for allowing us to see her new history of British Columbia, *The West beyond the West* (Toronto, 1991), before publication, and to Olive Dickason for permitting us to read the first draft of her new history of Amerindians in Canada. We also are very grateful to our Developmental Editors, Anne Venables Eigner and Irene Cox, as well as to Editorial Co-ordinator Marcel Chiera, Acquisitions Editor Sheila Malloch, and Editorial Director Heather McWhinney at Holt, Rinehart and Winston of Canada. We also thank Darlene Zeleney for a skilful copy edit. Any errors or important omissions in *Origins* and *Destinies*, of course, are our responsibility.

To our wives, Barbara, Lilianne, and Nancy, for their support throughout the preparation of both editions, we owe debts too enormous to describe.

x

PUBLISHER'S NOTE TO INSTRUCTORS AND STUDENTS

This textbook is a key component of your course. If you are the instructor of this course, you undoubtedly considered a number of texts carefully before choosing this as the one that will work best for your students and you. The authors and publishers of this book spent considerable time and money to ensure its high quality, and we appreciate your recognition of this effort and accomplishment. Please note the copyright statement.

If you are a student, we are confident that this text will help you to meet the objectives of your course. You will also find it helpful after the course is finished, as a valuable addition to your personal library.

Since we want to hear what you think about this book, please be sure to send us the stamped reply card at the end of the text. This will help us to continue publishing high-quality books for your courses.

xi

Contents

CONTENTS

xvi

xvii

CONTENTS

xx

List of Maps

xxi

List of Time Lines

The First Peoples

The first question of Canadian history remains unanswered: We still do not know for certain the place of origin of the first inhabitants of what was to become Canada. Indian elders argue that their ancestors emerged from this continent, while most archaeologists contend that early human beings migrated here from Siberia, although they debate among themselves when this migration first occurred. All experts do agree, however, that the original inhabitants of North America were living on this continent at least ten thousand years before the Europeans' arrival.

Origin of the First Peoples of North America

Many Canadian Indian elders accept as a spiritual truth—one revealed in sacred myths, dreams, and visions—that their ancestors originated in North America. They believe that their origin myths are as valid as those of the Judaeo-Christian tradition. Young Blackfoot-speaking children in present-day southern Alberta learn many stories about Napi or "Old Man," the creator of the world. Other Canadian tribes have their own explanations of the earth's beginnings, but the Blackfoot's is one of the most descriptive and most complete.

In the beginning, water covered the entire world. One day, the curious Napi decided to find out what lay below. He sent a duck, then an otter and a badger, but they all dived in vain. Then Napi asked a muskrat to plunge into the depths. He was gone so long that Napi feared he had drowned. At last the muskrat surfaced, holding a ball of mud. The Old Man took this lump and blew on it until it was transformed into the earth. Napi then piled up rocks to make mountains, dug out river and lake beds and filled them with water, and covered the plains with grass. He made all the birds and animals and, finally, people. He taught the men and women how to hunt and how to live. His work completed, the Old Man climbed a mountain and disappeared. Some say Napi's home is in the Rocky Mountains at the head of the Alberta river that bears his name— The Oldman.[1]

This spiritual belief is vital, for it offers a key to understanding the first peoples of Canada, their cultures, and their rights to the land. Canada is their homeland, the place where they have always lived. The aboriginal peoples' stories also contain moral lessons that reveal their worldview.

Modern scientists base their theories exclusively on observable data in the natural world. Their discussion of the origin of our species ignores the spiritual universe entirely—the Old Testament's Book of Genesis as well as the Blackfoots' story of Napi. On the basis of archaeological and geological evidence, scientists have argued that human beings did not evolve independently in the Americas, but that they migrated from Siberia.[2] Some archaeologists have recently posited that other migrations may have occurred by sea, principally to South America from across the Pacific.

Archaeologists believe that *Homo habilis*, the first direct ancestor of modern-day human beings, appeared nearly two million years ago in Africa. A more advanced form, *Homo erectus*, followed, approximately one and a half million years ago, in Asia, Africa, and Europe. About one hundred thousand years ago, *Homo sapiens neanderthalensis*, or Neanderthal man, emerged. Physical evidence of fully modern humans—that is, early hominid bones—dates back thirty-five to forty thousand years. All such evidence has been found in Africa, Asia, and Europe, not in the Americas. This leads most archaeologists to conclude that the human species originated outside of the Americas.

It is widely accepted among archaeologists that the early inhabitants of North America crossed over from Siberia during the last Ice Age. With so much of the earth's water locked in ice, sea levels dropped and the continental shelf became exposed in certain areas, one of which was the shallow region of the Bering Strait. From the strait a broad level plain, Beringia, emerged. This land bridge, which was more than thirteen hundred kilometres wide in places, existed throughout much of the period from seventy thousand to fourteen thousand years ago, when the cold climate was so dry that glaciers could not form.

Beringia is believed to have been a rich steppe-tundra with many species of large, cold-adapted grazing animals. It served as a highway for animals passing back and forth between Asia and the Americas. Many archaeologists believe that an ice-free corridor existed along the eastern slope of the Rockies at certain times, providing the animals—and, later, human beings—with a pathway southward. An ice-free coastal corridor may also have existed. Thus, human beings, after crossing the Beringia land bridge, may have travelled by water between the unglaciated pockets of land. Whether by foot or boat or a combination of the two, human beings gradually advanced southward. They spread throughout North, Central, and South America, eventually crossing more than fifteen thousand kilometres from Alaska to Patagonia, at the tip of South America. Canada's high Arctic was the last region to be populated, roughly four thousand years ago, as the ice retreated.

Three Archaeological Hypotheses

Scientists do not agree on when the migration from Siberia occurred. The three main schools of thought on the subject may be referred to as the radical, the liberal, and the conservative. Supporters of the radical theory contend that humans may have entered the Americas as early as 120 thousand to 80 thousand years ago. There is, however, no incontrovertible evidence of such an early arrival. More modest in their claims, the liberals argue that the first humans probably migrated to North America beginning about 30 000 B.C. The liberals support their hypotheses by referring to sites that, despite the absence of human skeletal remains, have good evidence of early human occupation. One such site is Monte Verde in Chile, South America, which, at its lowest level of occupation, has evidence of a simple stone technology dating back as far as thirty-three thousand years. In Canada, an exciting archaeological discovery was recently made in the northern Yukon's Bluefish caves, now believed to be the oldest known archaeological site in the country. Bone and stone artifacts indicate that the site may have been occupied fifteen to twenty thousand years ago.

3

The conservatives reject both the radical and the liberal views. They accept as evidence only those artifacts found in sealed deposits with organic matter that can be radiocarbon-dated. In addition, they limit themselves to distinctively styled artifacts—objects worked in much greater detail than those cited by the radicals and liberals. One example is the so-called fluted point, a stone projectile point with one or more flutes, or hollowed-out channels, that allowed for the attachment of the point to a wooden or bone shaft. The earliest known distinctive weapon or fluted point that the conservatives accept comes from Fort Rock cave in eastern Oregon and is radiocarbon-dated at approximately 11 000 B.C.

The discovery in 1927 of a fluted point between the ribs of an extinct bison excavated near the town of Folsom in northeastern New Mexico also provided concrete archaeological proof that humans had reached the Americas while the animals of the last Ice Age were still present. The Folsom point dates back to about 8500 B.C. A fluted-point site in central Nova Scotia, Debert, is contemporary with Folsom, as are two other Canadian sites—the Vermilion Lakes (in what is now Banff National Park) and Charlie Lake Cave, north of Fort St. John, British Columbia. All three sites confirm the presence of human beings at least ten thousand years ago.

About 8000 B.C. a drastic change in climate occurred in the northern hemisphere. For reasons still not fully understood, the great ice sheets (more than three kilometres thick) that once covered roughly 97 percent of present-day Canada began to melt. The run-off so raised the sea level that thousands of kilometres of coastline were flooded. The land bridge ceased to exist and the Bering Strait was created. The melting ice progressively freed up present-day Canada and the northern United States for human occupation.

The ecology changed as well. The absence of ice sheets in formerly glaciated territories meant that wind and rainfall patterns shifted. Forests replaced grasslands, and deserts developed. As habitats changed, some animals became extinct, especially such large grazing animals as mammoths (giant elephants), American camels, and a very large race of bison that foraged on the grasslands. Although the warmer climate opened up the northern half of the continent for settlement, it also contributed to the disappearance of many valuable game species in the period from twelve thousand to nine thousand years ago.

4

Civilizations of the Americas

About five thousand years ago the ice receded to approximately its present northern position and the climate became similar to today's. The Bering Strait attained its present width of approximately eighty kilometres, and land animals could no longer cross between Siberia and Alaska. People still made that journey, but no longer did they come from Asia's inland centres; they were sea-mammal hunters and fishers who traded across the strait. The Native American nations grew largely as a result of natural population increase, not as a result of migration.

In the millenium that followed, the Amerindian population of present-day Canada underwent major economic and social developments. The peak of technological and social complexity in the Americas, however, was achieved in present-day Mexico, Central America, and the Andes of Peru, where population densities were the highest on the two continents. Agriculture and rich sea resources formed the basis of these civilizations, since a permanent food supply (based for the agricultural communities on corn, beans, and squash) made a settled life possible. The first large, permanent communities appeared during the period from 3500 to 2000 years ago. They eventually became large centres with temples and other large structures such as plazas, chiefs' houses, and highways, all constructed with carved and painted stone.

The New World civilizations developed without the aid of Europe's domesticated animals—horses, oxen, and donkeys. The principle of the wheel was known (wheeled toys have been found in various parts of

Mexico), but the idea remained undeveloped, since without animals for transport (other than the dog and, in the Andes, the llama) these civilizations had little use for it. The New World also lacked ample supplies of usable copper and tin, which would have allowed for the replacement of stone tools with more efficient ones. The Peruvians did make a few tools from metal washed down in the streams, but in Mexico and the Yucatan there is evidence of only stone tools.

Despite the absence of the wheel and of metal tools, the natives made remarkable advances and achievements. The Maya in Central America developed a sophisticated system of mathematics, applying the concept of zero five hundred years before the Hindus did. The Maya were also skilled in astronomy, and worked out a year of 365 days as well as the cycle of the planet Venus. They were able to calculate eclipses and they recorded their calculations in a writing system that was both pictographic and phonetic. In the Andes, irrigation was highly developed, as was the building of bridges and roads. The Incas erected stone walls using enormous rocks cut to fit so tightly that a knife blade could not be pushed between two blocks. They also did metalwork of the highest quality, in gold and silver.

5

THE MOUND BUILDERS

The ancient Indian agriculturalists of the Americas carried corn from its place of origin (probably southern Mexico) and adapted it to their own various climates. About two thousand years ago, farming—and, with it, settled life—replaced gathering and hunting in certain sections of the present-day United States. The so-called Mound Builders of the Ohio River valley were one of the most interesting groups affected by the agricultural revolution. They constructed gigantic sculptured earthworks in geometric designs, sometimes in the shape of humans, birds, or serpents. Some of these constructions were nearly twenty-five metres high. The Mound Builders' culture evolved slowly, but, by roughly two thousand years ago, it had developed considerable complexity.

Archaeologists have located thousands of mounds used as burial sites and have excavated several earthen-walled enclosures, including one enormous fortification with a circumference of more than five kilometres, enclosing the equivalent of fifty modern city blocks. The Mound Builders participated in an extensive trading network. Among the artifacts found in the mounds of the Ohio peoples, there have been large ceremonial blades chipped from obsidian (a volcanic glass) from deposits in what is now Yellowstone National Park in Wyoming; embossed breastplates, ornaments, and weapons made from copper nuggets from the Great Lakes; decorative objects cut from mica sheets from the southern Appalachians; and ornaments made from shells and shark and alligator teeth from the Gulf of Mexico.

The Mound Builders' culture declined about 500 A.D., due perhaps to attacks by other tribes or to severe changes in climate that undermined agriculture. Another similar culture from farther to the west, one based on intensive agriculture, replaced that of the Mound Builders. Centred around present-day St. Louis, it extended over most of the Mississippi watershed, from Wisconsin to Louisiana and from Oklahoma to Tennessee. From 700 A.D. to 1000 A.D. the influence of this Mississippian culture was felt to the east, among the less technologically advanced Indian tribes. Indeed, it transformed those societies. The Iroquoian-speaking tribes of the Lower Great Lakes and the St. Lawrence Valley adopted the agricultural traditions of the Mound Builders and the Mississippians.

POPULATION GROWTH

6   Agriculture could support a larger population than could hunting and gathering, as the cultivation of as little as 1 percent of the land greatly increased the food supply. Recent estimates of the aboriginal population of the Americas in the mid-fifteenth century run as high as one hundred million people, or approximately one-sixth of the human race at that time. It is believed that the population north of Mexico may have reached ten million before European contact. Native populations achieved such numbers because they lived in a relatively disease-free zone, and many tribes, including the Iroquoians living in present-day southern Ontario and southwestern Quebec, had domesticated high-yield cereals and tubers, which allowed them to feed a large population. Approximately half a million people lived on the land that was to become Canada, roughly half of them along the Pacific coast and in present-day southern Ontario, the principal population centres.

The Europeans who came to the Americas were entering two continents that, in some areas, had populations as high as those of their homelands. The Europeans reduced these American populations drastically, however, by unintentionally bringing with them diseases that the natives of the Americas had never before experienced. The natives' ancestors had travelled through an Arctic environment in which many of the diseases found in temperate and tropical climates did not survive. Moreover, the migrating groups were biologically too small to sustain those diseases. Consequently, the native population lacked defences against contagious diseases such as smallpox and measles. Alfred Crosby, a biological historian, wrote that, "In theory, the initial appearance of these diseases is as certain to have set off deadly epidemics as dropping lighted matches into tinder is certain to cause fires."[3] The death rates after European contact in some areas of the Americas reached 90–95 percent. By the early twentieth century the entire population of Amerindians in Canada and the United States was less than one million, or 10 percent of the population that was present at the moment of European contact (according to the generally accepted estimate).

Classifying Canada's Amerindian Population

Canada's Amerindian population has been classified on the basis of three distinct categories: linguistic, tribal, and cultural. Each (particularly the first two) is less than fully satisfactory. A division according to linguistics reveals that Canada today contains eleven separate indigenous language families. One of these is Eskimo-Aleut, which includes the language spoken by the Inuit. There are ten Indian language families. A language from one family differs as much from that of another as English does from Chinese; within families, languages are related to each other in the same way that English is related to, say, Dutch.

Ethnologist Michael Foster has classified Canada's first languages. Seven of the ten Indian language families (Salishan, Tsimshian, Haidan, Wakashan, Tlingit, Kutenaian, and Athapaskan) are found in British Columbia. The Siouan-speaking group is found only on the prairies and in the foothills of the Rockies. The Iroquoian speakers live in eastern Canada. The Algonquian (or Algonkian) linguistic family, the largest group, extends from the Atlantic coast to the Rockies. Throughout the Yukon and the Northwest Territories and the northern sections of the four western provinces live speakers of Athapaskan languages. As nearly as can be determined, fifty-three distinct languages are spoken in Canada today, and there were probably more in the past. It is believed that slightly less than half the current aboriginal population have retained knowledge of their mother tongue.

This linguistic classification of the Amerindians unfortunately leads to the linking together of widely desperate tribes that had nothing in common except their language family, and to the separation of neighbouring groups that differed only in their speech. The Micmac Indians of the present-day Maritime provinces and the Blackfoot of the prairies, for instance, although separated by four thousand kilometres, are joined together in the Algonquian linguistic family; in reality, they lived entirely different lives, in total unawareness of each other's existence. Conversely, the Haida Indians of the Queen Charlotte Islands resembled their mainland neighbours, the Tsimshians, in everything except their language, which was totally unrelated.

The classification of Canada's original inhabitants by political, or tribal, categories also poses problems. Tribes—that is, groups of people bound together by a common culture and language and acting as a unit in relations with their neighbours—certainly existed. Among some groups, though, the ties between the various bands were not strong. The

7

8

LINGUISTIC FAMILIES

Algonquian	Wakashan
Iroquoian	Tsimshian
Siouan	Haidan
Athapaskan	Tlingit
Kootenayan	Eskimoan
Salishan	Beothukan

Source: Adapted from P.G. Cornell, J. Hamelin, F. Ouellet, and M. Trudel, *Canada: Unity in Diversity* (Toronto, 1967), 14.

Aboriginal language families within the boundaries of present-day Canada: an approximate guide for the period from the sixteenth to the eighteenth century.

more remote bands diverged considerably in dialect and, in some cases, had so readily assimilated the customs of alien peoples around them that they lost all feeling of political unity with their far-distant relatives.

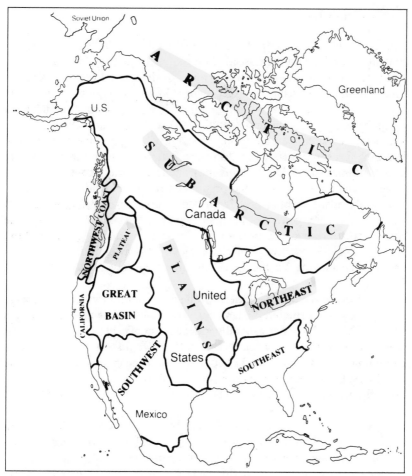

Source: Reprinted, by permission, from the *Handbook of North American Indians*, vol. 4, *History of Indian–White Relations* (Smithsonian Institution, Washington, D.C., 1988).

North American Indian culture areas. Rather than an authoritative representation of actual territories at any one time, this map should be regarded as a rough guide to contiguous groups that had, or have similar cultures and histories.

NATIVE CULTURE AREAS

The anthropologists' concept of culture areas provides the best description of Indian groups in present-day Canada, because it recognizes how climate and regional resources influence the development of societies and technologies. Native North American societies can be classified into six culture areas: Northwest Coast, Plateau, Plains, Subarctic, Arctic, and Northeast. An examination of each culture area might serve to enhance our understanding of Canada's original inhabitants before European contact.

Northwest Coast

The Northwest Coast is rich in marine resources. The Coast Range in British Columbia and the Cascade Mountains in the states of Washington and Oregon cut off the maritime peoples of the coastal regions from the inland hunters and fishers—except where low-lying regions, such as the Columbia River valley, allowed for contact. The coastal inhabitants fished for herring, smelt, eulachon (candle-fish), halibut, and several species popularly called cod. In addition, sea mammals were numerous: whales, seals, sea lions, porpoises, and sea otters. Salmon became the basic staple of the coastal people. The Indians speared, netted, and trapped salmon in huge quantities, then sun-dried or smoked it for year-round use.

The abundant rainfall and moderate temperatures produced a lush vegetation. The Northwest Coast peoples used the cedars and firs of the coastal rain forest for houses, for dugout canoes, and for woodworking crafts (carved boxes, bowls, dishes, ladles). This availability of supplies and food made the Pacific Coast the most densely populated area in Canada.

The Northwest Coast peoples lived the year round in villages that were usually located in sheltered island coves or on channels near the mouths of rivers. Each village was generally independent of others, but on occasion (particularly at times of war), several villages would join together. Their communal activities included the potlatch or large ceremonial feast. The Northwest Coast peoples organized potlatches to mourn the dead, to celebrate the investiture of new chiefs, or to mark the completion of a new house.

In contrast to the other culture areas in Canada, a hierarchical social structure evolved on the Northwest Coast. At the bottom were slaves taken in war; then came everyone else, in a very precise social ranking.

Archaeologists believe that the ancestors of the native peoples of the Northwest Coast had resided in the same territories in which the Europeans first found them for at least the previous two thousand years. The linguistic complexity of the region—with its nineteen distinct languages—suggests that, linguistically, it is an "old area" and the most likely starting point for migrations of successive groups to the east and to the south. The Northwest Coast culture area extended from northern California to the Alaskan panhandle.

Plateau

The Plateau culture area, the smallest of the six, takes in the high plateau between the coastal mountains and the Rockies in British Columbia. It extends southward through western Montana, Idaho, and eastern Washington and Oregon. The Canadian portion of the Plateau area is essentially the same as that locally described as "the interior" of British Columbia. Hot, dry summers and cold winters are common throughout the Plateau. In Canada the Plateau societies include the Kutenai (or Kootenay) in the east, the Interior Salish in the west, and the Athapaskan-speaking groups to the north. The Plateau Indians depended on salmon, and thus their populations were largest downriver, where the fish were most abundant. In dress, customs, and religion, these transitional Plateau people resembled the Plains' tribes far more closely than they did the Northwest Coast groups. In contrast to the Pacific bands, they were semi-migratory, non-agricultural, and small in population.

Plains

11

East of the Plateau region lies the Plains (or Great Plains) culture area, in the broad central region of North America west of the Mississippi and Red River valleys and east of the Rockies. It is an area in which open grasslands predominate, with tall grass in the east and short grass in the west. Like the Northwest and Plateau areas, the Plains area extends north – south, from northern Alberta and Saskatchewan and western Manitoba to Texas. The region has a continental climate—hot, dry summers and cold winters. In the eighteenth century, tribes belonging to three linguistic families lived on the Canadian Plains: the Algonquian, the Athapaskan, and the Siouan.

For nearly ten thousand years, the Great Plains Indians specialized in the communal hunt of the buffalo, or bison. Indeed, the buffalo, which fed on the grasslands, was the foundation of the Plains culture. Its hide furnished the Plains peoples with lodge covers, warm overcoats, bedding, and moccasins. The Indians made shields from the thick hide of the buffalo's neck, carved spoons and drinking cups from its horns, and created thread and bow string from sinew. The Blackfoot termed the buffalo's flesh "real meat," implying that all other meat was inferior.

Natives hunted the buffalo on foot in small nomadic bands of roughly fifty to a hundred people, since this number could most effectively handle a drive. These drives required excellent organization, particularly in the foothills, where the buffalo were stampeded over the edges of cliffs. Archaeologists have found some of the earliest evidence of human presence in North America on the Great Plains, at sites associated with buffalo hunting that are nearly ten thousand years old. One such location is Head-Smashed-In Buffalo Jump, a World Heritage Site in the Oldman River valley near Fort Macleod in southwestern Alberta. It is one of the largest and best-preserved of all the jumps in North America, and one that remained in use until the "horse days."

12

Photo by Edward S. Curtis. Glenbow Archives, Calgary/NA-1700-156.

A Blackfoot couple with horse-drawn travois.

THE HORSE

The horse had originally existed in the Americas, but then it disappeared. Its reintroduction in Mexico by the Spaniards in the sixteenth century transformed Plains culture. Until the return of the horse, the dog was North America's only domesticated animal used to transport goods. The horse reached the Canadian Plains by the 1730s through intertribal trade and raiding. The horse made buffalo hunting much more efficient, since the people no longer had to follow the herds on foot. Mounted hunters could simply surround or chase a buffalo herd without having to drive it into an enclosure or over a cliff.

The Plains peoples adapted the dog *travois* (a device made of two trailing poles on which was attached a platform or net for holding a load) for use with the horse. With a horse-drawn *travois*, a person could carry a load of 150 kg, in contrast to one of about 35 kg pulled by a dog. In addition, a horse could travel twenty kilometres a day—twice as far as a dog could. With the horse, people did not have to lighten their loads as much as they had before—they could carry more than just the basic necessities. They could keep extra suits of clothing, additional buffalo robes for winter, and more dried provisions.

Subarctic

To the north lies the Subarctic culture area, a region much less densely populated than the Plains. It extends across the Canadian Shield, from the Labrador coast to the mouth of the Yukon River. Except where it meets the Rocky Mountains, the land is low-lying and covered with coniferous trees. The subarctic area's northern boundary is near, but below, the tree line. Although the winters are long and harsh, the forests provide shelter. Members of two linguistic families lived in the Subarctic: in the west, the Athapaskan-speaking groups, or "Dene" (pronounced "de-ne" or "de-nay" and meaning "the people"); and in the east, the Subarctic Algonquians.

The Subarctic peoples lived in summer encampments consisting of several hunting bands (perhaps a hundred people) and situated at good fishing sites. In the autumn they broke up into bands that scattered in search of food. They lived in isolation in their hunting territories from early autumn until spring. Approximately twenty-five to thirty people, closely related either by family ties or by marriage, comprised a hunting band. A senior, respected male directed the group and, in consultation with the other men, decided where and when they would hunt and camp. Many of the Dene and Algonquians relied heavily on the moose, whose importance to them was comparable to that of the buffalo to the Plains peoples. Because of the thin distribution of game animals over vast areas of the boreal forest, Subarctic human population densities were among the lowest in the world.

13

Arctic

Immediately to the north of the Subarctic, beyond the tree line, lies the Arctic culture area. For about eight months of the year, most of the Arctic is snow-covered and extensive portions of its seas are frozen. The broad area of the Arctic generally includes most of Alaska, Canada north of the tree line, and Greenland. The human inhabitants of this area are the Inuit, sometimes called Eskimo, who, generally speaking, live on the northern tundra.

Today, all of the people known as Inuit speak languages related to one another, which suggests that these languages derived from a single ancestral tongue. They are distantly related to the languages of the Chukchi, Koryak, and Itel'men peoples of northeastern Siberia and are unrelated to those of any Amerindian tribe. This supports the theory that the Inuit originated relatively recently in Asia. Racially as well, the Inuit are more closely related to Siberian peoples than to the native North American populations to the south.

The Inuit's ancestors developed the ability to survive winters on the treeless tundra. Surprisingly, the Arctic can provide hunters and fishers with a basic subsistence. Although there are fewer species of animals the farther one travels from the equator toward the poles, the populations of those same few species are relatively large. In certain areas, migration and the availability of food lead to dense seasonal concentrations of many species, such as caribou, walrus, and seals.

Over the centuries the Arctic peoples, known to archaeologists as Paleoeskimos, developed hunting techniques to allow for a more efficient exploitation of their environment. As early as four thousand years ago they had become the primary inhabitants of Arctic Canada. The people of what archaeologists have termed the Dorset culture developed new objects and tools suited to their environment—the soapstone lamp, snow houses, and dog sleds. The Dorset Paleoeskimo culture emerged about twenty-five hundred years ago.

By 1000 A.D. an Alaskan people, the Thule, the direct ancestors of the modern Inuit, had entered the central Arctic. They appear to have caused the disappearance of the Dorset people, either through warfare or by absorbing them into their own communities. The Thule immigrants introduced a sophisticated sea-hunting culture to the area east of Alaska. By about 1400 A.D. a sparse Thule population occupied most of Arctic Canada north of the tree line. Modern Canadian and Greenlandic Inuit are descended from them.

14

Northeast

The Northeast (or Eastern Woodlands) culture area extended roughly from the Atlantic region westward to the Upper Great Lakes, south to Ohio and Virginia, and north to the southern boundary of the eastern Subarctic. The Northeast Indians hunted a variety of large game, particularly deer, as well as smaller game. They also fished and gathered edible wild plants and roots. Climate and soil conditions south of the Canadian Shield allowed some tribes to grow corn, beans, and squash. Speakers of languages belonging to two linguistic families lived in the Northeast: the Algonquians, a migratory people primarily dependent on hunting and fishing; and the Iroquoians, a semi-nomadic and agricultural people. The many tribes of the Algonquian family occupied the northern part of the region, while the Iroquoians inhabited much of present-day southern Ontario and neighbouring New York State.

THE ALGONQUIANS

The Algonquian-speaking tribes were numerous on the eve of European contact. The Micmac lived in the Maritimes and the closely related Malecite, in present-day western New Brunswick. North of the St. Lawrence and east of the St. Maurice River were the Montagnais. The Algonquins (Algonkins), the tribe that gave its name to the Algonquian linguistic family, lived in the Ottawa valley. (Note that the tribal name ends in "-quin" and that of the linguistic family in "-quian.") Still farther west were the Nipissings on Lake Nipissing, the Ottawas (Odawa) on Manitoulin Island in Lake Huron, and the Ojibwas (Chippewas) around Lake Superior. The Beothuk lived in Newfoundland. Now extinct, the Beothuk might also have been Algonquian speakers, but the available evidence is inadequate for firm conclusions.

Although many Algonquian groups grew some crops, hunting and fishing were the principal source of food for those north of the Great Lakes. During the winter they broke up into family groups to hunt for deer, elk, bear, beaver, and other game animals. In the early spring they met at maple groves to gather and boil the tree sap. The women undertook some agricultural work in the summer, when the men fished. During the fall they gathered wild rice, and farther south they harvested corn.

15

Several winter hunting groups apparently joined together for summer fishing. As anthropologist Bruce Trigger has written, each fishing band had a name, its own territory, and its own leader, although this leader had relatively little power or authority. The men of these male-centred hunting groups usually married women from neighbouring bands, thus maintaining friendly ties. Adjacent bands sharing a common language and customs were generally known as a tribe—but their unity was really more cultural than political, since the band was the only clearly defined political unit.[4] The Algonquians, unlike the Iroquoians on the eve of European contact, had no central governing authority. Two Iroquoian confederacies in the Great Lakes area were the Huron, and Five (later Six) Nations. These confederacies were governed by councils in which each of the founding tribes, or nations, had representatives.

THE IROQUOIANS

Initially, the Northeast peoples were primarily hunters and gatherers, but gradually many in the area south of the Canadian Shield adapted to agriculture. Crops of Mexican and Central American origin played an important role in the development of Iroquoian culture. About 500 A.D. corn appears to have spread northward from the Ohio and Illinois areas, adapting to the shorter growing season and the more rigorous climate. Some form of tobacco probably entered eastern Canada as early as twenty-five hundred years ago and beans appeared about a thousand years ago.

With the addition of beans, which are high in protein, rapid population growth occurred, since the combination of corn and beans partially freed the people from having to supplement their corn diet with animal protein.

Initially, the Iroquoians' small-scale gardening supplemented their traditional hunting and fishing, but later these roles were reversed: hunting and fishing came to supplement farming. The Iroquoians in the vicinity of the lower Great Lakes came to depend on their crops for up to four-fifths of their food. Increased reliance on agriculture meant that village sites had to be moved every ten to fifteen years, when the soil and the available firewood became exhausted. As Iroquoian society went from hunting to farming, women assumed the tasks of planting, cultivating, and harvesting the crops (the men cleared the fields). By taking over the major responsibilities of farming, the women freed the men for hunting, fishing, trading, and warfare.

16   The only societies that could afford the luxury of war were those that controlled their environment to a significant degree (as did the Iroquoian farmers) or that enjoyed an ample food supply (as on the Pacific coast or on the Plains, after the arrival of the horse). There is evidence of hostilities among the farming communities of southern Ontario from as early as 800 A.D. From the end of the fourteenth century the Iroquoians maintained heavily fortified villages with as many as three log palisades and with platforms from which stone throwers and archers could defend the townsite.

The Iroquoian peoples lived in villages of up to fifteen hundred inhabitants (and, in some exceptional cases, even more). Several families belonging to the same clan lived together in dwellings called "longhouses," which consisted of a framework of saplings, often arched in a barrel shape, covered with sheets of bark. Stretching more than half a football field in length, a large longhouse reportedly housed up to thirty families, although smaller structures usually accommodated about ten. The Iroquoians divided the longhouses into apartments that were usually occupied by closely related families. A corridor ran down the middle of the house, and families on each side shared fireplaces.

The families in the longhouse would usually be related through the female line (ideally, sisters and their families). The core of any household consisted of a number of females descended from a common ancestor. When a man married, he moved to his wife's home, where authority was invested in an elderly woman. In Iroquoian society the older women had real social and political power. The matrons of the appropriate families elected the chiefs, who were men; these women could also vote out of office any chief who displeased them.

Aboriginal Canada on the Eve of European Contact

The Iroquoian cultures had changed rapidly in the period immediately preceding European contact. Larger settlements had developed, tribes and possibly confederacies had evolved, and, in some cases, warfare was being waged on an expanded scale.

The two most prominent groups among the Iroquoians in the sixteenth century were the Hurons, located south of Georgian Bay, and the Iroquois, or the League of the Five Nations, who occupied the territory south of the St. Lawrence and Lake Ontario, from the Richelieu River in the east to Lake Erie in the west. In the St. Lawrence Valley lived another group of Iroquoians, neither Huron nor Iroquois, now called the Laurentian Iroquois.

17

Five hundred years ago the way in which each Amerindian group lived was largely decided by the nature and the abundance of the resources of the land that it occupied. The division of the groups into culture areas parallels almost exactly the country's geographical areas: the west coast, the interior of British Columbia, the prairies, the northern Canadian Shield, the eastern woodlands, and the Arctic. In addition to cultural differences, there was linguistic diversity: More than fifty languages, belonging to eleven linguistic families (one Inuit and ten Indian), existed among the Native peoples of the six culture areas.

On the eve of European contact, each of the Amerindian communities within present-day Canada administered its own affairs in its own language, following its own cultural pattern. The members of each community decided where they would hunt, fish, and, in certain cases, raise crops. They traded with their neighbours. In short, these self-governing individuals ruled themselves, completely oblivious to the presence of pale-faced human beings on a distant continent.

NOTES

[1]This paraphrasing of the Blackfoot origin story is based on the account given in John Ewers, *The Blackfeet* (Norman, 1958), 3–4.
[2]Alice Kehoe includes a very important discussion on this subject in the chapter entitled "Conflict of Opinion on the Origin of Native American Population," in her *North American Indians: A Comprehensive Account* (Englewood Cliffs, N.J., 1981), 1–4.
[3]Alfred W. Crosby, "Virgin Soil Epidemics as a Factor in the Aboriginal Depopulation in America," *William and Mary Quarterly*, 3rd series, 33 (1976): 290.
[4]Bruce G. Trigger, *The Indians and the Heroic Age of New France* (Ottawa, 1977), 6.

> ### Related Readings
>
> R. Douglas Francis and Donald B. Smith, *Readings in Canadian History: Pre-Confederation*, 3d ed. (Toronto, 1990) contains an important article relating to this chapter: Jacques Rousseau and George W. Brown, "The Indians of Northeastern North America," 3–16.

BIBLIOGRAPHY

Three valuable overviews by anthropologists are Alice B. Kehoe, *North American Indians: A Comprehensive Account* (Englewood Cliffs, N.J., 1981); R. Bruce Morrison and C. Roderick Wilson, eds., *Native Peoples: The Canadian Experience* (Toronto, 1986); and Alan D. McMillan, *Native Peoples and Cultures of Canada: An Anthropological Overview* (Vancouver, 1988). Diamond Jenness's older study, *The Indians of Canada* (Ottawa, 1932) should still be consulted as well.

J.V. Wright's *Six Chapters of Canada's Prehistory* (Ottawa, 1976) reviews the archaeological record. An up-to-date summary is Alan Lyle Bryan's "The Prehistory of the Canadian Indians," in *Native Peoples*, edited by Morrison and Wilson, 22–44; see also his study, *New Evidence for the Pleistocene Peopling of the Americas* (Orono, Maine, 1986). An excellent popular account is Robert McGhee's *Ancient Canada* (Ottawa, 1989). Liz Bryan's *The Buffalo People: Prehistoric Archaeology on the Canadian Plains* (Edmonton, 1990) is another useful introduction. Henry F. Dobyns, *Native American Historical Demography: A Critical Bibliography* (Bloomington, Indiana, 1976) provides useful demographic information. For details on the impact of disease, consult Alfred W. Crosby, "Virgin Soil Epidemics as a Factor in the Aboriginal Depopulation in America," *William and Mary Quarterly*, 3d series, 33 (1976): 289–99; and also his *Ecological Imperialism: The Biological Expansion of Europe, 900–1900* (Cambridge, England, 1986).

Short reviews of the culture areas appear in *The Canadian Encyclopedia*, 2d ed. (Edmonton, 1988), 1436–48. Surveys also appear in *Native Peoples*, edited by Morrison and Wilson; Kehoe, *North American Indians*; and McMillan, *Native Peoples and Cultures*. Two of the volumes in the series *Handbook of North American Indians* are invaluable: June Helm, ed., *Subarctic*, vol. 6 (Washington, 1981), and Bruce G. Trigger, ed., *Northeast*, vol. 15 (Washington, 1978). See also Robert McGhee, *Canadian Arctic Prehistory* (Toronto, 1978) for the Arctic culture area. A useful study on Native languages is Michael K. Foster's "Canada's First Languages," *Language and Society* 7 (Winter–Spring 1982): 7–16; as well as the entry by him ("Native Peoples, Languages") in *The Canadian Encyclopedia*, 2d ed. (Edmonton, 1988), 1453–56.

The early maps in R. Cole Harris, ed., *Historical Atlas of Canada*, vol. 1, *From the Beginning to 1800* (Toronto, 1987), are based on the most recent archaeological discoveries and contain a wealth of new information about the first inhabitants of present-day Canada. The most up-to-date summary of our current understanding of Canada's Amerindians before European contact is contained in a forthcoming book by Olive P. Dickason entitled *Canada's First Nations: A History of Founding Peoples.*

Time Line: 18 000 B.C.–1500 A.D.

18 000– —Human beings are believed to have lived in the
13 000 B.C. Bluefish caves in the northern Yukon, Canada's
oldest known archaeological site.

13 000 B.C.—Niagara Falls is created as the glaciers recede.

3000 B.C. —The glaciers in the north retreat to approximately
their present northern position, and the climate
comes to approximate today's.
—Construction of Stonehenge in England and the
pyramids in Egypt.

1500 B.C.– —Rise of the great Amerindian civilizations in
1 A.D. present-day Mexico, Central America, and Peru.

1 A.D.– —Development of the Mound Builders' culture in
500 A.D. present-day Ohio.

500 A.D. —Inhabitants of present-day southern Ontario began
to grow corn, allowing for the development of
societies based on agriculture.

700 A.D.– —Rise of the Mississippian culture in the Mississippi
1000 A.D. Valley.

1000 A.D. —Entry of the Thule, the direct ancestors of the
modern Inuit, into the central Arctic.

1500 A.D. —Existence of peoples within present-day Canada who
can be classified as belonging to six culture areas
and among whom more than fifty languages,
belonging to eleven linguistic families (one Inuit
and ten Indian), were spoken.

Before —Formation of the League of the Five Nations.
European
Contact

The Europeans' Arrival

The strange boat carrying the tall leafless tree from which a gigantic white blanket was hung must have amazed the hunters along the Labrador and Newfoundland coast. They believed that the world ended somewhere beyond the horizon. Never before in their long history had anyone seen such a sight emerging from the edge of the world. Upon the small sea monster's back rode beings with hair on their faces and with skin like the underbelly of a fish. It was about 1000 A.D., and the aliens were the Norse, who, for a brief period, explored the Atlantic coast from their base in Greenland. After an interval of nearly five centuries, other Europeans followed in quick succession: the English, the Portuguese, the French, the Spanish, and the Basques.

The dearth of source materials, however, makes writing an account of the Europeans' arrival in what was to become Canada a formidable task. The only information we have for the period up to the seventeenth century is a few Norse sagas and several European explorers' journals. We have no direct accounts by the original inhabitants and few narratives by the early European mariners, fishermen, and fur traders. Morris Bishop, a modern biographer of Samuel de Champlain, who founded Quebec in 1608, put it best when he wrote, "In reading history one must always be impressed by the fact that our knowledge is only a collection of scraps and fragments that we put together into a pleasing design, and often the discovery of one new fragment would cause us to alter utterly the whole design."[1] With that caution, we may proceed to a rough sketch of the Europeans' arrival in present-day Canada.

Arrival of the Norse

Irish monks were probably the first European navigators both interested in voyaging westward and capable of reaching North America. In the early Middle Ages, tales circulated about the celebrated Irish saint, Brendan, who was said to have found new lands by sailing west in the sixth century. But none of these accounts can be proven.

From the ninth to the twelfth century, Scandinavia was the leading European sea power, with a commercial empire extending from Russia in the east to Sicily in the south and to Normandy, Ireland, and Greenland in the west. The Norse were the Western world's best navigators. Their occupation of parts of Greenland was a continuation of their voyages from the European mainland: to the Faeroe Islands, roughly 300 km north of Scotland, by 800 A.D.; to Iceland by 870 A.D.; and to Greenland by 985 A.D. Without compasses (which were introduced only in the twelfth century) the Norse estimated their position on the seas by measuring the location of the North Star with the aid of a very crude device. (On their way home from Iceland to Norway, they occasionally landed in Ireland or Scotland by mistake.)

Eric the Red (Eirikr Thorvaldsson), the founder of the Norse settlements on Greenland, was driven to explore by more than a Viking's sense of adventure. Exiled from his native Norway for murder, he escaped to Iceland, only to become involved in a feud there. Banished for more killings, he fled farther west, toward a land that storm-driven sailors had reportedly sighted. After sailing about 800 km west, he found a vast uninhabited subcontinent. On its west coast, this land had green, reasonably level pastures and impressive fiords and headlands, all of which reminded him of his native Norway. Rich in game animals, with a sea full of fish and large mammals such as seals and walrus, the land could support many Icelanders. Eric named the inviting, unoccupied country "Greenland," which was an accurate description of what he had seen. On returning to Iceland, he encouraged others to migrate with him to this promising land. Accompanied by fourteen or fifteen shiploads of Icelanders, the Norse adventurer founded two settlements. The Icelanders persevered, raising cows, horses, sheep, pigs, and goats. Recent excavations of the remains of Eric's own farm have uncovered a surprisingly large and comfortable establishment, built with thick walls of stone and turf to protect against the chilling winds.

In 986 A.D., the second year of Eric's settlement of Greenland, Bjarni Herjölfsson, the owner of a ship that traded between Norway and Iceland, went to join Eric in Greenland. En route, he and his crew met with stormy and cloudy weather and were driven off course for several days. When the weather cleared they sighted a flat land covered with woods. As this country did not fit the description that he had of Greenland, Bjarni sailed north until he reached that country. Bjarni was thus the first known

European to sight eastern North America (probably Labrador, roughly four days' sailing from Eric's Greenlandic settlements), although he never landed there.

Eric's second son, Leifr (or Leif) Eiriksson, grew up hearing the tales about Bjarni and the forested land to the south. Timber was a precious commodity on Greenland, which had no trees. In the year 1001, at the age of twenty-one, Leif assembled a crew of thirty-five and set out to explore the lands southwest of Greenland.

Experts now agree that Leif's expedition sailed past Baffin Island, which he called "Helluland" (Flat Stone Land). Farther south he landed in a forested area—probably the coast of central Labrador—and named it "Markland" (Wood Land). Continuing on, he reached an attractive location with a moderate climate, which he named "Vinland" (Wineland) for its plentiful "wineberries" (probably wild red currants, gooseberries, or mountain cranberries). Scholars have placed Vinland anywhere between Labrador and Florida. After wintering in Vinland and doing more exploring, Leif and his crew took in a cargo of timber and "wineberries" and set sail for Greenland. They had not encountered any other human beings during their stay.

In the opening decade of the eleventh century, the Norse sponsored several expeditions southwest from Greenland. Leif's brother, Thorvaldr, led the next voyage to Vinland. With his crew of thirty he reached the Vinland houses and settled there for the winter, catching fish to supplement provisions brought from Greenland. During the next summer, Thorvaldr explored the coast to the south, meeting no one.

23

CONFLICT BETWEEN THE NORSE AND THE NORTH AMERICAN NATIVES

Violence characterized the first recorded contact between the Europeans and the North Americans. During the second summer, Thorvaldr and his men apparently followed the coast northward, where they encountered nine *skraelings* (barbarians), as the Norse called them, sleeping under three "skin boats" on shore. The Norse murdered eight of the nine. The native North American who escaped later returned with others in a fleet of skin boats (because of this reference in the Vinland Sagas, some experts believe these *skraelings* were not Indians but Inuit using kayaks). In the skirmish that ensued a *skraeling* arrow hit Thorvaldr, mortally wounding him. The crew returned to Vinland and then to Greenland the following spring. A few brief, usually hostile, encounters followed on subsequent expeditions. Hostile relations with the natives prevented the establishment of a permanent colony.

A final attempt to colonize Vinland was led by Freydis, Eric the Red's daughter. From the eleventh to fourteenth centuries the Greenlandic

Norse returned to buy wood from the *skraelings*, but they never again tried to colonize the area.

THE HISTORICAL VALUE OF THE NORSE SAGAS

Many questions about the Norse remain unanswered. We know of Eric the Red, Bjarni, Leif Eiriksson, and the later Viking explorers not from journals and accounts by first-hand witnesses but from sagas or stories passed on orally from generation to generation over the course of two or three hundred years before being written down. These sagas, told by expert storytellers, were designed to hold an audience spellbound; in the retelling many of the original facts were no doubt embellished and then re-embellished. Thus, although the tales mingle legend and fiction with reality, they undoubtedly have some basis in fact. In 1960 researchers who used these sagas as clues located a Norse settlement on the northern coast of Newfoundland—proof that the Norse visited Canada.

24

The first and only widely accepted Norse site in North America was discovered by Helge Ingstad and excavated by his archaeologist wife, Anne Stine Ingstad. At l'Anse-aux-Meadows in northern Newfoundland (see page 343), archaeological crews unearthed the remains of eight sod-walled structures similar to those constructed by the Norse in Iceland and Greenland. Radiocarbon-dating of Norse artifacts found at the site indicated a date of occupancy in the vicinity of 1000 A.D.—the date of the Vinland expeditions. Among the artifacts were two small objects of great importance: one was a bronze pin, used by the Norse to fasten their cloaks on the right shoulder in order to leave their arms free to wield a sword; the other was a spindle whorl used by Norse women to make yarn from wool (indicating that perhaps there were women in the first Norse settlement in North America). The absence of a midden (or refuse heap) containing bones and other debris, together with the fact that none of the houses had been rebuilt or had major repairs, hints that the occupancy lasted only a few years at most.

THE NORSE IN GREENLAND

Archaeologists have also found evidence of Norse trading (but not settlement) in Canada's Arctic archipelago. The Norse voyaged north to trade along the Greenlandic coast and west to Baffin and Ellesmere islands as late as the fourteenth century. Norse specimens, including ship rivets, chainmail pieces, two pieces of woven woolen cloth, oak pieces, barrel-bottom fragments, and many copper and iron pieces, have been excavated on the east coast of Ellesmere Island.

The Greenland settlements had vanished by the early fifteenth century, certainly by 1450. At the height of Greenland's prosperity, an estimated 2000–4000 people, and perhaps as many as 6000, lived there. In the thir-

teenth century, however, Greenland's climate became colder and threatened agriculture on the island. Furthermore, the settlements' prosperity,
precariously built on the walrus-ivory trade, was doomed when the Portuguese began importing African elephant ivory. Finally, the Black Death
epidemic of 1349 struck Norway and Iceland severely, killing one-third
of the population—a loss that cost the Norse their command of the
seas. The annual ship that brought vital supplies from Norway no longer
appeared.

Entry of the Portuguese and the Spanish

The Portuguese had replaced the Scandinavians as the leading European
sea power by the fifteenth century. Portuguese experiments in shipbuilding resulted in a fast, new sea-going vessel, the caravel. This longer and
narrower ship with two masts became the discoverers' standard ship.
Christopher Columbus's three vessels were all caravels.

25

The Portuguese advances came quickly. Like the Norse, they island-
hopped across the Atlantic. By 1420 they had reached Madeira and by
1427 the Azores, which lie a third of the way across the Atlantic. But then
their voyages across the Atlantic ceased, for they were setting out into the
western ocean at latitudes at which strong westerly winds make sailing
dangerous. Checked in the mid-Atlantic, they focussed their attention
instead on discovering a sea route around Africa to India. In 1488 the
Portuguese expedition of Bartholomeu Dias rounded the Cape of Good
Hope, and within ten years the Portuguese reached India.

EUROPE'S INTEREST IN EXPANSION

At least three impulses led the Portuguese—and later the Spanish, the
French, the English, and the Dutch—to expand beyond Europe. The first
was curiosity, the desire to find a better land than that in which they lived.
Second, from the thirteenth century onward, they sought a route to "the
Indies," as China, Japan, Indonesia, and India were then collectively
called. For want of refrigeration, preserving meat required spices, which
commanded very high prices. Finally, the Europeans voyaged overseas to
convert the "heathen" to Christianity.

Why did the Europeans become the great discoverers at the end of the
fifteenth century? Why not the Chinese or the Arabs? Both of the latter
groups had extensive maritime experience. Arabs living on the western
and northwestern shores of the Indian Ocean were at least as far advanced
in the sciences required for seafaring (astronomy, geography, mathematics,
and navigation) as their European contemporaries.

Long before the Portuguese had begun to travel along the west coast of Africa, the Arabs had explored the east coast of that continent to the Mozambique channel opposite the island of Madagascar, which lies about fifteen hundred kilometres north of the Cape of Good Hope. But the Arabs felt no need to go farther, since their territories included the rich variety of tropical plants and animals, as well as minerals, that Europe sought. The Arabs on the Indian Ocean were "already there."

Similarly, well over a thousand years before the extensive voyages of the Portuguese, the Chinese had evolved a strong maritime tradition. By the early fifteenth century, they had built a remarkable navy that traded with the Islamic world for at least five hundred years. The Chinese had introduced the compass to Europe two to three centuries earlier, and they had developed elaborate navigational charts showing detailed compass bearings. The Chinese went to other lands not as traders or conquerors but to broadcast the greatness and the wealth of China, the Central Kingdom. The expeditions sent out by the Chinese emperor in the early fifteenth century were the largest and most elaborate ever seen; one, in fact, consisted of nearly forty thousand crew members and a flotilla of more than three hundred ships. But a great withdrawal began in the mid-1430s, when the Chinese emperor ordered officials to suppress all seafaring. Just as the Europeans began to set out on their great explorations, landbound China sealed its borders. The Central Kingdom, which considered itself the centre of the world, no longer ventured abroad.

26

THE VOYAGE OF COLUMBUS, 1492

In ancient times it was believed in Europe that Asia could be reached by sailing west from the Atlantic coast. Aristotle, the Greek philosopher, said that it was possible to cross from Spain to the Indies. Two thousand years later, many Europeans held the same view. When the Italian mariner Christopher Columbus proposed his expedition to the king and queen of Spain, he did so essentially in these terms: Let the Portuguese take the long eastward route around Africa to the Indies; I will find the direct route across the Atlantic.

At the age of forty-one, Columbus already had extensive seafaring experience. Under the Portuguese flag he had sailed from above the Arctic Circle nearly to the equator and from the Aegean Sea west to the outer Azores. In 1492 he sailed south to the Canary Islands, avoiding the strong westerly winds of the North Atlantic, and then west, reaching the Caribbean. Columbus returned convinced that he had reached the Indies—in 1492 no one dreamed of the existence of what would be called the "New World." He named the original inhabitants of the Americas "Indians."

THE EUROPEANS' INITIAL PERCEPTIONS OF THE INDIANS

Many European expansionists perceived the Indians as threatening people who had to be controlled and whose culture had to be transformed according to Christian principles. The French later called them *salvages* or *sauvages*, people both rude and fierce living in a state of nature more like wild animals than humans.

Columbus's first voyage led to fierce maritime rivalry between Spain and Portugal. In 1493 the king and queen of Spain approached Pope Alexander VI and asked him for the right to evangelize in the territories they had recently "discovered." The Pope drew a line of demarcation through the mid-Atlantic, from the north pole to the south. By the Treaty of Tordesillas in 1494 both Spain and Portugal agreed to move the Pope's line of division one hundred leagues farther west. Everything to the west of the line belonged to Spain, while the land to the east belonged to Portugal. (This division brought a portion of present-day Atlantic Canada and much of Brazil into Portugal's sphere.)

27

The English and the French Reach the North Atlantic

Other European nations refused to accept the Spanish – Portuguese treaty. When news of Columbus's first two Atlantic voyages to "Asia" reached England, King Henry VII sponsored his own expedition, selecting John Cabot (Giovanni Caboto), an Italian mariner like Columbus, to lead it. The merchants of the English port of Bristol, anxious to secure direct access to the spices of the east, bore all costs.

An experienced mariner, Cabot had been to Mecca for the spice trade. Once he learned of Columbus's journey to islands off the coast of "Asia," Cabot resolved to reach the Indies by a shorter northern route. He first sought support in Seville and Lisbon. When that attempt failed he tried England, where in 1496 Henry VII granted him letters patent to sail, making the Italian navigator his agent over any new-found lands.

Cabot set sail from Bristol, England's westernmost port, on May 20, 1497, in the *Matthew*, a fast and able craft. Unlike the Norse, the Italian navigator had the benefit of compass, quadrant, and traverse table. On June 24 he reached land, probably Newfoundland. Here, claiming the territory for Henry VII, he planted the flags of England and Venice. He explored no farther, perhaps because he had only a small crew and wished to avoid conflict with hostile natives. Instead, he fished off what he believed was the coast of Asia. The seas so swarmed with fish that the sailors caught them simply by letting down and drawing up baskets weighted with stones. He had found the great continental shelf of Newfoundland, the shallow areas called banks, which were favourite breeding places of the cod. Cabot also discovered to the south a large passage (the Gulf of St. Lawrence) that he thought was a direct route to China and India.

Encouraged by this information, the English king sponsored a second voyage the following year. In May 1498 Cabot sailed again from Bristol with five ships. Shortly out of port, one vessel turned back in distress to Ireland, and Bristol never heard of the fate of the other four. With Cabot's disappearance, followed shortly by the death of Henry VII, English interest in the search for a Northwest Passage to the Orient temporarily lapsed. Nevertheless, John Cabot's first voyage announced England's arrival in the Americas. The voyage also brought the Grand Banks fishery to the attention of the fishing fleets of England, France, Spain, Portugal, and the Basque country, on the frontier of Spain and France. Thus was born the first great European business in North America—fishing.

THE PORTUGUESE IN THE NORTH ATLANTIC

Soon after Cabot came the Portuguese. For the most part, Portugal focussed its attention on the sea route to Africa and on Brazil, which it claimed in 1500. Yet, at least in the Azores, there was still interest in the discovery of the Northwest Passage to the Orient. The Azoreans believed that the "new lands" discovered by Cabot lay to the east of the line of demarcation—hence, within Portugal's sphere.

A *lavrador* (small farmer), João Fernandes, received letters patent from the Portuguese king in 1499 to search for islands in the Portuguese half of the world. His voyage was of no significant geographic interest, but it led to the naming of a large section of Canada's Atlantic coastline. In 1500 Fernandes reached Greenland. When he first sighted the huge land mass, Fernandes humorously called it "Tierra del Lavrador," Land of the Farmer. A century later, when mapmakers learned of the old Norse name "Greenland," they revived it and shifted the name Labrador to the south.

In 1500 the Portuguese sent another expedition under Gaspar Corte-Real, who sailed to a land that became known in the sixteenth century as "Tierra Nova de Corte Real": Newfoundland. The Azorean sea captain knew how rich west Africa had been as a source of slaves for Portugal, and he sought a new source in Tierra Nova. When he returned in 1501, he kidnapped fifty-seven Indians and sent them back to Europe with his brother Miguel. But Gaspar Corte-Real and his crew never returned. Like Cabot and his four ships, he was lost with all hands, as was Miguel when he came back to search for his brother.

Despite the dangers of navigating the uncharted North Atlantic, the Portuguese fishermen annually fished the Grand Banks and the coastal waters of Newfoundland. They sailed extensively along the outer Newfoundland coast. Several place names, now corrupted in English or French versions, testify to their travels: Cape Race (from *raso*, shaved), at the southeastern corner of Newfoundland; Fermeuse Harbour (from *fremoso*, beautiful), about halfway from the cape to St. John's harbour; Cape Spear (from the Portuguese *de espera*, hope), just south of St. John's harbour.

Since the Corte-Real expeditions did not produce any riches, the Portuguese lost interest for two decades in North Atlantic exploration. But around 1520 João Alvares Fagundes made a voyage along the south coast of Newfoundland and into the Gulf of St. Lawrence. Upon his return, the Portuguese shipowner asked the Portuguese king for the same rights granted to the Corte-Real brothers. Assuming that the papal ruling of 1494 granted Portugal sovereignty over the area, the King gave Fagundes complete ownership of this region. Fagundes then obtained colonists from Portugal and the Azores and established the first European colony in northeastern North America since the Norse.

The Portuguese probably settled on Cape Breton Island, but, after a year or so, difficulties arose with the local Indians. Jean Alfonce, a French navigator, recorded the colony's fate several years later: "Formerly the Portuguese sought to settle the land . . . but the natives of the country put an end to the attempt and killed all those who came there."

29

FRENCH INTEREST IN THE NORTH ATLANTIC

Of all the European powers in the early sixteenth century, France was perhaps the best situated to dominate northeastern North America. After Fagundes's failure, Portugal had little interest—apart from the cod fisheries—in this supposedly poor region of the New World. France, however, had twice the population of Portugal and Spain together, and six times that of England. It also had more ocean-facing territory and as many (or more) seaports as England, and far greater wealth. Yet due to France's involvement in European conflicts, François I did not become involved in North Atlantic exploration until 1524.

Asia remained France's objective. Two areas across the North Atlantic remained to be searched for a passage to the Orient: that between Florida and Newfoundland (the most promising) and that between Labrador and Greenland. The French selected an Italian mariner, Giovanni da Verrazzano, as commander of their expedition. Verrazzano searched the North American coast from the Carolinas to Gaspé. At one point, he believed he had found a route to Asia. Just north of what is now North Carolina, beyond a narrow strip of coastline, he saw a mirage. He thought he had seen an immense, oceanlike body of water. The error had a long life. For many years afterward, cartographers placed the Pacific Ocean just north of Florida, almost reaching the Atlantic. Gradually, as more became known about the continent, the mapmakers placed the Pacific farther away from the shores of the Atlantic. But as late as the mid-eighteenth century, one European map still showed a sea connected to the Pacific covering much of present-day western Canada.

Despite Verrazzano's failure to find a passage leading from the Atlantic to Asia, France now had a relatively clear and full picture of the eastern North American coastline. Verrazzano's discoveries were not immediately followed up, however, as France went to war against the Hapsburgs (the rulers of Austria, the Low Countries, and Spain). These conflicts prevented the sponsorship of a second voyage.

Only a few months after Verrazzano's voyage, the Spanish-sponsored expedition of Esteban Gómez in 1524–25 resurveyed the Atlantic coast from Florida to the Grand Banks. Not wishing to return empty handed, Gómez kidnapped a large number of Indians on the New England or Nova Scotia coast and took them back to Spain to sell as slaves. The Spanish king freed the fifty-eight Indians who reached Spain alive, but their subsequent fate is unknown. (The fate of Gómez is known: in 1538 Indians ambushed and killed him and the members of his gold- and silver-seeking expedition on the banks of the Paraguay River in South America.)

30

Jacques Cartier's Three Voyages

Verrazzano's successor was Jacques Cartier, a mariner from the wealthy port of Saint-Malo in Brittany, northwestern France. Fishermen from Saint-Malo and other northern French ports had already sailed to the Grand Banks and inshore Newfoundland. Cartier probably gained his first maritime experience on these runs. In late April 1534, Cartier left Saint-Malo with two ships and sixty-one men in search of a passage to China and India. The expedition reached the Strait of Belle-Isle between Labrador and Newfoundland in late May. Unimpressed with the area, Cartier called it "the land God gave Cain," after the Biblical wasteland.

Cartier then entered the Gulf of St. Lawrence, and landed on present-day Prince Edward Island, which he believed was part of the mainland. Next, he sailed northward to Chaleur Bay, which divides Quebec from New Brunswick. Here the French met Micmac Indians. Cartier's journal contains the first reference since the Vinland Sagas to a trading exchange between Indians and Europeans—one initiated by the Indians themselves, who "set up a great clamour and made frequent signs to us to come on shore, holding up to us some furs on sticks." Before Cartier's arrival, European fishermen had no doubt traded with these Indians, who brought furs to exchange for the newcomers' iron knives, kettles, and axes.

When the French moved north to Gaspé they encountered Iroquoian Indians who had come from the interior to fish. Unaccustomed to trading with Europeans, they had brought no furs with them. The French gave the Iroquoian Indians "knives, glass beads, combs, and other trinkets of small value" to win their friendship. The French kidnapped two sons of the chief, Donnacona, and took them back to France to learn French, so that they could serve as guides on the next voyage.

It was standard practice among early Europeans in the Americas to capture natives and to take them back to Europe as proof of having reached the new lands. Often, the Amerindians did not survive the voyage across the Atlantic; those who did often died in Europe, unable to fight off illnesses that did not exist in the Americas and to which they had not developed immunities. Such was not the case with Donnacona's sons, Taignoagny and Domagaya, however; they lived, and assisted Cartier on his next expedition.

CARTIER'S YEAR IN THE ST. LAWRENCE VALLEY, 1535–1536

Cartier accomplished much in one summer, locating and charting the Gulf of St. Lawrence. The next year (1535) he returned with three ships and sailed up the St. Lawrence to the Indian village of Stadacona (present-day Quebec), the former home of Cartier's guides Taignoagny and Domagaya. Cartier recorded a word that his two guides used to refer to their home: "They call a town, *Canada*."[2] En route, Cartier gave the name St. Lawrence to a cove at which he stopped, after the Christian martyr whose feast day it was (August 10). The entire gulf and the great river later obtained the same name.

31

The Iroquoians at Stadacona saw the French as powerful and valuable trading partners. But when Cartier told Chief Donnacona that he intended to travel inland, the chief strongly objected. The Stadaconans had the customary right to a monopoly over the upriver traffic. They wanted to hold on to that monopoly and barter the interior groups' furs for more of the precious European iron tools.

Cartier paid Donnacona no heed and travelled westward in early October. By his own estimate, more than a thousand natives greeted him at Hochelaga, a palisaded town of fifty longhouses, much more impressive than Stadacona. That afternoon Cartier climbed the summit of the hill he called Mont Royal (which eventually became pronounced "Montréal"). From this vantage point he had a magnificent view of the well-cultivated cornfields and the longhouses below, but he also sighted the Lachine rapids to the west, which no boat larger than a canoe could pass. The French stayed just one day, then returned downriver. It was too late to depart safely for France, so he and his men wintered at Stadacona.

The story of the winter of 1535–36 at Stadacona is one of mounting tensions. Patterns of behaviour were established that continued long after Cartier's time. First of all, Cartier refused to recognize that the Indians had any land rights. Second, he had travelled upriver without first obtaining Donnacona's permission, and thereby interfered with the Stadaconans' trading rights. In addition, the French who had been left behind built a

32

Source: Adapted from P.G. Cornell, J. Hamelin, F. Ouellet, and M. Trudel, *Canada: Unity in Diversity* (Toronto, 1967), 22.

Jacques Cartier's first two voyages, 1534 and 1535–36.

small fort during Cartier's absence—an act that infringed on the Indians' land rights.

The winter, much longer and colder in Canada than in France, was a nightmare for the French. By January and February ice nearly four metres thick locked in the ships, and on land the snow was more than a metre deep. To add to the sailors' problems, scurvy broke out. Twenty-five (one-quarter of Cartier's men) died before the French learned the Indians' cure from Domagaya: boiling the bark and leaves of the *annedda* (white cedar) to make a brew with a high content of ascorbic acid (vitamin C).

Despite the Indians' help, Cartier remained antagonistic to Donnacona and his people. Anxious to obtain more information about the lands to the west, particularly the rich "kingdom of the Saguenay" that the Indians had spoken of, the French mariner kidnapped Donnacona, his two sons, and three of his principal supporters. The French believed this fabulous land to be rich in gold and silver, a second Mexico. (In reality, stories of the "Saguenay" probably referred to the native copper deposits around Lake Superior.) After promising to return his hostages the following year, Cartier left with them in the spring of 1536. Four children presented to Cartier by Donnacona and the chief of a neighbouring village went along as well. The ten Indians never saw "Canada" again.

33

Cartier entered the port of Saint-Malo in mid-July 1536, after an absence of fourteen months. Although he had not discovered great wealth, he had nonetheless made some important contributions: he proved that New-foundland was an island, charted much of the Gulf of St. Lawrence, and recorded in his journal the existence of a great river flowing from deep in the new land's interior—the St. Lawrence. His geographical exploration was not to be surpassed by any other French explorer except Champlain, in the early 1600s.

THE CARTIER–ROBERVAL EXPEDITION, 1541–1542

War between France and Spain delayed Cartier's third voyage until 1541. This time, the French navigator was to found a colony and locate the famed "kingdom of the Saguenay" and the Northwest Passage. The expedition split into two groups, with Cartier wintering at Cap Rouge, about fifteen kilometres upriver from Stadacona. His superior, Jean-François de La Roque de Roberval, followed the next year. At Cap Rouge, Cartier unloaded cattle and supplies and planted crops, making it quite clear that he and the 150 French colonists had come to stay. Very little information has survived regarding the settlement that winter, but it was later reported that the Indians killed thirty-five Europeans.

By the spring, Cartier had had enough. With a cargo of iron pyrites and quartz that he thought were gold and diamonds, he sailed for France. A French proverb still used in Brittany and Normandy owes its origin to this episode: "*Faux comme un diamant du Canada*" (fake as a Canadian diamond).

Roberval had with him some two hundred settlers. They had a terrible winter at the site of Cartier's settlement, which they rebuilt. Fifty colonists, ignorant of the cure, died from scurvy. The next summer Roberval returned to France. An inscription on a French map of 1550 explains the reasons for the colony's failure: "It was impossible to trade with the people of that country because of their austerity, the intemperate climate of said country, and the slight profit."

France, still at war with Spain, and soon to be torn by a civil war between Roman Catholics and Protestants, left Canada to its native inhabitants. French fishermen, whalers, and traders continued to come in great numbers, but colonization was not attempted again for another half-century.

The harsh climate, hostile relations with the Indians, and the failure to find gold combined to give Canada a poor image in France. In the late 1550s France directed its colonization efforts towards Brazil instead and, in the early 1560s, toward the present-day southeastern United States.

After Cartier and Roberval

European fishers maintained contact with northeastern North America in the mid-sixteenth century. Between March and October of each year, large fishing fleets—Portuguese, Basque, French, and English—gathered there. They supplied the markets of western Europe and the Mediterranean with the "beef of the sea" (cod). The Newfoundland fishery had become big business. With an estimated eight to ten thousand fishermen visiting annually, it provided a livelihood for twice as many men as did the fisheries of the Gulf of Mexico and the Caribbean combined, where the great Spanish fleets sailed.

The fishermen used two methods of preserving fish. In the "green" or "wet" fishery, the fishermen salted the catch directly on board ship. In the "dry" or "shore" fishery, they took the catch ashore and dried it on drying racks, or "flakes" (see Chapter 17). The "dry" fishermen became the first Europeans to establish summer settlements along the Atlantic coast of what is now Canada. Some "dry" fishermen obtained furs from the Indians as souvenirs and for their own use.

THE BASQUES' WHALE FISHERY

Basque whalers joined the cod fishermen in the early sixteenth century, and established a whale fishery in the Strait of Belle-Isle. It flourished for half a century. Sixteenth-century Europeans treasured whale oil as a prime source of light, an all-purpose lubricant, an additive to drugs, and a major ingredient of scores of products such as soap and pitch. At its peak, the fishery employed about two thousand men, who remained in Newfoundland–Labrador waters for six months each season, until mid-January. At the Basque shore stations, Inuit and Indian groups could obtain European materials on an annual basis from fixed locations in southern Labrador, perhaps on the Gaspé coast as well. Marc Lescarbot, the early French chronicler, noted that the Native people trading along the Gaspé shore during the first decade of the seventeenth century spoke a Basque–Algonquian trade language that was "half Basque." This became a "contact" language, used in speaking to the Europeans.

ENGLISH ACTIVITY IN THE NORTH ATLANTIC AND THE ARCTIC　　*35*

The English established fishing posts in the eastern part of the Avalon Peninsula in southeastern Newfoundland, while the French visited along the island's southern and western shores. In August 1583 Sir Humphrey Gilbert repeated Cabot's act of taking formal possession of Newfoundland for England. His colonizing expedition, however, proved unsuccessful. It was destroyed by a mutiny ashore and by storms at sea.

England sponsored a number of expeditions north of Newfoundland in the late sixteenth and early seventeenth centuries. In 1576, only a few months before Sir Francis Drake left to plunder Spanish shipping in the Pacific, Martin Frobisher, thirty-seven years old and a mariner of great repute sailed on a more peaceful mission—to open a passage to India and China by way of the Northwest.

Off Baffin Island, Frobisher encountered Inuit who came to trade meat and furs for metal objects and clothing. The Inuit showed that they were no strangers to European ships by doing gymnastic exercises in the ship's rigging. They had no doubt already encountered vessels of the Newfoundland fishing fleet and had probably traded with the fishermen, from whom they obtained iron. Frobisher himself discovered this when, in a skirmish with the Inuit, he was struck by an iron-tipped arrow.

Frobisher failed to find a strait either on this first journey or on his two subsequent voyages in 1577 and 1578. Ten years later the expert seaman and navigator John Davis followed up on Frobisher's work in three successive summers (1585–87), but he did not meet with success. The necessary maritime technology for the penetration of the Arctic Archipelago simply did not exist in the late sixteenth century. It was as impossible a goal for that age as a landing on the moon would have been for the nineteenth century.

"Encounter with Eskimos." A watercolour by John White, an artist who travelled with Martin Frobisher on his expedition in 1577 to Baffin Island.

European Trade with the Amerindians

Unfortunately, little contemporary information has survived about how North American Indians and Inuit perceived the first Europeans they met. The information that does exist attests to the Indians' amazement at the range and abundance of material goods that the white man possessed. The Iroquoians of the Great Lakes called the Europeans "iron-men."

The Europeans' metal tools and weapons were worth many animal skins to the Indians. The newcomers' steel axes lightened the labour of gathering firewood. Their copper cooking pots were not fragile like the Indians' pottery vessels or perishable like their wooden boxes and birch-bark kettles. Steel knives were far more durable than stone knives. Steel awls and needles made sewing and the working of hides and leather much easier.

European trade goods immediately entered the extensive Indian trading networks, and interior groups obtained them long before they ever saw a European. Archaeology has confirmed, for example, the presence, by the early sixteenth century, of European trade goods among the Seneca south of Lake Ontario, an Iroquoian tribe located hundreds of kilometres from the Atlantic.

Yet, if the natives of North America initially regarded the European newcomers with awe (interpreting their possession of metal objects as evidence of some great supernatural power), the amazement quickly passed. Missionary reports from the early seventeenth century reveal that the Indians had noted the slowness of the French in learning how to use canoes, snowshoes, and everything else that seemed commonplace to the Indians.

37

The original inhabitants of present-day Atlantic and Arctic Canada witnessed the arrival of the first Europeans—the Norse—around 1000 A.D., and of the English, Portuguese, French, Spanish, and Basques five centuries later. The early European navigators crossed the North Atlantic at great personal risk. John Cabot, the Corte-Real brothers, and Sir Humphrey Gilbert lost their lives in the course of their explorations. In the words of Samuel Eliot Morison, the American maritime historian, "North America became a graveyard for European ships and sailors."[3] Yet the Europeans persisted in crossing the North Atlantic. Some came in search of a profitable Northwest Passage to China and the Indies. Others—the vast majority—were lured by the promise of economic gain in the cod and whale fisheries, and later in the fur trade. Yet, as late as 1600, no permanent European settlement existed in present-day Canada.

NOTES

[1]Morris Bishop, *Champlain: The Life of Fortitude* (Toronto, 1963; first published 1948), 26.
[2]H.P. Biggar, ed., *The Voyages of Jacques Cartier*, published from the original with translations, notes, and appendices (Ottawa, 1924), 245. For an important discussion of other possible origins of the word "Canada," see Olive P. Dickason, "Appendix 1: Origin of the Name 'Canada'," in *The Myth of the Savage and the Beginnings of French Colonialism in the Americas* (Edmonton, 1984), 279–80.
[3]Samuel Eliot Morison, *The European Discovery of America: The Northern Voyages, 500–1600* (New York, 1971), xi.

38

Source: Adapted from M. Trudel, *Introduction to New France* (Toronto, 1968), 24.

Locations of Amerindian groups in present-day eastern Canada at the beginning of the seventeenth century.

Related Readings

R. Douglas Francis and Donald B. Smith, *Readings in Canadian History: Pre-Confederation*, 3d ed. (Toronto, 1990) contains the following essays relevant to this topic: Keith Matthews, "The Nature and the Framework of New-foundland History," 149–58, and Jacques Rousseau and George W. Brown, "The Indians of Northeastern North America," 3–16. Arthur J. Ray's "Fur Trade History as an Aspect of Native History," 51–63, discusses whether the fur traders exploited the native North Americans.

BIBLIOGRAPHY

Two delightfully written summaries of the early European explorers' accounts are available: Samuel Eliot Morison's *The European Discovery of America: The Northern Voyages, A.D. 500–1600* (New York, 1971) and Daniel J. Boorstin's *The Discoverers: A History of Man's Search to Know His World and Himself* (New York, 1983). Less colourful in its presentation but very informative is David B. Quinn's *North America from Earliest Discovery to First Settlements: The Norse Voyages to 1612* (New York, 1977). The primary texts are available in David Quinn, ed., *New American World: A Documentary History of North America to 1615*, 5 vols. (New York, 1979). For an archaeological perspective on the arrival of the first Europeans, see Robert McGhee, *Canada Rediscovered* (Ottawa, 1991). Economic aspects are briefly reviewed by Michael Bliss in *Northern Enterprise: Five Centuries of Canadian Business* (Toronto, 1987). *The Dictionary of Canadian Biography*, vol. 1, *1000–1700* (Toronto, 1966) contains many useful biographical portraits.

For the Norse experience in Greenland and North America, see Kate Gordon (with an essay by Robert McGhee), *The Vikings and Their Predecessors* (Ottawa, 1981) and Robert McGhee's "Contact between Native North Americans and the Medieval Norse: A Review of the Evidence," *American Antiquity* 49, 1 (1984): 4–26. Helge Ingstad tells the story of the discovery of the Anse-aux-Meadows site in his *Westward to Vinland: The Discovery of Pre-Columbian Norse House-sites* (London, 1969). Peter Schledermann's "Inuit Prehistory and Archaeology," in *A Century of Canada's Arctic Islands*, edited by Morris Zaslow (Ottawa, 1981), 245–56, reviews the recent finds of Norse objects on Ellesmere Island.

Bruce Trigger's *The Children of Aataentsic: A History of the Huron People to 1660*, vol. 1 (Montreal, 1976) provides background information on the reaction of the St. Lawrence Valley Indians to Cartier and Roberval. See also Trigger's *Natives and Newcomers: Canada's "Heroic Age" Reconsidered* (Kingston and Montreal, 1985). For an understanding of the Cartier–Roberval expeditions, consult the following two surveys: Olive Patricia

Dickason, *The Myth of the Savage and the Beginnings of French Colonialism in the Americas* (Edmonton, 1984) and Marcel Trudel, *The Beginnings of New France, 1524–1663* (Toronto, 1973). Cornelius Jaenen reviews the cultural interaction between the French and the Indians in *Friend and Foe* (Toronto, 1976). Leslie C. Green and Olive Dickason examine the ideology that motivated the European occupation of the Americas in *The Law of Nations and the New World* (Edmonton, 1989).

On Basque activity in northeastern North America, see Selma Barkham, "A Note on the Strait of Belle-Isle during the period of Basque contact with Indians and Inuit," *Etudes/Inuit/Studies* 4 (1980): 51–58; and "The Basque Whaling Establishments in Labrador, 1536–1632: A Summary,"*Arctic* 37 (1984): 515–19. A well-illustrated series of articles (including contributions by James A. Tuck and Robert Grenier) entitled "Discovery in Labrador: a 16th-Century Basque Whaling Port and its Sunken Fleet" appeared in the *National Geographic* 168, 1 (July 1985): 40–71. Daniel Francis reviews Basque whaling in the early chapters of *A History of World Whaling* (Markham, Ont., 1989). Peter Bakker has written an article on the Basque–Algonquian trade language, "Basque Pidgin Vocabulary in European–Algonquian Trade Contacts," *Papers of the 15th Algonquian Conference*, edited by William Cowan (Ottawa, 1988), 7–15. Laurier Turgeon surveys European fishermen's activities in the area in "Pour redécouvrir notre 16e siècle: Les pêches à Terre-Neuve d'après les archives notariales de Bordeaux," *Revue d'histoire de l'Amérique française* 39 (1985/86): 523–49. Consult also James Axtell's chapter, "At the Water's Edge: Trading in the Sixteenth Century," in his book *After Columbus: Essays in the Ethnohistory of Colonial America*, (New York, 1988), 144–81. The ecological consequences of the European arrival in the waters off northeastern North America are reviewed by Farley Mowat in his popular study, *Sea of Slaughter* (Toronto, 1984).

The impact of the Europeans on the relationship to nature of the Amerindians of northeastern North America is reviewed by Calvin Martin, *Keepers of the Game: Indian–Animal Relationships and the Fur Trade* (Berkeley, 1978). This controversial study must be supplemented by Shepard Krech III, ed., *Indians, Animals and the Fur Trade: A Critique of Keepers of the Game* (Athens, Georgia, 1981).

A survey of the Frobisher and Davis expeditions in Arctic waters appears in L.H. Neatby, *In Quest of the North West Passage* (Toronto, 1958). William W. Fitzhugh's essay, "Early Contacts North of Newfoundland before A.D. 1600," in *Culture in Contact: The European Impact on Native Cultural Institutions in Eastern North America, A.D. 1000–1800*, edited by William W. Fitzhugh (Washington, 1985), 23–43, reviews the period between the Norse expeditions and those of Davis and Frobisher.

For excellent maps on early European exploration, see R. Cole Harris, ed., *Historical Atlas of Canada*, vol. 1, *From the Beginning to 1800* (Toronto, 1987).

40

Time Line: 985–1663

985	—Eric the Red founds Norse settlements in Greenland.
1001	—Leif, son of Eric the Red leads an expedition to northeastern North America; in the following decade, attempts to establish permanent Norse settlements fail.
1450	—Norse settlements on Greenland have disappeared.
1492	—Christopher Columbus reaches North America; in the belief that he is in Asia, he calls the inhabitants "Indians."
1497	—John Cabot (Giovanni Caboto), an Italian navigator in the English service, lands in northeastern North America.
1524	—Giovanni da Verrazzano, Italian navigator in the French service, explores much of the Atlantic coast between Florida and the Gulf of St. Lawrence.
1534	—Jacques Cartier's first voyage for the King of France.
1535–36	—Cartier's second voyage, during which he visits Hochelaga (present-day Montreal) and winters at Stadacona (present-day Quebec City).
1541–42	—The Cartier–Roberval expedition ends disastrously with the abandonment of the attempted French settlement.
1576	—Martin Frobisher makes the first of a number of attempts by the English to find the Northwest Passage to India and China through Arctic waters.
1603	—Samuel de Champlain accompanies the Gravé expedition to northeastern North America.
1605	—Port-Royal Founded.
1605–07	—The French spend two winters at Port-Royal in present-day Nova Scotia.
1606	—At Port-Royal, Marc Lescarbot presents his *Théâtre de Neptune*, the first play written in present-day Canada.
1608	—Champlain begins to build a fortified trading post at the narrows of the St. Lawrence, or "Québec," as the French transcribed the Algonquian term for "strait."
1609	—For the first time, Champlain and the French clash with the Iroquois.

41

1610   —John Guy establishes an English colony at Cupids on Conception Bay. This is the first year-round British colony in what is now Canada.

1615   —First Roman Catholic missionaries reach the Hurons.

1627   —Establishment of the Company of One Hundred Associates, formed to speed up the development of the colony of New France.

1629–32   —The English seize and occupy Quebec for three years.

1634   —The Jesuit Fathers reopen the Huron mission.

Mid-1630s   —A series of epidemics sweep the Huron country.

1635   —Champlain dies on Christmas Day.

1639   —The Jesuits build Sainte-Marie, a permanent mission headquarters in Huronia.

1642   —The Société de Notre-Dame founds a new settlement on the island of Montreal; later it becomes known as Montreal.

1645   —The Founding of the Habitants' Company, to replace the debt-ridden Company of One Hundred Associates.

1649   —Fall of Huronia. The Five Nations defeat the Hurons in a quick military campaign.

1653   —French coureurs de bois replace the Hurons as the middlemen of the fur trade.

1660   —Dollard's last stand at Long Sault.

1662   —The French fortify Plaisance (Placentia) on the western coast of the Avalon Peninsula, and expand the colony begun there in 1660.

The Beginnings of New France

A small fur-bearing animal, the beaver, was the real founder of New   *43*
France. In the late sixteenth century furs commanded high prices in
Europe. No fabric then available rivalled the warmth, wearability, and
beauty of furs, which were in great demand for the clothing of both the
men and women of the upper classes. Persons of importance wore them
to display their rank and wealth. Fur coats, muffs, wraps, gloves, fur-
trimmed garments and, most important, wide-brimmed beaver hats all
came into fashion.

The beaver had become almost extinct in Europe, and merchants eagerly
sought even cast-off Indian beaver robes. When the robes were worn or
slept in, the long guard hairs of the beaver pelts loosened and fell out,
leaving only the soft underfur. Hat makers could then process the under
fur into a smooth felt unequalled by any type of woven cloth. By the
end of the sixteenth century hundreds of French traders were sailing to
Tadoussac, at the mouth of the Saguenay River in Quebec, to bargain for
pelts.

Jacques Cartier's three voyages established a French claim to the Gulf
of St. Lawrence, but international recognition of that claim came only
with successful occupation. The development of the fur trade brought the
French back permanently, and convinced the French government to bring
the trade under the control of a monopoly. For a private fur-trading
company to obtain the monopoly, it had to fulfill two promises: first, to
promote colonization and, second, to send Roman Catholic missionaries
to Christianize the Indians.

Rise of the Fur Trade

In the Gulf of St. Lawrence and along the Atlantic coastline, the fur trade began as a by-product of the fishing industry in the mid-sixteenth century. By coming back each year to the same locality, the French had established good trading relationships with the local Indians. In the 1580s, as the demand for furs increased in Europe, several French merchants began to send out ships commissioned solely to trade.

Fur was an ideal product for the European traders: it could not be produced at home, it was light in weight and easily packaged and transported, and, in the early years, it was highly profitable. The Indians, already skilled traders wanted to barter for European metal goods. They brought in pelts that had already been worn, which caused the long guard hair to fall out, leaving only the fine, smooth fur, ideal for hat felt. The Amerindians also sold pelts (that were dried immediately after skinning, and later combed in Europe to remove the long guard hairs).

44

Initially, the Indians did not perceive that the trade posed any danger to their independence. But, in reality, the fur trade had revolutionized the Indians' way of life. By the early seventeenth century, the Algonquians on the Atlantic coast had lost much of their former self-sufficiency and had become increasingly reliant on the Europeans. Furthermore, the fur trade had transformed the coastal groups from hunters and fishers into trappers. Prior to European contact, the Micmac spent more than half the year living on the coast, since the sea supplied as much as 90 percent of their diet. Their desire for trade goods, however, caused them to spend longer periods each year hunting inland for fur-bearing animals. This change in their traditional activities affected their winter diet. They no longer accumulated their usual summer food stores and instead relied partly on the dried foods they received in trade.

Tadoussac, at the mouth of the Saguenay River, became the Europeans' principal centre for trade on the Gulf of St. Lawrence. Pre-existing trading networks led from there to Hudson Bay in the north and to New England in the south. In the mid-1580s, as many as twenty vessels at a time could be seen at Tadoussac in the summer.

Trade reached such a volume by the 1590s that the French Crown established a monopoly to control it. But the monopolists' colonization schemes proved expensive. Early attempts all failed: the French colonists suffered a disastrous winter at Tadoussac in 1600–1601, when only five of the sixteen settlers survived the winter. An outpost established in 1598 on Sable Island (about two hundred kilometres off the coast of present-day Nova Scotia, close to the fishing grounds) also failed.

In 1603 a distinguished French official, Aymar de Chaste, Vice-Admiral of France, obtained the monopoly over the fur trade. He appointed as his representative in America François Gravé Du Pont, an experienced captain who had already made fishing voyages up the St. Lawrence. His mission now was to determine whether the St. Lawrence Valley could support settlement. On Gravé's ship in 1603, as a sort of observer-chronicler, sailed Samuel de Champlain, a young seaman in his twenties. The two men remained partners for nearly thirty years and together helped establish the first permanent French settlement in the Americas.

Samuel de Champlain

Considering Champlain's important role in the founding of New France, suprisingly little is known about his background. He was probably born about 1580 (and not 1570, as was formerly believed) and most likely came from Brouage, on the Bay of Biscay in western France—one of the principal sources of salt for the fishing fleet. At an early age he had gone to sea and had become a competent ship's captain and an authority on navigation. The earliest references to him document his service in the royal army. As a soldier in his mid-teens, young Samuel was toughened by service in a Renaissance European army whose soldiers' actions, in the words of E. Pocquet, a French historian, could be summarized by five phrases: to steal possessions, to carry off cattle, to burn homes, to kill men, and to rape women.[1]

45

After his army service Champlain undertook a voyage to the West Indies that kept him away from France for two and a half years. He returned to France in 1601. Two years later Aymar de Chaste invited him to sail with Gravé.

Much had changed among the population native to the St. Lawrence Valley since the journeys of Cartier and Roberval. Champlain saw large numbers of Algonquians at Tadoussac and small groups at several encampments along the St. Lawrence, but no Iroquoians, who had mysteriously left.

Unfortunately, we have only hypotheses, and no complete accounts, of the St. Lawrence Valley from the time of Cartier and Roberval to that of Champlain. Harold Innis, a Canadian economic historian, believed that the Laurentian Iroquoians were driven out of the St. Lawrence Valley and from along the Gulf coast by eastern Algonquian tribes. They had obtained iron weapons before the Laurentian Iroquoians, which gave them a technological advantage in warfare.

Recently, Bruce Trigger, an anthropologist who has done extensive research on the ethnohistory of northeastern North America, has advanced another theory. Trigger speculates that raids by the Iroquois living in present-day New York State led to the expulsion of the St. Lawrence Iroquoians. He proposes that the landlocked New York Iroquois became anxious for European trade goods but found them difficult to obtain from either the Saint Lawrence Iroquoians or from the Algonquians.

The Mohawk, the most easterly tribe of the Five Nations Iroquois, in desperation attacked the natives of the St. Lawrence Valley. In the ensuing raids they dispersed the Laurentian Iroquoians, some of whom may have moved west to join the Huron on Georgian Bay on Lake Huron. Archaeologists, he says, have established that European goods had reached all of the New York Iroquois tribes by 1600. These, Trigger surmises, must have been largely obtained as booty from the Laurentian Iroquoians. Although both explanations for the disappearance of the St. Lawrence Iroquoians are plausible, the data is lacking to reach any definite conclusions.

Following Cartier's route as far as Montreal, Gravé and Champlain made a careful examination of the St. Lawrence Valley during the summer of 1603. They learned much about the *pays d'en haut*, the country north and west of the St. Lawrence Valley. They also learned for the first time of a nation called the "good Iroquois" (the Huron) who lived by a great lake to the northeast (Lake Huron). The natives also told them about the geography of the interior and the existence of Lakes Ontario and Erie, and the extraordinary Niagara Falls. These Algonquians had a good working knowledge of the lower Great Lakes since their trading network reached the Hurons' country on Lake Huron.

With the end of summer, Gravé and Champlain returned to France. De Chaste had died during their absence, and Pierre Du Gua de Monts was granted the monopoly.

The First French Settlements in Acadia

Today we take for granted that Quebec was the natural site for France's first permanent settlement in present-day Canada. In reality, however, the French initially rejected this location. From 1604 to 1607 de Monts, accompanied by Gravé and Champlain, who served as cartographer, searched elsewhere for the best place to establish a colony. To escape the competition of traders who refused to respect the monopoly of the French St. Lawrence fur trade, they sailed south to the present-day Maritime provinces, a region with a climate milder than that of the St. Lawrence region and one potentially rich in mineral resources. They also searched for a more southerly location for the colony in the hope that the coastline might reveal a shortcut to Asia. In 1604 many Europeans still believed that the inlet of the great western sea, reported by Verrazzano nearly a century earlier, existed not far to the west of the Atlantic coast.

Armed with vice-regal powers and a ten-year trading monopoly, de Monts led his colonists to the south coast of Nova Scotia. They sailed up the Bay of Fundy and entered the Annapolis Basin, which Champlain named Port-Royal (see page 32). The party crossed to the New Brunswick shore, passed a large river (which they named the Saint John), and wintered on a small island near the mouth of the St. Croix River, now on the border between Maine and New Brunswick. Roughly half of the expedition's seventy-nine men died of scurvy before spring, and many more were close to death. The losses suffered in all of these early European attempts to found colonies in the New World were incredibly high. Starvation and disease took many lives.

After a summer exploring the coastline, the French stayed the next winter at Port-Royal. The colony formed there became the first agricultural settlement of Europeans on soil that is now Canadian. The French again explored the coastline the following summer and then wintered at Port-Royal.

After two years of considerable expenditures in Acadia, unsuccessfully searching for mineral resources and the Northwest Passage, de Monts realized the area's limitations. He simply could not enforce his fur-trade monopoly along the winding and indented coasts of the Maritimes. An entrepreneur needed only a ship, a crew, and a supply of trade goods to sail to the Maritimes to make his fortune. Annually, about eighty ships poached on de Monts's domain. Furthermore, his profits were insufficient to cover the cost of maintaining a post at Port-Royal.

47

Champlain stayed at Port-Royal for his third and final winter in 1606–1607. For the first time the French had a successful winter and, in fact, enjoyed themselves, thanks largely to the Order of Good Cheer founded by Champlain. The order, the first social club in Canada, required that every gentleman at Port-Royal take turns at becoming chief steward and caterer for a day. Ceremoniously wearing the chain of office, each steward prepared meals and made out the next day's menus. In friendly rivalry each man vied with the others to serve game and fish in abundance, in addition to the ever-present bread and salt cod. They sang favourite old songs and composed new ones on the spot. In 1606 Marc Lescarbot, a lawyer in the party, presented *Théâtre de Neptune*, the first theatrical production in Canadian history. Despite the improved situation that winter, de Monts could no longer afford to sponsor Port-Royal.

Ironically, the very year that the French temporarily abandoned Acadia, the English settled permanently in North America. In 1607 the Virginia Company established the colony of Jamestown in southeastern Virginia.

The Founding of Quebec

In 1608 Champlain and Gravé led an expedition back to Quebec, where they could control access to the interior and prevent competition from other traders. Champlain, as de Monts's agent, constructed a *habitation*, a collection of wooden buildings built in the form of a quadrangle and surrounded by a stockade and moats. The *habitation* stood in the shadow of a towering cliff above it, at the very point where the St. Lawrence suddenly narrows before widening out once more. (*Kebek* is the Algonquian word for "strait" or "narrow passage.") Champlain's post became the heart of the first permanent French settlement in present-day Canada.

Gravé left Quebec with a load of furs in mid-September, leaving Champlain and twenty-seven others at the new post. Once again, the French were ill prepared for a severe Canadian winter. Twenty of the twenty-eight died, two-thirds from scurvy and one-third from dysentery. Seemingly indestructible, Champlain himself was smitten with scurvy but survived. The following summer he set out to strengthen his relationship with the Algonquian Indians—the Montagnais in the Quebec area and the Algonquins in the Ottawa Valley.

In hindsight, one might ask why the Native people did not oppose the French occupation of Quebec. Like other Europeans, the French did not recognize the Indians' rights to the land. They officially claimed the St. Lawrence Valley simply on the basis of Jacques Cartier's voyages. And, as a Christian nation, they believed they had the right to occupy non-Christians' lands without even having to consult the original inhabitants. In fact, they soon began to make grants of land to new colonists.

Nonetheless, the Indians of northeastern North America did regard the land as theirs. Each Montagnais band around Tadoussac and Quebec, for example, occupied a specific territory; the boundaries were well known and usually well defined by recognizable geographical features. But the French were fortunate to have entered a war zone. The Montagnais welcomed the French traders because they were armed with muskets, which provided the Montagnais with security against Iroquois raids. The trading post at Quebec also ensured that the Montagnais could obtain badly needed iron goods.

Early French–Indian Relations

No sooner had the French established Quebec and concluded an alliance with the Algonquians, their Indian trading partners, than the latter asked Champlain to join their war parties against the Iroquois. Since he depended on them for furs, Champlain obliged. In 1609 he joined the Algonquians and some Hurons in an attack on the Iroquois to the southwest. The harquebuses, French guns used by Champlain and two of his men, so frightened the Iroquois that they lost the battle of Lake Champlain. The next summer Champlain and his Indian allies again defeated a Mohawk war party near the mouth of the Richelieu River.

The Franco-Algonquian alliance proved invaluable to the French, in that they learned a great deal from the Algonquians. They adapted themselves to the Indians' means of transport, since, with the exception of a few footpaths around Quebec there were few roads, so it was possible to travel only by boat—indeed, only by birchbark canoe, as the natives did. When the rivers froze, the French had to use Indian toboggans and snowshoes (with which they wore Indian moccasins). They also relied on the Indians' food supply. As late as 1643, Quebec was almost entirely dependent on Indian hunting for its supply of fresh meat. The French also learned from the Indians how to make maple sugar, and they began to gather wild berries, particularly blueberries, as the Indians did, as well. The Algonquians also trained the first French colonists how to survive winters in the interior of North America.

In Brazil the French had begun the practice of sending young men to live with the Brazilians to learn their languages and their way of life. Champlain also wanted cultural go-betweens, or as they would become known in Canada, coureurs de bois (literally, "runners of the woods") men who would cement France's economic and political alliance with the Algonquians and the Hurons.

In 1610 Champlain arranged to have a young Frenchman, still in his teens (probably Étienne Brûlé, one of New France's first coureurs de bois), live with the Hurons, with whom the French wanted to open direct trade. In return, Champlain took Savignon, brother of a Huron headman and roughly the same age as Brûlé, into his custody.

From Brûlé and Savignon the French learned about the Huron Confederacy, an alliance of several tribes with a population of thirty thousand. The Hurons' trading area extended as far as Lake Superior to the west and, through their contact with the Algonquians on the north shore of Lake Huron, as far as James Bay to the north. The Hurons offered the Algonquian hunting tribes corn in return for furs, which they now gladly retraded with the French for European trade goods.

Champlain made his last wilderness journey in the summer of 1615, one to strengthen the Franco-Huron alliance. As traffic increased on the Ottawa River, the Iroquois raids reached a new intensity, and the Algonquins badly needed allies. In return for their assistance, the Algonquins permitted the Hurons to travel downriver to trade directly with the French. In 1615 the Algonquins also allowed the French passage along the Ottawa, a privilege denied them four years earlier.

While in Huronia, Champlain concluded treaties of friendship with individual Huron headmen, affirming French support in their wars provided that they continued to trade with them. By joining a large war party of Hurons and Algonquins against the Iroquois, he convinced the Hurons of his concern for their well-being. Henceforth, the French could live securely among their Huron allies. And although the Hurons still had to pay tolls to the Algonquins for using the Ottawa River, they continued to take their own furs to New France. By the 1620s the Hurons supplied between one-half and two-thirds of the furs obtained by the French.

49

Champlain served, in effect if not in title, as the governor of New France. He kept the tiny trading post at Quebec alive, thanks to his establishment of a firm economic alliance with the Algonquians and Hurons.

The Company of One Hundred Associates

The colony, which existed only to collect furs, grew slowly. During the winter of 1620–21, no more than sixty people lived at Quebec. Thanks to the co-operation of the Indians, the fur trade required few Europeans. Furthermore, there was no incentive for Europeans to settle and farm in the northern colony. To whom would farmers have sold their produce? No market existed.

Thus, New France remained pathetically small compared with the other European colonies in the New World, which were located in areas of greater agricultural potential. The English colony of Virginia, for example, with an economy based on tobacco (a crop that attracted a great deal of capital and required many immigrants), had two thousand inhabitants, or twenty times New France's population, by 1627. Even the newly established Dutch colony of New Netherlands in the Hudson River valley had two hundred settlers by 1625.

In 1627, the French government, observing such successes in America, decided to end New France's total dependency on furs. The decision was made by the king's new chief adviser, Cardinal Richelieu. A period of disorder had afflicted France from 1610 (the year of the assassination of King Henry IV) until peace was restored in 1624. In that year Louis XIII handed the government over to the capable Cardinal Richelieu, who became the master of France for a period of eighteen years (1624–42). The cardinal worked to unify France under the Crown and to make France the leading nation in Europe, with strong colonies overseas.

Richelieu intended to extend French overseas commerce and authority through mercantile trade. Mercantilism, the dominant economic philosophy of Europe, held that colonies existed to enrich the mother country by exporting raw materials and by importing finished manufactured products from the mother country. Like every other European government of the day, the French looked upon overseas colonies as areas to be exploited. Only French ships could carry the goods to and from the colony. From its overseas colonies Richelieu believed that France could draw strength and riches to increase its stature in Europe.

The cardinal sponsored a new company called the Compagnie des Cent-Associés ("Company of One Hundred Associates"), which obtained working capital from one hundred investors to develop and exploit New France's resources and to encourage Roman Catholic missionary activity (Protestants were barred from participation). The company became the seigneur (discussed in Chapter 5) of all the lands France claimed in North America. It had a monopoly on all commerce, including the fur trade, and the right to cede land to settlers in seigneurial tenure. In return for its trade monopoly, the company promised to bring out four thousand settlers, all French and Roman Catholic, within fifteen years, and to promote Native missions.

Unfortunately for New France, the project began at the worst possible time: war had just broken out between France and England. In 1627 the Kirke brothers, English privateers, seized Tadoussac and captured, off the shores of the Gaspé, the French ships that were bringing four hundred settlers to New France. In 1629, the English attacked Quebec itself. Cut off from France, and their provisions long exhausted, Champlain and his starving garrison surrendered in July 1629. Champlain and the ailing Gravé left Quebec in the general French evacuation.

Still New France's greatest champion and lobbyist, Champlain urged the French ambassador in England to begin negotiations for the return of Quebec. For three years, the St. Lawrence remained closed to the French, which meant heavy losses for the One Hundred Associates. Charles I, who had married Louis XIII's sister, refused to hand back the captured territories until his French brother-in-law paid his sister's full dowry. Finally, when Louis XIII agreed to hand over all sums outstanding, the English left the St. Lawrence and Port-Royal in Acadia. In 1632 the One Hundred Associates could finally resume the program established in 1627. Returning to New France in 1633, Champlain undertook one last major initiative. He founded a post above Quebec in 1634 at Trois-Rivières.

Champlain deserves full credit for establishing New France, the Laurentian colony in northeastern North America. With the founder's death on Christmas Day, 1635, the effective leadership of the fur-trading colony passed into the hands of the religious orders, in particular, the Jesuits.

Contribution of the French Religious Orders

Champlain wanted the neighbouring Algonquian Indians on the St. Lawrence to form settlements and farm, as the French did; he also wanted them to intermarry with French people, in order to build up the French population. The first French missionaries assigned the task of transforming the Indians into French people were the Récollets, a branch of the Franciscan Friars, who did not have a large financial base. At first they believed the task would be relatively easy. Three Récollet priests and a lay brother arrived at Quebec in 1615, and five years later, they opened a monastery close to the settlement. The Récollets initially hoped their seminary would train a Native clergy for the colony, but they found the

Indians had no desire to assimilate into French society. The seminary soon closed for lack of students and funds.

In an attempt to solve their financial problems, the Récollets sought to collaborate with the Society of Jesus (commonly known as the Jesuits), a wealthy and powerful order founded by Ignatius Loyola a century earlier. From 1625 to 1629 the Jesuits assisted the Récollets in establishing missions in New France. This highly disciplined order, renowned for its ability to attract able candidates, often of high rank, was also known for its willingness to take on the most dangerous tasks. Jesuits had already served in the front lines of the Roman Catholic church's campaign to reclaim Protestant Europe. These highly educated men would write some of the best contemporary descriptions of New France in their reports back to France, called the *Relations*. (These publications are invaluable to historians today as first-hand records of early New France.)

After the English occupied New France in 1629, Cardinal Richelieu gave the Jesuits a monopoly over the Canadian mission field. Their work then began in earnest. Yet when they opened a school for Indian children, they encountered the same problems as the Récollets had.

Enlisting Indian students was difficult. Parents often refused to let their children go, and finally the priests had to give presents to the parents in order to gain students for the seminary. Many Indian students ran away and others became ill and died. The deaths increased the parents' resistance to their children's schooling, as did the French custom of physically punishing children, a practice foreign to the Indians' approach to childrearing.

When Ursuline nuns arrived in the colony in 1639 they came with the specific purpose of instructing Indian girls. Over the next thirty years the nuns succeeded, with difficulty, in teaching a few girls to read and write. In 1668 Marie de l'Incarnation, founder of the Ursuline Order in New France, wrote, "We have observed that of a hundred that have passed through our hands we have scarcely civilized one. We find docility and intelligence in these girls but, when we are least expecting it, they clamber over our wall and go off to run with their kinsmen in the woods, finding more to please them there than in all the amenities of our French house."

THE JESUITS' WORK WITH THE ALGONQUIANS

The Jesuits learned the Indian languages, introduced schools, and provided medical care to the Indians. To help fight the strange new diseases, such as smallpox and measles, that arrived with the Europeans, the Indians eventually accepted the nuns' offer to care for the sick. The Indians left the aged and the infirm at what they called the "house of death" (since the mortality rate there was so high) and thus avoided killing or abandoning to die those who could not travel to the hunting territories.

Like the Récollets before them, the Jesuits encouraged the Algonquians to settle down. They believed a nomadic life was contrary to the laws of the church and incompatible with Christian life. The Jesuits also felt that the Algonquians would accept the new religion more easily if they would live in the French manner, in settled agricultural communities.

To accomplish their goal, the Jesuits hired workmen to help the Montagnais clear farmland and build a small village at the foot of the cliff of Cap aux Diamants (where Jacques Cartier's men had mined for diamonds a century earlier), about seven kilometres southwest of Quebec. Upon receiving the fortune of Noël Brulart de Sillery, formerly a minister and ambassador of the king, the Jesuits gave the name St. Joseph de Sillery to the reserve of approximately thirty-five hundred hectares.

By 1641 the Sillery reserve contained some 30 families, in all, about 150 baptized Amerindians. A few Montagnais lived in completed one-room houses and the others in bark wigwams. Some Algonquians from Trois-Rivières joined them in clearing land and planting crops. But the constant threat of Iroquois attacks checked the development of the community. Throughout the 1640s, the village men frequently left for long periods on war parties, at which time those left behind abandoned the village for the safety of Quebec. Sillery then became a ghost town. Disease also struck, carrying away a number of the important converts. The village itself was divided into a Christian faction and a somewhat larger non-Christian faction. An Iroquois raid in 1655 and a fire in 1656 that destroyed the mission residence, the church, and most of the small houses finished off the Indian village of Sillery. It never recovered. By 1663 French farmers occupied most of the Sillery land.

The Jesuits made an important contribution to education in New France. In 1635 they established a college for Amerindian boys at Quebec, and classes began that year. This school was the first institution of higher learning north of Mexico, established a year before Harvard University in Massachusetts. Four years later, in 1639, the Jesuits encouraged the Ursulines and the Hospital nuns of Dieppe to begin a school for girls and a hospital at Quebec.

The church, in effect, became the second industry of the colony. The Jesuits, Ursulines, and the Hospital nuns came in number to serve the Indians and in turn brought out *engagés*, or indentured workers on three-year contracts, to help them. These newcomers created a market for agricultural produce in the colony. Upon being discharged, some *engagés* stayed and began to farm.

THE FOUNDING OF MONTREAL

The church supported the colony and helped to expand settlement. The Jesuits worked with the Société de Notre-Dame de Montréal, an association of priests and laypeople founded in 1639 in Paris. The Société initially raised a considerable amount of money and obtained a grant to purchase the island of Montreal.

Paul de Chomedey de Maisonneuve, a thirty-three-year-old career soldier, led the first settlers sent out to establish the colony. At Quebec the citizens did their best to discourage Maisonneuve and his band of forty colonists from continuing up the St. Lawrence, then beset by Iroquois attacks. Maisonneuve replied that if every tree on the island were changed into an Iroquois, his honour would still oblige him to found the new religious colony on the island of Montreal.

The Société de Notre-Dame believed that a mission settlement remote and independent from the main settlement at Quebec would attract Indians to settle permanently around it, once it was endowed with a church, a school, and a hospital. Then the Indians could be converted to Christianity. The organizers chose the former site of Hochelaga, located at the confluence of the Ottawa and the St. Lawrence rivers, which could be easily reached by the Algonquian-speaking tribes.

54

In 1642 the settlers arrived at their destination on the island of Montreal and established farms on the grassy areas where the villages of the Laurentian Iroquoians once stood. Despite an initial burst of enthusiasm, the settlement grew slowly. The only sizable influx of new settlers, one hundred in all, arrived in 1653. Two factors prevented the expansion of the remote colony of Montreal: the Société's quick loss of enthusiasm for its missionary enterprise, and raids by the Iroquois. In 1663 the Sulpicians, another French religious order, took over the direction of the settlement and became the seigneurs of the island of Montreal.

The Habitants' Company

The Company of One Hundred Associates never overcame the effects of the English occupation of Quebec between 1629 and 1632. By the early 1640s it stood on the verge of bankruptcy, heavily in debt and unable to supply the funds needed to maintain and defend the colony. The leading settlers in 1645—a group of fifteen businessmen, at most—took matters into their own hands and formed the Compagnie des habitants ("Habitants' Company"). While reserving its rights of ownership over all of New France, the Company of One Hundred Associates ceded the fur monopoly to the Habitants. Henceforth, however, the Habitants' Company had to pay the costs of administering the colony. This included payments to the governor and the military officers for the maintenance of forts and garrisons, the upkeep of the clergy, and the responsibility of bringing twenty male and female settlers to the colony each year.

New France in the Mid-1640s

In 1645—a decade after Champlain's death—the French colony in the valley of the St. Lawrence contained six hundred residents and a few hundred *engagés*. Clerical intervention in the 1630s had increased the population greatly, but the colony still remained smaller than a single large Iroquoian village. This slow growth is puzzling when one considers the advantages of emigrating from France. Landless peasants or workers settling in Canada could obtain all the land they wanted. Moreover, they could enjoy privileges denied their class in France and they could avoid paying royal taxes.

Nevertheless, emigration from France to New France was unpopular—Canada seemed to hold little appeal for the majority of French people, and the French government offered little incentive for them to emigrate. French Protestants who might have been tempted to leave certainly had no incentive to do so after 1627, when both Protestant worship and teaching were forbidden in Canada, as the French now termed the St. Lawrence Valley. The obvious dangers and discomfort of emigrating also discouraged many. First, the would-be colonists faced the dangers of crossing the North Atlantic, a voyage that took anywhere from three weeks to more than three months. On these voyages, if headwinds continued too long, food supplies would sometimes run out, and then scurvy would take its toll. (If fewer than 10 percent of the ship's company died during a crossing, the captain considered the voyage most successful).

The peasants and artisans who arrived safely faced the challenge of clearing the virgin forest. A man could clear one hectare a year at best. Much of this difficult work had to be performed in the summer months, when the black flies and mosquitoes made life intolerable. In addition to the hardships of crossing the North Atlantic and the difficulties of clearing land, the new arrivals faced the danger of Iroquois raids, which resumed in earnest in the 1640s. Every man—and many women—capable of bearing arms had to be ready at all times to fight for their lives. Furthermore, the early settlers, at least initially, were not dressed warmly enough and found the winters excruciatingly cold.

All this having been said, emigrants did leave France in the 1630s and 1640s in the hundreds. They left for the French Antilles, in the Caribbean, and for the islands of Martinique and Guadaloupe in particular, where, despite warfare with the local Carib Indians, employment could be had. Unlike the northern fur trade, tobacco and cotton required a great deal of unskilled labour. Within a decade the white population of the French Antilles was estimated at seven thousand. Emigrants from France saw little economic opportunity in New France in the mid-1640s, and this best explains the colony's small population.

The fur trade had made the colony. New France depended on the thousands of Algonquians and Hurons who hunted, trapped, and prepared the beaver pelts, and then carried them hundreds of kilometres to Quebec. Within a generation, France had advanced a thousand kilometres into the interior, establishing a firm trading alliance with the Hurons. But in early 1649 it was doubtful whether New France, with a resident population of barely one thousand, could survive in the face of determined Iroquois attacks.

NOTE

[1]E. Pocquet, *Histoire de Bretagne* 5: 320; cited in Morris Bishop, *Champlain: The Life of Fortitude* (Toronto, 1963; first published 1948), 8.

BIBLIOGRAPHY

Marcel Trudel provides an overview of the period in his *The Beginnings of New France, 1524–1663* (Toronto, 1973). A shorter summary appears in W.J. Eccles's *The Canadian Frontier, 1534–1760* (New York, 1969). His later work, *France in America* (New York, 1972), also contains information on the early French colonies in the Caribbean, as well as New France and Acadia. Allen W. Trelease reviews the Dutch colony along the Hudson River, in *Indian Affairs in Colonial New York: The Seventeenth Century* (Port Washington, N.Y., 1971; first published 1960). Contemporary maps and illustrations appear in André Vachon, in collaboration with Victorin Chabot and André Desrosiers, *Dreams of Empire: Canada Before 1700* (Ottawa, 1982).

For Indian affairs, Bruce Trigger's *The Children of Aataentsic: A History of the Huron People to 1660*, 2 vols. (Montreal, 1976) and his *Natives and Newcomers: Canada's "Heroic Age" Reconsidered* (Kingston and Montreal, 1985) are invaluable; a shorter summary appears in his Canadian Historical Association Booklet (no. 30) entitled *The Indians and the Heroic Age of New France* (Ottawa 1977; revised edition, 1989). Denys Delâge's *Le Pays Renversé: Amérindiens et Européens en Amérique du Nord-Est, 1600–1664* (Montréal, 1985) also provides a complete overview. An older study, A.G. Bailey's *The Conflict of European and Eastern Algonkian Cultures, 1504–1700* (Toronto, 1969; first published 1937), is still valuable, particularly for the information on the Micmac and Montagnais. Ruth Holmes Whitehead and Harold McGee's *The Micmac: How Their Ancestors Lived Five Hundred Years Ago* (Halifax, 1983) provides a good popular review of the Micmac; see also Virginia Miller's "The Micmac: A Maritime Woodland Group," in *Native Peoples: The Canadian Experience*, edited by R. Bruce Morrison and C. Roderick Wilson (Toronto, 1986), 324–52. Arthur J. Ray's *Indians in the Fur Trade* (Toronto, 1974), E.E. Rich's *The Fur Trade and the Northwest to 1857* (Toronto, 1967), and Carolyn Gilman's *Where Two Worlds Meet: The Great Lakes Fur Trade* (St. Paul, Minn., 1982) cover the economic aspects of early Indian–European contact. An excellent article written for the

Italian Canadian Studies Association is John A. Dickinson's "Les Amér-indiens et les débuts de la Nouvelle-France," *Canada ieri e oggi*, vol. 3 (Bari, Italy, 1986), 87–108; see also Brian Young's and John A. Dickinson's first chapter, "Native Peoples and the Beginnings of New France to 1650," in their *Short History of Quebec: A Socio-Economic Perspective* (Mississauga, Ont., 1988), 11–34. J.B. Jamieson reviews the disappearance of the St. Lawrence Iroquians in his article "Trade and Warfare," *Man in the North-east* 39 (1990): 79–86.

Three well-written biographies of Champlain are available: Morris Bishop, *Champlain: The Life of Fortitude* (Toronto, 1963; first published 1948); S.E. Morison *Samuel de Champlain: Father of New France* (Boston, 1972); and Joe C.W. Armstrong, *Champlain* (Toronto, 1987). Marcel Trudel has contributed the entry on Champlain in the *Dictionary of Canadian Biography*, vol. 1, *1000–1700* (Toronto, 1966), 186–99. For an understanding of Champlain's Indian policy one must, however, supplement these studies with Trigger's *Children of Aataentsic*, and his *Natives and Newcomers*. Champlain's "real" birth date (most likely around 1580, not 1570 or 1567) is analyzed by Jean Liebel, in "On a vieilli Champlain," *Revue d'histoire de l'Amérique française* 32, 2 (septembre 1978): 229–37.

Valuable sources on the subject of the Algonquians in the St. Lawrence Valley include James P. Ronda's "The Sillery Experiment: A Jesuit–Indian Village in New France, 1637–1663," *American Indian Culture and Research Journal* 3, 1 (1979): 1–18; and Cornelius J. Jaenen, "Problems of Assimilation in New France, 1603–1645," *French Historical Studies* 4, 3 (1966): 265–89, as well as his *Friend and Foe: Aspects of French–Amerindian Cultural Contact in the Sixteenth and Seventeenth Centuries* (Toronto, 1976). François-Marc Gagnon examines early French racial attitudes in *Ces hommes dits sauvages: L'histoire fascinante d'un préjugé qui remonte aux premiers découvreurs du Canada* (Montréal, 1984). Olive Dickason's *The Myth of the Savage and the Beginnings of French Colonialism in the Americas* (Edmonton, 1984); John Webster Grant's *Moon of Wintertime: Missionaries and the Indians of Canada in Encounter since 1534* (Toronto, 1984); and James Axtell's *The Invasion Within: The Contest of Cultures in Colonial North America* (New York, 1985) are very useful for their review of missionary activities in New France. For a review of European opinions about the land rights of aboriginal peoples in the Americas, see Leslie C. Green and Olive Dickason, *The Law of Nations and the New World* (Edmonton, 1989), and Cornelius Jaenen, *The French Relationship with the Native Peoples of New France and Acadia* (Ottawa, 1984). Biographical articles appear in the *Dictionary of Canadian Biography*, vol. 1: see in particular the entries on Jacques Noël, p. 520; François Gravé du Pont, pp. 345–46; Pierre Du Gua de Monts, pp. 291–95; Étienne Brûlé, pp. 130–33; Marie Guyart, dite Marie de l'Incarnation, pp. 351–59; and Paul de Chomedey de Maisonneuve, pp. 212–22.

The early history of the settlement at Quebec is reviewed in John Hare, Marc Lafrance, and David-Thiery Ruddel *Histoire de la Ville de Québec,*

57

1608–1871 (Montréal, 1987). Jean Poirier conclusively establishes that "Quebec" is an Amerindian place name in his "L'Origine et la signification du nom de lieu Québec," *Onomastica Canadiana* 72, 1 (juin/June 1990): 1–10. For the early history of Montreal, consult Gustave Lanctôt, *Montreal under Maisonneuve, 1642–1665*, translated by Alta Lind Cook (Toronto, 1969). Winter in New France is the subject of Pierre Carle's and Jean-Louis Minel's *L'Homme et l'hiver en Nouvelle-France* (Montréal, 1972).

Valuable maps of early Acadia and of New France are contained in R. Cole Harris, ed., *Historical Atlas of Canada*, vol. 1, *From the Beginning to 1800* (Toronto, 1987).

The Resistance of the Iroquois

Although both the Huron and the Iroquois confederacies belonged to the   *59*
same linguistic family and shared the same culture, the early chroniclers
of New France praised the former and condemned the latter. In any
discussion of the struggle between the Iroquois and the Hurons, therefore,
one must keep in mind the highly biased nature of the written source
materials. Unfortunately, we have no contemporary accounts by the Iroquois. Yet we do have a story, handed down by word of mouth from
generation to generation, of the Iroquois' perception of their enemies. The
account, in several variations, tells of the founding, in what is now upstate
New York, of the League of the Five Nations, or the League of the
Iroquois, by the following tribes (from east to west): the Mohawks, the
Oneidas, the Onondagas, the Cayugas, and the Senecas. After the Tuscaroras, from the Carolinas, joined the confederacy in the early eighteenth
century, it came to be called the Six Nations. The story provides a rich
source of information about the values of the *Houdenosaunee* ("people of
the longhouse"), as the Iroquois call themselves.

Formation of the League of the Iroquois

The founders of the League of the Five Nations conceived it as the nucleus
of a larger union. Historians, including Paul A.W. Wallace, now generally
agree that the confederacy was established by the late fifteenth century.
Wallace studied various versions of the myth and consulted with members
of the Six Nations to write *The White Roots of Peace*, the story of how
Dekanahwideh, the culture hero of the Iroquois, brought the Great Peace
to Iroquoia.

The core of the narrative begins with Dekanahwideh's arrival in the
country of the Iroquois. The Iroquoian nations at this time often raided

Source: Adapted from M. Trudel, *Introduction to New France* (Toronto, 1968), 28.

The Iroquoian groups of the lower Great Lakes in the early seventeenth century.

each other's villages and suffered attacks by the powerful Algonquians as well. Order and public safety had broken down, and Dekanahwideh found his way into Iroquoia blocked by a notorious cannibal. Immediately the peacemaker went to the cannibal's house and, finding it empty, climbed onto the bark roof and waited. Lying prone on the roof, he peered straight down through the smoke hole to create his own reflection on the surface of the water in the kettle below.

When the cannibal returned, he placed his victim's body in his cooking pot. But while bending over the kettle, he saw Dekanahwideh's face reflected from the water's surface. Thinking the image of wisdom and strength was his own, he became greatly disturbed, because he had never dreamed that he possessed such noble qualities. He stepped back and began to think about the brutal life he had been leading. In revulsion, the cannibal emptied the kettle of its human contents and resolved henceforth to stop his killing. Just then, Dekanahwideh came down from the roof and explained the Great Spirit's Message of Peace and Power. When the cannibal accepted it, Dekanahwideh gave him the name Hiawatha, which meant "he who combs," for he would comb the twists out of people's perverted minds.

61

The lawgiver and his new spokesman visited the five warring nations and, with varying degrees of difficulty, persuaded each of them to come under the Tree of Peace and to form a union called the *Kanonsionni*, or the Longhouse. Dekanahwideh then planted the Tree of Peace, a great white pine with healthy white roots that extended to the four corners of the earth, allowing all nations of good will to follow those roots to their source and to take shelter with the others under the great tree. On top of the tree, he placed an eagle to warn of danger. Then he put antlers on the heads of the fifty chiefs representing the Five Nations and gave them the Words of the Law.

A new political structure was thus erected to maintain peace among the Iroquois and gradually to draw the surrounding tribes into the league. In the eyes of the Iroquois, the fact that the Hurons refused to come under the tree of peace proved that they were an evil, hostile people.

Their belief in this story of the founding of the confederacy helps explain the Iroquois' feelings of superiority over their neighbours: it was among the Iroquois that the tree of peace was first planted. The Five Nations stood at the centre of the universe. In the late 1640s this belief gave them great self-confidence and a strong sense of purpose.

The Missionaries' Arrival in Huronia

At the time of French–Indian contact in the seventeenth century, the Hurons and the Iroquois were at war. A desire for war honours and prestige no doubt contributed to the hostility. Participation in a war party, if successful, raised a man's standing in his clan and village. It increased his chances of an advantageous marriage and his hopes of one day becoming a village leader. Moreover, the necessity of avenging the dead led to more warfare, since the Iroquois and the Hurons believed the souls of the dead could not rest in peace until they had been avenged. This led to an escalation of the feud between the two hostile groups.

With the arrival of the Europeans, economic motives joined those of prestige and the blood feud as causes of Indian warfare. Both the Iroquois and the Hurons needed a steady supply of furs in order to buy European trade goods.

The struggle between the Iroquois and the Hurons was of immense importance to New France. By the 1620s the Hurons had become the principal economic partners of the French, exchanging corn and European goods with the neighbouring Algonquians for furs. The Algonquians, in turn, traded as far north as James Bay and along the shores of Lakes Michigan and Superior.

62 As elsewhere on the continent, the fur trade and the goods that it brought stimulated the development of a richer culture among the Hurons. They began to decorate their pottery with more complicated patterns and use iron knives to produce more intricate bone carving. Their rituals became more elaborate.

THE JESUITS AND THE HURONS

After the French established an economic alliance with the Hurons, they secured the right to send Roman Catholic priests to Huronia. Champlain despatched Récollet missionaries in 1615, and then Jesuit fathers in 1627. As a necessary precondition for the renewal of the Franco-Huron alliance after the English ended their occupation of Quebec, the French insisted that the Hurons allow Jesuits to live in Huronia. Reluctantly, the Hurons agreed. In 1634 Jean de Brébeuf and two companions reopened the Huron mission. Dressed in black gowns from neck to foot, wearing broad-rimmed black hats, and with iron chains and black beads hanging from their belts, the "Black Robes" went from village to village to spread the Christian gospel. They were met by the Native people with apprehension and a growing fear, particularly after the epidemics of European diseases broke out.

The Jesuit order spared none of its resources in its effort to build up the mission. In addition to priests, the Jesuits used French lay workers (donnés), whose contracts assured them of lifetime support but no wages. Once the Jesuits had thoroughly mastered the Huron language, they communicated their ideas to the would-be converts. They also used non-verbal methods: pictures of holy subjects or of the sufferings of lost souls; religious statues; coloured beads as prizes for successful memorization; ceremonies, chants, and processions on holy days or on such occasions as baptisms, marriages, and funerals. They decorated the churches with crosses, bells, and candles, creating a colourful visual display. Yet, in this initial period, their efforts to welcome Hurons to the church led to few conversions. The Jesuits made some progress, but the gulf between the two societies remained great.

For the Hurons, the meaning of existence was to maintain harmony with nature. Human beings were not superior to other entities in the natural world, but were equal partners. Their sacred stories explained the fundamental relationships of the universe: the relationship between man and earth, between man and animals, between the sun and the moon, between sickness and health. Christianity differed from the Hurons' religion in viewing the world as provisional, one preparatory to the new order of God's kingdom. John Webster Grant, the Canadian religious historian, wrote that if the Indian's religious symbol was the circle, the Christian's "might well be an arrow running from the creation of the world through God's redeeming acts in history to the final apocalypse."[1] The two world views thus clashed.

63

To gain a Huron audience, the Jesuits emphasized the similarities between the Hurons' faith and their own. They pointed out that both believed in a supernatural power that influenced their lives, one which the Hurons located in the sun or sky and the Jesuits in heaven. Both Huron shamans and Roman Catholic priests encouraged personal contact with the supernatural. At puberty, every young Huron man was expected, through fasting and a vision quest, to find his own guardian spirit. The Jesuits similarly encouraged spiritual quests and valued fasts and vigils. The common reliance on prayer revealed a shared conviction that divine power controlled warfare, caused rain or drought, and gave health or disease. Finally, both Jesuits and Hurons accepted the idea of an afterlife; for Indians it was a pleasant place where life continued essentially as on earth, and for Christians it was heaven.

These common elements aside, the differences between the two religions were enormous. The chief difference lay in the Christian insistence that only one deity ruled the universe, in contrast to the Hurons' belief that many supernatural beings existed. The Jesuits, even when they had mastered the language, found it difficult to translate many ideas, such as that of the Trinity and the Incarnation.

Marriage was definitely a controversial matter. The Jesuits found the Hurons' sexual behaviour aberrant. Among the Hurons divorce was easy and frequent, in contrast with the Jesuits' ideal of the indissolubility of marriage. Since Huron children by custom belonged to the mother, divorce did not endanger family stability—the Hurons did not see how lifetime marriage was superior to their own custom. Moreover, they could not understand the Jesuits' practice of sexual self-denial.

Human sinfulness and the need for salvation were also important areas where the Jesuits found no common ground with the Hurons. Of course, the Indians distinguished between good and evil conduct, but they had

no concept similar to the missionaries' idea of universal guilt, of a fundamental inadequacy in human nature. Like most native North Americans,
the Hurons believed that almost all people would experience the same
pleasant afterlife, regardless of how they had lived on earth. For the Jesuits,
there was both a heaven and a hell. The only way to escape hell was
through Christianity. This concept of a place of torment proved very
difficult to convey to the Hurons.

The Jesuits tried to convince the Hurons that biblical standards were
worth accepting. They argued for some changes in the Huron culture: the
curtailment of easy divorce; the observance of marriages that were binding
for life; and an end to frequent feasts and undue reliance on dreams. The
Hurons saw, though, that the missionaries threatened to subvert their
value structure and way of life, since the Jesuits would have them stop the
rituals they regarded as essential to successful hunting, good health, and
survival. As a Huron chief complained to Brébeuf, "You are talking of
overthrowing the country."

NEW EPIDEMICS STRIKE HURONIA

The French brought with them more than European trade goods and a
Christian missionary message. Unknowingly they brought to Huronia
diseases of European origin that devastated the Hurons and their neighbours. Although we do not know the nature of the first three epidemics
in the mid-1630s, we do know that smallpox raged in 1639. The epidemics
killed more than half the Huron population, reducing it to ten thousand.
The Hurons lived in half-empty communities. Since old people and children died in the greatest number, the Hurons lost much of their traditional
religious lore, which tended to be the preserve of the elderly. The death
of so many children foretold a serious shortage of warriors in the next
decade.

In the late 1630s the Jesuits suffered from the Hurons' belief that they
were sorcerers who brought disease. The Hurons recognized three major
sources of illness: natural causes, unfulfilled desires of a person's soul
(alleviated by a form of dream-fulfilment), and witchcraft. It was not
surprising that the Hurons blamed the new diseases on their visitors,
whom the last and most serious epidemic had not touched. The Jesuits'
celibacy suggested that the "white shamans" were nurturing great supernatural power for the purposes of witchcraft. They seemed to be causing
death by their incomprehensible rituals, since after they touched sick
babies with drops of water, many died.

As the epidemics became more severe, the Hurons' fear of the Jesuits
increased. Longhouses and even whole villages refused them entry. The
Hurons harassed and threatened the Jesuits and their workmen. On at
least two occasions, in 1637 and 1640, general Huron councils discussed
the death penalty for the missionaries or at least the possibility of forcing

the sorcerers to return to the St. Lawrence Valley. Yet they pursued neither course of action. Many of the leading chiefs realized that the Hurons had no other source for European goods than the French, and by the late 1630s they believed that they could not live without these goods. Since trading relations with the French had to be maintained, they continued to tolerate the missionaries.

HURON CHRISTIAN CONVERTS

During the epidemics of the mid-1630s the missionaries under Jean de Brébeuf's direction worked in selected Huron villages, spending most of their time mingling with the villagers. Jérôme Lalemant, the new superior of the Huron mission, changed this policy in 1638. He constructed a permanent mission headquarters of stone and timber buildings. Begun in 1639, Sainte-Marie included residences, chapels, workshops, and a hospital within its fortified walls. Adjacent to Sainte-Marie, the Jesuits cleared fields and planted crops.

65

Inspired by accounts of the Jesuits' missions in Paraguay in South America, Lalemant hoped that the Huron converts might be led to settle at Sainte-Marie and to adopt French customs. When they refused to leave their villages and abandon their clans, he established permanent Jesuit residences in the major Huron towns. The priests visited other villages on assigned circuits.

In the early 1640s conversions began to increase. Several factors contributed to this. No doubt the Jesuits' repeated explanations of the two faiths' common themes helped. The Jesuits' own unquestioned bravery during the Iroquois attacks influenced others to convert. Simple economics also influenced many Huron traders. As anthropologist Bruce Trigger has pointed out, French traders and government officials accorded the Christian Indians far greater honour and gave them additional presents at Quebec and Trois-Rivières. Another incentive to convert came from the French policy of selling guns only to those Indians who were baptized. In 1648, when only 15 percent of the Huron population had been baptized, more than half the traders who came to Trois-Rivières were already Christians or were receiving instruction.

Thanks to the dedicated efforts of the Jesuits, their stressing of the common bridges between the two faiths, and the obvious economic advantages of conversion, by 1646 the Huron Christian community numbered five hundred and was growing.

The development of a Christian faction in Huronia, however, seriously divided the community. The priests forbade converts to participate in public Huron feasts and celebrations, and they had to abandon all their traditional religious practices. To avoid involvement in Native rituals, Christian warriors often refused to fight alongside traditionalists. Conver-

Why the Hurons Accepted Christianity

In the 1640s an extraordinary event occurred; large numbers of Huron Indians in good health accepted Christianity. Before 1639 the Jesuits' attempts to Christianize the Hurons met with success mostly with individuals who were on the point of death, yet by 1648 they had converted several thousand people. Had it not been for the Iroquois defeat of the Hurons in 1649–50 and their subsequent dispersal, the Jesuits' dream of establishing a Roman Catholic Huronia might have been realized. The massive conversion of Hurons to Christianity in the last years of Huronia has recently aroused new interest among historians.

The impact of disease offers one explanation for the Hurons' sudden receptiveness to Christianity. From 1635 to 1640 a series of epidemics carried away more than half the population. The Hurons lost many of their most skilful leaders and craftspeople, and this had the effect of increasing their dependence on trade with the French. Anthropologist Bruce G. Trigger, in his 1968 article "The French Presence in Huronia," identified the economic motives, among other factors, that led many Hurons to convert. They sought, through conversion, "to receive preferential treatment in their dealings with traders and officials in New France," and in particular, to be able to secure guns, which were given only to converts. In fact, as Trigger points out, "in 1648, when only 15 per cent of the Hurons were Christian, half of the men in the Huron [trading] fleet were either converts or were preparing for baptism" (*Canadian Historical Review* 49 [1968]:134; reprinted in R. Douglas Francis and Donald B. Smith, eds.,

Readings in Canadian History: Pre-Confederation, 3d ed. [Toronto, 1990], 36.)

Trigger's secular explanation of the Jesuits' success in his later two-volume work, *The Children of Aataentsic: A History of the Huron People to 1660* (Montreal, 1976), greatly annoyed historian Lucien Campeau, himself a Jesuit. Referring to Trigger's work as "malheureusement biaisée et peu exacte sons l'aspect historique" [unfortunately biased and not very historically accurate] (p.18), Campeau wrote a full account of his order's work among the Hurons in order to prove that the Hurons understood the Christian message as it was preached to them and that that message was the primary reason for their conversion (*La Mission des Jésuites chez les Hurons, 1634–1650* [Montreal, 1987]). In reply, Trigger pointed out that Campeau had failed to examine the most recent ethno-historical research in preparing his study. Moreover, he was too ready to accept, uncritically and at face value, the Jesuits' account of their mission work. "What we have here is splendid hagiography but very old-fashioned historiography" ("Review of *La Mission des Jésuites chez les Hurons, 1634–1650* by Lucien Campeau," *Canadian Historical Review* 69 [1988]:102). By putting a human face on the discussions, biography can be useful in humanizing historical controversies. Yet, in the case of the Hurons, the would-be-biographer faces incredible obstacles. As Bruce Trigger has written in *The Children of Aataentsic*, "For the majority of Indians whose names have been preserved, only a few isolated events are recorded and even a skeletal life history of such individuals remains beyond our grasp" (vol. 1, p. 22). Fortunately, however, Trigger was able to use the Jesuit Relations to provide an account of the Christian convert, Joseph Chihoatenhwa (*The Children of Aataentsic*, vol. 2, pp. 550–51, 565–67, 594–95, 598–601). Expanding upon Trigger's sketch, John Steckley, an anthropologist and student of the Huron language, has completed a short biography, one of three included in his *Untold Tales: Three 17th Century Huron* (Ajax, Ont., 1981). In Chihoatenhwa's case, economic factors apparently played very little part in his decision to accept Christianity, as he traded with the neighbouring Petun Indians, and not with the French. Steckley argues, as does Trigger, that Joseph Chihoatenhwa converted in 1637 for reasons deep within his Amerindian culture. "As a Christian, Chihoatenhwa did have, or believed he had, a source of power on which he could draw, a spiritual source not unlike that upon which a pre-contact Huron shaman could rely.... The priest appeared to have an effective medicine when no other was forthcoming; a preventative or cure which Chihoatenhwa accepted much [as] he would have in earlier times accepted the curing vision or dream of a powerful shaman" (pp. 9–10).

Historians, anthropologists, and ethnohistorians radically differ about the causes of the Hurons' conversion to Christianity, but all agree on the importance of the phenomenon and on the richness of the Jesuits' descriptions of their efforts to convert the Hurons.

67

sion on occasion also resulted in divorce and in the Christian warriors' expulsion from their wives' or mothers' longhouses.

The Final Struggle between the Hurons and the Iroquois

At the very time when disease had weakened them and their internal cohesion had been reduced by the growth of a Christian faction, the Hurons faced their greatest military threat from the Iroquois. The invitation issued to the Hurons to join the Five Nations had been refused. In the 1640s, with a shortage of beaver pelts in their own territory, the Iroquois needed an increased supply to purchase European goods. The Huron country was adjacent to the fur-rich areas around the Upper Great Lakes that the western Iroquois wanted to exploit.

THE ESCALATION OF HOSTILITIES

Guns made the Iroquois a much more formidable foe. By about 1639 they had begun to obtain firearms from English traders in the Connecticut Valley and then directly from Dutch traders on the upper Hudson River. Thus equipped, they could raid the tribes living to the north much more readily than they could before. The longer and heavier Dutch guns were superior to those that the French sold to their Christian converts.

By the late 1640s the Iroquois had gained superiority in firearms. Bruce Trigger estimates that in 1648 the Hurons probably had no more than 120 guns, while the Iroquois had more than 500. These early guns were clumsy to handle and in many ways were little better than the bow and arrow, but their thunderous noise and their ability to inflict mortal wounds made them a source of terror. They also increased the self-confidence of those who owned them.

The successful Iroquois attacks of the early 1640s contributed to the growth of a faction of Huron traditionalists who were prepared to end the Huron Confederacy's trading alliance with the French. These Hurons believed that peace with their enemies the Iroquois—with whom they were at least closely allied in customs and speech—was preferable to cultural extinction through association with the Jesuits. In the end, however, the majority of the traditionalists mistrusted the Iroquois more than they did the French, and opted to side with the Christian Hurons in opposing the termination of the French alliance. The defeat of the anti-Jesuit Hurons ended organized resistance to the missionaries. By 1649, about half the Huron population had been baptized.

In mid-March 1649 the Iroquois brought the Jesuit experiment to an abrupt halt. Without warning, a large Iroquois army struck a small Huron village, killing or capturing all but ten of the four hundred people living there. They used the village as a base camp to destroy other settlements. Hurons who had been earlier captured and adopted by the Iroquois played a leading role in the attacks. The adopted Hurons, together with the Iroquois, tortured the French priests they captured, regarding them as sorcerers responsible for the destruction of their country. Familiar with the frequent baptizing of dying children, the attackers repeatedly baptized Father Jean de Brébeuf and Gabriel Lalemant (the nephew of Jérôme Lalemant, now the superior of all the Jesuits in Canada) with boiling water, then further tortured and finally executed them.

Over the course of the campaign, seven hundred Hurons died or were captured. The attacks threw the surviving settlements into chaos. The Hurons, seeing their position as untenable, burned their villages and deserted them. Hunger and contagious diseases claimed many Huron refugees who spent the winter on Christian Island, in Georgian Bay. A small number of survivors eventually accompanied the Jesuits to Quebec, where the order established a fortified mission for them on Île d'Orléans, just east of the town. Others joined the Algonquians to the north. In the next few years, a number of Hurons voluntarily joined the Iroquois. Their former villages lay destroyed in their old homeland of Huronia, and their cornfields reverted to forest.

68

THE RESISTANCE OF THE IROQUOIS

ADOPTION OF CAPTIVES

After defeating the Hurons, the Iroquois attacked and dispersed other Iroquoian peoples: first the Petuns, then the Neutrals, and then the Eries. The Five Nations adopted large numbers of the captives, just as they had previously taken in many Hurons. Due to a serious depletion in their own numbers (through disease and frequent warfare), the Iroquois needed to find replacements. As the neighbouring Iroquoians had the same mixed economies of agriculture, hunting, and fishing, and shared related languages and similar religious beliefs, they were ideal candidates for adoption.

The Fall of Huronia

The fall of Huronia greatly disrupted the fur trade on which New France's economy depended. Yet, as Bruce Trigger notes, "The situation would have been far worse for the French if the Huron traditionalists had been able to conclude an alliance with the Iroquois."[2] The diversion of furs to the Dutch on the Hudson River and the consequent bypassing of the St. Lawrence would have ruined the fur-trading colony. As it was, only in the short run did the dispersal of the Hurons hurt the colony's economy—in the long run, it helped it. Because the Hurons could no longer supply food to the northern Algonquians, the latter became a new market for the colony's farmers. Historian John Dickinson has noted also that in the 1650s the majority of the *engagés* began to stay in the colony after their contracts had expired. Farming expanded, as did the French fur trade.

By 1653, the French coureurs de bois (see Chapter 3) had begun to replace the vanquished Huron middlemen in the fur trade. They went inland to live with the Algonquians of the upper Great Lakes, or the "Ottawa," as the French called them, and to take their furs to New France. In 1654 Médard Chouart Des Groseilliers canoed into the interior, returning two years later with a rich cargo of furs. (Des Groseilliers' brother-in-law, Pierre-Esprit Radisson, accompanied him on later journeys, including one in 1659 to the far end of Lake Superior, where they heard of a "Bay of the North Sea" hundreds of kilometres to the north.)

In the early 1650s New France suffered greatly and almost collapsed from the Iroquois attacks. A mere fifty men held Montreal, the advance guard of the settlements. Even at Trois-Rivières and at Quebec few went out to work their fields because of the ever-present danger. Between 1650 and 1653 the Iroquois killed thirty-two French settlers and captured twenty-two. The Iroquois' use of guerilla war tactics, their avoidance of open combat in favour of ambush, and the speed and unexpectedness of their attacks demoralized many of the colonists. As Marie de l'Incarnation,

National Archives of Canada/C-3108.

The battle at Long Sault on the Ottawa River assumed epic proportions for French Canadian nationalists in the early twentieth century. Writers such as Abbé Lionel Groulx (1878–1967) wrote of Dollard as the soldier-saint who saved Montreal in 1660. *Above:* The painting by the famous Quebec artist M.-A. de Foy Suzor-Côté (1869–1937), completed in 1926, is entitled *Le combat de Dollard des Ormeaux 1660. Opposite:* Abbé Groulx, in a photo taken in 1960, holds his book *Dollard, est-il un mythe?* [Dollard, is he a myth?]

70

the founder of the Ursuline order in New France, recalled in a letter to her sister, the Iroquois "made such ravages in their regions that we believed for a time that we should have to go back to France."

With the outbreak of war between the Iroquois and the Eries to the west, New France obtained a five-year truce with the Iroquois in the mid-1650s. However, fighting resumed in the late 1650s and early 1660s. For the French, the struggle took on the atmosphere of a holy war. By this time, though, the population had increased in number and the colony was no longer in such danger as it had been in the early 1650s. The population tripled, from 1050 permanent French residents at the end of 1651 to nearly 3300 in 1662. The colony had grown thanks to new opportunities for farming.

A RENEWAL OF THE IROQUOIS ATTACKS

In the late 1650s and early 1660s New France developed effective measures against Iroquois attacks. A small detachment of soldiers patrolled the St. Lawrence from Trois-Rivières to Montreal, the most exposed settlement.

National Archives of Canada/C-16657.

The French organized militia units and erected stockades. They also came to realize that the Iroquois could best be fought using Indian tactics, and so adopted them.

The French took their first initiative against the Iroquois in the spring of 1660. The military force consisted of Adam Dollard Des Ormeaux, an ambitious young soldier recently arrived from France with sixteen other young Frenchmen, and Annaotaha, an experienced Huron warrior with several dozen warriors. They left Montreal intending to ambush a small Iroquois war party on the Ottawa River. The Frenchmen and their Huron allies knew that the Iroquois raided and hunted for furs in the Ottawa valley every winter.

To his horror, Dollard encountered an Iroquois invasion army. Instead of a small band of Iroquois hunters at Long Sault, northwest of Montreal, the French and their allies faced three hundred warriors on their way to rendezvous with four hundred more who awaited them at the Richelieu River. The Iroquois besieged the hastily built Franco-Huron fort, then waited for reinforcements from the south before making the final assault. In the interim, some of the adopted Hurons in the Iroquois camp persuaded a number of the Hurons who were with Dollard to join them. Since the French had turned over several Huron refugees to the Iroquois not long before, most of the Hurons felt no obligation to fight to the death. Only five Frenchmen were alive when the Iroquois took the fort. One was tortured to death immediately; the others were also tortured, but three managed to escape. It was from them that the French learned of the incident.

Historian André Vachon summarized the accomplishment of Dollard and his companions in repelling an attack on Montreal: they "diverted the Iroquois army temporarily from its objective in 1660, thereby allowing the settlers to harvest their crop and escape famine and allowing Radisson to reach Montreal safe and sound with a load of furs."[3] (In the late nineteenth and early twentieth centuries, French Canadian historians resurrected Dollard as a national French Canadian hero. In French-speaking Quebec, May 24 is known as Dollard Day.)

The Iroquois raids continued. Between 1660 and 1661, fifty-eight settlers were killed and fifty-nine captured. New France could not truly prosper until the Iroquois raids stopped. Pierre Boucher, governor of Trois-Rivières, warned in 1663 of the constant danger: "A wife is always uneasy lest her husband who left in the morning for his work, should be taken or killed and that never will she see him again."

Security finally came for the habitants when, in 1663, King Louis XIV elevated the tiny colony to a royal province of France. The previous year, he had sent one hundred troops to New France and in 1665 dispatched another twelve hundred, under veteran officers. The following year, in 1666, the French made two attacks on the Iroquois country in present-day New York State. The Iroquois, who were also then involved in a war with the Susquehannock (Iroquoian-speaking Indians living in present-day Pennsylvania), made peace with the French in 1667. Twenty years of peace followed for the St. Lawrence Valley. The truce allowed the colony to advance in the 1660s as dramatically as it had in the 1650s.

The Iroquois and the French, 1667–1701

Tension continued between the Five Nations and the French in the Great Lakes area. To obtain furs, the Iroquois sent raiding parties in the late 1660s to the Illinois country, but this interfered with French exploration of the Mississippi valley. The tribes in the Illinois refused to accept the Iroquois invitation to ally themselves with the Iroquois League and turned to the French, who promised aid and protection. Relations between the Five Nations and the French deteriorated every year as the Iroquois increased their raids against the Illinois Indians, now French allies.

At the same time that the Five Nations attacked the Illinois to the west, they attempted to improve their relations with the northern Algonquians in order to obtain their furs. This seriously troubled the French. The establishment of Hudson's Bay Company posts on James Bay and Hudson Bay in the 1670s had already diverted northern furs to the English. If the Five Nations took more furs from north of the Great Lakes to the Atlantic seaboard, New France would lose its leading export.

The Iroquois had colonized the north shore of Lake Ontario in the 1660s, and they used their settlements as bases for trading with the northern Algonquians. These developing trade links frightened the French, who established the post of Cataraqui, or Frontenac (at present-day Kingston), in 1673 to control the trade at the eastern end of Lake Ontario. Around 1680 the French also briefly maintained a fort at Niagara to control the trade at the western end of Lake Ontario.

The French ended the truce with the Iroquois in the mid-1680s. They wanted the Five Nations to cease their attacks on the Illinois Indians and to stop trading the northern Algonquians' furs to the English. An attempted invasion of the Iroquois country in 1684 under the leadership of Governor Le Febvre de La Barre was a fiasco. When provisions ran out and fever ravaged the governor's troops, he was forced to sign a humiliating peace treaty with the Iroquois that eventually led to his dismissal as governor.

In 1687 the French persuaded the Algonquians to join nearly two thousand French troops on a second expedition to the Iroquois country. The invaders burned a number of villages, destroyed cornfields, and looted graves. The war was now fully underway. In 1689 the Iroquois, with the aid of the English, retaliated by attacking the French settlement at Lachine, about fifteen kilometres west of Montreal. According to a French account, fifteen hundred Iroquois laid waste the open country: "the ground was everywhere covered with corpses, and the Iroquois carried away six-score captives, most of whom were burned."

73

The early 1690s marked the high point of the Iroquois' success against the French—but then their fortunes turned. The settlers (by necessity now skilled in the techniques of guerilla warfare), together with fifteen hundred regular troops sent from France, gained the upper hand. By 1693 the Five Nations were suffering very heavy losses as a result of both war and disease. In the face of the Algonquians' attacks, they could no longer maintain their forward position on the north shore of Lake Ontario. Their numbers fell from more than ten thousand in the 1640s to less than nine thousand at the turn of the century, despite massive adoptions of other Iroquoians.

IROQUOIS CHRISTIAN CONVERTS

The presence of Jesuit priests in their villages during the truce also weakened the Iroquois, especially during the period from 1668 to 1686. The priests attracted Christian converts from the Iroquois villages in present-day New York State to their mission at Sault Saint Louis (Caughnawaga, now Kahnawake) near Montreal. By 1700, an estimated two-thirds of the Mohawks, the most easternly of the Five Nations or Iroquois Confederacy, lived in the Montreal area.

Conversion to Christianity also weakened the indigenous belief systems of the Iroquois. The Jesuit *Relations* report, for example, that when ritual demanded that Garakontié, a leading Christian convert, recite "the genealogy and origin of the Iroquois ... he always protested that what he was about to say was merely a formula which is usually followed on such occasions, but that it was not true"; indeed, he said it was "simply a story, and that Jesus was the sole Master of our lives."

Many of the Jesuits' Iroquois converts were recently adopted Hurons and other prisoners, a fact that indicates the Five Nations had not yet had enough time to assimilate fully all their adoptees. In the mid-1660s several Jesuit missionaries established that adoptees constituted two-thirds or more of the population of many Iroquois villages. The recently adopted Iroquois no doubt weakened the unity of the Five Nations' communities.

THE SOUTHWARD MIGRATION OF THE ALGONQUIANS

The Algonquians considered themselves the allies, not the subjects, of France. In 1671 the French had claimed possession of the Great Lakes in the presence of a great convocation of tribes at Sault Ste Marie. Fourteen Amerindian nations witnessed the raising of a cross and of a post bearing France's coat of arms. The Algonquians, however, had an entirely different understanding of the proceedings, as evidenced by their oral history of the event. (The latter has been recorded by William Warren, a nineteenth-century Native historian.) The Indians believed that the French had simply asked "for permission to trade in the country," and that the French

74

king's representative had, in return, "promised the protection of the great French nation against all their enemies."[4]

Having secured their ties with the French, and having seen the Five Nations Confederacy in such a weakened state, the Algonquians advanced south from Lake Superior and the north shore of Lake Huron to occupy the former Huron, Petun, and Neutral homelands. By coming south, the Algonquians acquired rich new hunting and fishing grounds. Some even acquired a new name: The English colonists on the Atlantic Coast termed all the newcomers in the area bounded by Lakes Ontario, Erie, and Huron either Chippewa or Ojibwa. But they reserved a new name, Mississauga, for the Ojibwa on the north shore of Lake Ontario. In 1640 the Jesuit fathers first recorded the term *omisagai* (Mississauga) as the name of an Algonquian band near the Mississagi River on the northwestern shore of Lake Huron. For unknown reasons, the French, and later the English, applied this name to all the Algonquians settling on the north shore of Lake Ontario. Only a tiny fraction of these Indians could have been members of the actual Mississauga bands, but once recorded in the Europeans' documents, the name became the one most commonly used. The Ojibwa, of course, continued to call themselves by their own name of *Anishinabeg*, meaning "human beings."

PEACE ESTABLISHED, 1701

The English made peace with the French in 1697. This truce led the Iroquois to reconsider their own conflict with the French. In 1700 they made an offer to the French, who convened a council with them at Montreal. Combat fatalities, the exodus of Roman Catholic converts to New France, and disease had all greatly weakened the Iroquois. The Five Nations had had approximately 2570 warriors in 1689; by 1700, there were only 1230.

The Iroquois made peace with the French and thirteen western tribes in August 1701. To ensure that the Iroquois continued to serve as a buffer between the English colonies and New France, the French allowed them to continue to trade some northern furs with the English. In turn, the Iroquois promised their neutrality in any future colonial war between France and England.

In the short term, the Iroquois had seriously hindered the expansion of New France. The colony's very existence was in question after the dispersal of the Hurons and after the Iroquois raids on the tiny French settlements in the St. Lawrence Valley in the early 1650s. Yet, in the long term, the destruction of Huronia actually contributed to New France's growth. Agriculture became more profitable as the colony inherited the Hurons' former role as "provisioners" to the Algonquians. In addition, the French in the late 1650s and early 1660s entered the interior themselves to trade

directly for the Algonquians' furs, and the coureurs de bois helped reinforce the existing Franco-Algonquian alliance. Together, the French and
their Algonquian allies defeated the Five Nations in the late 1680s and
1690s. The peace treaty of 1701 marked the end of the great Iroquois
resistance to French expansion.

NOTES

[1]John Webster Grant, *Moon of Wintertime: Missionaries and the Indians of Canada in Encounter since 1534*
(Toronto, 1984), 24.
[2]Bruce G. Trigger, *Natives and Newcomers: Canada's "Heroic Age" Reconsidered* (Kingston, 1985), 335.
[3]André Vachon, "Dollard Des Ormeaux," in *Dictionary of Canadian Biography*, vol. 1 (Toronto, 1966),
274.
[4]William M. Warren, *History of the Ojibwa Nation* (St. Paul, Minn., 1885; reprinted 1957), 131.

Related Readings

R. Douglas Francis and Donald B. Smith, *Readings in Canadian History: Pre-
Confederation*, 3rd ed. (Toronto, 1990) includes Bruce G. Trigger, "The
French Presence in Huronia: The Structure of Franco-Huron Relations in
the First Half of the Seventeenth Century," 16–48. W.J. Eccles, "Society and
the Frontier," 94–112, outlines the Indians' influence on the French.

BIBLIOGRAPHY

A number of studies exist on the relationship between the People of the
Longhouse and the French. William Fenton provides an overview in "The
Iroquois in History," in *North American Indians in Historical Perspective*,
edited by Eleanor Burke Leacock and Nancy Oestreich Lurie (New York,
1971), 129–68. Mary A. Druke briefly reviews this relationship in "Iroquois
and Iroquoian in Canada," in *Native Peoples: The Canadian Experience*,
edited by R. Bruce Morrison and C. Roderick Wilson (Toronto, 1986),
302–324. On Amerindian–European relations in general during this period
see Bruce G. Trigger, ed., *Northeast*, vol. 15 of the *Handbook of North
American Indians* (Washington, D.C., 1978), and Denys Delâge, *Le Pays
Renversé: Amérindiens et Européens en Amérique du Nord-Est, 1600–1664*
(Montréal, 1985).

Bruce Trigger's summary in *Natives and Newcomers: Canada's "Heroic
Age" Reconsidered* (Montreal, 1985) covers the period ending in 1663.
Trigger has also written *The Indians and the Heroic Age of New France*,
Canadian Historical Association, Booklet no. 30 (Ottawa: 1977; rev. ed.,
1989). Francis Jennings reviews the period from the 1600s to 1744 in *The
Ambiguous Iroquois Empire* (New York, 1984), and in his sequel, *Empire of
Fortune, Crowns, Colonies and Tribes in the Seven Years War in America*
(New York, 1988). A new study of the Iroquois and their relations with
neighbouring Indian groups is Daniel K. Richter and James H. Merrell,

Beyond the Covenant Chain: The Iroquois and Their Neighbors in Indian North America, 1600–1800 (Syracuse, N.Y., 1987). A useful collection of articles is Francis Jennings et al., eds., *The History and Culture of Iroquois Diplomacy: An Interdisciplinary Guide to the Treaties of the Six Nations and Their League* (Syracuse, N.Y., 1985).

Paul A.W. Wallace relates the story of the founding of the League of the Iroquois in *The White Roots of Peace* (Philadelphia, 1946). A shorter version by the same author entitled "Dekanahwideh" appears in the *Dictionary of Canadian Biography*, vol. 1, *1000–1700* (Toronto, 1966), 253–55. Christopher Vecsey comments on other versions in "The Story and Structure of the Iroquois Confederacy," *Journal of the American Academy of Religion* 54 (1986): 79–106. William Engelbrecht relies on archaeological as well as oral data to determine the league's origins in his article "New York Iroquois Political Development," in *Cultures in Contact*, edited by William W. Fitzhugh (Washington, D.C., 1985), 163–83. Anthony F.C. Wallace (son of Paul A.W. Wallace) has written a complete study of one of the Iroquois tribes in *The Death and Rebirth of the Seneca* (New York, 1969). On the status of women in Iroquois society, see the collection of essays edited by W.G. Spittal, *Iroquois Women: An Anthology* (Ohsweken, Ontario, 1990).

There are a number of excellent studies on the Hurons. Bruce G. Trigger's *The Huron Farmers of the North*, 2d ed. (Fort Worth, Texas, 1990) is the best starting point. See also Conrad Heidenreich's *Huronia: A History and Geography of the Huron Indians, 1600–1650* (Toronto, 1971), and his article "The Natural Environment of Huronia and Huron Seasonal Activities," in *People, Places, Patterns, Processes: Geographical Perspectives on the Canadian Past*, edited by Graeme Wynn (Toronto, 1990), 42–55, as well as Elisabeth Tooker's *An Ethnography of the Huron Indians, 1615–1649* (Washington, D.C., 1964). The fullest review is provided by Bruce Trigger in *The Children of Aataentsic: A History of the Huron People to 1660*, 2 vols. (Montreal, 1976).

Good short summaries of the Jesuits' contact with the Hurons are contained in Henry Warner Bowden, *American Indians and Christian Missions* (Chicago, 1981), 59–95, and in James Axtell, *The Invasion Within: The contest of Cultures in Colonial North American* (New York, 1985). These can be supplemented by John Webster Grant's *Moon of Wintertime: Missionaries and the Indians of Canada in Encounter since 1534* (Toronto, 1984). A full review is provided by Father Lucien Campeau in *La Mission des Jésuites chez les Hurons, 1634–1650* (Montréal, 1987). S.R. Mealing has edited *The Jesuit Relations and Allied Documents* (Toronto, 1963), a one-volume anthology of selections from the *Jesuit Relations*. In her book, *Chain Her by One Foot: The Subjugation of Women in Seventeenth-Century New France* (London, 1991), Karen Anderson argues that the Jesuits introduced the subjugation of women by men in the Huron's egalitarian society.

Several useful articles for an understanding of the French and the Iroquoians include John A. Dickinson, "Annaotaha et Dollard vus de l'autre côté de la palissade," *Revue d'histoire de l'Amérique française* 35 (1981–82): 163–78; John A. Dickinson, "La guerre iroquoise et la mortalité en Nouvelle-France, 1608–1666," *Revue d'histoire de l'Amérique française* 36 (1982–83): 31–54; John A. Dickinson's "Les Amérindiens et les débuts de la Nouvelle-France," in *Canada ieri e oggi* (Bari, Italy, 1986), vol. 3, 87–108; Richard Haan, "The Problem of Iroquois Neutrality: Suggestions for Revision," *Ethnohistory* 27 (1980): 317–30. Daniel K. Richter, "War and Culture: The Iroquois Experience," *William and Mary Quarterly*, 3d series, 40 (1983): 528–59; and Daniel K. Richter, "Iroquois versus Iroquois: Jesuit Missions and Christianity in Village Politics, 1642–1686," *Ethnohistory* 32 (1985): 1–16. Specific explanations of the Hurons' defeat are discussed in Brian J. Given, "The Iroquois Wars and Native Arms" and Susan Johnston, "Epidemics: The Forgotten Factor in Seventeenth Century Native Warfare in the St. Lawrence Region," both published in *Native People, Native Lands*, edited by Bruce Alden Cox (Ottawa, 1988), 3–31. Keith Otterbein has two articles in *Ethnohistory* on the same topic: "Why the Iroquois Won: An Analysis of Iroquois Military Tactics," vol. 11 (1964): 56–63; and "Huron vs. Iroquois: A Case Study in Intertribal Warfare," vol. 26 (1979): 141–52.

Marcel Trudel reviews the French colony from 1645 to 1663 in *The Beginnings of New France, 1524–1663* (Toronto, 1973). For French views of the Iroquois, see *Word from New France: The Selected Letters of Marie de l'Incarnation*, translated and edited by Joyce Marshall (Toronto, 1967). The impact of the Iroquois attacks on the French settlers is discussed in Norman Clermont, "Les générateurs de frissons," *Recherches amérindiennes au Québec* 19, 2–3 (1989): 117–27. The best treatment of Dollard is that by André Vachon in the *Dictionary of Canadian Biography*, vol. 1 (Toronto, 1966): 266–75. The basic documents relating to Dollard's expedition are contained in Adrien Pouliot and Silvio Dumas, *L'Exploit du Long-Sault, Les témoignages des contemporains* (Québec, 1960). For the growth of settlement in New France during the 1640s and 1650s, see Lucien Campeau, "Le peuplement de la Nouvelle-France, opération civilisée," in his *La vie quotidienne au Québec* (Sillery, Québec, 1983), 107–23. A very good short overview of early New France is provided by Brian Young and John A. Dickinson, "Native Peoples and the Beginnings of New France to 1650," in *A Short History of Quebec: A Socio-Economic Perspective* (Mississauga, Ont., 1988), 11–34. The story of the Trudeau family in Canada appears in Thomas J. Laforest, *Our French-Canadian Ancestors* (Palm Harbour, Fla., 1981). Useful maps showing France's inland expansion appear in R. Cole Harris, ed., *Historical Atlas of Canada*, vol. 1, *From the Beginning to 1800* (Toronto, 1987).

Province de France: The Society, 1663–1760

From the 1650s onward the small French colony in the valley of the St.   79
Lawrence grew steadily. A new market for French farm produce opened
up among the Algonquians after the scattering of the Hurons in 1649–50.
French traders entered the interior to gather and bring out furs, thus
expanding the trade. Decades of warfare with the Iroquois forged a sense
of unity among the settlers. More than seventy years of intermittent
struggle with England's American colonies, from 1689 to 1760, also helped
to fashion a new Canadian identity.

During the course of one decade, the French Crown strengthened the
colony's economic infrastructure and introduced new political institutions
that lasted nearly a century. Three men transformed New France between
1663 and 1672: King Louis XIV; Jean-Baptiste Colbert, the king's
Minister of the Marine; and Jean Talon, the first intendant, the official
responsible for the civil administration of the colony. They worked to
make the St. Lawrence Valley into La Nouvelle France—a new France
overseas. By the early eighteenth century, however, an unforeseen development occurred—the habits and the mentality of the French began to
change in the North American setting. A new people, the *Canadiens*,
emerged.

The First Half-Century of Royal Government, 1663–1713

Louis XIV, the young French king, sought to create a dynamic French
presence in North America by making New France a *province de France*,
a colony directly under his control. New France became a province, with
the same administrative structures that the other French provinces had,
under the supervision of Jean-Baptiste Colbert, one of the king's most
loyal advisers. As Minister of the Marine, or to use the more modern term,

Minister of Colonies, Colbert attempted to make mercantilism succeed for France. He believed that, in order to prosper, a nation had to sell more goods than it purchased. If New France could produce more than it cost to administer, the colony could help to make France rich. It would supply France with natural products and, in return, purchase the mother country's manufactured goods.

From New France, the minister wanted the following: furs; timber (including ship masts), which France had formerly had to import from Scandinavia and Russia; and minerals. In addition, Colbert sought to develop a triangular trade network among New France, the French possessions in the Caribbean, and France itself. New France could export fish, wheat, peas, and barrel staves to France and the French West Indies; the islands could export rum, molasses, and sugar to Canada and France; and France could send its textiles and manufactured goods to Canada and the West Indies.

80 New France had to become more self-sufficient before the master plan could succeed. Colbert dreamed of making New France into a much more self-reliant, defensible colony, with a prosperous agricultural base in the St. Lawrence Valley and its own basic industries. The minister wanted it to become a "compact colony," one centred in the St. Lawrence Valley, without unnecessary forts and outposts on the periphery. He also opposed western expansion. Colbert's first objective was to strengthen the colony militarily. In the mid-1660s, he dispatched regular troops to New France, including one of the better units in the French army, the Carignan-Salières regiment of nearly eleven hundred men.

When the Iroquois made peace in 1667, the regiment in Canada was disbanded. Four hundred troops elected to stay in the colony. They were located at the colony's weakest point, along the Richelieu River between Lake Champlain and the St. Lawrence—the Iroquois' invasion route. With the establishment of peace, Colbert's program to transform New France into a profitable and well-populated colony based in the St. Lawrence Valley could begin.

Reform of the Seigneurial System

In fashioning this new royal province of France, the Minister of the Marine reformed what was known as the seigneurial system. Those landowners who had acquired large domains and who had done nothing to improve them, lost their lands to more energetic seigneurs. French immigrants to the colony were familiar with the seigneurial system, since it was the basis of land tenure in France. Peasant settlers, or *censitaires*, depended on a seigneur, or lord, who in turn was a vassal of the king. Title to all the land rested with the king, who granted fiefs, or estates, as he saw

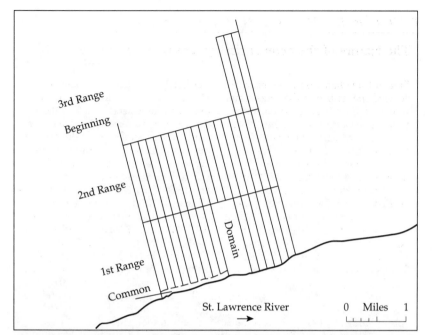

fit. The soil belonged to the seigneur, but the mineral or subsoil rights and all oak trees on the property belonged to the king. In 1627 the king granted the Company of One Hundred Associates (see Chapter 3) legal and seigneurial rights over the territory of New France; in 1633–34, the company in turn granted more than fifty seigneuries of varying size along the St. Lawrence between Quebec and Montreal. In return for their large rectangular estates fronting on the river and usually extending into the foothills behind, the seigneurs undertook to bring out the *censitaires*, or habitants as they were better known in Canada, who in turn paid them rent and dues.

Under royal government the intendant, among his other administrative duties, granted seigneuries and supervised the seigneurial system. On his arrival in 1665, Jean Talon, the first intendant of New France, made actual occupancy a condition of all future grants. Talon and his immediate successors also kept the size of the seigneuries relatively small to prevent the rise of a class of large landowners who might challenge royal authority. By 1700 the Crown had ceded almost all the riverfront from Montreal to below Quebec. Nearly two hundred seigneuries were open for settlement by 1715.

THE OBLIGATIONS OF THE SEIGNEURS AND THE *CENSITAIRES*

The intendant had to ensure that the seigneurs and *censitaires* fulfilled their mutual obligations. The seigneurs had to clear some of their seigneury,

The Nature of the Seigneurial System in New France

French Canadian historians have debated the nature of the seigneurial system in New France for more than a quarter of a century. Earlier historians, such as François-Xavier Garneau, held that the system was neither harsh nor oppressive. According to them, the institutions that France established in the St. Lawrence Valley, including the seigneurial system, had been purified in the new setting, their negative aspects removed by the French Crown. In 1899, historian Benjamin Sulte suggested that the seigneur in New France was not an exploiter but a "colonization agent" ("Le système seigneurial" in *Mélanges historiques*, vol. 1 [Montréal, 1918], 80 [text dates from 1899]; cited in Serge Jaumain et Matteo Sanfilippo, "Le Régime seigneurial en Nouvelle-France: Un débat historiographique," *The Register* 5, 2 [Autumn 1984]: 227). This traditionalist interpretation of New France as an open, egalitarian society dominated in Quebec until the mid-twentieth century.

A new critical view of the seigneurial system emerged in the 1960s and 1970s. In 1974 Louise Dechêne published her *Habitants et marchands de Montréal au XVIIe siècle*, (Montréal, 1974) a meticulous local study of the Montreal area that pointed to the oppressive nature of the seigneurial system in the late seventeenth century. She thus sided with fellow historian Fernand Ouellet, who, in his numerous writings from the 1960s to the 1980s, argued his belief that in the eighteenth century New France was a class-bound society. Both Dechêne and Ouellet maintained that seigneurial practices in the St. Lawrence Valley conformed to French patterns. In some cases, the customs in Canada were even more outdated than those in France. As Ouellet wrote in 1981, "In brief, the *ancien régime* society that had developed in the St. Lawrence Valley, far from being a modernized or purified version of that of the mother country, was in a sense more archaic" ("The Formation of a New Society in the St. Lawrence Valley: From Classless Society to Class Conflict," in *Economy, Class and Nation in Quebec: Interpretive Essays*, edited and translated by Jacques A. Barbier [Toronto, 1991], 33; originally published in French in the *Canadian Historical Review* 62, 4 [1981]: 407–50.

The division of opinion that exists among francophone scholars is also present among their anglophone counterparts. Richard Colebrook Harris, for instance, has endorsed many of the positions championed by traditionalist French Canadian historians. He questions the interpretation that farmers in New France occupied a position comparable to that of peasants in rural France during the last two centuries of pre-revolutionary France. "Rural Canada provided relative opportunity (cheaper land and higher wages) for ordinary people, and relative disincentive (higher labour costs, land of little value, and weak markets) for a landed elite" (New Preface to *The Seigneurial System in Early Canada: A Geographical Study*, 2d ed. [Montreal, 1984], xix). Harris argues that the rural population of New France was independent and self-reliant, and that it had opportunities for upward mobility. To a certain extent, W.J. Eccles, the leading anglophone historian of New France, has sided with the traditionalists. He wrote in *The Canadian Frontier, 1534–1760* (New York, 1969), p. 68, "The seigneurs were little more than land settlement agents and their financial rewards were not great."

The traditionalist viewpoint has been challenged by historian Allan Greer, the author of a monograph entitled *Peasant, Lord, and Merchant: Rural Society in Three Quebec Parishes, 1740–1840* (Toronto, 1985). Greer contends that "exploitation, domination, and the clash of interests were characteristics of rural Canada since the early years of the French regime" (p. xiv). In neither the francophone nor the anglophone historiography is there a consensus on the nature of the seigneurial regime in New France.

maintain a manor house, and reside there or have a responsible person living there throughout the year. They had to make land grants of up to eighty hectares to any genuine settlers who applied. Finally, on part of their land, they had to establish a flour mill for the use of their *censitaires*. Some seigneurs also maintained a court of law to settle minor disputes.

The *censitaires* also had responsibilities. They had to build their own house, clear the land granted them, and pay their seigneur the *cens* (a small cash payment) and *rentes* (another money payment). Together, these two different charges amounted to less than one-tenth of a *censitaire's* annual income. In a few seigneuries, the seigneur had the *droit de corvée* (right to forced labour) usually three days per year, determined in the contract with the *censitaire*. As part of their compulsory military service, they were also required by the Crown to work without pay for a day or two a year, doing general maintenance work on any seigneurial roads or bridges. By having accepted a grant of land, the habitants had to maintain the portion of road that passed through their farms. In return for all this, the habitants became virtual owners of their land, which they could pass on to their children. If they sold their land outside their families, however, they had to pay the seigneur a portion of the money they obtained.

Under royal government, the settlers became part of a well-organized social unit, and gained title to a tract of land. In time, the seigneur would build a manor house, a church, and a mill on the seigneury. Many seigneurs in pioneer times lived and worked as their habitants did, and this blunted the social distinctions that had prevailed in France. In the colony's early years, in fact, a handful of enterprising and ambitious settlers themselves became seigneurs. Pierre Boucher was one pioneer of modest means who managed to become a seigneur in early New France; in 1654, he was elevated to the governorship of Trois-Rivières. As historians Louise Dechêne and Fernand Ouellet argue, however, social distinctions did become important as the seigneuries became heavily settled and the opportunity for social mobility declined.

83

Immigrants by Sex and Decade 1608–1759

Period	Men	Women	Total
Before 1630	15	6	21
1630–1639	88	51	139
1640–1649	141	86	227
1650–1659	403	239	642
1660–1669	1075	623	1698
1670–1679	429	369	798
1680	486	56	542
1690–1699	490	32	522
1700–1709	283	24	307
1710–1719	293	18	311
1720–1729	420	14	434
1730–1739	483	16	499
1740–1749	576	16	592
1750–1759	1699	52	1751
Unknown	27	17	44
Total	6908	1619	8527

Source: R. Cole Harris, ed., *Historical Atlas of Canada,* vol. 1, *From the Beginning to 1800* (Toronto: University of Toronto Press, 1987), plate 45.

Growth of Settlement

To help populate the seigneuries, Colbert and Jean Talon worked to correct a social imbalance in the colony: there was an abundance of eligible bachelors, but a shortage of French women. In Montreal in 1663, for example, there was only one marriageable woman for every eight eligible men. Most widows remarried within a year of their husband's death.

THE DAUGHTERS OF THE KING

Colbert sought women who were strong enough for work in the fields and who had a good moral character. At first the French Crown selected orphanage girls, but when they proved not to be rugged enough, young healthy country girls were recruited. Many were not much older than sixteen. In the mid- and late 1660s French ships carried hundreds of the *filles du roi* ("daughters of the king") to Quebec, where the Ursuline and Hospital sisters looked after them. In all, the state sent nearly eight hundred *filles du roi*. The king even provided substantial dowries—"the king's gift"—usually consisting of clothing or household supplies.

The girls, kept under supervision in one place, chose their husbands themselves, most of them within two weeks after arrival. A young man in search of a wife had to declare his possessions and means of livelihood to the "directress" in charge of the girls. To encourage marriage, the government fined bachelors and denied them trading rights. Thus, there were many men seeking brides, and the women had a good deal of choice. Usually they sought first to find out if the suitor had a farm.

Even if the young man had begun a farm, a difficult life awaited these women, whose marriage contract bound them for life. They faced relentless work in clearing and maintaining their new family farms, for the women in New France toiled in the fields alongside the men. The severity of Canadian winters also came as a shock to the young French women. Fortunately, though, by the time the *filles du roi* arrived, the French settlers had learned to adjust to winter conditions. They now slaughtered animals at the onset of winter and hung the meat in icy cellars. By eating fresh meat and last season's vegetables through the winter, they escaped scurvy. They also learned to construct houses in ways that improved heat retention and heating efficiency—by digging cellars first and by putting fireplaces in the centre of the houses. In addition, they built roofs with steep angles that readily shed the snow. In the late seventeenth century the settlers introduced another improvement—iron fire boxes that produced four times more heat than conventional fireplaces did. Barns were built larger to store fodder for the winter and to keep domestic animals inside during the coldest weather.

To make the settlers' life easier, Colbert sent livestock to Canada at the Crown's expense. The first horses arrived in 1665. The Indians, who had never seen such animals, called them the "moose of France." Horses thrived in the colony. The habitants developed a particular fondness for them, and by the eighteenth century, even the poorest settler tried to keep one.

85

THE *ENGAGÉS*

In the mid- to late 1660s the Crown sent several hundred *engagés*, or indentured workers to the colony annually. Bound by a three-year contract, or *engagement*, to an established farmer, they received a modest wage. They were nicknamed "thirty-six months," since after that period they became free. Apparently, beginning in the 1650s, more than half stayed in the colony after their term of service ended. The system proved advantageous to both the seigneur, who used them to help clear his land, and to the *engagés*, who gained valuable knowledge of local conditions before they began farming on their own.

AN EARLY FRENCH IMMIGRANT

To put a human face on the early immigrants who came to New France, let us look at the experience of one man, Étienne Trudeau, from the city of La Rochelle in western France. This robust fellow, a master carpenter at eighteen, signed a contract for five years of military service in New France. Upon arrival in Montreal in 1659, he began service with the

Sulpician Fathers, who had hired him. Three years later he and two others were ambushed by fifty Iroquois. They fought back bravely and survived the attack.

In 1667, the year of the Iroquois peace treaty, the twenty-six-year-old Étienne married Adrienne Barbier, the daughter of a carpenter who was one of the original twelve colonists to arrive at Montreal in August 1642. Étienne and Adrienne had fourteen children; one child eventually settled in Louisiana, while three became voyageurs and went to the Great Lakes before their marriages. Étienne lived an active life as a farmer, carpenter, and stonemason. He died in 1712 at Montreal; his wife died several years later. Étienne Trudeau was the ancestor of all the Trudeaus of New France, including a ninth-generation descendant—Pierre Elliott Trudeau, prime minister of Canada from 1968 to 1979 and from 1980 to 1984.

THE SETTLEMENT OF THE ST. LAWRENCE VALLEY

Many immigrants died from disease, either on the voyage or in the colony itself, but New France's population grew rapidly nonetheless, from roughly three thousand in 1663 to almost ten thousand a decade later. By 1672, nearly four thousand men and women had been sent to Canada at the Crown's expense. French immigrants settled along the St. Lawrence from below Quebec to Montreal, and they cleared more land east of Montreal along the Richelieu River.

Throughout the French regime, the St. Lawrence remained the colony's main thoroughfare, both in summer by canoe or small boat and in winter by sleigh over the ice. Frontage along the water highway was always most sought after. In addition, the settlers wanted to be close to one another in the event of Iroquois attacks. Around Quebec the shores of the St. Lawrence already looked like one sprawling, unending village street, with the *censitaires'* whitewashed farmhouses huddled closely together. The narrow farms extending back from the river were often twenty times as long as they were wide.

The French state managed to stimulate significant population growth in the first decade of royal government, from 1663 to 1672. The women sent out in Colbert's great wave of immigrants married and produced large families. In the late seventeenth century the state encouraged births with what might be viewed as Canada's first baby bonuses. Couples with ten and more living children received a substantial gift of money. The imbalance in the ratio of males to females was corrected by the turn of the century. Despite disasters, such as the smallpox epidemic of 1701, which killed a thousand people, New France's population increase continued to be extremely high: the population doubled every twenty-five years, almost entirely as a result of the high birth rate rather than immigration.

In the colony's early years, women gave birth to eight or nine children on average (after 1700, the figure dropped to seven). One out of every five children, however, died before the age of one, hence the average "completed" family in the eighteenth century consisted of 5.65 children per couple. Babies were delivered at home by midwives. A new mother might have a woman friend stay for a week or so after the birth, and her own mother usually stayed with her for at least a month.

The remarkable example of one family in particular might give a sense of the prodigious population increase that occurred in New France. Pierre Tremblay arrived in the colony in 1647, and got married ten years later at Quebec. When he died, he left behind 12 children, 4 of whom were boys. His sons in turn had 15, 14, 14, and 6 children, respectively, and their descendants similarly had large families. By the year 1957, the 300th anniversary of Pierre Tremblay's marriage, there were 60 000 Tremblays in North America, all descended from this one marriage in New France.

THE RISE OF A *CANADIEN* IDENTITY

By the early eighteenth century, the residents of the colony called themselves *Canadiens*; some families had already been in Canada for two or three generations. A new French people, increasingly conscious of their separation from the French in France, were coming into being. They had even begun to speak *canadien-français*, a language with its own distinct expressions to describe Canadian realities—for example, *poudrerie* (drifting or powdering of snow), *cabane à sucre* (a cabin used at maple sugar time), and Indian words such as *canoë* and *toboggan*.

Thus, a common Canadian French was evolving. In the seventeenth century, France had many regional dialects; in fact, what would later be called standard French was still developing in Paris and the surrounding area. In the St. Lawrence Valley, however, the regional dialects eventually died out, because the newcomers from different areas of France intermingled, settling together in one area.

Colbert's Administrative Reforms

To mark New France's new status as a royal colony, Colbert established an authoritarian political structure modelled on that of the French provinces. At the top was Louis XIV. The king, however, delegated enormous powers to his ministers, particularly to Colbert. In effect, the government of New France resided with the Minister of the Marine, assisted by his *commis*, or secretary (the equivalent of a twentieth-century deputy minister in Canada). The most senior administrator in New France was the governor general, who symbolized royal authority. He and two other important officials, the intendant and the bishop, constituted the ruling triumvirate of the colony.

The Political Administration of New France

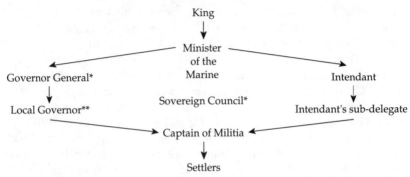

* The governor general, the intendant, the bishop, and the appointed councillors all belonged to the Sovereign Council.
** There was a local governor for each of the following: Acadia, Quebec, Trois Rivières, Montreal, Louisiana, Île-Royale.

Source: Adapted from Marcel Trudel, *Introduction to New France* (Toronto, 1968), p.156.

THE GOVERNOR

In New France the governor general was, almost without exception, a noble and a soldier. His chief task was to ensure that the other officials discharged their responsibilities honestly and efficiently. The Crown clarified the powers of the office after Louis de Buade, Comte de Frontenac, clashed repeatedly in the late 1670s with the Sovereign Council (which functioned as the colony's supreme court), and the intendant. Thereafter, whenever the governor entered into those jurisdictions, he had to justify his actions to the Minister of the Marine. Colbert made it quite clear that the governor should leave the work of the officers of justice alone, unless convinced that those officers were neglecting their duties.

The governor also had complete control over military affairs and diplomatic relations with the neighbouring Indian tribes and the English colonies to the south. The administration of Daniel de Rémy de Courcelle, governor of New France from 1665 to 1672, was marked by important campaigns against the Iroquois. His successor, the Comte de Frontenac (1672–82 and 1689–98), also spent much of his time dealing with the Indian nations and with the English colonies.

Two of the most celebrated governors of the eighteenth century were Philippe de Rigaud de Vaudreuil (1703–25) and his son, Pierre de Rigaud de Vaudreuil de Cavagnial (1755–60), the only Canadian-born governor of New France. The towns of Montreal and Trois-Rivières also had local governors answerable to the governor general (who also served as the governor of the Quebec area). These officials' functions were mainly military.

THE INTENDANT

The intendant, the official responsible for justice, public order, and finance, was second to the governor. He ran most of the daily affairs of New France. In France the king appointed intendants for each province. They were generally bureaucrats with sweeping powers, who applied the orders from the king and his ministers. The intendant was a skilled administrator with a good educational background and, usually, extensive legal training.

In New France the intendant urged the habitants to clear more land and experiment with new crops such as hemp and flax. In times of war the intendant had many military duties. He paid, fed, and clothed the troops and kept them supplied with arms and munitions. While the governor decided the military measures to be taken, the intendant provided the necessary supplies and labour. He was also responsible for the construction and maintenance of fortifications. As the population increased, the Crown appointed deputy intendants at Montreal, Trois-Rivières, and, later, Detroit. They were answerable to the intendant at Quebec.

89

The governor and intendant quarrelled often in the early years of royal government, largely because of their overlapping powers. These conflicts led the Minister of the Marine to define more clearly their respective roles and those of the other justice officers. Although the governor remained the supreme authority, the powers of the intendant were considerably enhanced. He quickly, for example, became the dominant figure in the Sovereign Council, the supreme administrative body for domestic matters in New France. Although ranked behind the governor and the bishop, the intendant came to preside over the council meetings. At the meetings the members never made motions or took votes; this meant, in effect, that the tribunal's verdicts were those of the presiding officer acting on the other members' advice. Three of the best-known intendants of New France were Jean Talon (1665-68, 1669-72), Gilles Hocquart (1731-48), and François Bigot (1748-60).

THE BISHOP

The bishop played a role in the political life of the colony, even though the powers of the office were significantly reduced after 1663. When the Sovereign Council was first established, the bishop ranked directly behind the governor. Thus, the first bishop, François de Laval, initially shared with the governor the responsibility of selecting the other council members from among the leading colonists. But after Laval clashed with the governor, he lost his right to share in the selection of councillors. Thereafter, the bishop's influence declined, and his attendance at the council became infrequent. The Crown respected the social and religious role of the church, but did not want it to become a political rival in the colony.

Musée du Séminaire de Québec, Québec.

This portrait of Bishop François de Laval (1623–1708) is attributed to the
Récollet friar Claude François (Frère Luc), ca. 1672. Bishop Laval, the colony's
first bishop, directed the diocese of Quebec from 1659 to 1684. He founded the
Séminaire de Québec in 1663.

Laval was followed by the puritanical Jean-Baptiste de La Croix de
Chevrières de Saint-Vallier (1688–1727), who served for nearly forty years.
He favoured a severe morality and waged war against drunkenness, blas-
phemy, dancing, and immodest dress. (Laval had spoken against women
appearing in church wearing fashionable gowns that revealed naked arms
and bosoms, but Saint-Vallier went farther and tried to stop women from
wearing low-cut gowns in their homes.)

At the beginning of the period of royal government, Louis XIV and Colbert feared the excessive authority of the clergy in New France. The Jesuits had, in effect, run the colony for thirty years. The governor and the intendant were instructed by the Minister of the Marine to make the church subordinate to the authority of the state. After 1663 the king himself nominated the bishop. The Crown contributed 40 percent of the colonial church's finances and used these subsidies to control the church.

THE SOVEREIGN COUNCIL

The Sovereign Council (Superior Council after 1703) both made laws and heard criminal and civil cases. Appeals could also be heard from lower courts. The members of the tribunal sat around a large table, with the governor, bishop, and intendant at the head (the governor in the centre, the bishop on his right, and the intendant on his left), surrounded by the councillors. As the amount of litigation in the colony increased, the council restricted itself to its legal functions, and the intendant enacted legislation.

91

THE LOWER COURTS

The lower courts in Quebec, Montreal, and Trois-Rivières stood below the Sovereign Council. The judges of these courts applied the municipal legislation drawn up by the Sovereign Council, such as regulations on street traffic, road maintenance, garbage disposal, and fire prevention. A few of the most populated seigneuries also had seigneurial courts, which heard minor civil disputes. In 1663 the law for the area around Paris, the so-called Custom of Paris (*coutume de Paris*), officially became the colony's legal code. Today's Civil Code in Quebec evolved from this "law of Canada."

In reforming the justice system in New France, Colbert took steps to ensure that justice would be provided with minimal expense to the state. First, he banned lawyers from practising in the colony; citizens argued their own civil cases in court. Notaries—not lawyers—drew up legal contracts. By 1700 the colony supported four notaries at Quebec, three at Montreal, and one at Trois-Rivières. Second, the Crown enforced a tariff of fees that legal officials, from judges down to bailiffs, could charge. All fees were very modest.

The courts operated in the same way that they did in France. When a crime was found to have been committed, the local magistrate or the attorney general of the Sovereign Council ordered an exhaustive investigation to gather all the evidence. The judge—or a member of the Sovereign Council delegated by the attorney general—interrogated anyone thought to have knowledge of the crime. If the evidence revealed a suspect, that person was apprehended and put in jail. The judge or attorney general then interrogated the prisoner under oath (at this point, the suspect still had not been informed of the charge against him).

This questioning and the taking down of statements was known as the *question ordinaire*. If, in important cases, the defendant being questioned proved reluctant to talk, torture could be used to extract a confession or the names of accomplices. This procedure was the *question extraordinaire*; it was employed against at least thirty men and women during the century of royal government.[1] The *maître des hautes oeuvres*, or master of the means of torture, bound boards to the defendant's shins, inserted wedges, and then struck them with a hammer, painfully crushing the bones of the accused. After each hammer blow the interrogators restated their questions until they were convinced that the prisoner was telling the truth. As legal historian Douglas Hay wrote, "If the truth had to be sought in the bones, nerves and sinews of an unwilling witness, that was unfortunate," but the investigator "considered it much as a surgeon would his exploratory operation."[2]

92

If the Sovereign Council heard the trial, the attorney general received all the evidence and testimony, laid it before the court, and added a summation. The members of the council subsequently discussed the report and gave their opinions. The intendant then delivered the verdict. The sentence was carried out either the same day or within a day or two.

THE CAPTAIN OF MILITIA

Colbert also established another institution, the office of captain of militia. In 1669 the intendant organized the entire male population between the ages of sixteen and sixty into militia units. He formed a company in each parish and appointed a captain from among the most respected habitants to command it. The office carried with it no salary, but it did bring considerable status and prestige; the captains became the most respected men in their communities. In addition to drilling the militia, supervising their equipment, and leading them in battle, the officers had other important civilian functions. The captains acted locally as the intendant's agents, communicating certain of his regulations and ordinances to the habitants and seeing that they were carried out. They also ordered the *corvées* for work on bridges and roads. During a *corvée*, even the local seigneur came under the militia captain's command. This new office thus prevented the seigneurs from becoming too powerful, as they were subordinate to the militia captains. Through the captains the people could make their wishes or complaints known to higher officials.

PUBLIC MEETINGS

Colbert made no provision for local self-government. New France would have no municipal governments, no mayors or town councils. Furthermore, people on their own could not call a meeting or public assembly. Government came from above, not from below. Even the magistrates of the Sovereign Council were appointed and paid stipends, and were dependent on the governor and the intendant.

The only elected office in the late seventeenth century (and for the remainder of the French regime) was that of church warden. Under royal government the power of the Crown was uncontested. Yet some flexibility existed. On occasion the governor and the intendant did make efforts to obtain the views of the people on issues that affected the general interest. Seventeen such assemblies were held between 1672 and 1700. On at least one of these occasions, the intendant subsequently acted to meet the wishes of the assembly. Thus, the people of New France had a limited say in the administration of their affairs, and, while not bound to do so, the authorities could legislate in accordance with their views. (Later, more adjustments were made. In 1709 in Quebec and in 1717 in Montreal the governor and the intendant also permitted the merchants to establish chambers of commerce. These bodies were asked to nominate one of their number to inform the governor and the intendant of measures to promote commerce in their towns).

93

The Failure of Colbert's Plan for a "Compact Colony"

Having set up a new administrative structure, Colbert sought capable men to fill the senior posts. These men, he hoped, would establish a self-reliant colony, or "a compact colony," in the St. Lawrence Valley. Intendant Jean Talon, a man of about forty who had been an intendant in France as well, began investigating New France's economic possibilities—discovering what the soil would grow, surveying the forests, and sponsoring expeditions to search for minerals. He also tried to develop a shipbuilding industry in the colony. The Crown sent skilled ship carpenters, tarmakers, blacksmiths, and foundry workers, as well as the necessary supplies. Three ships were built, but the industry never became profitable. The imported skilled workers demanded high wages. Iron had to be imported, and the industry required heavy capital outlays. In the end, ships cost much more to build in Canada than in France, and the program was curtailed.

Another disappointment was the failure to develop a large overseas trade with the West Indies. The loss of two of Talon's ships at sea certainly helped to end the experiment. Moreover, the handicaps were great—New France's ships could sail south only in the summer months, which was the hurricane season in southern waters. The French ships had to run the gauntlet of English privateers in wartime, and other nations' privateers infested the waters at all seasons. Finally, the Canadians had to compete with New England mariners, who could sell wheat and fish at a lower price year round. For these reasons, then, New France failed to secure a foothold in the West Indies market.

Of the industries in New France, fishing offered the greatest promise. Colbert provided subsidies for the necessary equipment. But Canadian fishermen faced several disadvantages, the foremost being the failure to establish salt works in the colony, which meant a reliance on France for a supply of salt. In addition, many of the fishing firms were managed by French merchants in France, whose ships sailed directly from French ports to the Grand Banks, and returned directly to France without ever landing in New France and purchasing Canadian fish.

One of Talon's enterprises, though, did make a strong beginning—a brewery at Quebec. Cheap beer brewed at Quebec proved popular. Other industries he promoted included the production of hats and shoes. Unfortunately for Colbert's hopes, however, everything Canada produced, except for furs and beer, could be obtained more cheaply elsewhere.

94 In 1672, the year Jean Talon left the colony, the infant industries died and the further dispatch of *filles du roi* ended. The Crown allocated no more funds because France had begun a costly war with the Dutch. As Colbert said in 1673, "His Majesty can give no assistance to Canada this year on account of the great and prodigious expense to which he has been put for the maintenance of more than 200 000 men and a hundred ships." New France had to depend solely on the fur trade, which remained its main economic activity.

Colonial administrators in New France also contributed to the failure of Colbert's "compact colony" ideal by using their positions to advance their own interests. The first prominent governor, Louis de Buade, Comte de Frontenac, in the 1670s openly favoured the expansion of the fur trade for his own profit and at the expense of the economic development of the St. Lawrence Valley. As business historian Michael Bliss wrote, "The idea that people with power should *not* use it to enrich themselves is a very modern notion. In the seventeenth and eighteenth centuries virtually all administrators of government—in Britain, France, and all their colonies—expected to gain personally from possession of their offices."[3]

Economic Development after the Treaty of Utrecht, 1713–1760

In 1713, the British and French signed the Treaty of Utrecht (see Chapter 6), after which the St. Lawrence Valley enjoyed an unprecedented peace until 1744. The thirty-year truce allowed New France to consolidate itself economically and socially. Many French Canadian historians look upon the thirty years of peace as New France's Golden Age. The diversification of the colony's economy had finally begun.

Once again, the French government supported economic initiatives in New France, which this time proved successful. The number of flour mills in the colony increased by 50 percent between 1719 and 1734. The fishing industry also grew, with fish and seal oil becoming export products. Gilles Hocquart, the intendant, established tanneries at Quebec, Lévis, and Montreal.

The Crown also worked to improve transportation. A road link was essential for farmers to take their growing surpluses to market. In 1737 the intendant completed the first royal highway, which connected Montreal and Quebec, and greatly facilitated travel. A return trip by water from Montreal to Quebec might take several weeks, while the trip by coach over the King's Highway could be completed in as little as nine days. The highway opened up to settlement new lands north of the St. Lawrence. The road would become the colony's lifeline in the summer of 1759 when the British fleet gained control of the St. Lawrence.

95

INDUSTRY

Private citizens also worked to develop the colony's industrial resources. Beginning in the 1720s, Canadian businessmen established small shipyards along the St. Lawrence. Intendant Gilles Hocquart helped with subsidies and tried to build on this privately stimulated economic growth by establishing state-owned shipyards. Canadian workers were to be employed in sailmaking, rope manufacturing, tar works, foundries, sawmills, and tool and machinery making.

The intendant, however, promoted the building of large ships, even though Canada's resources were better suited for small ones. In the 1740s the royal shipyard at Quebec constructed nine warships. Labour costs proved too high, however, and in the 1750s the shipyard built and launched only five naval vessels.

Canada's first heavy industry, the St. Maurice Forges near Trois-Rivières, was established in 1729. But under its second owner, serious technical errors and lax administration caused the company's ruin. In 1741 its directors declared bankruptcy, at which point the Crown, which had given large subsidies, intervened. Production under royal administration fluctuated greatly from year to year, but for a few years profits were reported. The ironworks employed about one hundred workers, who produced sizable quantities of cooking pots, pans, soup ladles, and stoves, as well as cannons and cannonballs.

AGRICULTURE

By 1700 agriculture had replaced the fur trade as the leading economic activity in New France, with three out of four Canadian families involved in farming. This greatly changed the colony's economic structure. From 1706 to 1739, the Canadian population increased 250 percent, and the amount of land under cultivation increased 430 percent. Wheat generally occupied about three-quarters of cultivated farm land, so the colony became self-sufficient in wheat and flour. (Wheat, in fact, made up one-third of the colony's exports by the 1730s.) The habitants also grew peas, oats, rye, barley, buckwheat, and maize. Surprisingly, the vegetable that in the early nineteenth century became the staple food of the habitants' diet was not grown in the colony: it was the English who introduced the potato to the St. Lawrence Valley after 1760.

Market conditions limited production of both produce and livestock. The towns of New France were not large, and many town dwellers kept their own gardens and livestock. But an increase in the population and the opening of an export market in the eighteenth century improved the situation. Flour, biscuits, and peas were exported regularly to the new French fortress at Louisbourg on Cape Breton Island as well as to the French West Indies. The habitants needed to produce a surplus to pay church tithes and seigneurial dues and to purchase the things they could not make themselves.

The unlimited supply of land and the high productivity of the new soil discouraged farmers from applying the intensive agricultural methods that were commonly used in Europe. As the good land became exhausted, the farmers cleared more. Conservation was an unknown concept in New France.

The Society of New France in the Eighteenth Century

During the eighteenth century, agriculture was the mainstay of the colony, but about one-quarter of New France's inhabitants lived in towns. Royal officials and military officers dominated life in Quebec, Montreal, and Trois-Rivières. In terms of social ranking in New France, these senior administrators stood at the top. Most were French from France and in the colony they dominated the Sovereign Council and held the top positions in the civil-service hierarchy. At the local level, however, the greater number of judges were Canadian born.

THE MERCHANTS

The merchants, or the bourgeois, constituted another social group in New France. The nature, size, and strength of this group became the focus of much debate among historians in the 1950s and 1960s (see Chapter 9). Historians questioned whether New France had a significant class of French Canadian entrepreneurs and whether an active bourgeoisie existed in the colony. The effects of the British Conquest were also debated in this regard. Some historians, among them Maurice Séguin, Guy Frégault, and Michel Brunet, argued that it did exist; others, such as Jean Hamelin and Fernand Ouellet, disagreed. Hamelin and Ouellet contended that the existence of monopolies and state control over the economy had stunted the development of a national bourgeoisie. Was French Canada's dynamic entrepreneurial class wiped out as a result of British domination, or did such a class ever exist?

Although a conclusive answer is not possible, it can be said that the metropolitan French appear to have controlled the biggest commercial operations connected with the profitable wholesale trade. They had the necessary funds and contacts to obtain adequate supplies in France. These French merchants provided most of the imported manufactured goods at Louisbourg and Quebec. About two-thirds of the colony's external trade was handled by French merchants and their Quebec agents.[4] The Canadian merchants dominated only the smaller-scale retail trade. Thus, while much work remains to be done on this subject, a picture emerges of a strong metropolitan French presence in large-scale commerce and of a French Canadian dominance in smaller-scale trading.

97

In the eighteenth century the fur trade was carried on by scores of small partnerships. The companies usually consisted of three or four partners who obtained a three-year lease on the trade at a particular fur-trading post. (At Niagara, Detroit, and Michilimackinac, however, French military commanders controlled the fur trade.) The members of the partnership shared in the profits or losses according to the percentage of the capital they had invested. The partners obtained trade goods from the large Montreal merchants, usually on credit at 30 percent interest. These French merchants marketed the furs through their agents at home in France.

WOMEN IN THE WORKPLACE

Women in eighteenth-century New France frequently ran small businesses that sold cloth, clothes, furs, brandy, and utensils. During their husbands' absences in the interior, the fur traders' wives and daughters often looked after their stores and accounts. A number of widowed merchants' wives continued their husbands' businesses. Well-versed in the affairs of her fur-trader husband, Marie-Anne Barbel decided to continue his business after his death in 1745. She also expanded his real estate holdings and began a pottery works. She was one of Quebec's well-to-do merchants until the Seven Years' War ruined her fur-trade operation. Much of her property was destroyed in the British bombardment of Quebec's Lower Town in 1759.

Other women also began successful commercial careers. Agathe de Saint-Père, Madame de Repentigny, headed a textile firm—New France's first—in the early eighteenth century. This energetic businesswoman ransomed nine English weavers held prisoner by the Indians and hired them to teach Canadian apprentices the trade. Soon she had twenty looms operating, turning out coarse cloth and canvas. Marie-Charlotte Denys de la Ronde, the widow of Claude de Ramezay, governor of Montreal, operated a sawmill, a brick factory, and a tile works. Her daughter, Louise de Ramezay, owned a flour mill, a tannery, and sawmills.

Throughout New France married women shared in the work of their husbands. At busy times of the year, they helped in the fields. In the urban areas, artisans' and merchants' wives assisted their spouses. Both rural and urban women often kept the family accounts and managed the servants (if there were any) or the apprentices, in the case of artisans.

98

THE *ENGAGÉS* IN THE FUR TRADE

Ranking below the middle-sized French Canadian retail merchants were the small-scale traders and the voyageurs, or *engagés*. These individuals carried the products of the country to the town, and vice versa; the voyageurs, under contract as *engagés* (as was increasingly the case after 1700), travelled thousands of kilometres from the St. Lawrence Valley.

Every year, 400–500 people received permission to enter the fur trade around the Great Lakes or in the Upper Mississippi valley. Possibly as many as five to six times that number went without permission. Little is known of these people. According to the historian Gratien Allaire, the majority were recruited around Montreal.[5] His research also reveals that the *engagés* tended to be habitants from rural areas seeking to supplement their farm incomes.

TRADESPEOPLE

The colony had about two thousand trades workers by the 1740s. The most numerous in the construction industry were carpenters and masons; in transportation, navigators and carters; and in the food industry, bakers and butchers. As a rule, craftsworkers owned all their own tools and worked in small workshops attached to their homes. The French authorities often accused Canadian workers of being headstrong and insubordinate; their self-confidence and independence were frowned upon by the administrators from Old France, where the average person had little, if any, personal freedom or opportunity for personal advancement.

THE HABITANTS AND THEIR WAY OF LIFE

The habitants comprised the largest group in the colony. By the 1740s the oldest seigneuries had two (in some cases, three) rows of farms stretching back from the river. The habitants paid no direct taxes (apart from the occasional tax for local improvements), whereas in France the peasants paid between one-third and one-half of their income in taxes. In addition, the habitants' tithes were only half the rate that was required at the time in northern France.

The majority of the habitants apparently ate well. Pork and game, particularly venison and wild hare, were staple meats, being served almost every day. Gradually, though, wild game came to be relied on less and less as it became harder to obtain near the settled areas. The pig remained a mainstay of the habitants' diet because it was inexpensive to keep (it would eat anything from acorns to kitchen scraps) and because, as the old folk saying in both France and New France put it, "You can eat everything but the squeal." Fish was also part of the core diet of the French settlers, as was buckwheat, a hardy cereal used to make bread, pancakes, and porridges. Maple syrup was the chief source of sweetening.

99

Vegetables from the garden, particularly peas and fèves (the large tough-fibred beans from Normandy that were brought to the St. Lawrence Valley), were favourites. Dried peas and beans could be stored for years and then made into tasty soups. And because legumes absorbed the flavour of either smoked or salted pork fat well, the habitants frequently used pork in their recipes for pea soup and baked beans.

The *Canadiens* also enjoyed such fruits as apples, plums, and cherries. Apple trees that were brought from the northwest of France thrived in the cool, moist Canadian climate. Wild fruits, especially raspberries, red and black currants, and cranberries, were to be had for the picking.

As for beverages, wealthy habitants could obtain tea and coffee from the traders, but these goods were costly. Milk, in contrast, was cheap and plentiful. Cider was drunk at all meals. The well-to-do could afford wine imported from France, while the habitants drank the cheaper beer brewed in the colony or, indeed, beer that they brewed themselves.

Farmers in New France detested being called "peasants." As the Finnish traveller Pehr Kalm noted in 1749, "The gentlemen and ladies, as well as the poorest peasants and their wives, are called Monsieur and Madame." The habitants had more personal freedom than did their counterparts in France. The royal officials in New France repeatedly complained that the independent-minded Canadians always pleased themselves and paid little attention to the administrators' directives.

The habitants' lives centred on their farms, which they cultivated with their families' help. The *curé* and the captain of militia were the habitants' links with the outside world. As in France, the *curés* were responsible for the registration of births, deaths, and marriages.

THE NOBILITY AND THE MILITARY

The nobility kept alive the military and aristocratic values of Old France in Canada. In general, the sons of the nobles became military officers, obtaining commissions in the Troupes de la Marine, or colonial regular army.

The military was a very important element in the community—especially considering that the St. Lawrence Valley had enjoyed only 50 years of complete freedom from war in the course of New France's 150-year existence. Every year, the Crown spent large sums for the maintenance of soldiers in New France. About fifteen hundred regular French troops garrisoned the posts during the early eighteenth century. Within the army, there was tension between the French and the Canadian-born officers. In the army, as in the militia, Canadian leaders had a moral authority over the Canadian troops that French officers lacked. Unlike the French, Canadian troops had adapted to, and preferred, a different type of warfare—what in the twentieth century would be called guerilla warfare.

The Church in New France

During the years of royal government, and particularly during the years of the great migration from France in the late 1660s and early 1670s, the church suffered from an acute shortage of personnel. As late as 1683 the intendant reported that three-quarters or more of the habitants heard mass only four times a year. The shortage of priests would remain a serious problem until well into the nineteenth century.

The parish priests played an important role in those communities they could regularly visit, a role that has been aptly described by sociologist Jean-Charles Falardeau as follows: "The Canadian curés were pastors of communities lacking resources, organization and, most of the time, local leaders. They soon became also the real leaders of these communities."[6]

Yet historians such as W.J. Eccles and Cornelius Jaenen, while not denying the church's central role, distance themselves from such an interpretation. They stress that the people of New France showed a surprising independence from the church. When, for instance, the Crown decided that the populace should pay tithes (or ecclesiastical taxes) for the support of a secular clergy, and the bishop stipulated that it be at the rate of one-thirteenth of the produce of the land, the people protested. The bishop reduced his demand to one-twentieth, and eventually had to accept only one twenty-sixth of the grain. To make up the difference, the Crown provided the clergy with annual subsidies. Only when more land came into production in the early eighteenth century did many parish priests become relatively well off.

The frequent *ordonnances* of the intendant provide further proof of the independence of many *Canadiens* from the clergy. Repeatedly the intendant directed the inhabitants of the parishes with priests to pay more respect to them. He prohibited walking out of church as soon as the priest began his sermon, standing in the lobby arguing, brawling during the service, and even bringing dogs into church.

The clergy did, however, enjoy the respect of the community for what today would be called social services. During the early history of New France, the church established the first clerically administered social institutions. These endured, in many cases, into the twentieth century. The clergy were actively involved in teaching, nursing, and other charitable work. In 1760 the nearly 100 diocesan or parish priests in the colony were assisted by 30 Sulpicians (a religious order that had begun work in the colony in 1657), 25 Jesuits, 24 Récollets (who had returned in 1670), and more than 200 nuns belonging to six religious communities.

101

Schooling was the preserve of the church in the colony, and all the religious communities assumed some responsibility for education. Generally speaking, it appears that only the urban dwellers benefited in number from the schools, which were located in the largest towns. In a study of three rural parishes in mid-eighteenth century New France, historian Allan Greer discovered that only approximately 10 percent of the men and women could sign their marriage act. The percentage in the urban centre of Trois-Rivières, in contrast, was approximately 50 percent.[7] The Quebec Seminary ran the Petit Séminaire, the most important elementary school in the colony. The Jesuit College at Quebec provided male students with a post-secondary education equivalent to that which could be obtained in a provincial town in France. The Congrégation de Notre-Dame and the Ursuline order established elementary schools for girls in the larger centres.

Along with education, the church provided welfare services and maintained charitable institutions. Three women's religious communities and two men's communities became involved in this work. Each of the three principal towns in New France had a Bureau of the Poor, which served as a relief centre and employment agency. Those who were too elderly or too infirm to work (and who were not being cared for by their children at home) were placed in institutions at Montreal or Quebec, along with the chronically ill, the insane, and women of "loose morals" (the latter were put there to be reformed by the hospital nuns). To help pay for these institutional services, the church held about one-tenth of the seigneurial lands in the St. Lawrence Valley. By the 1750s it held about one-quarter of the land. In the colony's final years, more than one-third of New France's population lived on church seigneuries, providing the clergy with a substantial revenue.

Musée du Québec

This painting by French Canadian illustrator Henri Julien (1852–1908) is entitled *La Chasse-Galerie*. It illustrates a very popular tale of the fur trade, which involved Satan's promise to a group of voyageurs to get them to their homes in New France for New Year's Eve on condition that they did not utter the name of God or touch a cross or a church steeple along the way. If they did, the Devil would claim their souls. The tale allowed for all kinds of variation—sometimes Satan won; other times, he failed. The legend never lost its appeal, as listeners never knew how it would turn out.

POPULAR RELIGION

Popular religion remained strong in New France. Many *Canadiens* in the rural areas believed in magic and witchcraft. Tales of flying canoes, werewolves, and encounters with the devil were told to generations of Canadian children. But these tales were harmless in contrast with the real belief in sorcerers. Individuals who today would be recognized as suffering from mental illness were then believed to be possessed by demons, and considered sorcerers. The clergy were frequently called on to perform exorcisms on such individuals with the aid of prayers, candles, and holy water. Even the clergy supported the principle that anyone believed to have been a sorcerer should not be buried in sanctified ground. New France, however, never knew the hysteria that swept through part of New England in the 1690s, as exemplified by the infamous witchhunts of Salem. No executions occurred in New France as punishment for occult practices.

THE CANADIANIZATION OF THE CLERGY

Gradually, the clergy became "Canadianized." The training of a native-born Canadian secular clergy had long been an objective of the church. The seminary at Quebec trained Canadian priests at its theological college.

During the eighteenth century the parishes in New France came to be staffed increasingly by Canadians. In 1760 Canada had about one hundred parishes, most of them run by diocesan clergy, about four-fifths of whom were Canadian. Tensions, however, existed between the Canadian-born clergy at the lower levels of the church's administration and the French-born clergy who dominated at the top.

The Amerindian Population

The settled areas of Canada contained a small non-French population. Several thousand Indians lived in five major settlements in the St. Lawrence Valley: the Hurons at Lorette near Quebec; the Abenakis from present-day Maine at Saint-François, east of Montreal; and the Iroquois at Caughnawaga (Kahnawake), St. Régis (Akwesasne) and the Lake of Two Mountains (Kanesatake or Oka), all west of Montreal. More than simply a desire to convert the Indians to Christianity led the French to establish Native villages near their own settlements. They sought a buffer against Iroquois and English invaders. But the existence of these Amerindian settlements had an unanticipated side-effect—it speeded up the expanding contraband fur trade between New France and the American colonies, in which both the Roman Catholic Iroquois and the Abenakis participated.

Historian Peter Moogk has noted that the Christian Indians of New France sometimes raised the children of French Canadians, as a consequence of the fact that unmarried pregnant women in the colony faced prosecution as criminals.[8] Some women concealed their pregnancies, then left their babies to perish. The death penalty could be imposed in such cases. A few unwed mothers gave their babies to the Indians to raise instead. The midwives who assisted these women with their deliveries helped them escape detection. Indians also adopted and raised American children who had been taken as captives during Franco-Indian raids.

As the French needed the resident Indians for protection and for assistance in their raids against the English, they could not afford to antagonize them by rigorously enforcing French laws. Thus, although they regarded the Amerindians in the colony as French subjects, they granted them what might best be termed "special status." As historian W.J. Eccles has written, the French avoided addressing the basic question of whether or not the Indians were subject to French law "by tacitly granting [them] something akin to diplomatic immunity." The French did not usually prosecute

Amerindians for breaches of the peace, "for one good reason; to have attempted to do so with any degree of vigor would have alienated the Indians, and this the French could not afford to do."[9]

AMERINDIAN AND BLACK SLAVES

A slave class in Canada existed to help meet the acute labour shortage. From the late 1680s, Indian slaves from the Upper Mississippi valley began arriving in New France on a regular basis. These *panis* (or Pawnees, the name of a single tribe, which was used despite the fact that the slaves were taken from many other tribes as well) were sold to the French by other Indians. Blacks captured during raids on the English colonies or brought in from the French West Indies also increased the number of slaves in the colony. The rare black slaves were sold at an average price twice as high as that received for the more numerous Indian captives, because the blacks had greater resistance to disease than did the Indians.

104

The Canadians traded slaves like cattle, at the marketplace or at auction. Slavery, which was an urban phenomenon, enjoyed great popularity among the governors of New France: Rigaud de Vaudreuil, governor from 1703 to 1725, owned eleven slaves, while the Marquis de Beauharnois, in office from 1726 to 1746, owned twenty-seven. But merchants, traders, and the clergy were the biggest slave owners. Indian and black slaves worked at the convents and hospitals operated by nuns in Quebec and Montreal. Between the 1680s and about 1800, there was a total of approximately four thousand slaves in French Canada. They lived short lives: for Indian slaves, the average age at death was about eighteen, and for blacks, twenty-five.

By 1754 New France's French Canadian population had reached fifty-five thousand. What had begun as an offshoot of Old France became a new community in Canada. Little by little, the French had become *Canadiens*, with values, manners, and even attitudes that differentiated them more and more from the metropolitan French. The *Canadiens* resented the assumption of superiority by the military and ecclesiastical leaders of Old France. The French officer Louis-Antoine de Bougainville, who came to Quebec in 1757, was struck by the increasing differences between the French and the *Canadiens*: "We seem to belong to another, even an enemy, nation."[10]

NOTES

[1]André Lachance, "Tout sur la torture," *Le Magazine Maclean*, décembre 1966, 38.
[2]Douglas Hay, "The Meanings of the Criminal Law in Quebec, 1764–1774," in *Crime and Criminal Justice in Europe and Canada*, edited by Louis A. Knafla (Waterloo, 1981), 77.
[3]Michael Bliss, *Northern Enterprise: Five Centuries of Canadian Business* (Toronto, 1987), 44.
[4]Bliss, *Northern Enterprise*, 70.

[5]Gratien Allaire, "Fur Trade Engagés, 1701–1745," in *Rendezvous: Selected Papers of the North American Fur Trade Conference*, 1981, edited by Thomas C. Buckley (St. Paul, Minn., 1984), 22.

[6]Jean-Charles Falardeau, "The Seventeenth-Century Parish in French Canada," in *French-Canadian Society*, vol. 1, edited by Marcel Rioux and Yves Martin (Toronto, 1964), 27.

[7]Allan Greer, "The Pattern of Literacy in Quebec, 1745–1899," *Histoire sociale/Social History* 11, 22 (November 1978): 299.

[8]Peter N. Moogk, *"Les Petits Sauvages*. The Children of Eighteenth-Century New France," in *Childhood and Family in Canadian History*, edited by Joy Parr (Toronto, 1982), 27.

[9]W.J. Eccles, *The Canadian Frontier, 1534–1760* (New York, 1969), 78.

[10]Bougainville quoted in Guy Frégault, *Canada: The War of the Conquest*, translated by Margaret M. Cameron (Toronto, 1969), p. 64. On this important point see the comments of George G.F. Stanley in *New France: The Last Phase, 1744–1760* (Toronto, 1968), 272.

Related Readings

R. Douglas Francis and Donald B. Smith, *Readings in Canadian History: Pre-Confederation*, 3d ed. (Toronto, 1990) contains a number of articles that deal directly with this topic: W.J. Eccles' "Society and the Frontier," 94–112; John F. Bosher, "The Family in New France," 112–23; and Jan Noel, "New France: Les femmes favorisées," 123–46.

105

BIBLIOGRAPHY

For a study of the domestic life of New France in the late seventeenth and early eighteenth centuries, see W.J. Eccles, *Canada Under Louis XIV, 1663–1701* (Toronto, 1964); the introductory chapters of Brian Young and John A. Dickinson, *A Short History of Quebec: A Socio-Economic Perspective* (Toronto, 1988), 11–102; and Dale Miquelon, *New France, 1701–1744* (Toronto, 1987). Developments in France are reviewed in Pierre Goubert's *Louis XIV and Twenty Million Frenchmen* (New York, 1970). Two helpful surveys of New France in the eighteenth century are the chapter by Jacques Mathieu, "Un pays à statut colonial (1701–1755)," in *Histoire du Québec*, edited by Jean Hamelin (Montréal, 1976), 183–230, and the beautifully illustrated *Taking Root: Canada from 1700 to 1760*, by André Vachon, with the assistance of Victorin Chabot and André Desrosiers (Ottawa, 1985). Useful guides for the period 1663–1760 are provided in W.J. Eccles, *The Canadian Frontier, 1534–1760* (Toronto, 1969) and his *France in America* (New York, 1972; rev. ed., 1990); as well as in Marcel Trudel, *Introduction to New France* (Toronto, 1968). In *Northern Enterprise: Five Centuries of Canadian Business* (Toronto, 1987), Michael Bliss reviews the economic life of New France, as does Alice Jean E. Lunn in her older study, *Développement économique de la Nouvelle-France, 1713–1760*, translated from the English by Brigitte Monel-Nish (Montréal, 1986). Lunn's work was originally presented as a Ph.D. thesis at McGill University in 1942, but was published only recently, and in French rather than the original English.

A number of important articles by W.J. Eccles have been reprinted in his *Essays on New France* (Toronto, 1987). Terence Crowley, in " 'Thunder Gusts': Popular Disturbances in Early French Canada," *Historical Papers/*

Communications Historiques 1979, pp. 11–32, reviews civil discontent in the colony. Louise Dechêne describes Montreal in the seventeenth century in *Habitants et marchands de Montréal au XVIIe siècle* (Montréal, 1974), and in the eighteenth century in "La croissance de Montréal au XVIIIe siècle," *Revue d'histoire de l'Amérique française* 27 (1973/74): 163–79; the latter article appears in English translation as "The Growth of Montreal in the 18th century," in *Canadian History Before Confederation*, 2d ed., edited by J.M. Bumsted (Georgetown, Ont., 1979), 154–67. John Hare, Marc Lafrance, and David-Thiery Ruddel review urban life at Quebec in *Histoire de la Ville de Québec, 1608–1871* (Montréal, 1987).

For further information on other aspects of the social history of New France, see the following historical pamphlets published by the Canadian Historical Association: Marcel Trudel, *The Seigneurial Regime* (Ottawa, 1956); W.J. Eccles, *The Government of New France* (Ottawa, 1965); and Cornelius J. Jaenen, *The Role of the Church in New France* (Ottawa, 1985). Cornelius Jaenen's full study of religious life in New France is also entitled *The Role of the Church in New France* (Toronto, 1976). Several important essays on New France's society appear in Fernand Ouellet, *Economy, Class and Nation in Quebec: Interpretative Essays*, edited and translated by Jacques A. Barbier (Toronto, 1991). Two accounts of the seigneurial regime are William Bennett Munro's now-dated *The Seigneurs of Old Canada* (Toronto, 1922), and Richard Colebrook Harris's *The Seigneurial System in Canada: A Geographical Study* (Madison, 1966; rev. ed., Montreal, 1984). Legal historian Douglas Hay comments on French law in New France in his article "The Meanings of the Criminal Law in Quebec, 1764–1774," in *Crime and Criminal Justice in Europe and Canada*, edited by Louis A. Knafla (Waterloo, Ont., 1981), 77–110. Historian André Lachance reviews the question of torture in his "Tout sur la torture," *Le Magazine Maclean*, décembre 1966, 36–39, 41–42. Jean-Charles Falardeau's "The Seventeenth-Century Parish in French Canada" appeared in *French-Canadian Society*, vol. 1, edited by Marcel Rioux and Yves Martin (Toronto, 1964), 19–32. An interesting article on witchcraft is Jonathan L. Pearl's "Witchcraft in New France in the Seventeenth Century: The Social Aspect," *Historical Reflections* 4 (1977): 191–205. References to music in New France are contained in Helmut Kallmann, *A History of Music in Canada, 1534–1914* (Toronto, 1960). The best short summaries of the fur trade are by W.J. Eccles: "Fur Trade," in *The Canadian Encyclopedia* 2d ed. (Edmonton, 1988), 856–57, and "The Fur Trade in the Colonial Northeast," in *History of Indian–White Relations*, edited by Wilcomb E. Washburn, vol. 4 of the *Handbook of North American Indians* (Washington, D.C., 1988), 324–34. On the *engagés*, see Gratien Allaire, "Fur Trade Engagés, 1701–1745," in *Rendezvous: Selected Papers of the North American Fur Trade Conference 1981*, edited by Thomas C. Buckley (St. Paul, Minn., 1984), 15–26. An overview of the contraband trade is provided by Jean Lunn in "The Illegal Fur Trade Out of New France," Canadian Historical Association, *Report*

(1939), 61–76. Marcel Trudel has written a short history of slavery in New France in "Ties That Bind," *Horizon Canada* 18 (1985): 422–27. A short article on the French language in Canada, written by the linguist Gaston Dulong, appears in *The Canadian Encyclopedia*, 2d ed. (Edmonton, 1988), 847. Allan Greer examines the question of literacy in "The Pattern of Literacy in Quebec, 1745–1899," *Histoire sociale/Social History* 11, 22 (November 1978): 295–335. For a view of New France in 1749, see Pehr Kalm's *Travels in North America*, 2 vols. (New York, 1966) for his descriptions of Canadian life and customs. A delightful account of early French Canadian food and cooking customs is Jay A. Anderson's "The Early Development of French-Canadian Food Ways," in *Folklore of Canada*, edited by Edith Fowke (Toronto, 1976), 91–99.

For the activities of women in New France, consult Micheline Dumont et al., *Quebec Women: A History* (Toronto, 1987), and Lilianne Plamondon, "A Businesswoman in New France: Marie-Anne Barbel, The Widow Fornel," in *Rethinking Canada: The Promise of Women's History*, edited by Veronica Strong-Boag and Anita Clair Fellman (Toronto, 1986), 45–58. An excellent overview is "French Women in the New World," Chapter 2 of Alison Prentice et al., *Canadian Women: A History* (Toronto, 1988), 41–64.

Peter N. Moogk studies the children of eighteenth-century New France in *"Les Petits Sauvages,"* in *Childhood and Family in Canadian History*, edited by Joy Parr (Toronto, 1982), 17–43. The story of the Tremblay family (cited in the chapter) is told in Jacqueline Darveau-Cardinal's "De l'origine et de l'histoire de quelques patronymes canadiens," *La revue française de Généalogie 11 (1981): 20–23.*

Two valuable historiographical articles on the economic and social history of New France are Serge Jaumian and Matteo Sanfilippo, "Le Régime seigneurial en Nouvelle-France: Un débat historiographique," *The Register* 5, 2 (Autumn 1984): 226–47, and Robert Comeau and Paul-André Linteau, "Une question historiographique: Une bourgeoisie en Nouvelle-France?" in *Économie québécoise*, edited by Robert Comeau (Montréal, 1969), 311–23. Serge Gagnon's *Quebec and Its Historians: The Twentieth Century* (Montreal, 1985) contains several interesting historiographical essays on New France. Fernand Ouellet's historiographical survey, "The Formation of a New Society in the St. Lawrence Valley: From Classless Society to Class Conflict," appears in *Economy, Class, and Nation in Quebec: Interpretative Essays*, edited and translated by Jacques A. Barbier (Toronto, 1991), 5–39. For biographies of prominent individuals in New France, see *Dictionary of Canadian Biography*, vols. 1–4 (Toronto, 1966, 1969, 1974, 1979); and for valuable maps of the St. Lawrence colony, consult R. Cole Harris, ed., *Historical Atlas of Canada*, vol. 1, *From the Beginning to 1800* (Toronto, 1987). The most recent survey of New France is Jacques Mathieu's *La Nouvelle-France, Les Français en Amérique du Nord, XVIe–XVIIIe siècle* (Québec, 1991).

107

The Anglo-French Struggle for a Continent

108   At about the same time that the French settled Quebec, England established its first colonies in North America: Virginia in 1607; Newfoundland in 1610; and Massachusetts in 1620. Others followed on the Atlantic seaboard, and in 1664 the Dutch colony of New Netherlands passed into English hands and was renamed New York. The English also sponsored expeditions into the huge inland sea north of New France. Henry Hudson led the English expedition that in 1610–11 first located the immense body of water the size of the Mediterranean Sea. A little more than half a century later, an English company established a string of fur-trading posts around Hudson Bay.

Conflict arose between England and France in the late 1680s when the two empires confronted each other in the interior of the North American continent. Contrary to Colbert's directives, New France in the 1670s and 1680s had established forts around the Great Lakes to the Mississippi River. Even after the fur trade became uneconomical in the mid-1690s, the French resolved to stay for strategic reasons. The French, in fact, subsidized the fur trade to retain their military alliance with the inland Indian tribes. European claims to the contrary, the Indians remained the sovereign powers beyond the St. Lawrence Valley and the Appalachian Mountains.

Founding of the Hudson's Bay Company

The English preceded the French in the exploration of the area north of New France. On his return from a voyage in the Dutch service to the river that now bears his name in New York, Henry Hudson was sent by financial backers on an expedition to discover the Northwest Passage. In early June 1610 he entered an ice-bound strait previously noted (in the 1570s and

1580s) by English Arctic explorers Martin Frobisher and John Davis. Both the strait and the inland sea into which it led were later named after him. Although Hudson and his men spent a terrible winter on the east coast of James Bay, the following spring the determined captain announced that their search for the Northwest Passage would continue. His crew mutinied and seized Hudson, his son, and seven others, setting them adrift to die. Eight of the twelve mutineers returned alive to England, where they falsely reported that the expedition had found the Northwest Passage. Nothing is known of Henry Hudson's fate. The Welsh navigator Sir Thomas Button crossed Hudson Bay in 1612 but failed to find Hudson or a passage to the Indies.

Other English expeditions followed until 1631, when it became clear that, even if a Northwest Passage existed, it would not be commercially viable as a trade route. Since both the Dutch and the English had already begun to make the longer but less hazardous journey around Africa to India and China, the lure of the Northwest Passage diminished.

109

Ironically, two renegade French coureurs de bois, Pierre-Esprit Radisson and Médard Chouart Des Groseilliers (Mr. Radishes and Mr. Gooseberry, as the English called them), who had found no support in New France for their plan to trade in the rich fur country south of Hudson Bay and James Bay, directed the English to that area. In 1668, a group of English merchants under the patronage of Prince Rupert, a cousin of King Charles II, sponsored Groseilliers's expedition, which was to winter on Hudson Bay and return with a cargo of fur. The enterprise proved so successful that in 1670 Charles II gave the Hudson's Bay Company exclusive trading rights and property ownership to all the lands within the area drained by the rivers flowing into Hudson and James bays (nearly half the area of Canada today). No one consulted the Indians about this charter to "Rupert's Land."

French Expansion to the North and West

The English now threatened New France's fur trade from two sides—the upper Hudson River valley and Hudson Bay. The collapse of the Huron trading system in 1649 left a vacuum and greatly facilitated the English establishment on Hudson Bay. In response, the French in the early 1670s dispatched overland expeditions to Hudson Bay, Lake Superior, and the Mississippi River to establish French claims to these areas.

Frontenac, who became governor in 1672, openly promoted further westward expansion. His ally in this was René-Robert Cavelier de La Salle, a daring and ambitious fur trader. Both Frontenac and La Salle knew that a fortune in furs awaited the first French traders to reach the Indians in the Mississippi valley. Early in 1682 La Salle reached the Mississippi delta,

Source: Adapted from Richard I. Ruggles, *A Country So Interesting: The Hudson's Bay Company and Two Centuries of Mapping, 1670–1870* (Montreal and Kingston, 1991), 27.

European knowledge of Canadian territory in 1670.

where he raised the royal arms of France. The French explorer claimed all the land drained by the Mississippi River and its tributaries for the King of France and named the huge valley Louisiana, after Louis XIV. La Salle's own attempt to found a colony in Louisiana ended in failure—and his assassination in 1687—but settlement was successfully undertaken twenty years later.

In the mid-1670s Montreal traders built Michilimackinac at the junction of Lakes Michigan and Huron, which became the starting point for the fur trade along the Upper Mississippi and beyond Lake Superior. Soon French trading posts dotted the entire area from the Ohio River to Lake Superior and north to Hudson Bay.

War with England's American Colonies

Frontenac's successors faced an increasingly difficult military situation in the 1680s. After the French ended their truce with the Iroquois in the mid-1680s, the Five Nations (with the encouragement of the English) resumed their raids on New France. Few in number and scattered over a vast area, the French realized more than ever the importance of co-operation with their Algonquian allies. The coureurs de bois then became the colony's greatest strength, because they could be used to revitalize France's Native alliances in the interior.

111

The Iroquois raid in 1689 on Lachine, a settlement west of Montreal, launched in retaliation for a French attack on several Iroquois villages two years earlier (see Chapter 4), led to a new round of conflict between the French and the Iroquois along with their allies, the English colonies. Sent back to New France as governor in 1689, Frontenac launched French Canadian and Indian hit-and-run raids against the English settlements. At Schenectady, New York, and Salmon Falls, New Hampshire, the French and Indian raiding parties broke into homes and scalped men, women, and children. *La petite guerre*, the war of ambush and surprise, was waged by the Canadian militia and their Algonquian allies under the direction of regular French officers. It continued for nearly a decade, until the Treaty of Ryswick in 1697 between England and France brought four years of peace. But in 1701, the very year that New France's conflict with the Iroquois ended, war broke out again with England.

FRANCE'S NEW NORTH AMERICAN STRATEGY, 1701

France developed a new North American strategy in 1701 and held to it for the remainder of the French regime. Economically, Canada was a liability for France. With a glut of furs in France, the fur trade had ceased to be of any real economic benefit. But rather than retreat from the Great Lakes and the Mississippi valley, the French chose to stay, for strategic reasons. To keep the Indians in the French alliance, they would, if necessary, subsidize the fur trade. France had to prevent the English expansion into the West. Thus, the French fur-trading empire was retained for non-economic reasons. No more attention was paid to Colbert's idea of a "compact colony" on the banks of the St. Lawrence. Instead, the French began preparations for a chain of posts linking the Great Lakes to the Gulf of Mexico. Louis XIV also ordered that a new settlement, to be named *détroit* ("the straits"), be built at the narrows between Lakes Erie and Huron. Detroit would bar English access to the northwest and maintain French control of the upper Great Lakes. With their Indian allies, the French planned to contain the English within the coastal strip between the Alleghenies and the Atlantic.

New France in Wartime

The war that began between the English colonies and New France in 1689 ultimately would be resolved only in 1760—more than three-quarters of a century later. In the initial struggle New France had three main handicaps. First, the colony's population was small in comparison with the total number of British Americans who outnumbered the French by nearly twenty to one. A second weakness of the tiny colony lay in the precariousness of its economy. Only one export industry existed—the heavily subsidized fur trade—and it was extremely vulnerable in wartime when the transport of furs from the interior could be cut off. New France's third weakness lay in the relatively small scale of its agriculture, which was also vulnerable to disruption in wartime. Even in good years, the habitants produced only a small surplus. In wartime, they had a deficit, because militia service pulled the habitants off the land. War also meant increased dependence on France for food and war materials at a time when the sea lanes to and from France became exposed to attack by the English.

The French colony did, however, have a number of strengths. Effective political leadership was perhaps the most important. The reforms of 1663 had left New France with a unified command structure in times of war. Subject only to annual review, the governor had complete control over the marshalling of the colony's resources, its negotiations with the Indians, and the planning of its war strategy. Nature had provided New France with a second strength—natural defences. The Adirondacks of New York, the Green Mountains of Vermont, and the White Mountains of New Hampshire and Maine all protected the French colony from a direct attack from the south. Two of the three gateways to the St. Lawrence—the river itself (closed half of the year by ice) and the Hudson River–Lake Champlain–Richelieu River waterway—could be sealed. Quebec commanded the St. Lawrence River, and a system of forts existed on the Richelieu (later to be complemented by fortifications at the southern end of Lake Champlain). The only gateway that could not be effectively shut off was the western approach from Lake Ontario. Inadvertently, the Iroquois were responsible for building up the third strength of the French. By example, they had taught the habitants the techniques of guerilla warfare. A cadre of tough and versatile French raiders had emerged from the wars with the Iroquois in the Illinois country—men who subsequently became Frontenac's most-valued troops in his raids against English frontier settlements in New England and New York.

NEW FRANCE'S ALGONQUIAN ALLIES

France's Algonquian allies constituted her fourth great asset. The French had very close trading (and, hence, military) ties with the Abenakis from Maine, many of whom had sought refuge from the expanding New England in Canada, and with the Micmacs and Malecites in the Maritimes.

France also had loose alliances with the Great Lakes Algonquians: the Ojibwa, Ottawa, Potawatomi, Miami, and Illinois. Moreover, the Canadian fur traders and fort commanders had cultivated the friendship of the Algonquians by giving them gifts and presents. While the English benefited from the Iroquois' support in the 1680s and 1690s, the majority of the Amerindian groups in northeastern North America sided with the French.

113

DIVISIONS AMONG THE ENGLISH COLONIES

Another great advantage for the French arose from the divisions among the English colonies in the late seventeenth century. A great deal of friction existed in English America, arising in part from differences in origin and religion. Its numerical superiority was more apparent than real. Furthermore, not all the colonies felt threatened by the French; consequently, they were not prepared to fight. The colonies of the Carolinas, Virginia, Maryland, and Pennsylvania, for instance, believed themselves to be quite safe behind their mountain barriers. New York and Massachusetts shielded Rhode Island and Connecticut. In the north, only two highly populated colonies—Massachusetts and New York—supported the struggle.

Of the two English colonies that fought New France, New York might have proved Canada's match had the colony's non-Indian population not been divided in the 1690s between the descendants of the original Dutch colonists and the new English settlers. The Dutch in the north showed little enthusiasm for offensive operations in the name of the English king, and consequently New York posed little threat to New France. Massachusetts, though, did launch a naval attack on Quebec in 1690.

NEW FRANCE'S "LUCK"

New France's final great advantage over the English came about through what might be called simple luck. Sir William Phips of Massachusetts, after taking Port-Royal in Acadia in 1690 (see Chapter 7), returned to

Boston to take command of a naval expedition of more than thirty vessels with twenty-three hundred men. Fortunately for the survival of Canada, Phips's ships took two months to reach Quebec: en route, smallpox had broken out and swept through his ranks. Arriving at Quebec late in the season and fearing entrapment in the ice, Phips withdrew after consuming almost all of his gun powder bombarding the Quebec citadel. Grateful residents of Quebec named the newly built parish church at Place Royale, Notre-Dame-de-la-Victoire.

Luck intervened again in the second round of the contest. In 1711, England made a final, decisive strike against New France. An armada under Sir Hovenden Walker was organized, and England supplied 5300 troops, building up the fleet's strength to nearly 6500, while 2300 troops worked their way up the Lake Champlain route by land. New France was thus invaded by a force equal to half the total French population of the St. Lawrence Valley. Fortune intervened. In fog and gales at the mouth of the St. Lawrence the English lost ships and nearly 900 men. The Walker expedition turned back. Once again, Quebec's thankful citizens renamed the little church in the lower town—this time, to Notre-Dame-des-Victoires. (The church still stands today.)

The Treaty of Utrecht, 1713

The Treaty of Utrecht in 1713 settled the war, one in which the French had more than held their own ground. At the outset of the peace negotiations in 1713, the French occupied York Factory, the most important Hudson's Bay Company post on Hudson Bay. They had possession of Port-Royal in Acadia and retained Detroit and their forts on the Great Lakes. The establishment of Louisiana had consolidated their position in the Mississippi valley. Yet the peace treaty did not reflect these strengths.

At the bargaining table at Utrecht, New France paid for Louis XIV's European losses. France had to make concessions, and Louis XIV decided to make them in North America. The French Crown ceded all claims to Newfoundland, except for fishing rights on the north shore, and renounced its claims on Hudson Bay. The French recognized British suzerainty over the Iroquois confederacy, and surrendered control over what the English called Nova Scotia, handing the major French Acadian settlements over to the English. Without having been defeated in a single major battle, the Canadians were defeated in the Treaty of Utrecht.

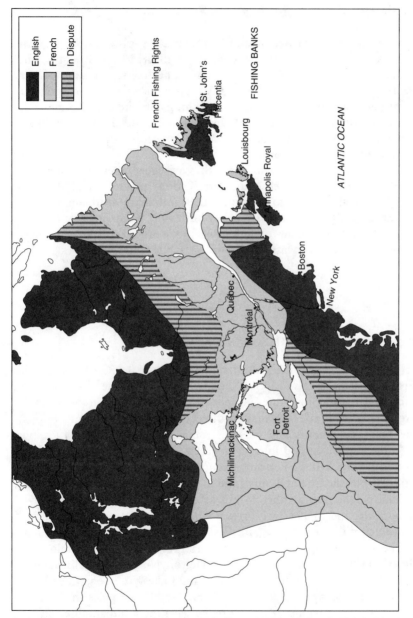

Source: Adapted from P.G. Cornell, J. Hamelin, F. Ouellet, and M. Trudel, *Canada: Unity in Diversity* (Toronto, 1967), 38.

Declared French and English spheres of interest after the Treaty of Utrecht, 1713. Beyond the palisades of the French and English forts, the Indians controlled all of the interior.

Military Preparations, 1713–1744

France's forfeiture of Acadia and Newfoundland was a serious strategic setback for New France. But the French still held Cape Breton Island, and, in an attempt to redress the situation, they constructed the military fortress of Louisbourg there in 1717. Although essentially a garrison town, Louisbourg also became an important fishing port and a vital commercial centre for the fur trade among France, Quebec, and the West Indies. It became one of the busiest ports in colonial America—fourth after Boston, New York, and Charleston.

To protect the major towns in the St. Lawrence Valley, governor Philippe de Rigaud de Vaudreuil built fortifications at Quebec and Montreal. The French also moved to strengthen their military position on the Great Lakes and on Lake Champlain. They built Fort Saint-Frédéric on Lake Champlain, at the narrows of the lake near its southern end. Saint-Frédéric closed off the main invasion route into Canada from New York.

THE WAR AGAINST THE FOX INDIANS

While strengthening their military position on the Great Lakes, the French became involved in an Indian war west of Lake Michigan. The Fox tribe, wishing to retain their position as middlemen in the fur trade, prevented the French from making direct contact with the Dakota (Sioux), the Fox's neighbours and enemies immediately to the west. Friction with the French turned into open warfare from 1714 to 1717. The first campaigns checked the Fox only temporarily, and conflict broke out again in 1728. For the first and only time in the Great Lakes area, the French incited neighbouring tribes to kill off the Fox. This, however, proved impossible, and in 1737 the French authorities conceded the futility of continued military action against the tribe and granted them a pardon.

The strength of the French in the interior rested on the "gift diplomacy" they so skilfully practised. Each year at Detroit, Niagara, Michilimackinac, and other posts around the Great Lakes and Lake Winnipeg, where Pierre Gaultier de Varennes et de La Vérendrye established posts in the 1730s and 1740s (see Chapter 18), the French gave their Indian allies gifts of guns, ammunition, and supplies. The Indians regarded the annual gifts as a form of rent for the use of the land on which the French forts stood and also as a fee for the right to travel across their territory. The Indians remained in complete possession of their lands and limited French rule to the tiny confines of their trading posts, and to their towns and settlements in the St. Lawrence Valley.

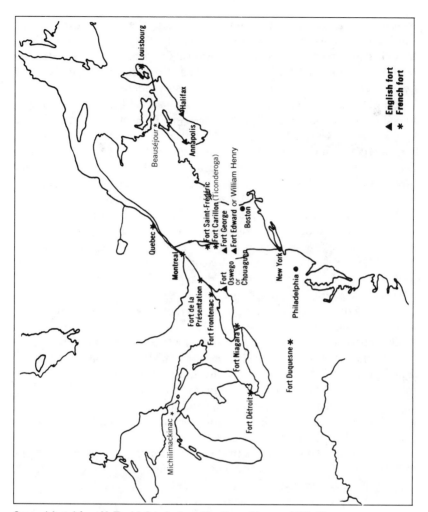

Source: Adapted from M. Trudel, *Introduction to New France* (Toronto, 1968), 88.

The struggle for a continent: English and French fortifications, 1713–1758.

117

THE OUTBREAK OF WAR AND THE FALL OF LOUISBOURG

Apart from the war with the Fox tribe to the west and the Micmac raids against the British in Nova Scotia, the period 1713–44 was relatively peaceful. This tranquillity ended in 1744 with the outbreak of war in Europe between France and England. The business community of New England welcomed the opportunity of attacking Cape Breton (Île Royale). If it fell, they could secure a monopoly of the North Atlantic fisheries. Governor William Shirley of Massachusetts organized an expedition of more than four thousand colonial militia to attack the French fortress. In spite of the many years spent on construction, the walls on the town's southern and northern flanks were extremely weak. The defenders also lacked adequate provisions and munitions. The attackers bombarded the town heavily for nearly seven weeks, reducing it to ruins. Finally, with no help expected from France, the defenders surrendered.

Louisbourg's fall caused great anxiety in Canada and revealed the precariousness of France's position in the interior. It opened the gates of the St. Lawrence, clearing the way to Quebec. Fortunately for New France, England could not mount an invasion of Quebec in 1745. Prince Charles Edward Stuart, "Bonnie Prince Charlie," had just rallied his Highland forces in Scotland. Until the English defeated Prince Charles at Culloden Moor in April 1746, they could not send troops elsewhere.

France realized the importance of Louisbourg, and attempted to retake it in the summer of 1746, assembling a force of seven thousand. The naval expedition, though, proved to be one of the most unfortunate ever undertaken by the French. In Nova Scotian waters, scurvy and smallpox took a terrific toll. On October 5 it was reported that nearly six hundred men had died and fifteen hundred more were too weak to do anything. The fleet returned to France without having attained a single one of its objectives, and at the cost of thousands of lives.

The continued possession of Louisbourg by the English had very serious consequences for the French. It prevented supplies of ammunition and trade goods, so badly needed for the Indian trade, from reaching the interior. This led to the defection of many of France's Great Lakes Indian allies. Fortunately, hostilities with England ceased in 1748, and the French were able to rush trade goods to the interior, ending the Indian's hostility.

France now knew that without its great Atlantic port it would lose the interior of North America, perhaps the St. Lawrence Valley as well. During the peace treaty negotiations at Aix-la-Chapelle in 1748, France therefore sacrificed its conquests in the Netherlands as well as the city of Madras in India in order to regain Louisbourg.

Rivalry in the Ohio Country

The Treaty of Aix-la-Chapelle in 1748 proved to be no more than a glorified ceasefire. The next clash came in the Ohio country. The governor of New France refused to concede this strategic region (the natural highway to the West) to the English. In 1753 the Marquis Duquesne, the new governor of New France, made the occupation of the Ohio River a top military priority. He sent a French military expedition to clear a route from Lake Erie to the forks of the Ohio River, and the following year he commanded French soldiers to build Fort Duquesne at the forks of the river.

As early as November 1753, Virginia's governor received British authority to use force, if necessary, to oust the French from the king's dominions. (Virginia considered English territory to include the area at the forks of the Ohio.) In early 1754 the governor sent George Washington, a twenty-two-year-old militia officer, and a number of Indian allies to expel the French. In the late spring of 1754, Washington's party of militiamen and Indians ambushed a small French detachment sent to order them to withdraw from the area. These were the first deaths in what was to become a larger war. The Seven Years' War thus began in America two years before the first shots were fired in Europe.

After the clash, Washington withdrew to a temporary fortification that the Virginians called Fort Necessity, about a hundred kilometres from Fort Duquesne. The French quickly prepared an attack on the Virginian "assassins." Under cover of a nearby woods, a force of five hundred French, Canadians, and Indians opened fire on the Virginians and soon overpowered them. The French allowed Washington and the Virginians to return home, but their defeat brought all the wavering Indian bands into the French alliance.

New France at the Outset of the Seven Years' War

By the mid-1750s New France had built up its military strength considerably. The population of Canada had tripled since 1713, to more than fifty-five thousand in 1755. New farmlands had been cleared along the Richelieu River, southeast of Montreal; along the Ottawa, northeast of Montreal; and along the Chaudière, south of Quebec. More people could be called up to fight and more farm produce could be provided. Finally, transportation had improved over the last half century. Road building allowed expansion back from the waterfront, thereby facilitating better communication.

Many weaknesses also existed. First, New France's elongated frontier was a liability; it took, for example, a year to exchange letters between Quebec and New Orleans. To protect French interests, the Crown built a string of forts from Louisbourg to Fort Duquesne, but many of these outposts were simply trading posts grown into wooden forts. Second, the Franco-Algonquian alliance was precarious. The Canadians could hold the interior only as long as they retained the support of the Great Lakes Indian tribes. Third, although the population of New France had increased to more than fifty-five thousand, the population of the American colonies was now more than one million. American settlement extended nearly two hundred kilometres from the coastline. Fourth, although the eight thousand militia of the colony could be called up quickly, few of them knew the guerilla techniques that their grandfathers and great-

119

grandfathers had mastered. Fifth, the growing friction between the French and the Canadian-born in the army officers' ranks weakened New France.

A sixth weakness of New France lay in its economy—although agricultural productivity had improved, the colony still could not feed its more than six thousand regular troops, as well as the varying numbers of Indians and militia who had to be supplied in wartime. Another problem existed as well: the need for farm labour to harvest crops made it impossible for the French to go on lengthy offensives.

More troubling than all these shortcomings was the new unity of the American colonies. The co-ordination of strategy under a British commander-in-chief did much to draw the English colonies together. In addition, the colonists wanted to defeat New France in order to end the border raids and to gain access to the rich farmlands of the Ohio valley. Nine colonies with populations larger than that of New France gave the English colonists a manpower advantage of roughly twenty to one. The foodstuffs available to them were enormous. In 1755 the governor of Pennsylvania claimed that his colony alone could export enough food to provide for an army of one hundred thousand. Pennsylvania's iron industry already competed with the iron industry of the mother country.

New France's Successes, 1754–1757

In its early years, however, the war for North America went badly for the British. In 1755, General Edward Braddock planned a four-pronged offensive aimed at taking four French forts: Duquesne, Niagara, Saint-Frédéric, and Beauséjour (the latter on the Isthmus of Chignecto between Nova Scotia and present-day New Brunswick). Since France and Britain were still officially at peace in 1755, Braddock's offensive did not aim at the conquest of New France but merely at rolling back France's empire in North America.

Braddock himself took command of the assault on Fort Duquesne, with a strike force of 1000 regulars and 1500 colonial troops. It took two months for the force to make its long march over the mountains—to clear roads and drag cannon and supplies. The spirits of the advance column of 1450 men were high when they finally arrived within fifteen kilometres of Fort Duquesne. Then came an ambush. The French and their Indian allies unleashed a barrage of gunfire at the scarlet-coated regulars and blue-coated Virginians, inflicting 1000 casualties. Braddock was killed, and his army destroyed.

Immediately after receiving news of the defeat at Duquesne, the British postponed their expedition against Fort Niagara. In the attack on Fort Saint-Frédéric in the Lake Champlain area, they did no better than a draw. The newly appointed, Canadian-born governor, Pierre de Rigaud de Vaudreuil de Cavagnial (the Marquis de Vaudreuil), immediately built Fort Carillon at the northern end of Lake George. Carillon, so named because it was located where the falling waters produced the sound of bells, became New France's first line of defence for the St. Lawrence Valley.

The Anglo-Americans scored their only clear-cut success in Acadia. Thanks to the assistance of Thomas Pichon, a traitorous French officer, the British took Fort Beauséjour and, with it, French Acadia. The fall of Beauséjour cleared the way for an attack from Halifax on Louisbourg and for the drastic measure of expelling the Acadians, then approximately ten thousand strong, from peninsular Nova Scotia (see Chapter 7).

With the exception of Beauséjour, the French and their Indian allies humiliated the larger English colonies and the British army in 1755. Governor Vaudreuil wanted to keep up the momentum, fighting where the Canadians and the Indians excelled—in the forest. In 1756 he sent out more than two thousand Indians and Canadians in raids from Fort Duquesne. The Canadian guerilla bands caused so much terror in Virginia and Maryland that these two colonies stayed out of the war until 1758, fearing that the raids might trigger slave uprisings. The French gained control of the Great Lakes by capturing Fort Oswego at the eastern end of Lake Ontario, in 1756. The following year Vaudreuil attempted to take Fort William Henry, south of the French stronghold of Carillon (or Ticonderoga, as the English called it). This was a greater challenge, as Fort William Henry—unlike Oswego—lay at the end of a short and easy supply line and could be reinforced speedily from Albany. In addition, grain shortages were severe and persistent in Canada, and the limited provisions would not permit a long siege of the English fort.

121

A final problem arose: there was a growing rift between Governor Vaudreuil and the lieutenant general, the Marquis de Montcalm, the new French military commander in Canada. Fort William Henry did fall, but Montcalm refused to march against Fort Edward, the English post on the Hudson River, 25 kilometres to the south. For Vaudreuil, offence was the only defence, but Montcalm opposed such a strategy. He wanted to see a concentration of French and Canadian troops in the St. Lawrence Valley in order to protect Montreal and Quebec against the next English invasion. The French ministry resolved the dispute by putting Montcalm in command over Vaudreuil in military matters.

Britain Gains the Upper Hand

The entire aspect of the war changed in 1757 with the accession to office of William Pitt the Elder, the self-styled saviour of the British Empire. The new prime minister inspired a nation suffering defeat to make a greater effort, and made the American war and the conquest of Canada his major objectives. The British offensive of 1758 was aimed at the same four localities as the offensive of 1755, but on this occasion, the results were rather different. Braddock's previous offensive had clearly succeeded in only one of its four attacks; the campaign of 1758, however, would succeed in three.

Several factors explain the change in England's fortunes. First, Pitt decided in 1758 to commit large numbers of regular soldiers to America, men reliable under fire in set-piece European-style battles. Second, by 1758 the Royal Navy's blockade of France was so effective that there were no more major "escapes" of French support squadrons to Canada. Finally, Pitt greatly increased Britain's financial commitment to the war. More men, more ships, and more money made a significant difference in British fortunes in 1758 and 1759.

122

FRANCE'S REVERSES IN 1758

The first English objective in 1758 was Louisbourg, which, because of the effectiveness of the British blockade on France, lacked the protection of a fleet. The thirteen thousand attackers outnumbered the defenders three to one. To the British, the important factor was speed. Louisbourg had to be taken quickly if Quebec was to be captured in the same season. The defenders, however, held out for seven weeks—just long enough to rule out an expedition against Quebec in 1758.

The successful French defence at Carillon also served to prevent an attack on Canada in 1758. At Carillon, Montcalm faced an English army of fifteen thousand with only thirty-five hundred of his own men. Yet, Montcalm won. But the French success had its price. Indirectly, it cost the French both Fort Frontenac on Lake Ontario and Fort Duquesne in present-day Pennsylvania. As almost all the troops available in the colony had been concentrated at Carillon, Fort Frontenac, with its small garrison and inadequate walls, could not be defended against an English attack. The French themselves destroyed the important post in August 1758. They also abandoned Fort Duquesne. When an English army of seven thousand came within a few kilometres of Fort Duquesne, the French garrison blew the fort up and retreated. The English renamed the site "Pittsburgh," after their prime minister.

The largest single explanation for the English success in 1758 was the Royal Navy, which blockaded Canada. The navy allowed the English colonies to obtain troop reinforcements and supplies, but deprived New France of any major outside assistance. In 1759, New France faced odds of nearly three to one in ships, four to one in regular soldiers committed to North America, and ten to one in money.

NEW FRANCE IN 1759

In 1759 Pitt's determination to take the French colony became an obsession. With the great resources England had in America, it could attack both Quebec and Carillon in equal strength. New France, by contrast, with its limited resources, had to concentrate its strength in the most vital area, Quebec. At the capital, white-haired men and beardless boys turned out to defend their homeland. The Franco-Canadian army that gathered at Quebec in the summer of 1759 numbered about 15 000. From a population of only some 60 000, the presence of more than 10 000 French Canadians represented an extraordinary mobilization.

JAMES WOLFE AT QUEBEC

James Wolfe, thirty-two years old and for eighteen of those years a professional soldier, commanded the British invasion force sent against Quebec. He had performed very well at Louisbourg, and Pitt gave him a splendid army. All the troops had previous American experience. The strike force of 4000 included some of the best units in the British army. In all, the invasion fleet had 13 500 men.

The French defenders at Quebec faced several defensive problems in the summer of 1759. First, the city walls on the western side facing the Plains of Abraham had no gun emplacements, seriously weakening the city's defence. Second, the French made a monumental error: they left undefended the south bank of the river opposite the city, and shortly after their arrival the British established batteries there. From the Lévis heights they bombarded and largely destroyed the city. Worse still, under cover of this fire, the Royal Navy could transport its ships up the river beyond Quebec. In effect, the British army could land either above or below Quebec for an assault on the walled town.

All that summer, inland French-held garrisons continued to fall into enemy hands. By the end of June 1759 the British had reoccupied Fort Oswego. Fort Niagara succumbed to a British attack in late July. Rather than see the British take Fort Rouillé, France's small outpost in the area that the Indians called Toronto, the French burned it to the ground. (An obelisk on the grounds of Toronto's Canadian National Exhibition marks the fort's location.) The French had now lost control of Lakes Ontario and Erie, and the Ohio country. In addition, the French abandoned Forts Carillon and Saint-Frédéric and retreated northward to the head of Lake Champlain.

The Canadian historian C.P. Stacey aptly called James Wolfe a "Hamlet-figure"—a soldier who had enormous difficulty making up his mind.[1] This was his first independent command, and he could not decide where to attack. After several weeks of indecision, he made up his mind to strike Montcalm and his forces at Montmorency, just east of Quebec. Wolfe's

124

National Archives of Canada/C-357.

The Notre-Dame-des-Victoires Church after the naval bombardment of Quebec by the British in 1759. Note the extent of the war damage shown in this engraving by A. Bennoist, from a sketch by Richard Short, an English naval officer.

frontal attack on the French army's entrenchments failed, and the British retreated. The English commander spent the remainder of the summer systematically devastating the parishes around Quebec. On the south shore of the St. Lawrence, the British destroyed a thousand buildings, as well as the French Canadians' harvest.

THE BATTLE OF THE PLAINS OF ABRAHAM

Wolfe knew he had to obtain a foothold on the north shore and then force Montcalm into an open, European-style battle. Haste was essential, for the naval expedition had to leave the St. Lawrence before the onset of winter. Then luck intervened: the British found a small cove, Anse au Foulon, from which a narrow path led up the steep sixty-metre-high cliffs. Believing it to be impossible for an invasion force to climb the heights on the tiny path, the French had left it lightly guarded. Incredibly, they had also failed to establish a password for a French convoy expected to bring supplies on the night of September 12.

Until the moment Wolfe landed, Montcalm believed the British attack would come on the other side of the city or at its centre, never at Anse aux Foulons to the west. The British achieved complete surprise, as the

French sentries on the shore believed that the boats gliding past them belonged to the French convoy that was expected that night (in fact, the convoy had been cancelled). The British commander placed his few French-speaking officers in the forward vessels; in the dark, they answered the sentries' challenges satisfactorily. A half-hour before dawn on September 13, the British landed near the cove. Three waves of landing ships reached the shore in total darkness. The advance party, two abreast, then walked up the steep pathway and, without detection, gained the summit of the cliffs.

A series of risks paid off for Wolfe: the difficult naval landing succeeded and his advance guard of Scottish highlanders overpowered the French post, securing a foothold on the cliffs. If the French sentries had identified the British in time, they could have sounded the alarm and easily eliminated the advance guard as they climbed the cliffs.

By daybreak, Wolfe had deployed forty-five hundred highly trained British troops on the Plains of Abraham, the grassy field close to the unarmed western walls of the citadel. At this point, Montcalm made a fatal mistake. Without waiting for Colonel Louis-Antoine de Bougainville to arrive with his three thousand regulars stationed at Cap Rouge about fifteen kilometres upstream, Montcalm impulsively attacked. At about eight o'clock that morning, Bougainville learned of the enemy landing, but by the time he reached Quebec, it was too late.

125

The battle lasted less than half an hour. The two armies on the field were numerically equal, but the British had a force composed entirely of regular soldiers, while the French army included many badly trained militia members. The British held their fire until the French army was within forty metres of them. Wolfe was ready: to ensure accurate and concentrated fire power, he had deployed three-quarters of his men in a single line confronting the French. Then the British officers gave the order, "Fire." The muskets roared, and a second volley followed, breaking the French attack and causing the French army to retire in disorder. Wolfe, leading a picked force of grenadiers, was shot down and died on the battlefield. In the confusion after Wolfe's death, the French army retreated up the St. Lawrence by a circuitous route. Mortally wounded in the battle, Montcalm died the next day in Quebec. The British suffered about 650 casualties, and the French roughly the same. On September 18, Quebec, short of provisions and soldiers, and weakly fortified on its western side, opened its gates to the English in defeat.

NEW FRANCE'S FINAL YEAR, 1759–1760

The loss of Quebec was a serious blow to the French, but they still controlled the rest of the St. Lawrence Valley. Their army was intact. Everything now depended on which ships would arrive first in the spring. The French planned to launch a spring offensive to coincide with the

126

National Gallery of Canada.

The Death of General Wolfe. This dramatic and richly colourful painting by
Benjamin West (1738–1820), unveiled in London in 1771, has become one of
the world's most famous historical paintings. The fame of West's masterpiece
endures even though as early as 1901 A.G. Doughty and G.W. Parmelee in
their exhaustive documentary collection, *The Siege of Quebec,* 6 vols. (Quebec,
1901) pronounced it as "absolutely valueless as a historic representation," vol.
3: 223–225. Wolfe died, they claim, not in the centre of the action, but in a
corner of the battlefield, attended by not more than four men. The historian
Simon Schama provides a fascinating look at West and his painting of Wolfe in
Dead Certainties (Unwarranted Speculations) (New York, 1991): 21–39, 328–330.

arrival of ships from France. The vastness of the Gulf of Lawrence made
it impossible for the Royal Navy to control completely.

Before the ice left the rivers in April, the Chevalier de Lévis, Montcalm's
successor as French commander, marched his 7000 troops to Quebec.
James Murray, the British commander, had experienced a terrible winter,
one in which scurvy had reduced his garrison to about 4000. Lévis defeated
him at Ste-Foy, immediately west of the city (near the site of Université
Laval today). This battle proved bloodier than the Plains of Abraham,
with about 850 casualties on the French side and nearly 1100 on the
English side.

Victorious Lévis proceeded to besiege Quebec. Short of ammunition
and supplies, Lévis—and all of New France—prayed for French ships to
reach Quebec. But British seapower had dealt a fatal blow to the French
navy at Quiberon Bay off western France in November 1759. English ships
arrived first at Quebec in mid-May, and no French ships were sighted.

Lévis had to raise his siege. The rest of the year's operations were a forgone conclusion.

At Montreal that September, Lévis and 2000 troops confronted 17 000 British and American troops coming from three directions. After the French capitulated on September 8, 1760, the British took possession of Montreal. Canada passed into British hands.

Disarmed and obliged to swear an oath of allegiance to the British king, the *Canadiens* awaited the announcement of their ultimate fate. Many feared that Britain would deport them all, just as she had expelled the Acadians from their homeland. The future of the Amerindians also remained in question, despite the fact that Article 40 of the capitulation at Montreal in 1760 guaranteed them protection for the lands they occupied. Article 40 included this sentence: "The savages or Indian Allies of His Most Christian Majesty shall be maintained in the lands they inhabit; if they choose to reside there."

127

NOTE

[1]C.P. Stacey, *Quebec, 1759: The Siege and the Battle* (Toronto, 1959), 171.

Related Readings

Two articles in R. Douglas Francis and Donald B. Smith, *Readings in Canadian History: Pre-Confederation*, 3d ed. (Toronto, 1990), are useful for this topic: W.J. Eccles, "The Preemptive Conquest, 1749–1763," 175–98, and C.P. Stacey, "Generals and Generalship before Quebec, 1759–1760," 198–212.

BIBLIOGRAPHY

For an overview of French expansion into the interior of North America and New France's conflict with the English colonies, see the following works by W.J. Eccles: *The Canadian Frontier, 1534–1760* (Toronto, 1969); *France in America* (New York, 1972; rev. ed., 1990); *Essays on New France* (Toronto, 1987); and "The Fur Trade in the Colonial Northeast," in *History of Indian–White Relations*, edited by Wilcomb E. Washburn, vol. 4 of the *Handbook of North American Indians* (Washington, D.C., 1988), 324–34.

Four excellent volumes on the military events of the late seventeenth and eighteenth centuries are: I.K. Steele, *Guerillas and Grenadiers: The Struggle for Canada, 1689–1760* (Toronto, 1969); George F.G. Stanley, *New France: The Last Phase, 1744–1760* (Toronto, 1968); C.P. Stacey, *Quebec, 1759: The Siege and the Battle* (Toronto, 1959); and Guy Frégault, *Canada:*

The War of the Conquest, translated by Margaret M. Cameron (Toronto, 1969). The *Dictionary of Canadian Biography* (Toronto, 1966–) also contains important biographical sketches; of particular interest are C.P. Stacey's "James Wolfe" in vol. 3: 666–74; W.J. Eccles' "Louis-Joseph de Montcalm," in vol. 3: 458–69; and W.J. Eccles, "Pierre de Rigaud de Vaudreuil de Cavagnial," in vol. 4: 662–74. The best summaries of the two respective armies in the 1750s appear in vol. 3 of the *Dictionary of Canadian Biography*; see the essays by W.J. Eccles, "The French Forces in North America during the Seven Years' War:" xv–xxiii, and C.P. Stacey, "The British Forces in North America during the Seven Years' War:" xxiv–xxx.

Two overviews of the history of Louisbourg are J.S. McLennan's *Louisbourg from Its Foundation to its Fall, 1713–58* (London, 1918); and the short up-to-date booklet by Terry Crowley, *Louisbourg: Atlantic Fortress and Seaport.* Canadian Historical Association Historical Booklet No. 48 (Ottawa, 1990). For a review of the French forces, see also: Martin L. Nicolai, "A Different Kind of Courage: The French Military and the Canadian Irregular Soldier during the Seven Years' War," *Canadian Historical Review* 70 (1989): 53–75. A good introduction to Amerindian warfare is Leroy V. Eid's "The Neglected Side of American Indian War in the Northeast," *Military Review* 61, 2 (1981): 9–21. For a review of France's wars with the Fox Indians see Joseph L. Peyser, "The Fate of the Fox Survivors: A Dark Chapter in the History of the French in the Upper Country, 1726–1737," *Wisconsin Magazine of History* 73, 2 (Winter, 1989/ 1990): 83–110. Dated, but still useful, is J.E. Lunn, "Agriculture and War in Canada, 1740–1760," *Canadian Historical Review* 16 (1935): 125–36. An interesting study of the impact of the British invasion on the south shore of the St. Lawrence (east of Quebec, from Beaumont to Kamouraska) is Gaston Deschênes, *L'Année des Anglais: La Côte-du-sud à l'heure de la conquête* (Sillery, Québec, 1988). I.K. Steele reviews the crucial battle of Fort William Henry in 1757 in *Betrayals: Fort William Henry and the "Massacre"* (New York, 1990). Olive Dickason explains Louisbourg's alliances with Amerindians in "Louisbourg and the Indians: A Study in Imperial Race Relations," *History and Archaeology* 6 (1976): 1–206. Students will enjoy the five well-crafted biographies of ordinary Louisbourg citizens in Christopher Moore's *Louisbourg Portraits* (Toronto, 1982).

For an American perspective on the final struggle for the continent, see Samuel Eliot Morison's *Prehistory to 1789*, vol. 1 of his *Oxford History of the American People*, 3 vols. (New York, 1972).

Valuable maps depicting events of the Seven Years' War and the battles for Quebec, 1759–60, are contained in R. Cole Harris, ed., *Historical Atlas of Canada*, vol. 1, *From the Beginning to 1800* (Toronto, 1987).

Time Line: 1663–1764

1663	—Louis XIV makes New France a royal province under his direct control.
1665	—The Carignan-Salières regiment is dispatched from France to fight the Five Nations.
1667	—Truce between the French and the League of the Five Nations, or the Iroquois Confederacy, and the beginning of two decades of peace.
1670	—Founding of the Hudson's Bay Company.
1686	—The number of Acadians in present-day Nova Scotia grows to 800.
1687–1701	—Resumption of conflict between New France and the Five Nations.
1701	—Peace made by the Five Nations with the French at Montreal. The confederacy promises to remain neutral in all future conflicts between England and France.
1689–1697	—War between England and France
1702–1713	
1710	—The English capture Port-Royal and rename it Annapolis Royal.
1713	—Signing of the Treaty of Utrecht; New France gives up its claims to Hudson Bay, Newfoundland, and Acadia.
	—Under the Treaty of Utrecht, France cedes "Acadia" to England.
	—By the Treaty of Utrecht, Britain gains control of all of Newfoundland, except for the French Shore, representing about one-third of the island's western coastline.
1713–1744	—Thirty years of peace.
1719	—France begins the construction of its fortress of Louisbourg on Île Royale (Cape Breton Island).
1729	—The Commander of the annual naval convoy to Newfoundland is made the island's governor in the summer months.
1744–1748	—French and English again at war.
1749	—The British found Halifax.

1755	—The expulsion of the Acadians to the Thirteen Colonies and to England. Over a seven-year period, about 10 000 of the 13 000 are deported.
1756–1763	—Seven Years' War
1758	—Deportation of the Acadians from Île Saint-Jean (Prince Edward Island). —Nova Scotia's first legislative assembly meets in Halifax. —Louisbourg falls to the British.
1759	—Wolfe's victory on the Plains of Abraham, leading to the fall of Quebec.
1760	—The British conquer New France, and establish a military government until the signing of the peace treaty ending the war in 1763.
1763	—By the Treaty of Paris, New France becomes a British colony. —Chief Pontiac and the Great Lakes Indians wage an unsuccessful war of resistance against British rule. —The Royal Proclamation of 1763 recognizes the land rights of the Amerindians around the Great Lakes and creates the Province of Quebec in the St. Lawrence Valley. —The Treaty of Paris transfers Labrador from France to Britain. Apart from the years 1774–1809, when it was administered by the Province of Quebec and Lower Canada, Labrador has been in Newfoundland's jurisdiction.
1764–65	—First group of Acadians reaches Louisiana. Another large group arrives from France in 1785.
1764–1800	—Permission is granted in 1764 for the Acadians to resettle in Nova Scotia—about 3000 do. By 1800 the Acadian population in present-day Nova Scotia numbers 8000.

The Acadians

The French first used the name Acadia to distinguish the eastern or maritime part of New France from the valley of the St. Lawrence, or the western portion, which they called Canada. Under French rule Canada and Acadia remained separate colonies. Just where Acadia ended and Canada began was never clearly defined, but certainly Acadia included present-day New Brunswick, Nova Scotia, and Prince Edward Island. It was on the frontier between English- and French-dominated areas.

Since France's interests lay largely in Canada, with its fur trade and its agricultural settlement, Acadia was largely neglected. There was little contact between the two colonies, even before Acadia was granted to England by the Treaty of Utrecht in 1713. Gradually, cultural differences emerged between the Acadians and the French Canadians despite their common French origins and shared Roman Catholic faith. By the mid-eighteenth century the Acadians had become a people distinct from both the French Canadians and the French. Nonetheless, the English regarded them, along with the French, as a threat to British Nova Scotia, and in 1755 they deported them from their homeland.

Beginnings of French Acadia

The roots of French Acadia go back to 1604, when the French wintered on an island in the St. Croix River, on the present-day boundary between Maine and New Brunswick. They wintered again in 1605 and 1606 at Port-Royal in present-day Nova Scotia. With Champlain's founding of Quebec in 1608, however, France's colonization efforts became focussed on Canada, although French interest in Acadia never waned entirely.

Jean de Biencourt, Sieur de Poutrincourt, a French nobleman, came out with the first expedition of 1604 and left in 1607. In 1611 Poutrincourt brought back his family, several settlers, and two Jesuit priests, but his settlement failed after the pirate Samuel Argall struck from his base at Jamestown, Virginia, and destroyed Port-Royal. Argall's attack ruined Poutrincourt's French investors, and *Acadie*, as a European settlement, almost completely vanished until the 1630s.

With the arrival of Gov. Isaac de Razilly in 1632, France began its first serious attempt to colonize Acadia. Many of the settlers came from the west coast of France, near the Atlantic port of La Rochelle. Labourers skilled in harvesting salt from the salt marshes joined the contingent of several hundred colonists. In Acadia, rather than clear the forested upland areas, they used their skills to build dikes to reclaim the fertile land that the Bay of Fundy's strong tides flooded twice a day.

Razilly's death in 1636 proved catastrophic for the colony. Years of strife and confusion followed as three men vied for control of Acadia. In 1640 Charles de Menou d'Aulnay, Nicolas Denys, and Charles de Saint-Étienne de La Tour governed their own territories and claimed exclusive trading rights. A small civil war broke out among rival trading interests, and ended only in the mid-1640s.

In 1654 the struggle between France and England again touched Acadia, which lay as a wedge between the two expanding empires. The English conquered Acadia that year and held it until 1670. They saw it chiefly as a strategically located fishing zone and fur-trading area.

Acadian Society in the Late Seventeenth Century

During the British occupation of 1654–70, the Acadians initially espoused a spirit of accommodation rather than confrontation with their English rulers. Some Acadians learned to speak English. The generation of Acadian children born during the occupation had little knowledge of France.

At Port-Royal the average Acadian couple usually married in their early twenties, and had ten or eleven children, most of whom survived to adulthood. The population doubled every twenty years, a faster rate than in New France. By 1670 the colony had a population of about 400–500. The absence of war, famine, or epidemics (such as typhoid, smallpox, and cholera) accounts for the rapid population increase.

Although Port-Royal was Acadia's largest settlement, there were other small outlying communities on the Bay of Fundy and along the eastern coastline of present-day Nova Scotia. Acadian settlements were established in the 1670s and 1680s at Beaubassin (Amherst), Grand Pré (Wolfville), and Cobequid (Truro). With the addition of about forty families brought out after 1671, the population grew to more than eight hundred by 1686.

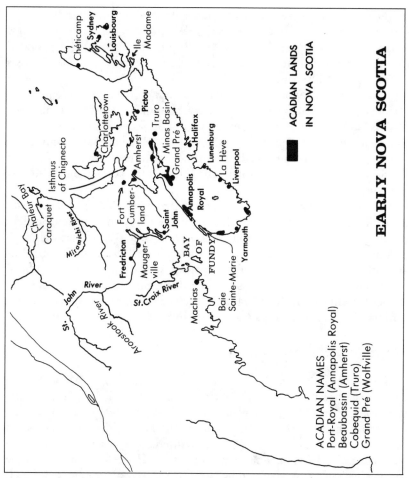

EARLY NOVA SCOTIA

ACADIAN LANDS
IN NOVA SCOTIA

ACADIAN NAMES
Port-Royal (Annapolis Royal)
Beaubassin (Amherst)
Cobequid (Truro)
Grand Pré (Wolfville)

133

Source: Adapted from P.G. Cornell, J. Hamelin, F. Ouellet, and M. Trudel, *Canada: Unity in Diversity* *(Toronto, 1967):* 121.

Major Acadian settlements in the early eighteenth century.

The Acadians developed a unique identity, with strong family kinship patterns. The settlers came from different areas of France, but once settled here they intermarried and developed a family network that crisscrossed the colony. Blood ties, common beliefs, and a system of mutual aid and solidarity thus united these first Europeans in Acadia. They developed their own speech patterns in an amalgam of various dialects—mostly French, a few English, and one or two Indian, merged and adapted into a single new language that reflected the Acadians' distinctive way of life and their need for a special vocabulary to describe it.

By the end of the seventeenth century, the Acadians had established themselves in the region's fertile and easily worked marshlands. Judging by the names they gave their settlements along the Bay of Fundy and the Chignecto Isthmus, which connects present-day Nova Scotia and New Brunswick, they were contented—Beaubassin ("beautiful pond"), Cocagne ("land of plenty"), and a settlement near Port-Royal called Paradis Terrestre ("earthly paradise," or "Garden of Eden").

In Acadian society the family and the church, rather than the seigneurial system that dominated Canadian society, became the most powerful institutions. The Crown granted seigneuries at Port-Royal, at Beaubassin (the first major village settled after Port-Royal), and along the Saint John River, but the seigneurs had practically no influence on the settlers' daily life. In the St. Lawrence Valley the intendant enforced the system, but in Acadia there was no such official.

The church was a much more important influence in Acadia than it was in the St. Lawrence Valley. No single religious order dominated Acadian development; the Jesuits, Capuchins, Récollets, and Sulpicians all took part in religious and educational work among the Acadians. The inhabitants often sought the advice of their priests, who came to act as unofficial judges in the disputes that arose among them. But the clergy did not rule the settlements. As in New France in the late seventeenth and eighteenth century, the Acadian clergy's authority over the populace was limited.

134

RELATIONS WITH THE INDIANS

The Acadians maintained good relations with the resident Micmac Indians, in part because they used the tidal flats, lands of little interest to the Indians. Unlike the New England settlers, who antagonized the Indians by seizing their lands and clearing away the forests, the Acadians posed no threat. As a result of this peaceful interaction, a few Acadian men married Indian women. The community at La Hève, for example, on the southeastern coast of what is now Nova Scotia, was a *métis* (mixed-blood) settlement. Until after the deportation of 1755, most settlements had at least one family in which one of the partners, usually the woman, was a Micmac or Malecite (from present-day western New Brunswick).

ACADIA AND NEW ENGLAND

The Acadians traded to the south with New England, rather than to the west with Canada or to the east with France. In many respects the colony on the Bay of Fundy became an economic satellite of New England more than of France. Acadian governors proved powerless to prevent the entry of American merchants and fishermen to the area. British merchants had such a flourishing business, in fact, that they built warehouses at Port-Royal. There they bought furs and surplus grain (wheat and oats) from the Acadians in return for products such as sugar, molasses, and rum from the West Indies and manufactured goods—knives, needles, dishes, and cloth—from Europe. The Acadians also travelled to Boston to sell their wheat and furs, and brought back cloth, tobacco, and pipes. In the late 1680s even the governor of Acadia bought stockings and shoes in Boston for the French garrison at Port-Royal.

Acadia Becomes Nova Scotia

New England wanted political as well as economic control over Acadia. When war broke out in Europe in 1689, the New Englanders got their opportunity. An invasion force of seven hundred New Englanders led by William Phips attacked Port-Royal in 1690. They easily overpowered the governor of Acadia and his garrison of one hundred troops and devastated Acadia's capital. The New Englanders held on to Acadia for seven years, until the signing of the Treaty of Ryswick in 1697, when France regained the colony (see Chapter 6).

135

With the outbreak of war in Europe in 1702, Acadia again became easy prey for seafaring raiders from New England. Despite the repeated attacks and looting, the Acadians, with little help from France, held their ground against the English until 1710. That year, determined to conquer Acadia, Britain supplied New England with money, arms, munitions, and naval aid; the American colonies provided additional men and supplies.

An expedition of thirty-four hundred men and thirty-six ships arrived at Port-Royal in September 1710. In face of this invasion force, the French governor held only a ramshackle fort with fewer than three hundred men. The French resisted for three weeks, then accepted the inevitable and surrendered in mid-October. The Treaty of Utrecht in 1713 put to rest the question of the ownership of the peninsula. Acadia became Nova Scotia, and the English changed the name of Port-Royal to Annapolis Royal. But Louis XIV did obtain certain guarantees for the Acadians. One clause of the treaty stipulated that they had the right to leave Nova Scotia and settle elsewhere. Originally, they had one year in which to make up their minds, but this was later changed to allow slightly more time.

Then, a rivalry for the allegiance of the Acadians began. France retained one territory in the Gulf of St. Lawrence—Île Royale (Cape Breton Island). Anxious to establish a strong colony there, the French tried to attract the Acadians. The Acadian community did send representatives to inspect the lands on Cape Breton, but the delegates reported negatively on the rocky soil. Few Acadians liked the idea of having to leave their rich lands and comfortable houses to pioneer once again. The English tried to prevent Acadians from leaving by forbidding them to construct boats or to sell their property and cattle. From the English vantage point, French immigration to Cape Breton would only reinforce the French presence and weaken Nova Scotia, which would lose successful farmers and their livestock. There was also the danger that the Acadians might destroy their homesteads and the restraining dikes as they left.

THE NEUTRAL ACADIANS

The English administrators of Annapolis Royal faced a major problem: how should a minority govern a majority? They insisted that the Acadians become British subjects by swearing an oath of allegiance. The practice of asking the inhabitants of a country to make an oath of loyalty was customary both when a new monarch succeeded to the throne and after a war. On five separate occasions the governors of Nova Scotia would try to force the Acadians to swear an oath, and each time the Acadians would insist on remaining neutral. As a border people between two rival empires, the Acadians wanted to proceed cautiously.

Finally, in 1717, the Acadians worked out the terms on which they would remain under British government: their adherence to Catholicism was to be respected, as was their neutrality in any future war against France. British officials were to recognize that they lived in Indian territory and that they would suffer Indian attacks if they aligned themselves militarily against the French, the Indians' allies. In 1730 the British finally agreed, insisting only that the Acadians take this mild oath:

> I sincerely promise and swear on my faith as a Christian that I will be utterly loyal, and will truly obey His Majesty King George the second, whom I recognize as the sovereign lord of Acadia or Nova Scotia. May God so help me.

The Acadians took the oath and thereafter most English people spoke of them as "the neutral French," the term the Acadians applied to themselves. For their policy of neutrality, they earned the wrath of both the French and the English. As historian Naomi Griffiths notes, "In 1748, the Acadians considered themselves Acadian, the French considered them unreliable allies, and the English, unsatisfactory citizens."[1]

THE ACADIANS' GOLDEN AGE: 1714–1744

For the next thirty years the Acadians prospered. Their high birth rate and their longevity led to a phenomenal population increase. In Port-Royal, 75 percent of the population reached the age of twenty-one, at a time when only 50 percent reached that age in France. In 1711 there were approximately 2500 Acadians; in 1750, more than 10 000; and in 1755, more than 13 000 (Louisbourg excluded). The Acadian population spread into settlements along the present-day New Brunswick shoreline, as well as the Île Saint-Jean (Prince Edward Island) and even into areas of present-day Nova Scotia that had been surveyed and reserved for future English immigration. Charles Morris, the surveyor general of Nova Scotia, visited

Beaubassin at the mouth of the Bay of Fundy in 1748 and left a vivid description of the Acadians' country: "a Number of Villages built on gentle rising Hills interspers'd with Gardens and Woods the Villages divided from each other with long intervalls of marshes and they at great distance bounded by Hills covered with Trees the Natural growth of the Country. Here may be seen rivers turning and winding among the Marshes then Cloath'd with all the variety of Grain."

The Acadians continued their traditional lifestyle: farming, fishing, hunting, and trading. They relied on their local priests or on the village patriarchs, to solve problems of land boundaries, cattle theft, and other legal matters. The text of the Treaty of Utrecht guaranteed them the free exercise of Catholicism, "insofar as the laws of Great Britain allowed." Although this guarantee was a contradiction in terms because English laws made very difficult the practice of Roman Catholicism in Britain, the British authorities in Nova Scotia allowed a broad interpretation of the clause and permitted the Acadians religious freedom.

137

The Roman Catholic church was allowed to minister to both the French and the Micmac populations. The missionaries gained great influence among the Micmacs, who numbered about one thousand in the early 1740s in peninsular Nova Scotia and probably another thousand on Île Saint-Jean, Cape Breton, and the mainland side of the Bay of Fundy. By the first half of the eighteenth century the Roman Catholic religion had become an integral part of the Micmac identity. Abbé Pierre Maillard developed a Micmac alphabet, allowing the Micmacs to learn selected prayers and chants and the catechisms.

The Society of Nova Scotia

In 1744 war broke out between England and France once again. The conflict lasted four years, and during it, the English captured Fort Louisbourg. But the peace treaty of 1748 restored the status quo. Louisbourg was given back to France, an act that angered the New Englanders who, at great expense and loss of life, had captured it.

England consequently felt obliged to fortify Nova Scotia, to make it a proper counterbalance to Louisbourg and a strong outpost of English power. The English had earlier committed themselves to making Nova Scotia an effective part of their North American empire. They now sought to make the Acadians into completely trustworthy subjects, to populate Nova Scotia with Protestant settlers, and to replace Annapolis Royal with a new military and administrative centre.

The new governor, Edward Cornwallis, then thirty-six years old (he was the uncle of the Lord Cornwallis who would surrender to the Americans at Yorktown in 1781), transported two thousand colonists to the port the

Micmacs knew as "Che-book-took" (at the biggest harbour), a name the English rendered as "Chebucto." Cornwallis renamed it Halifax, after the Earl of Halifax, the president of the English Board of Trade and Plantations, a committee of Crown appointees in London who handled the administration of Britain's North American colonies until 1768.

In 1750–51 the British also brought in approximately fifteen hundred "foreign Protestants," largely Germans, whom they settled at Lunenburg on the south shore of the peninsula, within easy reach of Halifax. British authorities transferred the seat of government from Annapolis Royal to Halifax. Cornwallis also introduced British institutions and laws, and he fortified the new settlement to equal the strength of Louisbourg. These measures, together with the construction of roads to the Acadian settlements and the introduction of a large English garrison, completely changed the balance of power in the colony.

138 Simultaneously, the French strengthened their position in what is now New Brunswick. While the English were constructing Halifax and bringing Protestant immigrants into Nova Scotia, the French increased their garrison at the mouth of the Saint John River and occupied the Chignecto Isthmus, building Fort Beauséjour (near present-day Sackville, New Brunswick) in 1750. Beauséjour protected their overland communications from Canada to Louisbourg.

THE MICMACS AND THE ENGLISH

The French had maintained their alliance with the Micmac Indians in the hope of using them against the English. The Micmacs needed little encouragement, since they were resentful of English encroachments on their hunting grounds. In addition, unlike the French, the British had refused to give them annual gifts in return for the use of Micmac land. The English seldom took the Micmacs into account where the question of land ownership was involved. As far as they were concerned, France had ceded its title to the land with the Treaty of Utrecht in 1713, and after that, it belonged to Britain.

Years of Micmac raids and harassment had followed the Treaty of Utrecht, with many of the attacks against the British taking place at sea. (The Micmacs had purchased European longboats after their first contact with French fishermen.) They captured dozens of English trading and fishing boats in the course of these attacks. With the outbreak of war between England and France in 1744, the Indian raids against the British in Nova Scotia reached a new level of intensity. Cornwallis responded by proposing drastic measures. One plan was to recruit fifty rangers locally and bring in another hundred from Boston, and to send them throughout the entire province to kill Micmacs. On October 2, 1749, the English governor issued his proclamation commanding all "to Annoy, distress, take or destroy the Savages commonly called Mic-macks, wherever they are found." In wartime the French paid the Indians for English scalps, just as the English paid for Indian scalps. Cornwallis again promised payment and added that any person found helping the Indians would this time be treated as one himself.

Cornwallis's drastic measures, however, never went into effect. London advised a milder policy, adding that experience in other parts of North America had indicated that "gentler Methods and Offers of Peace have more frequently prevailed with Indians than the Sword, if at the same Time, that the Sword is held over their Heads."

BRITAIN'S GROWING ANXIETY ABOUT THE ACADIANS

As frontier incidents and Micmac raids increased, Cornwallis became ever more doubtful of the Acadians' loyalty to Britain in the event of another war. In 1749 the governor commanded them to swear an oath of unconditional allegiance to Britain. He warned all those who refused that they would be deported. But when the Acadian delegates replied negatively to Cornwallis's ultimatum, he did not expel them, preferring to wait until British power became stronger in Nova Scotia.

The Acadians entered a period of much greater strain in the early 1750s. Between 1500 and 2000 Acadians left peninsular Nova Scotia by choice or by coercion (many were forced by French raiding parties to move to French territory north of the isthmus). Everyone was certain that war between France and Britain would soon break out once again. Yet four-fifths of the Acadians who remained in the colony believed that the governor, by his refusal to remove them, had, like other English governors before him, accepted their "neutral" status.

When Charles Lawrence became lieutenant governor of Nova Scotia in 1753 the Acadians expected the situation to remain the same. This time, however, they were wrong. First and foremost, Colonel Lawrence was a soldier. Like most soldiers, he knew only allies and enemies, not "neutrals." To him, the Acadians posed a definite threat in the event of another full-scale war. But in the early months of 1754, Lawrence did not consider expulsion to be justified. He believed that if the British confronted the Acadians firmly they would yield and agree to take the oath of total unconditional loyalty.

Expulsion of the Acadians

The outbreak of war in North America in 1754 and Gen. Edward Braddock's campaign in 1755 completely altered the military situation as well as Lawrence's view of the Acadians. In June 1755, Col. Robert Monckton, with a force composed largely of New England troops, captured Beauséjour and the rest of the French garrisons on the Chignecto Isthmus. Sufficiently impressed by the English victories, the Indians stopped their attacks. This allowed Lawrence to turn his attention to the Acadian question.

In July, Lawrence ordered representatives of the Acadians to appear before the Halifax Council, which advised the governor. Lawrence probably believed that the Acadians would capitulate quickly and agree to the oath. The council (which was dominated by military officers) made it quite clear that it would insist on an unqualified oath that the Acadians would support Britain in the event of war. (The council may have had ulterior motives in setting such strict terms: some of the twelve council members were perhaps eyeing the Acadians' rich lands along the Bay of Fundy; there were profits to be made in the evacuations, as well as in the resettlement of New Englanders in Nova Scotia.) On July 23, two days before the first Acadian delegates from the villages arrived, the news of General Braddock's catastrophic defeat near Fort Duquesne in the Ohio country reached Halifax. Casualties approached 40 percent, and the British commander himself had been killed. Nova Scotia's need for the Acadians to make a declaration of unequivocal allegiance to Britain, to recognize themselves as unconditional subjects of the British Crown, became all the more urgent.

The Acadian delegates presented their case before the council members, arguing that they had always been loyal to George II and would present to the English all their firearms as proof of their loyalty. They were prepared to abide by the oath they had sworn earlier, but not to take a new one. They asked to be considered as a neutral people, pointing out that between 1713 and 1755 they had never fought for France. Throughout the discussion, none of the delegates foresaw the catastrophe impending if they refused to swear the required oath. They underestimated the determination of Lawrence's council.

The final confrontation came on Monday, July 28. After hearing the delegates one last time, the council reached a decision. It endorsed the deportation of all Acadians under British jurisdiction who had refused to take the unqualified oath. Now, in the general hysteria after Braddock's defeat, the British were prepared to remove them. The Acadians' fate passed into the hands of two thousand hostile, anti-Catholic New England recruits working under the instructions of Lt. Gov. Charles Lawrence.

THE DEPORTATION BEGINS

The deportation began immediately after the council's decision. Lawrence attempted initially to prepare carefully for the evacuation, providing adequate cabin space on the ships and ample provisions for the duration of the journey. But, in the end, the evacuation was brutal and poorly planned. The English first herded the Acadians together at Annapolis Royal, Grand Pré, Beaubassin, and other settlements. As sending them to Cape Breton

The Expulsion of the Acadians: Was It Necessary?

Canadian historians have long disagreed about the necessity of the British expulsion of the Acadians in 1755. The controversy owes as much to the complexity of the question and the contradictions in the evidence as to differing perspectives. As historian Naomi E.S. Griffiths put it in her edited volume *The Acadian Deportation: Deliberate Perfidy or Cruel Necessity* (Toronto, 1969), "Acadian history 1710–1755 provides endless questions of fact and interpretation, problems about what actually happened and whether it was brought about intentionally or not.... As the years lead on to 1755, the problems which divide historians multiply, and the events of the expulsion itself have been so diversely treated that one sometimes wonders whether the authors are writing about the same events" (p.3). Some condemn the English, others believe that the Acadians themselves were to blame for their misfortunes. A third group contends that interference from Quebec and Louisbourg resulted in the tragedy.

The argument that the deportation was necessary was still being made in the 1950s. As late as 1956, popular historian Joseph Lister Rutledge summarized this position in his *Century of Conflict* (Toronto, 1956), a volume in the popular *Canadian History Series*, edited by Thomas B. Costain. "If ever a conquered people were treated with consideration by their captors, it was the Acadians.... The net result was generous and understanding treatment for people who represented a very stubborn breed indeed. This conquered people retained their land and freedom and the assurance of the exercise of their religion. The loyalty oath required

of them was generous to a fault" (p. 409).

Several English-language writers have argued that the expulsion should be seen solely as a military operation necessary for Nova Scotia's defence. Archibald McKellar MacMechan, professor of English at Dalhousie University, for instance, wrote as follows in 1913: "Before passing judgement on the men who conceived and executed this removal of an entire population, it should be remembered that they acted as did Louis XIV in expelling the Huguenots from France and the United States in expelling the tories. All were precautionary measures dictated by the need of national self-preservation; and they were regarded by those who took them as imperative in a dangerous crisis. Lawrence acted like the commander of a fort expecting a siege, who levels trees and houses outside the walls in order to afford the enemy no shelter and to give the garrison a clear field of fire" (*Canada and Its Provinces*, vol. 13, edited by A. Shortt and A.G. Doughty [Toronto, 1913], 98).

Most French-language historians have rejected the arguments advanced in defence of the expulsion. In the 1920s, French historian Émile Lauvrière wrote of Governor Lawrence's actions that "Only a criminal soul could devise such a plot in all its details" (quoted in N.E.S. Griffiths, "The Acadians," in *Dictionary of Canadian Biography*, vol. 4, *1771–1800* [Toronto, 1979], xxvi). French Canadian writer and Roman Catholic priest Henri Beaudé considered the deportation order entirely undeserved and "conceived in hate, a prejudice of race and religion" (*La déportation des Acadiens* [Montréal,

1918], 21–26; translated by and quoted in Griffiths, ed., *The Acadian Deportation*, 156).

In recent years, Naomi Griffiths has revealed the complexity of the decision to expel an entire people from their homes. She concludes her discussion of the expulsion in her sketch, "The Acadians," in the *Dictionary of Canadian Biography*, vol. 4, 1771–1800 (Toronto, 1979), "For the Acadians, however, whatever the motive the result was the same: the destruction of their society, the elimination of their communities, their exile to foreign lands" (p. xxvi).

or Canada would only serve to build up the French militia in the two French colonies, the English decided to disperse most of them among the Thirteen Colonies and to send some to England. Lawrence's troops, including those commanded by Col. Robert Monckton, the victor at Beauséjour, burned houses and barns to deprive those who escaped of shelter.[2] Within hours, the work of more than a century of toil was turned to ashes.

THE DESTRUCTION OF ACADIAN SOCIETY

The expulsion destroyed Acadian society. It broke up communities and dispersed closely knit families. Some fought back—for the most part, ineffectively. Abbé François Le Guerne, who remained in what is now southern New Brunswick until August 1757, reported that women and children took to the woods to escape deportation and to flee the English soldiers who had burned their property. Some eighty-six Acadians escaped by digging a tunnel from their barracks in their prison camp near Fort Beauséjour. On board a ship bound for the American colonies, an Acadian group seized their captors, sailed back to the Bay of Fundy, then fled overland to the upper reaches of the Saint John River. An estimated two thousand Acadians fled to Île Saint-Jean (Prince Edward Island). The refugees outnumbered the original Acadian residents on the island three to one.

Many died in the deportation. Storms at sea, a shortage of food and drinking water, and poor sanitary conditions meant that many ships lost more than one-third of their Acadian passengers. The *Cornwallis*, which left Chignecto with 417 Acadians on board, docked at Charleston, South Carolina, with only 210 still alive. The expulsions continued for seven years, until 1762.

The British military occasionally sent ships from the same village to different destination points. Inevitably, family members were separated. Massachusetts, New York, Pennsylvania, Maryland, Virginia, the Carolinas, and Georgia all received Acadians. For the most part, the Americans provided support and tried to settle the exiles in various small towns and villages, but these efforts were largely unsuccessful. Despite all prohibi-

142

tions to the contrary, the Acadians, footsore and half-clad, wandered from town to town, looking for family and friends. They remained outsiders in the communities where they were settled. Their mortality rate in the American colonies was high. An estimated one-third of those deported died from diseases that had been practically unknown to them before 1755—smallpox, typhoid, and yellow fever.

It is extremely difficult to estimate the number of Acadians expelled between 1755 and 1763. It is commonly accepted, however, that the British deported nearly three-quarters of the Acadian population of roughly 13 000. Approximately 7000 were sent away in the first year, 1755. By the time the policy was officially ended in 1762, another 2000–3000 had been deported.

The Acadians from peninsular Nova Scotia were split into small groups. Many who escaped to Île Royale (Cape Breton) and Île Saint-Jean (Prince Edward Island) were rounded up after the British took these two islands in 1758. (Of the two thousand captives taken on Île Saint-Jean in 1758, *143* seven hundred drowned when three of the transport vessels were lost at sea.) About fifteen hundred Acadians also fled to New France to establish homes near Quebec, Trois-Rivières, and Montreal. Others successfully made their way to Saint-Pierre and Miquelon, the two small islands off the coast of Newfoundland that France was able to retain under the peace treaty of 1763.

THE ACADIANS IN FRANCE AND LOUISIANA

One thousand Acadians had been sent to Virginia in 1756 and then immediately dispatched to England. (The Virginians argued that the Acadians were British subjects and that they were therefore entitled to England's support.) About one-quarter of them died from an epidemic of smallpox during their first summer in England. The remainder spent seven years in internment camps in England until France took them in 1763.

Many of the Acadians who settled in France in 1763 had difficulty adjusting to French society, which suggests that, although they spoke French and practised Roman Catholicism, they were a people distinct from the French. Acadians were not accustomed to the limitations that restricted ordinary French people in the eighteenth century: the *corvée* (enforced days of unpaid labour) and restrictions on travel within the country. The way of life in France was alien to them, and harsh. As one French lawyer noted, the Acadians were used to a bountiful country where the land was easily cultivated. At home they had eaten bread, butter, and meat and drunk milk; in France they looked down on fish, vegetables, and cider.

Not finding comfortable homes in France, seven shiploads of Acadians—nearly sixteen hundred people—sailed for New Orleans, Louisi-

Painting by Lewis Parker. Courtesy of Environment Canada—Parks Service, Atlantic Region.

The Expulsion of the Acadians from Île Saint-Jean, 1758. A re-creation by Lewis Parker of the arrival of ten British warships sent to evacuate the Acadian population of Île Saint-Jean (present-day Prince Edward Island). Lewis Parker (b. 1926) is one of Canada's foremost painters of historical scenes.

ana, in 1785, where they joined other Acadians who had settled there earlier. Some three hundred had arrived in 1764–65. Of those, some had initially sought refuge at Saint-Domingue (present-day Haiti), the French sugar island, but had eventually crossed over to New Orleans. In addition, about seven hundred Acadians from Maryland and Pennsylvania had arrived in Louisiana by ship between 1766 and 1770.

Although it was at that time a Spanish possession, Louisiana's main language was French, and the colony was officially Catholic. Like the Bay of Fundy area, Louisiana had large marshes that needed draining—work at which the Acadians had prior experience. Today, Louisiana has more than a million descendants of the Acadians. As the Acadian settlements spread across the Louisiana bayous and prairies, their neighbours shortened the French name "Acadien" to "Cadien" and, eventually, to "Cajun."

THE RETURN OF SOME ACADIANS

Permission was granted in 1764 for the Acadians to resettle in Nova Scotia, and a steady stream of wanderers returned—in all, an estimated three thousand. But since the Halifax authorities had set aside the Acadians' farms for New Englanders, they could not settle on their old lands.

By 1800 the Acadians in Nova Scotia numbered 4000 and in the new colonies of New Brunswick and Prince Edward Island, 3800 and 700 respectively—a result of high birth rates rather than the return of more exiles. They were concentrated around Baie Sainte-Marie in southwestern Nova Scotia and Chéticamp on Cape Breton Island (see the map on page 133). They also settled around Malpèque on Île Saint-Jean (which the English initially called St. John's Island, and later Prince Edward Island). Since the best vacant lands were in present-day New Brunswick, especially along its east coast, the majority of returned Acadians went there. Finding themselves in many of these locations on infertile land, most of the Acadians became fishermen rather than farmers. Subsequently they made a living from these lands, but it was at a much lower standard than what they had known on their well-developed farms before 1755.

Buffeted about for a generation, from 1755 to the late 1780s, the Acadians finally established a new Acadia, but one that was much less cohesive than the original one. They tried to rebuild their shattered communities, but many family units had been broken up. In the new Acadia the Roman Catholic clergy represented the only remaining French institution. *145*

It became customary in Acadian villages for the older people to tell of their experiences in the deportation. Indeed, the expulsion became the unifying event of Acadian experience. The tradition remained an oral one until American poet Henry Wadsworth Longfellow, who first heard the story in the early 1840s, recorded it in his poem *Evangeline*, which was subsequently published in several French translations. The story centres on Evangeline Bellefontaine, a seventeen-year-old *Acadienne* who is separated in the deportation from her lover Gabriel Lajeunesse. When, after a lifelong search, she finds him again, he is a broken old man. As she holds him in her arms, he dies. *Evangeline* confirmed for Acadians that they were a unique people with an identity of their own.

In 1979 Antonine Maillet, Acadia's great novelist, wrote a more convincing tale, *Pélagie-la-Charrette*. This is the story of an unconquerable woman, Pélagie, who, after the expulsion, spent a decade travelling in a cart drawn by a cow. With others she met along the way, she journeyed from Georgia back to Acadia. "When they built their carts," Maillet wrote, "they were just families. By the time they returned to Acadia they were a people."

It is tragic that the first European group to establish itself successfully in the present-day Maritime provinces received such treatment. But the Acadians lived in an area contested by two great European powers. Geography not only isolated them from their natural allies—the Canadians in the valley of the St. Lawrence—but also linked them closely with New England. The Acadians tried to maintain a balance between the two competing powers by keeping a strict neutrality. They succeeded for more than a century, until wartime hysteria won out and the British felt it necessary to expel the "neutral French."

NOTES

[1] Naomi Griffiths, *The Acadians: Creation of a People* (Toronto, 1973), 37.
[2] Ironically, the largest Acadian community today is in Moncton, New Brunswick—a city named in honour of Robert Monckton, who became lieutenant governor of Nova Scotia in December 1755.

Related Readings

Naomi Griffiths' article "The Golden Age: Acadian Life, 1713–1748," reprinted in R. Douglas Francis and Donald B. Smith, *Readings in Canadian History: Pre-Confederation*, 3d ed. (Toronto, 1990), 158–72, is a valuable introduction to the topic.

146

BIBLIOGRAPHY

Two good summaries of Acadian history are John Bartlet Brebner's *New England's Outpost: Acadia Before the Conquest of Canada* (Hamden, Conn., 1965; first published 1927), and Naomi Griffiths, *The Acadians: Creation of a People* (Toronto, 1973). For the early period, consult John G. Reid, *Acadia, Maine, and New Scotland: Marginal Colonies in the Seventeenth Century* (Toronto, 1981). Andrew H. Clark provides a historical geographer's view in *Acadia: The Geography of Early Nova Scotia to 1760* (Madison, Wis., 1968). See also Naomi Griffiths' "The Acadians," *Dictionary of Canadian Biography*, vol. 4, *1771–1800* (Toronto, 1979), xvii–xxxi. Jean Daigle's account, "Acadia, 1604–1763: An Historical Synthesis" in *The Acadians of the Maritimes*, edited by Jean Daigle (Moncton, 1982), 17–46, is very useful. There are two valuable studies of the Acadians on Île Saint-John (Prince Edward Island): D.C. Harvey's *The French Régime in Prince Edward Island* (New Haven, Co., 1926), and Georges Arsenault's *The Island Acadians, 1720–1980* (Charlottetown, 1989). *The Acadian Exiles* by Arthur G. Doughty (Toronto, 1964; first published 1915) is still worth reading. Guy Frégault's "The Deportation of the Acadians, 1755–62," chapter 6 in *Canada: The War of the Conquest*, translated by Margaret M. Cameron (Toronto, 1969), 164–200, provides a French Canadian historian's interpretation of events in Acadia in the 1750s. Various opinions on the issue of the expulsion appear in Naomi E.S. Griffiths, ed., *The Acadian Deportation: Deliberate Perfidy or Cruel Necessity?* (Toronto, 1969)

Several interesting articles on the Acadians are included in Phillip A. Buckner and David Frank, eds. and comps., *Atlantic Canada Before Confederation*, vol. 1, *The Acadiensis Reader* (Fredericton, 1985): Gisa Hynes, "Some Aspects of the Demography of Port-Royal, 1650–1755," 11–25; Naomi Griffiths, "Acadians in Exile: The Experiences of the Acadians in the British Seaports," 26–43; and Graeme Wynn, "Late Eighteenth-Century Agriculture on the Bay of Fundy Marshlands," 44–53. Robert G. Leblanc provides a short review of the expulsion in "The Acadian Migrations," *Canadian Geographical Journal* 81 (July 1970): 10–19. For the Acadians' arrival in Louisiana, see Carl A. Brasseaux, "A New Acadia: The Acadian Migrations to South Louisiana, 1764–1803," *Acadiensis* 15 (1985): 123–32. Griffin Smith, Jr., provides a modern view of the community in "The Cajuns: Still Loving Life," *National Geographic* 178, 4 (October 1990): 40–65. The history of the Micmacs in Acadia under French and British rule is recounted in Olive Patricia Dickason, "Louisbourg and the Indians: A Study in Imperial Race Relations," *History and Archaeology* 6 (1976): 1–206, and L.F.S. Upton, *Micmacs and Colonists: Indian–White Relations in the Maritimes*, 1713–1867 (Vancouver, 1979). The story of the founding of Halifax is told in Thomas H. Raddall's entertaining *Halifax: Warden of the North*, rev. ed. (Toronto, 1971).

Two overviews of the Acadians' history since the expulsion are the essays by George F.G. Stanley, "The Flowering of the Acadian Renaissance," in *Eastern and Western Perspectives*, edited by David Jay Bercuson and Phillip A. Buckner (Toronto, 1981), 18–46; and Léon Thériault, "Acadia, 1763–1978: An Historical Synthesis," in *The Acadians of the Maritimes*, edited by Jean Daigle (Moncton, 1982), 47–86. For a discussion of the Acadians' return from exile, consult Mason Wade, "After the *Grand Dérangement*: The Acadians' Return to the Gulf of St. Lawrence and to Nova Scotia," *American Review of Canadian Studies* 5 (1975): 42–65. Thomas R. Berger provides a lively review of the Acadians' past and present in "The Acadians: Expulsion and Return," in his *Fragile Freedoms: Human Rights and Dissent in Canada* (Toronto, 1981), 1–25. Biographical portraits of seventeenth- and eighteenth-century Acadians appear in the *Canadian Dictionary of Biography*, vols. 1–4 (Toronto, 1966, 1969, 1974, 1979). Maps of Acadian marshland settlement and of the Acadian deportation and return appear in R. Cole Harris, ed., *Historical Atlas of Canada*, vol. 1, *From the Beginning to 1800* (Toronto, 1987). Donald Lemon's *Theatre of Empire* (Saint John, 1987) contains many valuable maps of the Maritimes.

147

Nova Scotia and the American Revolution

148   After the British conquest of Canada, the Thirteen Colonies advanced toward independence. The new United States, however, would not include all of British North America. Nova Scotia, the new colony of Saint John's Island (created in 1769 and renamed Prince Edward Island in 1799), the island of Newfoundland, and the former French colony of Quebec would remain part of the British Empire.

Britain easily maintained control of the small, isolated colony on Saint John's Island, with its settler population of only one thousand recent British arrivals and Acadians. As for Newfoundland, its Anglo-Irish population looked eastward to Britain rather than southward to the Thirteen Colonies. Moreover, the town of St. John's was separated from Boston by more than fifteen hundred kilometres.

Nova Scotia, which then comprised the whole of present-day Nova Scotia and New Brunswick, had perhaps the most difficult time deciding whom to support, for the "fourteenth colony," as it was sometimes called, bordered on, and had the closest links with, New England. It may seem puzzling that the Nova Scotians did not join their fellow Americans in 1776—after all, more than half of Nova Scotia's approximately twenty thousand inhabitants were New Englanders with strong economic, cultural, and political ties with their former home. Why, then, did Nova Scotia not become the fourteenth state in the American union?

New England's Outpost

With the deportation of the Acadians in 1755 and the capture of Louisbourg in 1758, Americans began moving north. Almost everywhere, English names began to replace the former French or Micmac ones. The

British authorities wanted to attract loyal Protestant settlers in order to prevent the return of the deported Acadians. In October 1758, Governor Lawrence issued a proclamation throughout British America that invited settlers to claim the unoccupied Acadian farmlands. The circular described Acadia's eighty thousand hectares as "Plowlands producing Wheat, Rye, Barley, Oats, Hemp, Flax ... cultivated for more than a Hundred Years past, and never fail of Crops, nor need manuring." The Nova Scotian government promised to pay for New Englanders' transportation and give grants of forty hectares of land to each family head and twenty hectares for each additional family member.

In crowded, heavily settled southeastern Massachusetts, eastern Connecticut, and Rhode Island, the invitation had great appeal among the poorer farmers. Hundreds of fishermen who wanted to locate closer to the Grand Banks also came. By the end of 1763, thousands had left New England and sailed to Nova Scotia.

Most of the immigrants went to the Annapolis Valley in peninsular *149* Nova Scotia, to lands cleared and diked by the Acadians before their deportation, and to the area around Cumberland, near present-day Sackville, New Brunswick. A much smaller number entered the Saint John River valley, forming small frontier communities at the mouth of the river and at Maugerville (just south of present-day Fredericton), along the lower Saint John River.

The New England farmers and fishermen worked to create a new English-speaking Nova Scotia. But the lack of roads linking the settlements prevented regular communication. As historian George Rawlyk notes, "On the eve of the American Revolution, Nova Scotia was little more than a political expression for a number of widely scattered and isolated communities."[1]

Americans were still migrating to the forested lands north of the Bay of Fundy when hundreds of Acadians returned. In 1764 the British government permitted them to settle in Nova Scotia, providing that they disperse throughout the colony. Many returned not to their farms, which were now occupied by New Englanders, but to the Bay of Chaleur, on the present-day border between Quebec and New Brunswick. The settlement of Caraquet became a focal point for the region. Other Acadians lived on farms along the lower Saint John River.

Other immigrants came to Nova Scotia in the 1760s and 1770s: some 2000 settlers from Ulster in Northern Ireland; more than 750 from Yorkshire, England (many of whom settled on the Isthmus of Chignecto); and, in 1773, nearly 200 Scots (who settled at Pictou). They joined the original British residents of Halifax, the 1500 or so Acadians, and the approximately 1500 "foreign Protestants," largely Germans, who resided south of Halifax in the area around Lunenburg. New Englanders constituted about 60 percent of Nova Scotia's total population of nearly 20 000 in 1776.

THE IMPORTANCE OF HALIFAX

Halifax, as the only urban centre, became the colony's capital. It housed the military establishment and published the province's only newspaper. The upper level of Halifax society centred on the governor, his senior officials, and a group of merchants who had grown rich from army and navy contracts. A handful of smaller merchants and professional people also lived in the colony's capital. The rest of the city's population consisted of poor fishermen, carpenters, mechanics, and labourers.

Nova Scotia was given an elected assembly in 1758, but few rural members could afford the honour of taking their seats as unpaid members. As a result, a small clique of Halifax merchants controlled both the assembly and the governor's council. So influential were the merchants that they secured the recall of Gov. Francis Legge to England. Sent to the colony in 1773, the would-be reformer attempted to expose the spoils system operated by the large Halifax merchants. The merchants protested to London, threatening that Nova Scotia would join the American Revolution if Legge were not removed. Already fearful of developments in the Thirteen Colonies, London overlooked the evidence of corruption that Legge had unearthed and ordered the governor home in early 1776.

THE IMPACT OF THE AMERICAN REVOLUTION

The rhetoric of rebellion of the American colonies in 1775–76 found an audience in rural Nova Scotia. Many New Englanders in Nova Scotia resented the fact that in the late 1750s they had been promised constitutional rights and liberties similar to those enjoyed in New England, where the townships had considerable local autonomy. At annual town meetings, the voters had elected their officers and decided local issues. But in Nova Scotia in the 1760s, this form of township democracy was not practised; instead, London intended to build a tightly controlled, centralized government structure. The merchant-controlled assembly in Halifax, which strongly supported the governor, worked to eliminate local township government. It appointed justices of the peace to administer the local areas and did not allow the election of township officials.

As tensions mounted in the Thirteen Colonies, outer settlements in Nova Scotia began holding town meetings similar to those held in the American colonies. When Governor Legge called out one-fifth of the provincial militia in November 1775 and levied new taxes to meet the cost, petitions from the settlements of Truro, Cumberland, and Onslow voiced opposition to military service. The Chignecto settlers objected to the new tax and to the idea that the governor might force them to "march into different parts in Arms against their friends and relations." Like the Acadians of twenty years earlier, most Nova Scotian settlers sought neutrality. Yarmouth, for example, responded to the governor's request with the following statement:

> We were almost all of us born in New England, we have Fathers, Brothers, & Sisters in that country, divided betwixt natural affection to our nearest relations, and good Faith and Friendship to our King and Country, we want to know, if we may be permitted at this time to live in a peaceful State, as we look on that to be the only situation in which we with our Wives and Children, can be in any tolerable degree safe.

Realizing the seriousness of the discontent, Legge wisely retreated. He promptly suspended compulsory military service, allowed the militia to stay at home unless an actual invasion occurred, and cancelled the new taxes, thus effectively neutralizing much of the discontent that existed in the colony.

151

The Response to the American Revolution

The communities farthest from Halifax showed the greatest enthusiasm for the American cause. The town of Mathias on the vaguely defined border between Nova Scotia and Maine, the Maugerville settlement on the lower Saint John River, and the Chignecto–Cumberland region at the head of the Bay of Fundy became active centres of support for the revolution. Jonathan Eddy, a New Englander who farmed in the Chignecto region, took the lead in the development of a revolutionary movement in his area. He raised an invasion force of about 180 men and attacked British-held Fort Cumberland (the reconstructed French fort of Beauséjour) in 1776. He had no artillery and his force was smaller than that defending Fort Cumberland; moreover, few New Englanders on the isthmus openly supported Eddy's poorly trained, undisciplined, and badly led army. With the arrival of British reinforcements, Eddy's troops fled in disorder, and the English burned the homes and barns of Eddy's supporters. The following summer British naval vessels entered the Bay of Fundy and took control of the area.

Eddy's attempt to capture Fort Cumberland failed for a number of reasons. Historian John Bartlet Brebner points out that General George Washington, whom Eddy had approached for support, refused it because he knew that the Americans had "little energy or material available for side shows, no matter how admirable the cause and its proponents."[2] As well, British military power, in particular the Royal Navy, discouraged the Americans from making such an attempt. Brebner believes the Americans' lack of a navy and their failure to win sufficiently strong support among Nova Scotians best explain the revolutionaries' failure north of the border.

The Nova Scotians supporting the revolution "could make no headway because their friends in the rebellious Colonies had no navy and because they themselves could not assemble from the scattered settlements an effective force for unassisted revolt."[3]

THE RESPONSE OF THE INDIANS AND THE ACADIANS TO THE REVOLUTION

The English also obtained the neutrality of most of the thousand or so Micmacs and Malecites who held the balance of power north of the Bay of Fundy. By now the British had adopted the French techniques of gift diplomacy to win over the Indians, giving them presents of food, medicine, and ammunition. In addition, Britain seemed to them to be a stronger power than the American colonies, particularly after it extended its control over the Bay of Fundy and captured the coastline of northern Maine from the Americans. Thanks to the Indians, the upper Saint John River valley remained in the British zone throughout the war. The Acadians, for their part, now struggling to establish themselves in their new settlements, had no interest in becoming involved in the conflict between the two English-speaking groups.

GROWING ANTAGONISM TOWARD THE AMERICAN REVOLUTIONARIES

While the American insurgents were consolidating their hold on the former Thirteen Colonies, Nova Scotia was moving in a different direction, largely as a result of raids on the colony by American privateers. While the Royal Navy could locate and confront an invasion fleet, it had difficulty spotting single privateer ships. Ironically, the raids helped to make many once-sympathetic Nova Scotians antagonistic to the American revolutionaries. No Nova Scotian settlement (except Halifax) escaped the American raiders, who seized anything they could carry away. These attacks alienated wealthy citizens in ports such as Yarmouth, Lunenburg, and Liverpool, and prompted them to launch their own retaliatory raids against American shipping. By 1781 settlements in the Minas Basin and the Bay of Fundy area, which in 1775–76 had opposed increased taxes for military defence, now willingly accepted militia service and taxes to meet the cost of defending the colony.

Henry Alline and the New Light Movement

The unwillingness of many New Englanders in Nova Scotia to support the revolution can also be explained by what has been called the "missing decade" thesis.⁴ Although these recent immigrants held many New England values and still possessed an attachment to their old homeland, they had been absent during a crucial decade in New England's political development. They had no doubt heard the revolutionary rhetoric of the early 1770s about the growing British oppression and the need to defend New Englanders' liberties, but they were too preoccupied with the need to clear land and develop the fisheries to become involved. They simply wanted the political agents from both Maine and Halifax to leave them alone.

Nonetheless, during this period of acute disorientation and confusion, these settlers needed direction. In the late 1770s and early 1780s a religious gospel rather than a political one monopolized the attention of Nova Scotians. They became part of a great religious revival that centred on a charismatic young man named Henry Alline.

HENRY ALLINE

Henry Alline, who was born and raised in Rhode Island belonged to the Congregational church, the church to which most New England immigrants in Nova Scotia belonged. Henry received his early education at Newport. He was twelve when his family moved to Nova Scotia in 1760. They settled in one of the richest farming areas in the colony–the Minas Basin, near present-day Windsor. He received no further schooling, for no school existed in his township. Nor was there a church. Religion was preserved through family prayer, Bible reading, and religious discussions at home. But Henry came into contact with an evangelical group that emphasized the need for an intensely emotional conversion experience known as the "New Light."

In 1776, at the age of twenty-eight, Henry Alline began his career as an itinerant preacher. From the reminiscences of one of his early listeners, we know that Alline appeared "mighty in prayer," and never talked "about the world at all, except as urged by necessity." Committed to music as a means of teaching the faith, he was "a good singer and loved singing." Physically, he was of "middling size; straight, and very thin; of light complexion, with light curly hair, and blue eyes, with a solemn expression"; his dress was "neat but plain."

Initially, Alline confined his activities to Minas Basin, but three years later was ordained by several Annapolis Valley churches as an evangelist. Convinced that God had selected him to carry His message, Alline travelled constantly. The evangelist often rode as far as sixty to eighty kilometres in a day, bringing religion to rural people. His willingness to preach under all conditions struck a responsive chord among rural Nova Scotians, who were then still struggling on the brink of survival. They heard Alline's message and believed that Nova Scotia had become the new centre of

Christendom. Alline's message seems to have filled a spiritual vacuum in the frontier areas.

Nova Scotia's "New Light" communities chose political neutrality and worked instead during the years of the American Revolution to perfect their spiritual condition. Alline's religious revival diverted their attention away from the revolutionary struggle. He convinced many Nova Scotians that they were performing a special role–bringing the world back to God— and that it was Christ who merited their allegiance, not the British or the revolutionists.

The charismatic preacher returned to New England to bring back the purity of the Christian Gospel. He died of tuberculosis in New Hampshire in early February 1784, leaving behind him in Nova Scotia scores of disciples and hundreds of followers. After his death, his manuscript journals were copied and recopied by hand and circulated among his followers until they were published in 1806. George Rawlyk regards them as "one of the two or three most illuminating, honest, introspective accounts available concerning the spiritual travails of any eighteenth-century North American mystical evangelical."[5] His disciples, popularly referred to as Allinites, later became members of the Baptist church and carried on the teachings of the "Apostle of Nova Scotia."

154

The Loyalists

Throughout the Thirteen Colonies, a substantial number of Americans opposed the American Revolution and wanted to remain loyal to Britain. Historians now estimate that approximately 20 percent of the white American population of 1776 (roughly half a million people) became Loyalists.[6] They were strongest in New York, partly because the British occupied the city after the Battle of Long Island in the autumn of 1776 and partly because New York had a strong British aristocracy. The Loyalists were weakest in Connecticut, Massachusetts, and Virginia. Loyalists came from every class, race, occupation, religion, and geographical region. They supported Britain for many diverse reasons, ranging from personal loyalty to the Crown to a fear that the revolution would threaten individual freedoms.

Loyalists who came from the ruling class often had a vested interest, as colonial office holders, in maintaining the status quo. But a high proportion of Loyalists also came from religious and cultural minorities. Not yet having joined mainstream American society, recent immigrants from Europe (Germany, Holland, and the British Isles) and members of religious minorities (such as the French Huguenots, Maryland Catholics, and Quaker pacifists) held on to the British connection for fear that increased American power could result in a restriction of their freedoms. The Indian tribes, particularly the Iroquois, looked upon the Crown as the lesser of two evils, since it might slow down the advance of the American settlers westward, anxious as the Imperial power was to avoid the increased expenditures of more Indian wars. Blacks saw an opportunity to free themselves by joining the British and fleeing their owners.

Persecution of the Loyalists began as early as 1774, when it became more and more difficult to maintain neutrality in face of the approaching struggle. Appropriately, the term "lynch law," an informal system of law enforcement, originated to describe the treatment of Loyalists in Virginia. A favourite pastime was tarring and feathering outspoken Loyalists. The victim was stripped naked, smeared with a coat of tar and feathers, then paraded through the streets.

With the passing of the Declaration of Independence, the local revolutionary committees stepped up their activities against Loyalists. According to historians Wallace Brown and Hereward Senior, the committees' means of persuasion "ranged from mild social pressure to murder."[7] Various states disenfranchised, put in prison, banished, and fined "Tories" and confiscated their property as well. (In Loyalist-controlled areas, outrages were also committed against, and restrictions of civil liberties imposed on, those believed to be supporters of the revolution).

155

THE LOYALISTS' DEFEAT

The decisive battle of the war was fought on October 19, 1781, when Lord Cornwallis surrendered his army of seven thousand at Yorktown, Virginia. This battle really ended the revolutionary war, although the general peace was made two years later.

For many Loyalists, the two years between the disaster at Yorktown and the final signing of peace was the worst time of all. As the war wound down and the British began to evacuate southern ports such as Wilmington, Charleston, and Savannah, to which the Loyalists had fled for protection, persecution reached new levels. Several of the newly independent states subjected the Loyalists to double and triple taxation, and Congress invited the states to confiscate their property. Physical violence against Loyalists continued. It became clear that Britain had to do something for the Loyalists. The British continued to hold New York City and Long Island, and many Loyalists (at one point, thirty thousand) assembled there, awaiting evacuation.

At the peace negotiations, the American commissioners agreed that no further persecutions of Loyalists would take place. But while Congress urged the states to grant restitution and amnesty, it had no power to enforce its requests. Except in one or two states, every clause in the Treaty of Paris relating to the Loyalists was abrogated. When news of the preliminary peace reached the United States in the spring of 1783, the proscriptions, confiscations, and harassment began again.

The Great Migration to Nova Scotia

A great migration of thousands of Loyalists and their families began even before the peace treaty. Both during and after the war, the more influential Loyalists, such as royal officials, wealthy merchants, landowners, professionals, and high military officers, sailed for England to press their claims for compensation. The humbler element decided, for the most part, to settle in the remaining British colonies in North America.

Traditionally, the number of exiles has been estimated at 100 000, but this figure is probably inflated. Wallace Brown and Hereward Senior believe that British North America received more than 50 000 white, black, and Indian Loyalists; Bermuda no more than 100; the Bahamas about 2000; the British West Indies about 4000; and a few settled on the Mosquito Coast (now Belize, Central America). The British Isles received approximately 10 000, with a small number (mainly Germans), returning to the Rhine Valley. The overwhelming majority of the Loyalists were white, as Brown and Senior note, but there were also approximately 6000 black Loyalists who migrated to the Maritimes, Sierra Leone, the Bahamas, and the West Indies. Some 2000 Iroquois Indians also left New York. In all, 70 000 people—approximately the population of New France at the moment of the conquest—left the United States.[8]

The Loyalists favoured Nova Scotia over Quebec at a ratio of roughly two to one. Nova Scotia's fisheries, its large tracts of empty land, and the potential trade with the West Indies were well known. Nova Scotia, too, was the shorter trip by sea. Small groups of Loyalists had been finding their way to Halifax since 1775. The evacuation of New York in 1783, though, led to an unanticipated invasion. On April 26, 1783, the first or "spring" fleet set sail, carrying no fewer than seven thousand men, women, and children. Half the vessels went to Port Roseway on the south shore of Nova Scotia and the other half sailed to the mouth of the Saint John River. They went ashore at Saint John on May 18, now commemorated in New Brunswick as "Loyalist Landing Day." Other fleets followed in the summer and autumn.

THE LOYALISTS' FIRST SETTLEMENTS

The voyage from New York to either Halifax or the Saint John River usually took from one to two weeks, depending on the winds and the navigators' skill. About 14 500 people went to what became New Brunswick in 1784; about the same number went to peninsular Nova Scotia; of the remainder, 400 went to Cape Breton, about 500 to Prince Edward Island, and a few families to Newfoundland.

The smallest group of those who made their way to Nova Scotia came, surprisingly, from New England. As historian Neil MacKinnon notes, "The New England states seem to have been represented more by quality

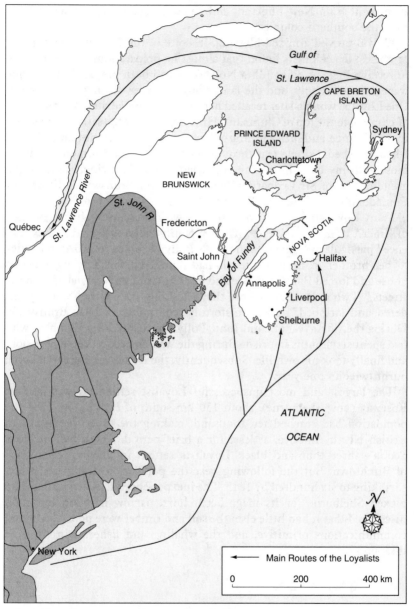

Loyalist settlement before 1800 in the Maritimes.

than quantity, leadership than numbers."[9] He estimates that of those who came to Nova Scotia, at least 40 percent came from New York state, 15 percent from the other middle colonies (particularly New Jersey),

20 percent from New England, and about 25 percent (black and white) from the southern colonies.

Arrival proved a mixed blessing. In spite of the British government's promises, the colonists found that almost no preparations had been made to receive them at Saint John. No shelter had been prepared, provisions were in short supply, and the land along the river was not yet surveyed. One Loyalist woman later recalled her thoughts immediately after landing: "I climbed to the top of Chipman's Hill and watched the sails disappearing in the distance, and such a feeling of loneliness came over me that, although I had not shed a single tear through all the war, I sat down on the damp moss with my baby in my lap and cried." (This individual became the grandmother of Sir Leonard Tilley, one of New Brunswick's Fathers of Confederation.)

Many Loyalists brought with them to New Brunswick vivid memories of American injustices. The Dribblee family of Long Island had experienced particularly harsh treatment. As Polly Dribblee recorded in a letter to her brother in England, rebels had plundered this Loyalist family's house and forced Polly Dribblee and her five children out "naked into the streets." Two more times before they left Long Island, they were "plundered and stripped." Their misfortune continued in New Brunswick. During their first year at Saint John, Polly's husband, Filer Dribblee, who had spent six months in prison during the war, entered a deep depression, and finally took his own life. Subsequently, the Dribblees' log cabin home burnt twice in one year.

The largest and most unsuccessful Loyalist settlement was at Port Roseway (now Shelburne), about 150 km south of Halifax. By 1784 the population had reached ten thousand, making the town the largest in British North America, at least for a brief period. About half of Nova Scotia's three thousand black Loyalists settled in Shelburne's suburb of Birchtown. But the following year the population declined sharply, shrinking to six hundred by 1815. The inexperienced Loyalist settlers had picked Shelburne for its magnificent long, narrow harbour, but soon discovered that it had little else: the soil and timber were poor, the inland communications primitive, and the whaling and fisheries in the area disappointing.

THE BLACK LOYALISTS

For the black Loyalists there were far more disappointments than the conditions at Shelburne. Among their ranks were men and women who had heeded the British proclamation of 1779 that offered freedom to any slaves who left their American masters and rallied to support the Crown. Some blacks had taken part in combat; others had served as spies, guides, nurses, and personal servants. Assuming they would enjoy equality with the white Loyalists, the free black Loyalists expected to receive govern-

National Archives of Canada/C-10548.

The Loyalist boomtown of Shelburne, Nova Scotia. Along with the Saint John River valley in New Brunswick, Shelburne was one of the first major areas of Loyalist settlement. The drawing by William Booth shows part of the town of Shelburne in 1789.

ment grants of land and provisions. Most, however, received no land, and those who did found themselves in possession of rocky tracts. Few obtained any provisions. Out of necessity, one of the landless later wrote, they must "cultivate the lands of a white man for half the product, which occupies the whole of our time." Finding their prospects poor and objecting to the servile jobs they had to take, almost half of the black Loyalists left Nova Scotia in 1792 to join a free black colony in Sierra Leone in West Africa.

Many of the white Loyalists also found economic conditions in Nova Scotia difficult. In one stroke the colony's population almost tripled, and the resources of "Nova Scarcity" (as the first refugee Loyalists termed the province) were insufficient to meet the demand. Not surprisingly, many soon left peninsular Nova Scotia. Some went to Upper Canada, others to England, many back to the United States, and a large number to what was then western Nova Scotia, soon to be named New Brunswick.

The Founding of New Brunswick

The privations and sufferings of the American refugees on the north shore of the Bay of Fundy were considerable, as so little had been done before their arrival. The future Loyalist leaders of New Brunswick subsequently began a partition movement to have the section north of the Bay of Fundy removed from the jurisdiction of the Nova Scotian governor and made a separate Loyalist province. Loyalists argued that the distance of the Saint John settlements from Halifax made it difficult to transact business with the capital. Moreover, they did not want to be under the rule of Nova Scotia, which they felt had done little for the war. Without admitting as much, they also realized that the creation of a new colony would provide administrative offices for themselves.

In the summer of 1784 Britain met their request and created the new colony of New Brunswick. Col. Thomas Carleton, the younger brother of Quebec governor Sir Guy Carleton, became the colony's first governor, a position he held for thirty years. In 1785 the major settlement at the mouth of the great river was named Saint John. Colonel Carleton gave the new capital, approximately one hundred kilometres north of Saint John, the name of Fredericktown (the "k" and "w" were dropped shortly thereafter), in honour of Prince Frederick, second son of George III.

160   Thomas Carleton selected Fredericton as the capital to promote inland settlement. Moreover, the up-river location had a distinct military advantage, as Carleton's two regiments of British troops could be garrisoned there and be safe from a sudden coastal attack.

The fear of an American attack was a real one, because the Americans claimed one-third of the province. The Treaty of Paris of 1783 established the Saint Croix River as the boundary between Maine and New Brunswick. Unfortunately, identification of the river was unclear because three rivers flowed into Passamaquoddy Bay. The Americans pressed for the most easterly river as the boundary. Fifteen years later, however, New Brunswick won its case by establishing that Champlain and de Monts had wintered in 1604–05 on Dechet's Island at the mouth of the most westerly river, which was indeed the true Saint Croix. They confirmed the site by conducting excavations on the island and revealing the ruins of the buildings as had been described by Champlain in his journal. New Brunswick thus emerged in roughly the form its founders had envisioned.

BUILDING A LOYALIST PROVINCE

The Loyalist immigrants in New Brunswick came from all levels of society, and most did not have a superior education. Slowly, they built a new society in the Saint John River valley. It was hard work even for the affluent, for New Brunswick had a severe shortage of labour. All who came to the province preferred to work for themselves and not for others. As W.S. MacNutt, the New Brunswick historian, wrote, "Judges of the Supreme court and other Loyalist patricians took to the fields to raise the fruits and vegetables necessary to livelihood."[10] Along the lower and middle reaches of the Saint John River a series of largely self-sufficient agricultural communities developed. The town of Saint John became the major urban centre, with a population of thirty-five hundred in 1785. The Acadians' settlements were located along the eastern and northern shores of New Brunswick.

Ironically, the very people whose allegiance had been critical in retaining western Nova Scotia for the Crown suffered the most. The new settlers encroached on vast portions of the Indians' hunting and fishing territories. The British claimed the land as Crown land and did not make purchases from the Indians. The Royal Proclamation of 1763 (see Chapter 9) under which the British negotiated land surrender treaties with the Indians, was observed in Upper Canada but not in the Maritime colonies. As historian Leslie Upton points out, the Micmacs and Malecites in 1782 "were no longer of account as allies, enemies, or people." The correspondence connected with the arrival of thirty thousand immigrants contains "not one word about the Indians who would be dispossessed by the new settlers."[11]

The Loyalists in Prince Edward Island

Several hundred Loyalists travelled to St. John's Island, where they constituted about one-fifth of the population. In Nova Scotia and New Brunswick the Loyalists were—eventually—looked after by the authorities and supplied with free land, government timber, and tools. On Prince Edward Island (as it was renamed in 1799), they became victims of treachery and duplicity.

In 1767 the British government, in a curious experiment, gave the entire island and many parts of Nova Scotia away. The system vaguely resembled the seigneurial system. The island was first divided into long belts of land, stretching from north to south. It was chosen by lot until all sixty-seven townships of roughly eight thousand hectares each had been granted to soldiers, politicians, and courtiers favoured by the British government. New landlords had to pay a small annual fee, or quitrent, for their land; they also had to promise to bring over settlers. Elsewhere, the government of Nova Scotia later practised *escheat*, the process of cancelling the large land grants. But Halifax could not end the grants on the island, as the absentee landlords had protected their lots by having the island established as a separate colony in 1769.

To attract Loyalists to their lands, the large landed proprietors assigned certain areas for colonization. They promised Loyalists grants of land with secure titles. But once the Loyalist settlers on the island had cleared their lands, erected buildings, and planted orchards, the proprietors denied written title deeds to those who wanted to become freeholders rather than tenants. Many obtained no redress and left in disgust without obtaining title or compensation. Those who remained fought for seventy-five years for justice. Only in 1860 would a land commission recommend that free grants be made to those who could prove that their ancestors had been attracted to the island by the original promises made to the Loyalists. A final attempt to resolve the land question would be made in 1873, in conjunction with Prince Edward Island's entry into Confederation.

Nova Scotia's land area was reduced now to the peninsula. (With the arrival of a late migration of Loyalists into Cape Breton Island in 1784, that island became a separate colony.) New England, the ancestral home of many of Nova Scotia's and New Brunswick's inhabitants, became a foreign country. In the early 1780s the hatred on both sides remained very strong. Gradually, though, the Loyalists' animosity to the newly independent United States receded. Communication began to be resumed in the late 1780s as time wiped out bitter memories of the years of struggle. Ties with relatives and friends had not been entirely broken. Letters and visits to and from the United States became more frequent. A number of Loyalists returned to the United States in the late 1780s, particularly when Britain allowed half-pay officers to receive their pensions while living outside the Empire. With time, American anger against the Loyalists subsided and the returning Loyalists found a cordial welcome. Cadwallader Colden, for example, the grandson of a royal lieutenant governor of New York, returned from self-imposed exile and was later elected mayor of New York City.

Slowly, the Loyalists and the New Englanders in the Maritimes lost many of their Yankee customs. One important cultural trait, though, did remain: their speech patterns in English. The New Englanders and the Loyalists spoke American English, which by the time of their arrival in the Maritimes in the mid- and late-eighteenth century was noticeably different from British English. Consequently, the English speech community that developed in the Maritimes was, in most respects, North American and not British.

The Loyalists made a considerable impact on Nova Scotia. Their arrival led to the creation of two new colonies—New Brunswick and Cape Breton Island (to 1820). Among the Loyalists were American colonists of many different class, ethnic, racial, and religious backgrounds. Regardless of those divisions, the Loyalist legacy contributed to a deep affection for Great Britain in what became Maritime Canada. It also contributed to a respect for evolution—rather than revolution—in the development of Maritime government.

NOTES

[1]George A. Rawlyk, "The American Revolution and Nova Scotia Reconsidered," *Dalhousie Review* 43 (1963–64): 379.
[2]John Bartlet Brebner, *The Neutral Yankees of Nova Scotia* (Toronto, 1969; first published 1937), 285.
[3]John Bartlet Brebner quoted in Rawlyk, "American Revolution," 380.
[4]This thesis was first advanced by Gordon Stewart and George Rawlyk in *A People Highly Favoured of God* (Toronto, 1972); see especially pp. 3–4 and 43–44.

⁵G.A. Rawlyk, *Ravished by the Spirit: Religious Revivals, Baptists, and Henry Alline* (Kingston and Montreal, 1984), 13.
⁶Paul H. Smith, "The American Loyalists: Notes on Their Organization and Numerical Strength," *William and Mary Quarterly*, 3rd series, 25 (1968): 269.
⁷Wallace Brown and Hereward Senior, *Victorious in Defeat: The Loyalists in Canada* (Toronto, 1984), 16.
⁸The estimates of the Loyalists' numbers are taken from Brown and Senior, *Victorious in Defeat*.
⁹Neil MacKinnon, *This Unfriendly Soil: The Loyalist Experience in Nova Scotia, 1783–1791* (Kingston, 1986), 59.
¹⁰W.S. MacNutt, *New Brunswick: A History, 1784–1867* (Toronto, 1963), 70.
¹¹L.F.S. Upton, *Micmacs and Colonists: Indian–White Relations in the Maritimes, 1713–1867* (Vancouver, 1979), 78.

Related Readings

For articles of interest on this topic in R. Douglas Francis and Donald B. Smith, *Readings in Canadian History: Pre-Confederation*, 3d ed. (Toronto, 1990), see James E. Candow, "The New England Planters in Nova Scotia," 214–19; George A. Rawlyk, "The American Revolution and Nova Scotia Reconsidered," 220–33; and W.G. Shelton, "The United Empire Loyalists: A Reconsideration," 234–43. The land question on Prince Edward Island is reviewed by Ian Ross Robertson in "The Prince Edward Island Commission of 1860," 433–42.

163

BIBLIOGRAPHY

The major events in the American Revolution are reviewed in Samuel Eliot Morison's *Oxford History of the American People*, vol. 1, *Prehistory to 1789* (New York, 1972). On the Loyalists, see Christopher Moore, *The Loyalists: Revolution, Exile, Settlement* (Toronto, 1984); Wallace Brown and Hereward Senior, *Victorious in Defeat: The Loyalists in Canada* (Toronto, 1984); and Robert S. Allen, *The Loyal Americans: The Military Role of the Loyalist Provincial Corps and Their Settlement in British North America 1775–1784* (Ottawa, 1983). The story of Polly Dribblee and her family is told in Wallace Brown, *The Good Americans: The Loyalists in the American Revolution* (New York, 1969). For an estimate of the number of Loyalists who came to Nova Scotia, see William H. Nelson, *The American Tory* (Boston, 1964) and Paul H. Smith, "The American Loyalists: Notes on Their Organization and Numerical Strength," *William and Mary Quarterly*, 3d series, 25(1968): 259–77.

For a general overview of Maritime history in this period, see W.S. MacNutt's *The Atlantic Provinces, 1712–1857* (Toronto, 1965), 76–102. Nova Scotia's response to the American Revolution is reviewed by John Bartlet Brebner in *The Neutral Yankees of Nova Scotia* (Toronto, 1969; first published 1937). George A. Rawlyk examines the question of the Nova Scotians and the revolution in depth in *Nova Scotia's Massachusetts: A Study of Massachusetts–Nova Scotia Relations, 1630 to 1784* (Montreal, 1973); see also his "Revolution Rejected: Why Did Nova Scotia Fail to Join the American Revolution?" in *Emerging Identities: Selected Problems and Interpretations in Canadian History*, edited by Paul W. Bennett and Cornelius J. Jaenen (Scarborough, Ont., 1986), 133–57.

For information on Henry Alline and his New Light Movement, consult Gordon Stewart and George A. Rawlyk, *A People Highly Favoured of God: The Nova Scotia Yankees and the American Revolution* (Toronto, 1972); J.M. Bumsted, *Henry Alline* (Toronto, 1971); and George A. Rawlyk, *Ravished by the Spirit: Religious Revivals, Baptists, and Henry Alline* (Kingston and Montreal, 1984).

Two bibliographical guides to writings on the Loyalists and their influence on the development of the Maritimes are Robert S. Allen, *Loyalist Literature: An Annotated Bibliographic Guide* (Toronto, 1982) and J.M. Bumsted, *Understanding the Loyalists* (Sackville, N.B., 1986). The impact of the Loyalists in New Brunswick is reviewed by Ann Gorman Condon in *The Envy of the American States: The Loyalist Dream for New Brunswick* (Fredericton, 1984). W. Stewart MacNutt reviews the same subject in the opening pages of *New Brunswick: A History, 1784–1867* (Toronto, 1963). Neil MacKinnon examines the Loyalists' first decade in Nova Scotia in *This Unfriendly Soil: The Loyalist Experience in Nova Scotia, 1783–1791* (Kingston, 1986). An earlier article by MacKinnon, "The Changing Attitudes of the Nova Scotian Loyalists towards the United States, 1783–1791," has been reprinted in Phillip A. Buckner and David Frank, eds. and comps., *Atlantic Canada Before Confederation*, vol. 1, *The Acadiensis Reader* (Fredericton, 1985), 118–29. Thomas Raddall's *Halifax: Warden of the North*, rev. ed. (Toronto, 1971) contains a lively review of the impact of the revolution and the Loyalists on Halifax. An interesting study of Shelburne, the great Loyalist centre, is Marion Robertson's *King's Bounty* (Halifax, 1983). J.M. Bumsted's *Land, Settlement, and Politics on Eighteenth-Century Prince Edward Island* (Kingston, 1987) focusses on developments in Prince Edward Island.

For information on the Maritime Indians during the American Revolution, see L.F.S. Upton, *Micmacs and Colonists: Indian–White Relations in the Maritimes, 1713–1867* (Vancouver, 1979). James W. St. G. Walker's *The Black Loyalists: The Search for a Promised Land in Nova Scotia and Sierra Leone, 1783–1870* (New York, 1976) is the most important secondary source on the experience of black Loyalists. Eleven portraits of Loyalists, including Phyllis R. Blakeley's "Boston King: A Black Loyalist," appear in Phyllis R. Blakeley and John N. Grant, eds., *Eleven Exiles: Accounts of Loyalists of the American Revolution* (Toronto, 1982). Maps of the Maritimes in the late eighteenth century appear in Donald Lemon's *Theatre of Empire* (Saint John, 1987).

Time Line:1767–1791

1767 —The lands of Île Saint Jean, called Saint John's Island by the British (and renamed Prince Edward Island in 1799), are granted to absent proprietors.

1768 —Guy Carleton replaces James Murray as governor of Quebec.

1769 —Saint John's Island becomes a separate colony.

1774 —The Quebec Act guarantees the continuation of French civil law and the Roman Catholic religion in the St. Lawrence Valley. The Province of Quebec's boundaries are extended to include the Great Lakes.

1775 —The Americans capture Montreal, but are defeated at Quebec, and are expelled in 1776 from the St. Lawrence Valley.

1776 —Jonathan Eddy's pro-American force unsuccessfully attacks Fort Cumberland.

—Most of the Micmac and Malecite Indians promise to remain neutral during the American Revolution.

—Henry Alline begins his career as an itinerant preacher.

1778 —The establishment of the Franco-American alliance.

1783 —Peace of Paris ends the American Revolutionary War. The Thirteen Colonies gain their independence as the United States of America.

—Thirty thousand Loyalist refugees arrive in Nova Scotia.

1784 —The colonies of New Brunswick and Cape Breton are created to accommodate the influx of Loyalists.

—Chief Joseph Brant and the Iroquois Loyalists settle on the Grand River in the western portion of the Province of Quebec.

1791 —The Constitutional Act of 1791 divides the province of Quebec into Upper and Lower Canada.

The Aftermath of the Conquest in Quebec, 1760–1774

With thousands of British troops massed at the gates of Montreal in early September 1760, the Marquis de Vaudreuil, governor general of New France, saw that there was no sense in continuing the struggle. Wishing to spare the colony further devastation and bloodshed, he resolved to surrender, and set about drawing up the conditions to offer the attackers. Certain of victory, however, General Jeffery Amherst, the British commander-in-chief, was not about to accept indiscriminately all the demands of the losers; in particular, he refused to accord the French the "honours of war"—the privilege, often conceded in that age to a defeated army, of marching out under arms with colours flying and drums beating. Vaudreuil capitulated anyway, thereby bringing upon himself the wrath of the French government, which was apparently far more interested in the fate of the French army than in that of the *Canadiens*. On September 22, 1760, Britain established military rule over Quebec by a proclamation issued by General Amherst. The British Conquest thus became a reality, at least militarily. But until the final peace treaty, the ultimate fate of the colony—whether it would be retained by Britain or restored to France—was not determined.

British Military Rule, 1760–1763

Wartime conditions were painful for the roughly seventy thousand *Canadiens* living in the St. Lawrence Valley. Quebec City was in ruins. During the prolonged siege of that fortress in the summer of 1759, Wolfe's troops also laid waste the south shore of the St. Lawrence as far as Kamouraska, 150 km downstream. The next year James Murray continued the ravages at Sorel and elsewhere. This devastation resulted in such severe food shortages that Murray, named military governor of the district of Quebec

National Archives of Canada/C-11043.

Canadian Artist Adam Sherriff Scott (1887–1980) created this scene two centuries after the event. The painting conveys how the French and English forces might have appeared on the day of capitulation at Montreal, September 8, 1760.

after the surrender, had to intervene to force merchants to sell hoarded grain stocks at uninflated prices.

From the French Canadians' perspective, the terms of capitulation were mild. They had feared worse. Their bishop had warned them in 1756 that, if they lost, they would suffer the fate of the Acadians—expulsion. Whether the British were practising enlightened self-interest or magnanimity, the results were the same: rather than encourage New France's inhabitants to depart, the British decided to try to make them loyal subjects of the Crown. The conquerors did refuse to guarantee the survival of French laws, customs, and institutions, but His Majesty's new subjects were allowed to retain their "entire peaceable property and possession of their goods, noble and ignoble, moveable and immoveable." They could also continue to practise the Roman Catholic religion. Priests and female (but not male) religious orders could continue to perform their functions.

Colonials wishing to return to France could do so. Thus, of the twenty-two hundred French troops that remained in Vaudreuil's desertion-plagued army, about three-quarters sailed home with their officers. Perhaps another two thousand French and *Canadiens*, including the richest members of colonial society, also crossed the Atlantic. New France thus lost its political and military elites.

War and its aftermath disrupted the colony's economy. Some merchants returned to Europe. Others were forced into bankruptcy. François Havy and Jean Lefebvre, French Huguenots, started transferring their assets from Quebec to La Rochelle when the Seven Years' War officially broke out in 1756. Hostilities made it virtually impossible for them to ship their furs across the sea, and after the battle of Ste-Foy, the French government's decision to suspend payments on all colonial paper money consummated their ruin. Moreover, the shelling of Quebec's Lower Town had destroyed much of the property of the local merchants. Marie-Anne Barbel (see Chapter 5), for example, who had administered the lucrative trading post at Tadoussac after the death of her husband, Louis Fornel, lost numerous properties in which she had invested her capital, including a general store she maintained at Place Royale. For her and other merchants suffering similar losses, the Conquest was disastrous.

168   The Conquest also placed the Roman Catholic church in a delicate and precarious position. First, the church suffered substantial property losses during the military campaign; then, numerous ecclesiastics returned to France. When Henri-Marie de Pontbriand, bishop of Quebec, died in June 1760, he left no successor. Without a bishop, new clergy could not be ordained. Worse, the Church of England now became the established church and the colony's Roman Catholic church could no longer count on the government to support it financially and legally.

The Proclamation of 1763

The Treaty of Paris, signed in 1763, formally ended the Seven Years' War. France ceded Canada to the British, who were not really sure that they wanted it. During the discussions of the terms of peace, Prime Minister William Pitt allegedly pleaded with his cabinet: "Some are for keeping Canada, some Guadeloupe. Who will tell me what I shall be hanged for not keeping?" The West Indian island of Guadeloupe, an important producer of sugar, could certainly bring substantial economic benefits to Britain. But, if only to avoid another series of wars with France in northeastern North America, the British government decided to retain Canada. The following year civil rule began, and the three military districts of Montreal, Trois-Rivières and Quebec were united into the province of Quebec, with James Murray as governor.

The peace treaty confronted Britain with a dilemma in North America. It now administered a large French population whose loyalty would naturally be doubtful in the event of renewed war with France. The new colonial masters thus hoped that the French population might be quickly assimilated—that is, Protestantized and Anglicized. Assimilation, however, could succeed only if large numbers of New Englanders migrated

WHERE   HISTORIANS   DISAGREE

The Impact of the Conquest of 1760

Most historians do not dispute the immediate effects of the Conquest. But in their evaluation of the longer-term repercussions, they strongly disagree. The debate among French-speaking historians is due to the fact that they have stressed different aspects and asked different questions. What happened to the church? What became of the traditional elites? What were the effects on French Canadian participation in Quebec's economy? How did life change for the habitants? Historians' evaluations have also differed because they have written at different periods and thus used different frames of reference.

In the aftermath of the Rebellions of 1837–38, the nationalist François-Xavier Garneau, recognized as French Canada's first major historian, portrayed the Conquest in his *Histoire du Canada* (8th ed., [Montréal, 1945], vol. 6) as a tragedy, the beginning of his people's "sufferings and humiliations" (p. 82). But in 1905, historian Benjamin Sulte, who revered British liberties, concluded that, on the contrary, it signified the passage from "a reign of absolute subjection under the Bourbons to the free and untrammelled life of constitutional government" (Cited in Ramsay Cook, *The Maple Leaf Forever: Essays on Nationalism and Politics in Canada* [Toronto, 1971], 102).

English-speaking historians have also shown a great range of opinion on the impact of the conquest. A.L. Burt wrote in his *The Old Province of Quebec* (Minneapolis, 1933) of the immediate past-conquest period, "The years of this military régime are of supreme importance in the history of Canada, for they planted in Canadian hearts that trust in British justice which has preserved the

country with its dual nationality from splitting asunder" (p. 56). Yet, a fellow English-speaking Canadian historian disagreed. Arthur Lower wrote of the "bitter agony of Canada" in 1760 in his *Colony to Nation: A History of Canada* (3rd ed., Toronto, 1957), "No one can suggest that the English conquest, as conquests go, was cruel or English government harsh. If the French in Canada had had a choice of conquerors, they could not have selected more happily than fate did for them. But conquerors are conquerors: they may make themselves hated or they may get themselves tolerated; they cannot, unless they abandon their own way of life and quickly assimilate themselves, in which case they cease to be conquerors, make themselves loved. As long as French are French and English are English, the memory of the Conquest and its effects will remain. Not until that great day comes when each shall have lost themselves in a common Canadianism will it be obliterated." (p. 64)

Many French Canadian clerical historians, horrified by the excesses of the French Revolution, suggested that, by conquering the colony, the British saved Quebec from the atheism of republican France. But Abbé Lionel Groulx, whose historical writings spanned more than six decades of the twentieth century, viewed the Conquest as a catastrophe. He believed that the events of 1759/1760 paralyzed French Canada's normal economic, social, and cultural development.

In the 1950s and 1960s, historians such as Maurice Séguin, Guy Frégault, and Michel Brunet argued that New France's bourgeoisie had been "decapitated" by the Conquest; the return to France of many of the colony's bourgeoisie inevitably condemned French Canada to economic inferiority. Other historians disagree. In "A Change in Climate: The Conquest and the *Marchands* of Montreal" (Canadian Historical Association, *Historical Papers* [1974]; reprinted in *Readings in Canadian History: Pre-Confederation*, edited by R. Douglas Francis and Donald B. Smith, 3d. ed. [Toronto, 1990]), his study of Canadian merchants involved in the fur trade, José Igartua stated that it was the new British system of business competition that was responsible for the economic decline of the French. "The Montreal merchants were not 'decapitated' by the Conquest; rather, they were faced in very short succession with a series of transformations in the socioeconomic structure

of the colony to which they might have been able to adapt had these transformations been spread over a longer period of time" (p. 269). Yet, Fernand Ouellet, doubts that a significant Canadian bourgeoisie even existed prior to the Conquest.

Historian Susan Mann Trofimenkoff, writing from a feminist perspective, has captured in one trenchant phrase what might have been the sentiments of many *Canadiens* as they faced the realities of defeat and foreign takeover: "Conquest is like rape" (*The Dream of Nation: A Social and Intellectual History of Quebec* [Toronto, 1982], 31). No consensus exists even yet on the nature of the impact of the Conquest, although there was surely no more significant event in French Canada's history.

north, but few showed any inclination to do so. Quebec's climate appeared too harsh and there was little desire to live among a "foreign" population with strange laws and customs. Prospective colonists much preferred to move west.

Thus, by the outbreak of the American Revolution, the habitants were not only still very Catholic and French, they were also, thanks to an astonishingly high birth rate of at least 55 per thousand annually, much more numerous. British concern for security in the face of mounting tension in the American colonies soon forced a major revision of imperial policy toward Quebec and the French Canadians. The change was put into statute law in the Quebec Act, adopted by the British Parliament in 1774.

PONTIAC'S RESISTANCE

In 1763 the Indian question posed a greater problem for Britain than did the treatment of the *Canadiens*. The Proclamation of 1763 dealt with growing unrest in vast territories acquired south of the Great Lakes and west of the Allegheny Mountains, where the Indians resented the encroachment of settlers on their lands.

Indian bitterness over land-grabbing by British Americans had been growing since the French surrender in 1760. Pontiac, a discontented Ottawa chief in the Detroit region, organized a pan-Indian confederacy and mounted the most formidable Indian resistance that the British had ever faced. The discontent arose from another source as well—a fundamental difference in French and English policy toward the Indians (see Chapters 6 and 7). In contrast to the "gift diplomacy" practised by the French, the English in the Thirteen Colonies had pursued a system of making treaties or outright purchases for the Indians' land. They made payments only once. After their conquest of the interior, the British put a halt to their enemies' policy of making generous annual payments to the Indians.

Sir William Johnson, superintendent of northern Indians, understood the need for payments to the Indians and urged a return to the French policy of supplying ammunition and presents. General Amherst refused and paid dearly for his stubbornness. In May 1763 the Indians attacked British garrisons and frontier settlements throughout the upper Mississippi and Ohio River basins. With the exception of Detroit, Pontiac and his confederacy captured every British post west of Niagara. The Indians killed, or captured, an estimated two thousand whites. So determined was the Indian resistance that General Amherst contemplated waging biological warfare. In a letter he advised one commander as follows: "You will do well to try to inoculate the Indians by means of blankets, as well as to try every other method that can serve to extirpate this execrable race." Although no evidence exists that Amherst carried out this policy, it is known that a Captain Ecuyer, in June 1763, gave a group of hostile Indians at Fort Pitt a present of two blankets and a handkerchief from the smallpox hospital.

171

Several factors then led the Indians to make peace. By autumn, Indian morale began to decline as Detroit remained in English hands and the Indians had to resume their hunting to bring in winter food supplies. The halt in the fur trade hurt as the Indians ran short of ammunition. Then came word of the peace treaty between the French and the English, signifying that the Indians could not expect French military aid from Louisiana. In addition, Pontiac's confederacy was dealt a fatal blow when old intertribal rivalries resurfaced, destroying the unity of his pan-Indian alliance. As a result, by late 1764, British military expeditions were able finally to quell Indian resistance.

The troubles justified British plans, already laid out by the Board of Trade and Plantations in London, to satisfy Indian grievances. The Proclamation of 1763, issued by the British in October at the height of the troubles, set aside a huge reserve west of the Allegheny Mountains for "the several nations or tribes of Indians with whom we are connected, and who live under our protection." The British agreed that they had no right to colonize Indian territory without prior purchase by the Crown and the consent of the affected Indian band. Colonial governors were forbidden to make any land grants or engage in any surveying in the area of the reserve. Trade relations were to be strictly managed by London.

This "ambitious programme of imperial control," as historian Pierre Tousignant describes the proclamation,[1] became the first legal recognition by the British Crown of aboriginal rights. Events soon showed, however, that without a substantial British military presence in the interior, the

An Amerindian council with the British. The Indians in Northeastern North America made wampum (cylindrical beads made of shell) belts. The wampum belt served as a mnemonic device to recall to the speaker a previous agreement or treaty. An engraving from a painting by Benjamin West from William Smith's *An Historical Account of the Expedition Against the Ohio Indians* (Philadelphia, 1766).

policy was unenforceable, because thousands of land-hungry Americans pushed over the mountains into the fertile Ohio country.

The *Canadiens* after the Proclamation of 1763

In creating the Indian territory the Royal Proclamation drastically reduced Quebec's territory to a rough quadrilateral along both sides of the St. Lawrence River, extending from what is today eastern Ontario to Gaspé (see page 186). It also provided the new province with governmental institutions, among them a council to assist the governor.

Other stipulations gave the *Canadiens* good reason to worry about the future: as Roman Catholics, they were to be excluded from all offices. Elected assemblies were promised, with a view to attracting English Protestant immigrants from the New England colonies. While awaiting the expected wave of settlers that would permit the British to remake Quebec into an English colony, those few English-speakers already living in Quebec could rely on "the enjoyment of the benefit of the laws of our realm of England."

173

The *Canadiens* occasionally expressed dissatisfaction with life under British rule. As before, some habitants attempted to avoid unpaid *corvées* required for roadworks by taking the wheels off their wagons. Moreover, they protested whenever the British raised the question of enlistment in the militia, which they did during the Indian troubles of 1763 and again at the time of the American invasion.

Complaints also arose about the functioning of the judicial system after military government ended in 1764. Historian A.L. Burt has pointed out that, prior to that date, the British used the militia captains as "the hands, the eyes, the ears, and the mouth of the government."[2] The position of *capitaine de milice*, which had existed for nearly a century, carried with it far more than the military responsibilities of commanding habitant militias. These militia captains were also magistrates who relied on the *coutume de Paris* (one of several legal codes that existed in France at the time) to reach their decisions. With the coming of civil government, however, they were cast aside and replaced by Protestant justices of the peace and bailiffs. Under English law, these new officers could go so far as to seize homes for minor debts, and they frequently jailed debtors. Inept justices of the peace were even accused of deliberately stirring up feuds so that they might charge fees to settle them. Sir Guy Carleton, who was sent to Quebec as lieutenant governor in 1766, commented wryly on the competence of some judges: "Not a Protestant butcher or publican became bankrupt who did not apply to be made a justice."

The legal disorder in the colony proved so great that Murray soon felt obliged to waive the laws disqualifying Roman Catholics from serving on juries or preventing Roman Catholic barristers from practising in courts. Unfortunately, no written statements by the habitants themselves exist to indicate their response to those reforms. Certainly, though, the governor's tolerance of Roman Catholic lawyers and jurors (and his allowance of some use of French civil law) helped to pacify the habitants. Governor Murray may have been correct in assuming that the *Canadiens* wanted "nothing but that plenty which the ravages of the war have deprived them of to make them entirely happy."

Furthermore, with the return of peace and reasonably good weather, agricultural production, notably of wheat, increased. So did both the marriage and birth rates of the habitants—a sure sign of better times.

Although the time was hardly a golden age, survival was possible in British-ruled Quebec. Pressures on the land in the old seigneurial region along the St. Lawrence were not yet intense and new concessions could be had with relative ease. Nor did the habitants feel threatened by increases in the "foreign," English-speaking population: excluding soldiers, there were barely five hundred British in the colony in 1765.

Moreover, the presence of British troops prevented any serious thought of uprising from taking hold among the seventy thousand French Canadians, especially at a time when they could not expect any help from France. In a realistic assessment, Murray commented that the *Canadiens* "hardly will hereafter be easily persuaded to take up arms against a nation . . . who will have it always in their power to burn or destroy."

174

URBAN LIFE

The degree of satisfaction among urban dwellers, particularly those of modest circumstances, is more difficult to judge. Even the term "urban" must be put in context. Barely 20 percent of the province of Quebec's citizens lived in towns, and even the largest of these were tiny communities by today's standards. Quebec, the largest centre, boasted scarcely more than seven thousand citizens in 1765; Montreal had barely five thousand. Beyond the new borders, the Detroit area contained perhaps another two thousand *Canadiens*.

Although these townspeople had access to certain goods and services that their country cousins lacked, they suffered important disadvantages. Wage workers, for example, had to contend with the seasonal nature of much of the available employment.

Disease and fire also caused untold misery. Epidemics due to contaminated water supplies and poor hygiene took many lives, especially among the old and the very young. Fires devastated urban areas. On May 18, 1765, Montreal suffered a great conflagration when a fire that began near the waterfront expanded to destroy more than a hundred houses, and thereby led to an acute housing crisis. The town was rebuilt, but the rising cost of land within the small city, with the ensuing increase in rents, pushed less-affluent citizens, such as artisans and labourers, beyond the town walls. Although the bourgeois rebuilt their homes from stone, the poor continued to use wood, which was much cheaper. In spite of ordinances requiring regular sweeping of chimneys and forbidding the use of wooden shingles, fires were a common occurrence.

THE OLD ELITES

The colony's traditional elites—the seigneurs and the clergy—faced difficult times after the Conquest. The seigneurs, many of whom had lived in town, were obliged to rely on the revenue from their seigneurial land and even to live there, but sparsely populated seigneuries produced precious little income. With the end of the French regime, the seigneurs also lost their privileged links with the state, as well as their military commissions.

Yet Gov. James Murray and his successor, Guy Carleton, entertained ambitions for this group, whom Carleton mistakenly viewed as having great influence with the habitants. Recognizing that the "nobles" had been deprived of "their honours, their privileges, their revenues and their laws," he recommended that the British show them sympathy in order to ensure their loyalty. Carleton's views attracted considerable support in London, and by 1771 additional royal instructions had been issued to ensure the perpetuation of the seigneurial system.

175

James Murray found policy pertaining to the Roman Catholic church more difficult to apply. No attempts were made to close the churches; both the articles of capitulation and the Treaty of Paris granted freedom of worship, though only "as far as the laws of Great Britain permit." (Although there was little persecution of Roman Catholics in England after 1689, anti-Catholic legislation remained in force until the early nineteenth century).

During the war Murray was strongly antipathetic to the Catholic church and identified the clergy as "the source of all the mischiefs which have befallen the poor Canadians." He obviously entertained considerable doubts about the church's loyalty. Many priests, particularly members of male religious orders such as the Jesuits and the Sulpicians, were French-born and were thus to be looked upon with suspicion. Moreover, London had instructed Murray to take measures to ensure that the *Canadiens* "may by degrees be induced to embrace the Protestant religion, and their children be brought up in the principles of it."

In time, however, Murray came to manifest a pragmatic attitude toward the Catholic church. He realized that, even with all the support of the colonial administration, the handful of Protestants in the conquered colony had no chance of converting the *Canadiens*. He also judged that the church enjoyed considerable influence with the habitants. By avoiding any open oppression of Roman Catholics and indeed rewarding loyal priests, the British administration, Murray reasoned, might even be able to rally the church's support. In the meantime, Murray and his officials kept a watchful eye on church activities and administration.

PRECARIOUS STATE OF THE CHURCH

The period immediately after the Conquest was a trying one for the church. Numbering close to 200 at the time of the Conquest, the Catholic clergy quickly declined, through deaths and departures to France, to fewer than 140 by 1762. Male religious orders were forbidden to recruit. The British army was quartered at the Jesuit property at Quebec, and the fate of the wealthy Sulpician community in Montreal was in doubt.

The female orders, also with about two hundred members in 1760, enjoyed greater tolerance, perhaps because most of the nuns had been born in Canada and also because the authorities appreciated the usefulness of their hospital work and other kinds of social assistance. In fact, the nuns were obliged to give priority to caring for wounded soldiers, though they were explicitly warned to leave their patients' souls alone. Nevertheless, the religious community of the Hôpital Général de Québec verged on bankruptcy and that of the Hôtel-Dieu de Montréal envisaged returning to France. Anxious to consolidate good relations with the British, the Ursulines at Quebec elected as their superior Esther Wheelright, an American captive who had been rebaptized Marie-Joseph and had become an Ursuline nun forty-five years earlier.

The most delicate problem that had to be solved was the replacement of Bishop Pontbriand, who died in 1760. Murray's instructions from London indicated that the "Popish hierarchy" should not be re-established. But after the New Englanders failed to come north, the governor needed someone with whom he could deal as the leader of French Canadian society. For the aristocratic Murray, it was quite natural that such a leader should come from the church. He was thus ready, in spite of London's directives to the contrary, to accept a "superintendent of the Romish religion." But when the Quebec cathedral chapter chose Étienne Montgolfier, superior of the Sulpicians, as candidate for bishop, Murray balked and made known his preference for Jean-Olivier Briand, vicar general of the diocese of Quebec, who had shown great respect for British authority. The chapter capitulated, and nominated Briand for the position instead.

With Murray's support and some rule-bending, the nominee for bishop sailed for London to lobby the British government for its approval of the post. After obtaining London's agreement, Briand went to France where Rome, conveniently overlooking the government meddling that had gone into his selection, named him bishop. In June 1766, six years after Pontbriand's death, the Canadian church at last had a new leader.

With a bishop installed, priests could now be ordained, though training them was another matter. Ecclesiastical discipline could also be more easily maintained; indeed, a firmer hand at the helm was necessary. Too

176

many priests had committed serious offences against discipline, and other petty breaches of the rules were even more common. Nor were the faithful above reproach, at least in the critical eyes of their clergy. Bishop Briand ceaselessly bemoaned wayward members of his flock who "confessed Christianity with their mouths while contradicting it by their conduct." Exasperated, he sometimes wondered if he would not have been happier ministering to a single parish.

Co-operation with the British brought the church obvious benefits. Bishop Briand even obtained an annuity from the governor for his "good behaviour." But the British exacted a high price for their concessions. After all, the governor had effectively chosen the bishop, and this represented a significant limitation of ecclesiastical authority. When, after eight years, Briand was finally permitted to name a coadjutor with the right to succeed him as bishop of Quebec, Carleton forced him to choose a man five years his senior who would attempt to run the diocese from the seclusion of his presbytery on the Île d'Orléans. When Briand named priests to *cures*, he sought Murray's approval. When he solicited the governor's approval to recruit foreign priests, Murray refused.

The governor used the church as a means of communicating with the general population. Pastoral messages in support of the state were forthcoming when Murray desired them. Priests made government announcements from the pulpits and on the church steps. Briand even offered prayers for King George III. To his critics, who thought him too obliging, he replied that the British "are our rulers and we owe to them what we used to owe to the French." Briand was trying to gain time until the situation of the church improved.

THE COMMERCIAL ELITES

Several hundred merchants involved in a wide variety of commercial pursuits, including the fur trade, vied for influence in Quebec. Many of these merchants were French-speaking. Some, however, were English-speaking, having arrived after the Conquest from Britain or the American colonies. This group quickly carved out for itself an important place in the local economy.

The respective fates of the two groups have long nourished historical controversy. On one side, historian Hilda Neatby maintains that French-speaking merchants had no difficulty in adjusting to British rule; they could get the credit they needed and, far from being worse off after the Conquest, participated in the general prosperity. On the other side, Michel Brunet sees the Conquest as establishing a new set of rules that placed the French at a decided disadvantage. For his part, Fernand Ouellet admits that the French merchants suffered a relative decline; indeed, research shows that British investments in the fur trade as well as in other sectors appear to have surpassed French investments by the early 1770s. But

Ouellet asserts that the French merchants themselves were much to blame for their own fate: they were too individualistic to build up the powerful associations that would have enabled them to remain competitive, and they were too conservative in their investments.

The difficulty of trade relations with France forced Canadian merchants to try to adapt to the new conditions. A few continued to import French merchandise to be sold in Canada. Others, like François Baby, successfully made arrangements to shift their commercial relations from France to England. But most French-speaking merchants possessed only meagre financial resources with which to undertake the post-Conquest struggle for control of the fur trade, the most dynamic sector of the economy. Moreover, the army usually chose British or American traders to supply its posts.

178 British merchants appeared to benefit from less obvious types of favouritism as well. When shipping space was scarce, for example, they were able to get their shipments aboard government vessels. They also appeared more at ease in lobbying governments, both in Quebec and in London. The English merchants were accustomed to the competitiveness that accompanied British trade policy, while in New France trade had been well ordered and state regulated. Still, the French did enjoy one advantage: the Great Lakes Indians preferred doing business with French families, such as the Cadots (Cadottes), St. Germains, and Grignons, who had intermarried with them, and had *métis* families.

Conflict between the Merchants and the Governor

Although English-speaking merchants benefited from the new context, they did not necessarily enjoy the favour of the aristocratic colonial governors. The arrogant Murray, for example, clearly preferred gentlemen such as the French Canadian seigneurs (with whom he could converse in excellent French) to English tradesmen, whom he considered "the most cruel, ignorant, rapacious fanatics who ever existed."

In return, the English-speaking merchants viewed Murray as a despot. They condemned him for the strict controls he imposed on the fur trade, conveniently ignoring the fact that British policy severely limited the governor's options. They denounced him for being too conciliatory to the colony's French-speaking Roman Catholic population, who happened to constitute more than 95 percent of the total, and they agitated for an assembly in which no Catholic would be allowed to sit. Finally, they petitioned the king for Murray's recall. Murray's troubles were compounded by the fact that, in the colony, authority was divided between himself, as civilian governor, and Ralph Burton, as military commander. Friction between the two, who formerly were warm friends, rapidly intensified. Murray sailed for England in June 1766, and, even though he successfully defended himself against the accusations of the British merchants and officially remained governor until 1768, he never returned to Quebec.

Murray's successor, Sir Guy Carleton, appeared to want to do a better job of redressing the merchants' grievances. He endorsed Britain's decision to lift the constraints imposed on the fur traders and to leave control of trade relations with the Indians to the colonial governments. Canadian merchants were pleased but began to complain increasingly of competition from wealthier traders from New York and Pennsylvania. Moreover, in responding to the merchants' complaints concerning Quebec's laws, taxes, and system of justice, Carleton could not overlook the necessity of ensuring the loyalty of the overwhelming majority of the population who, he prophesied, would people this country "to the end of time," barring some unforeseen catastrophe. Before long, the merchants vigorously censured his moderate policies and his sympathy for the seigneurs and higher clergy.

179

The Quebec Act

From the late 1760s, pressures in North America began to force London to consider changes in its administration of Quebec. Within the colony itself a tiny but vocal minority, mostly merchants, urged England to grant Quebec the liberties it had given the Thirteen Colonies. This group was convinced that appointed officials from London, many of them army officers, were incapable of recognizing that the commercial class constituted the very backbone of the colony and thus merited special consideration. French merchants supported some of their grievances, particularly in opposition to the seigneurs' own pretentions, but language and religion constituted a barrier to common action. While English-speaking merchants demanded that British commercial law apply to the colony, the *Canadiens* agitated in favour of a return to "our customs and usages." The English felt that, by right of Conquest only Protestants should occupy administrative positions in the colony. For the *Canadiens*, only equality between the king's old—that is, British—subjects and his new, French-speaking Roman Catholic subjects, was acceptable.

THE QUEST FOR SECURITY

For Britain, security in North America was paramount. The Quebec Act of 1774, which spelled out Britain's new policy, extended Quebec's frontiers into the Ohio region. The British hoped by this means to put an end to the virtual anarchy and ferocious competition among traders that plagued the territory. Quebec's economy depended far more on furs than did New York's, and giving the West to Quebec would thus preserve the economic balance. London also viewed annexation of the Ohio region to Quebec as a wise decision because the St. Lawrence traders and merchants had generally maintained good relations with the Indians there and, perhaps more important, they appeared to be the only traders capable of successfully competing with the original French traders who worked along the Mississippi.

Not surprisingly, the extension of Quebec's boundaries embittered the Americans (see page 186). They viewed it as a measure that effectively continued to seal off the West, which had been officially closed since the Proclamation of 1763. They also bitterly resented the recognition that the Quebec Act bestowed on the colony's despised "papists" by conceding "the free exercise of the religion of the Church of Rome" and by firmly recognizing the right of the Catholic church to collect tithes. The "tyrannical" act figured prominently among the grievances of the Americans when they launched their rebellion in April 1775.

The Quebec Act also put into law the significant concessions that Governors Murray and Carleton had already made to the seigneurs. Generally speaking, it retained the application of English criminal law but reintroduced French civil law with regard to property. This was an attempt to resolve the uneasy co-existence of two completely different legal systems.

The return of French civil law enraged the merchants but pleased the seigneurs. Britain now legally confirmed the existence of the seigneurial system and gave it a much-needed boost through the restoration of seigneurial dues.

Finally, this new constitution for Quebec substantially modified the structures of government in the province. It established an appointive Legislative Council that could make laws with the governor's consent. The governor could suspend or remove councillors. Significantly, these councillors could be Roman Catholics, since the act introduced a special oath that eliminated the need for public office holders to declare their acceptance of royal supremacy over the church or to deny belief in the central Roman Catholic doctrine of transubstantiation. Roman Catholics in Great Britain were not granted such political freedom until the late 1820s.

While pleased with the colony's new boundaries, the English merchants were furious that Parliament had denied them the elective assembly for which they had so often petitioned. The only plan put forth during the debate preceding the Quebec Act had been for an exclusively Protestant body. The British Parliament refused to place the colonial government in the hands of a few hundred English merchants, nor was it willing to countenance the establishment of a representative assembly that would be dominated by French-speaking Roman Catholics whose race and religion made them quite untrustworthy in the eyes of British Protestants.

The higher clergy and seigneurs may well have looked upon the Quebec Act as a veritable charter of French Canadian rights, but for the habitants the legal recognition given to the tithe and seigneurial dues was probably disappointing. Nevertheless, restoration of their system of colonization, which enabled the habitants to obtain land without having to purchase it, no doubt pleased them.

SECRET INSTRUCTIONS

The Quebec Act cannot be fully appreciated without considering the secret instructions that accompanied it and in many ways contradicted it. The instructions required the governor to weigh the possibility of law reform that would gradually introduce English civil law. They also explicitly detailed plans to subordinate the church to strict state control. Appeals to any "foreign ecclesiastical jurisdiction"—that is, to the pope—were forbidden. Protestant ministers could at some future date collect tithes from Roman Catholics. Clergy were to be permitted to marry. The government was to oversee the bishop's performance of all his official functions and to regulate seminaries. The religious orders were to disappear, with the Jesuits being given an extra push through the outright suppression of the order and the confiscation by the state of all its holdings. When the British had carried out all of these initiatives, the church itself would gradually wither away. That, at least, was the hope of the authors of the secret instructions.

181

Bishop Briand appears to have learned of these proposals, and they must have horrified him. Had all his efforts to improve the lot of the church in the years since the Conquest and to establish it as the leading French Canadian institution been to no avail? Were the British now going to push for the full Protestantization of the colony?

Carleton reassured Briand that he disapproved of the instructions and intended to ignore them. Understandably, Carleton's major preoccupation was with the security of the colony he governed. His conservative and aristocratic bias led him to favour the clergy and the large landowners, who would support the government if the Americans invaded. Carleton's preferences, however, caused him to exaggerate the influence of these elites on the general population. But did he have an alternative? Had he chosen to promote the objectives of the largely anti-French and anti-Roman Catholic English merchants and thus deliberately attempted to undermine the colony's traditional social institutions, would he have had any greater success with the rather independent-minded habitants?

Fifteen years after the Conquest, official British policy toward the new colony of Quebec was modified for a second time. Publicly, Britain gave the appearance of yielding to French and Catholic desires. George III declared that the act would have "the best effects in quieting the minds and promoting the happiness of my Canadian subjects." The French could now play at least a minority role in the administration of the province. The Quebec Act also showed that the British believed the Roman Catholic church was powerful and held considerable sway over the *Canadiens*. There was no quick way in which to Anglicize and Protestantize a colony that had attracted but a few hundred English-speaking Protestant immigrants, largely merchants. Not that the British rejected assimilation as their ultimate aim; it was simply not a realistic policy in 1774. A year later, with the outbreak of revolution to the south, it was even less feasible. Eventually, with the arrival of thousands of Loyalists who wished to cast their lot with Britain, the hopes of the assimilationists would revive. But for the moment, Quebec's population remained overwhelmingly French-speaking and Roman Catholic.

NOTES

[1] Pierre Tousignant,"The Integration of the Province of Quebec into the British Empire, 1763–91. Part I: From the Royal Proclamation to the Quebec Act," *Dictionary of Canadian Biography*, vol. 4, (Toronto, 1980), xxxii–xlix.
[2] A.L. Burt, *The Old Province of Quebec*, vol. 1 (Toronto, 1968; first published 1933), 28.

Related Readings

R. Douglas Francis and Donald B. Smith, *Readings in Canadian History: Pre-Confederation*, 3d ed. (Toronto, 1990) contains two important articles on this topic: S. Dale Standen, "The Debate on the Social and Economic Consequences of the Conquest: A Summary," 246–55, and José Igartua, "A Change in Climate: The Conquest and the *Marchands* of Montreal," 255–72.

BIBLIOGRAPHY

Although more than half a century old, A.L. Burt, *The Old Province of Quebec* (Toronto 1933; reprinted 1968) is the standard general work for the post-Conquest decades. Hilda Neatby added new research in her work *Quebec: The Revolutionary Age, 1760–1791* (Toronto, 1966). See also Pierre Tousignant's useful essay, "The Integration of the Province of Quebec into the British Empire, 1763–91. Part I: From the Royal Proclamation to the Quebec Act," *Dictionary of Canadian Biography*, vol. 4, *1771–1800*, xxxii–xlix.

Economic aspects of the period are reviewed in Fernand Ouellet, *Economic and Social History of Quebec, 1760–1850* (Toronto, 1980). Several essays on the same topics are included in his *Economy, Class and Nation in Quebec: Interpretative Essays*, edited and translated by Jacques A. Barbier (Mississauga, Ont., 1991). Important surveys of life in Quebec at this time include Allan Greer, *Peasant, Lord, and Merchant: Rural Society in Three*

Quebec Parishes, 1740–1840 (Toronto, 1985), and David T. Ruddel, *Quebec City, 1765–1832: The Evolution of a Colonial Town* (Ottawa, 1987).

On the impact of the Conquest, see Michel Brunet, *La présence anglaise et les Canadiens: études sur l'histoire et la pensée des deux Canadas* (Montréal, 1964), and his brief Canadian Historical Association booklet, *French Canada in the Early Decades of British Rule* (Ottawa, 1962); Cameron Nish, ed., *The French Canadians, 1859–1766: Conquered? Half-conquered? Liberated?* (Toronto, 1966); Dale Miquelon, ed., *Society and Conquest: The Debate on the Bourgeoisie and Social Change in French Canada, 1700–1850* (Toronto, 1977). The fate of French-speaking merchants is examined in José Igartua, "The Merchants of Montreal at the Conquest: A Socio-Economic Profile," *Histoire sociale / Social History* 8 (1973): 275–93, and in his article "A Change in Climate," given in the preceding Related Readings section. For recent examinations of the historiography of the Conquest, consult Claude Couture, "La Conquête de 1760 et le problème de la transition au capitalisme," *Revue d'histoire de l'Amérique française* 39 (1985/86): 369–89, and S. Dale Standen, "The Debate on Social and Economic Consequences of the Conquest: A Summary," in *Proceedings of the Tenth Meeting of the French Colonial Historical Society, 1984,* edited by Philip P. Boucher (Lanham, Md., 1985), 179–94. Ronald Rudin provides a short review of Quebec's embryonic English-speaking community in *The Forgotten Quebecers: A History of English-Speaking Quebec, 1759–1980* (Quebec, 1985). Finally, the major figures of these years all have biographies in various volumes of the *Dictionary of Canadian Biography,* an essential tool for this and other periods. For important maps of Quebec in this period, see R. Cole Harris, ed., *Historical Atlas of Canada,* vol. 1, *From the Beginning to 1800* (Toronto, 1987).

The following books and articles provide a good introduction to the Native history of the period: Francis Jennings, *Empire of Fortune: Crowns, Colonies and Tribes in the Seven Years War in America* (New York, 1988); Howard H. Peckham, *Pontiac and the Indian Uprising* (Chicago, 1971; first published 1947); Leroy V. Eid, "The Neglected Side of American Indian War in the Northeast," *Military Review* 61, 2 (1981): 9–21; W.J. Eccles, "Sovereignty-Association, 1500–1783," in his *Essays on New France* (Toronto, 1987), 156–81; Jacqueline Peterson, "Many Roads to Red River: Métis Genesis in the Great Lakes Region, 1680–1815," in *The New Peoples: Being and Becoming Métis in North America,* edited by Jacqueline Peterson and Jennifer S.H. Brown (Winnipeg, 1985), 37–71. Specific developments in the Province of Quebec are mentioned in Daniel Francis, *A History of the Native Peoples of Québec, 1760–1867* (Ottawa, 1983). Denys Dêlage's important article on the Iroquois communities in the St. Lawrence Valley reviews their history from the late seventeenth to late eighteenth century: "Les Iroquois chrétiens des 'réductions,' 1677–1770," *Recherches amérindiennes au Québec,* 21, 1–2 (1991): 59–70; 21, 3 (1991): 39–50.

183

The Impact of the American Revolution on Quebec, 1774–1791

184   The impact of the American Revolution on Quebec was virtually as great as that of the British Conquest. In the aftermath of the Conquest, the British failed in their attempts to attract English speakers to the colony. In contrast, the American Revolution led to the arrival of a sizable English-speaking population. The American victory forced those colonists who wanted to live under the British flag or who had supported Britain during the revolution to move to Nova Scotia and Quebec. In Quebec's case, the arrival of between twelve thousand and fifteen thousand Loyalists gave the province a significant English-speaking minority. This peaceful invasion set the stage for the heightened ethnic tensions that followed.

As for the Indians, the Six Nations Confederacy council declared its neutrality in what it perceived as a "family feud" between the British and their American offspring. Later on, however, the Indians could not avoid being drawn into the struggle. Most tribes of the confederacy living south of Lake Ontario favoured the British, and thus at the war's end had to migrate north as "Loyalists." Other tribes inhabiting the western portion of the colony below the Great Lakes found themselves living on American soil. For them, the American victory opened their lands up to settlement and signified the collapse of the Indian reserve policy, spelled out in the Proclamation of 1763 and strengthened by the Quebec Act of 1774. In the intensifying confrontation between Indians and settlers, the Indians could only momentarily resist the American advance; eventually, they had to move farther west or north.

The French Canadians and the American Invasion

From the early 1770s American radical propaganda denouncing British tyranny, lauding elective institutions, and proclaiming the people's rights and liberties circulated widely in Quebec. American agents roamed the countryside, appealing to the French Canadians to choose between making the rest of North America their "unalterable friends" or their "inveterate enemies." French-born expatriate Fleury Mesplet, sent to Quebec by Benjamin Franklin, set about printing and distributing pamphlets on liberty. He took up residence in Montreal, where, except during the years he spent in prison, the founder of *The Gazette* defended democratic ideals, first American, and then, after 1789, French.

The Continental Congress in Philadelphia decided early in the revolutionary war to invade Canada in order to prevent the British from concentrating their forces there and then sweeping down into the colonies. In September 1775 General George Washington's armies advanced into Quebec by way of Lake Champlain and Maine, and the French Canadians were compelled to choose sides. Both the clergy and the seigneurs, who were supporters of a traditional order that the American revolutionaries clearly threatened, urged the habitants to support the British cause and, indeed, to enlist. They had strikingly little success, however. When Gov. Guy Carleton proclaimed martial law and summoned the militia, the result was strong resistance and even mob violence. The experience embittered Carleton, who had written scarcely a few months earlier that the French Canadians were rejoicing over the Quebec Act and that "a Canadian regiment would complete their happiness."

185

CARLETON'S ROLE

After abandoning Montreal to the Americans in late November 1775, Carleton fled to Quebec, narrowly escaping the advancing American forces. He was not optimistic about Quebec's possibilities of successfully holding off the besiegers. As he put it: "We have so many enemies within, and foolish people, dupes to those traitors (i.e., the American rebels) . . . [that] I think our fate extremely doubtful, to say nothing worse."

The Americans, for their part, were confident of success. General Richard Montgomery boasted that he would eat Christmas dinner in Quebec City or in hell. In fact, he ate it in neither place. The assault came on New Year's Eve, and Montgomery was killed while attempting to scale the walls of the city.

In London the British government made preparations for an expedition to relieve Quebec. George III, whose mental instability was not yet such as to prevent him from appreciating the course of events, declared that "when such acts of vigour are shown by the rebellious Americans, we must show that the English lion when aroused has not only his wonted resolution, but has added the swiftness of the racehorse." Five months later, in May 1776, a fleet of British ships sailed up the St. Lawrence, and the ill-equipped and demoralized Americans hastily departed.

The Old Province of Quebec, 1763–1791.

Several British politicians demanded Guy Carleton's recall for not preventing the American retreat up the Richelieu and for not retaking the important fortress of Ticonderoga on Lake Champlain in preparation for the invasion of the Hudson River valley. Historian A.L. Burt also believed that the governor's inaction "ruined the campaign of 1776 and possibly altered the outcome of the war."[1] Actually, Carleton did try to march after the Americans but his troops, after weeks spent on crowded transport ships, needed frequent rest. Moreover, they appear to have consumed too many fresh vegetables and were plagued by an outbreak of the "flux." The British also lacked supplies, again through no fault of Carleton's.

According to historian R.A. Bowler, Carleton may have been overprudent, but he does not seem to have made strategical errors, and he should certainly not receive all the blame for the failures of the campaign.[2]

In 1777 the British conceived a plan to crush the revolt by striking down from Quebec to New York City, thus cutting the rebellious colonies in two. These hopes were dashed when a numerically superior American force surrounded and defeated the British at Saratoga, north of Albany. Thereafter, the British launched no more large-scale expeditions southward from the St. Lawrence.

The alliance of France with the American colonies in February 1778 changed the face of the war. A secret clause of the arrangement stipulated, however, that France should not invade Canada or Acadia; the Americans wanted no restoration of New France to France. Though Louis XVI wanted to weaken British power by assisting the Thirteen Colonies in gaining their independence, he did not favour an American conquest of Canada. Indeed, he hoped that a British Canada, by posing a continual threat to the Americans, would ensure the latter's dependence on France. Clearly, neither France nor the United States wished the other to possess Canada.

187

AMBIVALENCE OF THE HABITANTS

During the American expedition into Canada, many habitants seemed, if not to have welcomed the invaders, at least to have given them support. These folk may have been swept up by the Americans' heady notions of liberty and equality; probably they listened more readily to the Americans' denunciations of tithes and seigneurial rents, both firmly established by the Quebec Act. But linguistically and religiously, the invaders were akin to the conquerors, not the conquered, and there was little love lost for the *Bostonnais*. Like the Indians, the habitants felt little interest in this struggle, and most preferred to keep their neutrality as long as possible. When American fortunes improved and American soldiers were willing to pay good prices in coin for supplies, the habitants sympathized with them. But when the invaders failed to take Quebec and the long winter siege dragged on, and—even worse—when they began to pay for their provisions with paper money or simply not at all, the liberators' popularity fell precipitously.

With the retreat of the Americans, many French Canadians who had given them aid had to submit to British exactions and, in some cases, retribution. Throughout the war, military *corvées*, previously levied under the French regime, were still common, with the habitants being called on to furnish and transport materials for various construction works. They were not paid for their labour unless they were artisans. The correspondence of Frederick Haldimand, appointed governor of Quebec in 1777, shows that desertions from the military *corvées* were frequent and that, to avoid paying for the labour, the governor imposed fines and prison sentences on recalcitrant workers.

The church, too, attempted to reassert its authority. Bishop Briand worked hard to secure the repentance of those who had sided with the Americans. "I stand firm," he wrote in September 1776. "The rebel must retract publicly before being admitted to the sacraments, even at the hour of death." A hard core of intractable habitants remained. One, asked on his deathbed to recant, was reported to have spat back at the priest, "You sound like an Englishman." Having uttered these words, he turned his back and died.

Those habitants left in peace by troops on both sides, and able to cultivate their farms, benefited from a tripling of agricultural prices. In part, speculators caused this inflation by going out into the countryside and buying up crops. In an effort to control prices, the government intervened, just as it had in earlier days, by prohibiting exports and hoarding. But due to the determination of the grain speculators, the government's actions proved to be generally ineffective.

188

The rise in prices encouraged the habitants to clear and sow new land in order to increase their production of wheat and other farm products. Prosperity came to the countryside, but the towns suffered greatly as prices for flour and other basic necessities soared. Harvests were generally abundant but, in view of war needs, most of the crops were sold on the local market. Thus, grain exports to both the West Indies and Britain fell off considerably.

The American Revolution and the Indians

If the *Canadiens* were threatened and cajoled by both sides in the struggle, so were the Indians, particularly the Six Nations. The cost of their involvement in the conflict was heavy: the Iroquois League, which was several hundred years old, collapsed, and the Mohawks lost their lands along the Mohawk River and elsewhere. Britain's defeat forced two thousand Indians to abandon their homelands and migrate to the area that would become Upper Canada.

After the defeat of Pontiac, the British cultivated good relations with the Indians to ensure their military assistance. William Johnson, a large landowner in the Mohawk Valley who spoke Mohawk and served as the northern superintendent of Indian affairs, was instrumental in carrying out this policy. Johnson, whose companion was Molly Brant, the sister of Six Nations war chief Joseph Brant, played an important role in the lengthy negotiations to define a boundary for the Indian territory that took place after the Proclamation of 1763 and Pontiac's resistance. After his death in 1774, his successor and nephew, Guy Johnson, argued that the annexation of Indian territory to the province of Quebec (by the Quebec Act) showed the British government's solicitude for its Indian subjects and its desire to protect their territory from white settlement.

In 1775 the British instructed Guy Johnson to pressure the Iroquois to "take up the hatchet against His Majesty's rebellious subjects." Johnson failed, however, to neutralize American efforts to enlist the aid of the Oneidas and Tuscaroras, among whom an American Congregationalist minister had made converts. Johnson then came to Montreal and attempted to build up support for the British cause among the several thousand Iroquois living at Caughnawaga (Kahnawake), southwest of Montreal; Kanesatake (Oka), about fifty kilometres west of Montreal; and St. Regis (Akwesasne), a settlement on the St. Lawrence River about a hundred kilometres west of Montreal.

Thanks largely to the efforts of Joseph Brant, the Mohawks and some Senecas supported the British. The Onondagas and the Cayugas, though, declared their neutrality, while many Oneidas and Tuscaroras, as well as some of the Indians in the Montreal area, showed a preference for the Americans.

In 1779, however, American troops under Gen. John Sullivan invaded the Six Nations territory, indiscriminately punishing the Iroquois by burning crops and destroying villages. These attacks on the hitherto neutral Onondagas and Cayugas brought them over to the British side. One thousand Iroquois warriors retaliated by burning and pillaging American farms throughout the immense territory between the Ohio and Mohawk rivers.

By 1782, with the British on the verge of final defeat, Frederick Haldimand, the governor of Quebec, instructed commanders to limit themselves to purely defensive actions. The Indians, however, were not prepared to capitulate and only with difficulty did Haldimand's orders prevail.

THE INDIANS AND THE RETURN OF PEACE

Peace came, first in preliminary fashion at the end of 1782 and then finally in September 1783 with the Treaty of Paris. The Indians were not mentioned in the treaty, and the British recognized as American the area south of the Great Lakes. The Iroquois, though, had never acknowledged direct British sovereignty over their territory or the Crown's right to dispose of it. Outraged, Brant and the Indians were described as being prepared to "defend their own just rights or perish in the attempt . . . they would die like men, which they thought preferable to misery and distress if deprived of their hunting grounds." John Johnson (William's son), who had just replaced his cousin Guy as Indian superintendent, went with much trepidation to Niagara to negotiate with Brant. For his part, Governor Haldimand wanted to mollify the Iroquois and the Great Lakes Indians in order to prevent them from taking revenge on the British, whom

189

they now saw as their betrayers. The governor therefore urged the British to delay the surrender of the western posts of Oswego, Niagara, Detroit, and Michilimackinac, which were now on American territory (see Chapter 11).

Indian attempts to convince the Americans to recognize the boundary of the Proclamation of 1763 (and as later extended in the Treaty of Fort Stanwix in 1768) proved fruitless because the Americans intended to open the eastern part of the Indian territory to white settlement. In fact, hundreds of settlers had already crossed the former boundary line. The Indians thus had little choice but to cede extensive lands to the states of New York and Pennsylvania.

A disheartened Joseph Brant, backed by John Johnson, prevailed upon Haldimand to grant new lands to the Iroquois in the area north of Lakes Ontario and Erie. In 1783–84 the Indian Department purchased vast tracts of land from the Mississaugas, as the British called the Ojibwas on the north shore of Lake Ontario. It gave part of this territory (more than three hundred thousand hectares along the Grand River valley) to the Six Nations "to enjoy forever." Joseph Brant personally received land at what is now Burlington, as well as a house and a military commission. His sister Molly was also given a house, and her daughters married English military men and officials.

Loyalist Immigration

During and after the revolution, thousands of Loyalists, bitterly denounced as un-American by the victorious revolutionaries, fled northward across the border. Haldimand was overwhelmed and, at least with regard to tardy arrivals, suspected that they were more often land-hungry immigrants than genuine Loyalists. Many came to Quebec from upper New York and New England. They would immediately have settled in the area that was to become the Eastern Townships had not Haldimand, unsure of the location of the international border and perhaps fearing to settle an English-speaking population along it, forbidden them to do so. (The ban was lifted only in 1791.)

Nor did Haldimand wish the Loyalists to settle on the seigneurial lands along the St. Lawrence River where, he feared, conflicts with the French might erupt. He preferred that they move on to Nova Scotia, or that they migrate to the western portion of the colony that was to become Upper Canada in 1791. The Crown bore the costs of transporting the Loyalists and, after making the necessary agreements with the Mississaugas, assisted them in establishing their own farms (see Chapter 11).

The arrival of the Loyalists was encouraging for those British administrators who wanted to make Quebec into an English-speaking colony. For the first time since the Conquest, a significant contingent of English-speaking immigrants settled in the province. Quebec's population of British origin increased to at least 10 percent of the total non-Native population, estimated at about 160 000 in 1790.

Guy Carleton, now Lord Dorchester, having changed his mind about the *Canadiens*, showed a much more English outlook during his second tour of duty as governor of Quebec from 1786 to 1796. He had been greatly disappointed by the habitants' failure to rally to the British cause and was convinced that they had not been governed with a sufficiently firm hand. He took as his principal adviser William Smith, a Loyalist from New York whom he named chief justice. Smith looked forward to the day when the French would be assimilated by waves of English-speaking settlers from the United States.

Life of the Habitants

The departure of the Americans and the return of peace did not guarantee prosperity for the habitants. Agriculture, of course, depended largely on the weather and yields were highly uncertain. After a prosperous period in the mid-1770s came several very lean years. Drought ruined the crop in 1779 and the harvests of the early 1780s were also poor, spoiled by late springs or early autumn frosts. Only in the mid-1780s did the situation improve, and then not for long. In 1788, rust or smut resulted in a serious drop in production, and the large surplus of 1787 had already been shipped away by the time the extent of the damage was realized. The results were catastrophic. In the wake of the shortage, prices more than doubled and both the urban and the rural poor suffered. Many died from famine, particularly in the Montreal area. Not until 1791 did harvests finally climb back to prewar levels.

Increased production after 1791 necessitated larger markets, both at home and abroad. Fortunately for the colonial economy, the accelerating pace of industrialization, urbanization, and population growth in Britain meant that that nation would buy virtually all surplus grain available in Canada. In the aftermath of the American Revolution and the Napoleonic Wars in Europe, Canada's economy became ever more tightly integrated into the imperial economic system.

Even in relatively prosperous times, illness haunted the habitants. On several occasions they fell victim to smallpox, typhoid fever, and other diseases transmitted through the water supply. In the disastrous epidemic of 1784 the death rate climbed to an extremely high 45 per 1000. Medical practitioners in the colony (most of them without diplomas) numbered but a few dozen in the late eighteenth century. The majority were English speaking and lived in towns, at a time when 80 percent of the population

National Gallery of Canada, Ottawa.

Thomas Davies (ca. 1737–1812), an English military artist, completed this painting of Château-Richer on the Côte de Beaupré, east of Quebec City in 1787. It offers an excellent view of a mature rural landscape along the St. Lawrence in the eighteenth century. The wooden enclosures shown in the river and the tidal marshes are traps for eels.

was rural. Moreover, the number of inhabitants per doctor was rising sharply and the colony had no school of medicine to train new doctors. The profession lacked prestige (except perhaps for medical officers in the army) and doctors seem to have had difficulty finding paying clients: they often ran notices in the newspapers requesting payment. In rural areas, folk medicines obtained from the Amerindians during the French regime remained in use.

MERCHANTS AND COMMERCE

Most of Quebec's inhabitants survived by cultivating the land, but the fur trade was the province's principal source of commercial wealth. The grain trade fluctuated wildly, sales of fish products declined, and wood exports were just beginning to enter a period of dramatic expansion. In the late 1780s, however, furs still represented more than half of total exports— even though the fur trade was undergoing radical changes at the time. Government regulations in wartime, such as the preference accorded military cargoes on transport ships, had provoked numerous complaints from traders. With the American Revolution, Albany obviously ceased to be a centre for fur exports to Britain, a development that boosted the fortunes of the Montreal traders. But in 1794, when the British finally relinquished the Ohio country to the Americans, the Montreal merchants instantly lost an enormously productive region and now had to look to the west.

The most important development was that the industry became concentrated in the hands of fewer and fewer traders. The new barons of the North West Company, formed in the early 1780s, were almost all English speaking. The French, who tended to work alone or in small associations, were gradually being pushed out; by 1789 they supplied only 15 percent of the trade goods sent into Indian country. The surviving *Canadien* merchants could not pay the capital investment required for expeditions to the western posts. But *Canadiens* continued to provide most of the labour required in the trade.

At the same time, relations between the merchants and the colonial authorities went from bad to worse. The merchants' bitterness toward the Quebec Act intensified, and they petitioned London for its repeal. As noted earlier, they maintained that the province needed an elected assembly to defend their interests. As well, they demanded the granting of English commercial law, which would liberate them from French "custom and usage," as recognized in the Quebec Act. They sought recognition of legal rights, such as the right to trial by jury in civil cases, to protect them from the arbitrary authority exercised by the governor and appointed officials. The merchants also managed to arouse the ire of several public officials whom they personally attacked. Although the government did make some effort to redress their grievances, Haldimand in particular felt that most merchants were making their representations without considering the rest of society.

193

THE TRADITIONAL ELITES

In his relations with the merchants in the early 1780s, Governor Haldimand was simply treading the well-worn path of hostility already established by Murray and Carleton. All three were conservative, authoritarian, and generally unwilling to share power in the colony with any group. All three had the Legislative Council at their disposal, to which they appointed mostly government supporters, including some French-speaking seigneurs. The governors also had a few close advisers, such as the chief justice and the attorney general; many of them were inept and few had any sensitivity toward the colony's French-speaking majority.

Virtually the sole preoccupation of the governors in this troubled period was security. They treated the French seigneurial and clerical elites with a certain deference. They assumed that these elites controlled the *Canadiens*, and they favoured individuals they viewed as belonging to the upper ranks of society. All three governors were deeply suspicious of the ambitions of the colony's anglophone merchants and were thoroughly unimpressed by the latter's political pretensions.

SEIGNEURS

Historians have emphasized the governors' sympathies for the colony's traditional elites. The Quebec Act helped confirm the social and economic status of the seigneurs. Some, such as the military engineer Gaspard-Joseph Chaussegros de Léry, the military officer René-Amable Boucher de Boucherville, and the businessman François Baby, were named to the Legislative Council; several others received civil service or judicial appointments. When Carleton re-established the militia in 1777, seigneurs such as Baby, who had been loyal to Britain during the American invasion, regained their traditional military role.

The growth of Quebec's population and the increases in wheat production should have brought the seigneurs important economic benefits. The development of new lands and investments in roads and mills, however, required capital that most seigneurs did not possess. Seigneuries, therefore, began to pass into the hands of the British, to individuals such as Gabriel Christie, whose five properties assured his family material security with minimal risk. By 1784 more than one-quarter of the seigneuries, including the most lucrative, had British owners. The *censitaires* remained almost exclusively French, with English-speaking settlers preferring the freehold system of land tenure. Thus, despite the declining prestige of the seigneurs, the system itself appears to have served as a bulwark against assimilation.

The seigneurs belonging to Governor Carleton's councils often voted together as a sort of conservative French party, resisting plans for immigration and for the conversion of seigneurial grants to freehold tenure. When talk of enacting a new constitution that would introduce a popularly elected assembly increased in the late 1780s, seigneurs such as Baby and Boucher de Boucherville pleaded against setting up a body that would surely boost the fortunes of the anglophone merchants and thus endanger religion and property.

After the establishment of the Assembly, however, several seigneurs ran for office and, except for the merchants, they constituted the most numerous group in Lower Canada's first elected house. They also tended to speak of themselves as the representatives of the French Canadian nation, although French Canadian merchants hotly disputed this claim. Moreover, a slowly rising group of professionals, at first consisting of a few notaries and lawyers, more frequently challenged the seigneurs' attempts to assume leadership.

THE ROMAN CATHOLIC CHURCH

The church proved a much more complex problem for the British authorities. It was loyal to the Crown during the American Revolution, but the British tried to prevent it from becoming too strong and independent. Also, many of the strongly Anglican administrators of the colony scorned

"Romanism" and hoped that the French might eventually convert to Protestantism. While waiting for this transition, they certainly did not intend to support the institutions of the Roman Catholic church.

Ecclesiastical succession continued to pose a serious problem. Briand resigned in 1784 so that his assistant, coadjutor Louis-Philippe Mariauchau d'Esgly, then seventy-four years old, might become bishop and choose his own coadjutor before he died. D'Esgly picked the relatively youthful Jean-François Hubert, but Haldimand, then in England, was furious at not having been consulted. London then demanded that the old and senile Étienne Montgolfier be named in place of Hubert, but Montgolfier fortunately refused. Hubert was finally accepted and became bishop upon d'Esgly's death in 1788. Lord Dorchester then imposed as coadjutor the ambitious and worldly Charles-François Bailly de Messein, a strongly pro-British cleric whose relations with Hubert were often sorely strained.

The church confronted other equally serious problems, among them *195* the perennial question of clerical recruitment. Just after the Conquest, Quebec had three priests per thousand people. By 1788 this ratio had declined to only one per thousand; seventy-five parishes were without priests and the bishops seriously worried about the quality of parish religious life. The government opposed any attempts to relieve the shortage by bringing in priests from France, or even French-speaking priests from the Duchy of Savoy who were not of French nationality. Only after 1791 were some French priests, driven by the French Revolution to England, authorized to come to Canada.

Male orders such as the Jesuits and the Récollets were still prohibited from recruiting; together, the two orders accounted for only sixteen priests in 1790. Upon the death of the last Canadian Jesuit in 1800, the properties of that order were forfeited to the Crown. The Crown thus assumed title to the Jesuits' Indian mission lands at Kahnawake. As the Sulpician order remained intact, however, the British allowed it to keep its Indian mission at the Lake of Two Mountains, or Kanesatake (Oka).

Although female communities could continue to recruit, in practice they received few candidates because of their insistence on a dowry. The number of nuns in 1790—about 230—was scarcely higher than it had been in 1760. Church officials lamented the lack of discipline in the communities, complaining of nuns who were discourteous to their superiors, who maintained small business operations for their private needs, and who played cards too much.

British interference ensured the Canadianization of the clergy. Of sixty-four new priests appointed between 1784 and 1792, fifty-eight were born in Canada. The government did not persecute the Roman Catholic church in the usual sense of the term, but it did intervene constantly in church affairs in an effort to weaken and control the institution.

In the late eighteenth century, the church contributed greatly to Quebec's cultural heritage through the work of artists and sculptors hired to create religious art for churches. The Baillairgés, founders of a dynasty that occupied a prominent place in Quebec's art and architecture for five generations, executed the interior decoration of the reconstructed Notre-Dame cathedral in Quebec. Philippe Liébert, a painter and sculptor, devoted his considerable talents to church decoration in the Montreal region. Goldsmiths such as François Ranvoyzé showed imagination and versatility in the fabrication of hundreds of chalices and other religious objects.

Toward the Constitutional Act of 1791

196   While the church showed little interest in the colony's constitutional future, the merchants discussed it with increasing urgency. They wanted an assembly, preferably controlled by the province's tiny English-speaking minority. They saw themselves as responsible for economic growth and thus deserving of greater political power. Attorney General James Monk agreed that any assembly would have to overrepresent the English to avoid French domination. But Chief Justice William Smith felt that the English element had to be strengthened through immigration before representative government could be established.

Many French Canadian merchants and professionals also desired an assembly, since the French, as the majority, hoped to control this part of government. The merchants and professionals tried to persuade the habitants that an assembly would decide on the *corvées* and on militia laws—the implication being that a French-dominated legislative body would be unfavourable to both. But the seigneurs, who linked their interests and privileges to the maintenance of the status quo, warned that an assembly could be dangerous for the colony, for it might tax land. Moreover, the seigneurs were outraged by the prospect of their tenants becoming their political equals with the advent of elections.

Petitions and counter-petitions circulated. In reality, the great majority of the province's 150 000 "new subjects" (the *Canadiens*) probably had little understanding of, and even less interest in, the question. Their main preoccupation was simply in subsisting, an objective not easily attained in these often difficult years.

Although not thoroughly familiar with social conditions in Quebec, the imperial government had to arbitrate often-contradictory pressures and draw up the new constitution. William Grenville, Secretary of State for the colonies, drafted the Constitutional Act of 1791 that provided for the division of the province into two sections, Upper and Lower Canada, with the upper part possessing an English-speaking Loyalist majority. The reasons for the partition of Quebec were not economic or geographic, for the colony functioned as a single unit. Rather, Westminster's motivation was, as Grenville explained, to reduce "dissensions and animosities" among two "classes of men, differing in their prejudices, and perhaps in their interests."

Institutional Changes

The major new institution established in each of the Canadas was the elective assembly. Besides giving a voice to the population, this body could raise money through taxes for local expenditures, thus reducing the burden on the imperial treasury. At the same time, wary of what had happened in the American colonies, London moved to place the assembly under strong executive control that would apply restraint if the people's representatives got out of hand. A lieutenant governor was to be established in each province. He would appoint the members of the Legislative Council, the upper house. The Legislative Council's membership was intended eventually to be hereditary, like that of the British House of Lords. Thus, the "right men," that is, landowners, would be assured of a place in power. The Executive Council, also composed of appointed officials, would be the governor's personal cabinet. The governor enjoyed extensive veto powers and a measure of financial autonomy, thanks to the revenues from the Crown lands set aside by the Constitutional Act of 1791. (Other lands were reserved for the maintenance of a "Protestant clergy," intended to mean the Church of England.) Yet this remarkably equilibrated construction soon condemned Lower Canada's government to increasingly frequent and severe bouts of paralysis.

197

On account of property qualifications in England at this time, relatively few people there could vote in elections. Essentially the same qualifications applied in Lower Canada, but because of that colony's very different social structure, the great majority of male habitants obtained the right to vote. Still, suffrage was far from universal. Most urban labourers and domestics were disqualified because they neither owned property nor paid sufficient rent. The property qualification eliminated the great majority of women from the rolls, although only in 1834 did the Assembly of Lower Canada specifically disenfranchise women.

The electoral arrangements disappointed Lower Canada's English Protestants. They had petitioned so often for an assembly from which the French would be excluded, or at least in which there would be an English-speaking majority bolstered by further immigration. Montreal merchant Adam Lymburner lobbied in London for an arrangement in which the towns, where most of the English-speaking population lived, would get half the seats, even though the towns contained only about one-fifth of the total population. His avowed aim was to avoid putting the House in the "power of ignorant and obstinate men" who held "the absurd idea that it is the landholders' interest to oppress commerce." In fact, although the towns obtained only ten of the fifty seats, fully half of the candidates in the rural districts, in the first elections held in 1792, were also well-established merchants who could afford to travel.

With the Constitutional Act of 1791, Quebec obtained its third constitution in fewer than thirty years. The American Revolution and the arrival of thousands of Loyalists had made change imperative. Reactions to the new legislation varied widely. In Britain there was satisfaction that the new colony of Upper Canada would be free to grow under British law and British liberty, and that the French majority in Lower Canada, confined to the House of Assembly, could do little damage. Some, like William Pitt, even hoped that the French, seeing the British system at work in Upper Canada, would gradually adopt English laws and customs. In the meantime, no force would be required.

Certain Lower Canadian groups, such as the seigneurs, the professionals, and the merchants, thought that they could use the new institutions profitably. Most disappointed as a group were Lower Canada's ten thousand English. The Constitutional Act of 1791 led to their separation from the growing English-speaking population in the new colony of Upper Canada. Moreover, the English-speaking inhabitants of what now became Lower Canada obtained few of the reforms for which they had agitated and did not even succeed in getting the Quebec Act repealed. The only real compensation offered was the provision for the freehold system of land tenure in the area outside the seigneurial zone, in what became the Eastern Townships. Furthermore, the English were unsure of what to expect from the Assembly. The maintenance of a strong executive in British hands was but small consolation to the merchants. After all, the government had been in British hands since 1760, and yet the merchants were more often than not at loggerheads with the colonial administrators. Nevertheless, regardless of political changes, the English merchants' economic power was increasing. In 1791 they had reason to be optimistic about the future.

NOTES

[1]A.L. Burt, *The Old Province of Quebec*, vol. 1 (Toronto, 1968; first published 1933), 218.
[2]R. Arthur Bowler, "Sir Guy Carleton and the Campaign of 1776 in Canada," *Canadian Historical Review*, 55 (1974): 131–40.

Related Reading

As with Chapter 9, the following articles from R. Douglas Francis and
Donald B. Smith, *Readings in Canadian History: Pre-Confederation*; 3d ed.
(Toronto, 1990), will also be helpful for this topic: S. Dale Standen, "The
Debate on the Social and Economic Consequences of the Conquest: A
Summary," 246–55, and José Igartua, "A Change in Climate: The Conquest
and the *Marchands* of Montreal," 255–72.

BIBLIOGRAPHY

Hilda Neatby's synthesis, *Quebec: The Revolutionary Age* (Toronto, 1966),
reviews the political developments. Chapters 4 and 5 of Fernand Ouellet's
Social and Economic History of Quebec (Toronto, 1980) are also very useful.
On the American invasion, see Robert M. Hatch, *Thrust for Canada: The
American Attempt on Quebec in 1775–1776* (Boston, 1979); George A. Raw-
lyk, *Revolution Rejected, 1775–1776* (Scarborough, Ont., 1968); and George
F.G. Stanley, *Canada Invaded, 1775–1776* (Toronto, 1973). A critical exam-
ination of Carleton's wartime conduct may be found in R. Arthur Bowler,
"Sir Guy Carleton and the Campaign of 1776 in Canada," *Canadian Histori-
cal Review* 55 (1974): 131–40.

L.F.S. Upton, ed., *The United Empire Loyalists: Men and Myths* (Toronto,
1967) contains useful documents, while David V.J. Bell, "The Loyalist
Tradition in Canada," *Journal of Canadian Studies* 5 (1970): 22–33, evalu-
ates the impact of the Loyalists. The best study on the Six Nations is by
Barbara Graymont, *The Iroquois in the American Revolution* (Syracuse,
1972). The best review and most complete biography of Joseph Brant is
Isabel Thompson Kelsay, *Joseph Brant, 1743–1807: Man of Two Worlds*
(Syracuse, N.Y., 1984). For Native affairs in the St. Lawrence Valley in
this period, see Daniel Francis, *A History of the Native Peoples of Québec,
1760–1867* (Ottawa, 1983). Françoise Noël has studied the management of
a group of seigneuries in "La gestion des seigneuries de Gabriel Christie
dans la vallée du Richelieu (1760–1845), *Revue d'histoire de l'Amérique
française* 40 (1986/1987): 561–82. Church history is examined by Marcel
Trudel in "La servitude de l'Église catholique du Canada français sous le
régime anglais," Canadian Historical Association, *Report* (1963), 42–64,
and by Jean-Pierre Wallot in "Religion and French-Canadian Mores in
the Early Nineteenth Century," *Canadian Historical Review* 52 (1971):
51–94. Attempts to bring French-speaking priests from Savoy to Quebec
are described in Luca Codignola, "Le Québec et les prêtres savoyards,
1779–1784: Les dimensions internationales d'un échec," *Revue d'histoire
de l'Amérique française* 43 (1989/1990): 559–68. Information on women in
late eighteenth century Quebec appears in Micheline Dumont et al., *Quebec*

199

Women: A History (Toronto, 1987). The history of Quebec's English-speaking population is reviewed in Ronald Rudin, *The Forgotten Quebecers: A History of English-Speaking Quebec, 1759–1980* (Quebec, 1985). Pierre Tousignant studies the genesis of the Constitutional Act in "Problématique pour une nouvelle approche de la constitution de 1791," *Revue d'histoire de l'Amérique française* 27 (1973/1974): 181–234. Important studies of life in rural and urban Quebec include Allan Greer, *Peasant, Lord, and Merchant: Rural Society in Three Quebec Parishes, 1740–1840* (Toronto, 1985) and David T. Ruddel, *Quebec City, 1765–1832: The Evolution of a Colonial Town* (Ottawa, 1987). The *Dictionary of Canadian Biography* (Toronto, 1966–) includes sketches of merchants, statesmen, Indians, seigneurs, artists, and other personalities.

200

Britain's First Inland Colony: Upper Canada, 1791–1815

When the American Revolution broke out in 1775, the territory that
is now called Ontario was part of the Province of Quebec. The Royal
Proclamation of 1763 had reserved all this land for the Amerindians. The
only European settlement of any size was located on the outskirts of
present-day Windsor, where French Canadian farmers who supplied Fort
Detroit, just across the river, had established farms. In the late 1770s the
whole western portion of the Province of Quebec was one continuous
forest. As economic historians Kenneth Norrie and Douglas Owram have
written, "In the normal course of events, it would have been another
generation before significant European settlement intruded upon the
area."[1]

The American Revolution, however, led directly to the creation of
Britain's first inland colony in 1791. Canada became a place of refuge for
the defeated Loyalists. John Graves Simcoe, commander of the Queen's
Rangers (a Loyalist corps) in the revolution, and the first lieutenant
governor of Upper Canada, spent four years constructing the framework
for a colony intended to be the ideal home for Loyalist heroes. In the end,
however, the majority of settlers were Americans. On the eve of the
outbreak of the war of 1812, the American settlers in Upper Canada
outnumbered the Loyalists four to one. Could the northern colony resist
American conquest? Many Upper Canadians asked themselves the same
question when war was declared.

The Anishinabeg

At the close of the 1770s few European settlers lived in the present-day
southern Ontario peninsula. The Algonquian Indians in the area had seen
French forts established on the fur trade routes at Niagara, Detroit, and

Michilimackinac, but never in the interior. After the conquest of 1760 the English maintained these forts but made no attempt to begin settlements in what would soon become Upper Canada. By the outbreak of war in 1812, however, seventy-five thousand Europeans occupied the area, outnumbering the Native population roughly ten to one.

THE EARLY LAND PURCHASES

The Proclamation of 1763 (see Chapter 9) recognized the Great Lakes area as Indian country; hence, the Indians had to surrender that land to the Crown before settlement could proceed. Until the early 1780s present-day southern Ontario was the home of three closely related tribes: the Ojibwas (Chippewas), the Ottawas (Odawas), and the Algonquins—the three Algonquian tribes who called themselves the "Anishinabeg," meaning true human beings.

202   Sir Frederick Haldimand, the governor of Quebec from 1778 to 1784, arranged for the purchase of the land from the Mississaugas, as the British called the Anishinabeg along the north shore of Lake Ontario. The first settlement of Loyalist soldiers and refugees in the Niagara area had grown up across the river from Fort Niagara, at what is now Niagara-on-the-Lake. In order to provide farms for these settlers, the British, in 1781, paid the Mississaugas "three hundred suits of clothing" for a strip of land six and a half kilometres wide on the west bank of the Niagara River.

Other Loyalists had moved up the Hudson River valley to the St. Lawrence, where Haldimand housed them in refugee camps. Toward the end of the revolutionary war, another four or five thousand civilian refugees and ex-servicemen from several Loyalist regiments, along with roughly two thousand Six Nations Indians who had fought for the Crown, followed. Haldimand had to find homes for them as well. Fortunately, the governor's agents knew of good land along the St. Lawrence around the Bay of Quinte, at the eastern end of Lake Ontario, and in the Grand River valley, west of Lake Ontario. In an agreement in 1783, the Indians surrendered all the land from roughly present-day Gananoque to the eastern end of the Bay of Quinte, extending back from Lake Ontario "as far as a man can travel in a day." This was in exchange for guns, powder, ammunition for the winter's hunt, clothing for all of their families, and "as much coarse red cloth as will make about a dozen coats and as many laced hats."

In 1784 the British purchased the Niagara peninsula and gave the Grand River valley to the Six Nations. By the late 1780s the British believed that they had obtained title to the entire Niagara peninsula and the whole north shore of Lake Ontario, except for a large tract between the head of the lake (present-day Hamilton) and Toronto. The British regarded the transactions as simple real-estate deals—complete title to the surrendered area in exchange for trade goods, paid on a once-and-for-all-time basis.

Why did the Mississaugas accept these conditions? First, they were dependent on the European goods that were supplied by the traders and on the gifts that the English had given them annually since the suppression of Pontiac's resistance. Second, it appears that they did not believe they were selling the land once and for all. The Indians' pattern of land ownership and use differed from that of the British in the late eighteenth century. Among the Great Lakes Algonquians, an individual family could use a recognized hunting ground, fishing place, or maple sugar bush, but as soon as the family ceased to go there, it reverted to the collective ownership of the entire band. Most likely, the Anishinabeg regarded the initial agreement as one with tenants for the use of the land for as long as they practiced good behaviour. Third, the Mississaugas had a small population of about a thousand, divided into a dozen or more separate bands along the five hundred kilometres of lakefront. They could have resisted their British and Iroquois allies only with great difficulty. Thus, weakly organized, reliant on European trade goods, and believing that they were receiving presents in perpetuity for the use of their land, the Mississaugas agreed to the proposals.

203

Arrival of the Loyalists

Loyalist refugees arrived in large numbers on the north shore of Lake Ontario in 1784. The Crown helped them by bearing the costs of transporting them to their new homes and by providing them with large amounts of free land, as well as food, clothing, tools, seed, and shelter.

The land was allotted according to status and rank. Each family head could receive 40 ha, with an additional 20 ha for each family member. Non-commissioned officers could claim 80 ha, field officers 400 ha, and captains 280 ha. Subalterns, staff, and warrant officers were allowed 200 ha.

Loyalist settlements appeared throughout the province. About four thousand Loyalists had settled in the townships along the St. Lawrence–Bay of Quinte area by the autumn of 1784. Since many of them had been farmers in the old colonies, they gradually transformed the forest into orderly farms and settled communities. A large number of those who settled along the St. Lawrence were native-born Americans of German ancestry, and others were German regular soldiers who had fought as mercenaries for Britain.

Next in size to the St. Lawrence–Bay of Quinte settlements was the settlement at Niagara, a haven for the Loyalists of the frontier districts of Pennsylvania and New York. Only a relatively small number of Loyalists settled on the northwestern shore of Lake Erie and in the towns of Sandwich (within the present-day boundaries of Windsor) and Amherstburg. In 1796, when Detroit passed into American hands, the population of these two towns greatly increased. Many of Detroit's French citizens, wishing to retain their British allegiance, became Loyalists and crossed to the Canadian side.

Some Loyalists settled in the lower Thames River valley (below present-day Chatham) once the Crown purchased the land from the Anishinabeg in 1790. The Long Point peninsula of Lake Erie was the last major centre of white Loyalist settlement, the majority of its inhabitants having originally settled elsewhere.

IROQUOIS LOYALISTS

Approximately two thousand Iroquois Loyalists came to Upper Canada, leaving behind an equal number of their people. Of those that came across the border, the majority followed Joseph Brant to the Grand River Valley. They were mostly Mohawks, Cayugas, and Onondagas who had fought for Britain. Brant chose the location because of its proximity to their allies, the Senecas, who had decided to remain in western New York, and to the Upper Great Lakes Indians, whom he aspired to lead in a Great Lakes Indian Confederacy. A group of about a hundred Mohawks who were antagonistic to Brant followed Chief John Deseronto and settled on a tract on the Bay of Quinte.

Anxious to retain the Indians' support in the event of another war with the Americans, the British provided the Six Nations people on the Grand River with a church, a school, a sawmill, a gristmill, and an allowance for a schoolmaster, and £1500 as general compensation for their war losses. The Mohawks on the Bay of Quinte also obtained a school, a schoolmaster, and a church. In keeping with Indian Department policy, all the Indians received annual presents and, like the other Loyalists, clothing, tools, and provisions.

Loyalist Settlements

Historian Bruce Wilson has estimated that, in 1785, approximately 7500 Loyalists (5500 white and 2000 Indian) lived in the region extending west from Montreal into present-day Ontario. By 1791 the number of settlers in this area had risen to 20 000–30 000. New settlements had been established throughout the area extending north from the St. Lawrence up the Ottawa River to the Rideau. They were spread over fifteen kilometres around the Bay of Quinte and formed a narrow strip along the Lake Ontario shore from the Bay of Quinte to York, where farms extended twenty-five kilometres up Yonge Street.

National Archives of Canada/PA-237054.

York on Lake Ontario, Upper Canada, 1804, by Elisabeth Francis Hale (1774–1826). The watercolour shows the tiny capital of Upper Canada (population 435) hemmed in by the surrounding forest. Today's Front Street was then at the water's edge.

Settlers, mostly from rural New York and Pennsylvania, now occupied the narrow strip of good land below the escarpment around the Niagara peninsula and part way up the Lake Erie shoreline. From the concessions along the front of the Detroit River, settlement began to move along the south shore of Lake St. Clair, and the lower Thames River valley began to receive settlers.

LIFE OF THE LOYALISTS

Most of the early Loyalist settlers in Upper Canada were poor. Not until the wave of immigration from New Brunswick in the 1790s did Upper Canada receive what might be termed a Loyalist elite, composed of families such as the Robinsons, the Jarvises, and the Ryersons. The early Loyalists lived in military tents until they built their first homes, usually very humble dwellings. They preferred sites by the lakes and rivers, which were the principal means of communication before roads. Indian trails, although narrow (seldom exceeding 50 cm in width), were invaluable for travelling in the immediate area. To support themselves in the first year or so, the Loyalist settlers had to rely heavily on the Indians for food. On the open meadows, Indian corn or maize became the most important first crop. Once additional land was cleared, the settlers planted wheat. Indeed, the destruction of the forest became an obsession for the settlers. The potash made from the ashes of the burning trees could be sold for necessities.

The average Loyalist home was a log cabin, with one or sometimes two rooms. These cabins had no cellar or foundation, and the floor was often earthen. The cabin's dimensions were small, on the average no more than four metres by five. The roofs were constructed of bark or small hollowed basswood logs that overlapped like tiles. Oil paper, not glass, usually covered the windows. Since bricks were not available, the chimneys were built of sticks and clay or rough unmortared stones. Sometimes there was no chimney, and the smoke found its way out through a hole in the bark roof. Clay and moss filled the chinks between the logs. Some sticks of furniture or family heirlooms might have survived the journey to Upper Canada, but the bulk of the furniture was handmade. The cooking was done at an open fireplace. In summer there were plenty of flies and mosquitoes in the houses. Field mice and rats (introduced from Europe) infested the towns.

206

The new settlers in present-day southern Ontario wanted the land system that prevailed in the Province of Quebec to be changed immediately. The authorities obliged and allowed the settlers to participate in a system of freehold tenure, even though that system was officially illegal until 1791. The settlers could exchange land, by selling and purchasing it, well before the Constitutional Act of 1791 officially abolished the seigneurial system in the province it created—Upper Canada.

THE CONSTITUTIONAL ACT OF 1791

The Constitutional Act of 1791 brought the colony of Upper Canada into existence. It provided for freehold tenure and free land. (Settlers paid only the fees for issuing and recording land titles.) The legislation also set aside the equivalent of one-seventh of all lands granted in the future for "the Support and Maintenance of a Protestant Clergy." Unfortunately, just what constituted the "Protestant Clergy"—the Church of England only, or the Church of Scotland and other Protestant denominations as well—was not made explicit. This caused confusion and controversy. Initially, for instance, Governor Simcoe interpreted the phrase to refer only to the Church of England. In addition, the British government set aside another seventh of all lands as Crown reserves; the revenues from the sale or rental of these lands were to be used to fund the colonial government.

A "Truly British" Colony

John Graves Simcoe, an energetic and enthusiastic military officer then in his late thirties, became the first lieutenant governor of Upper Canada.

As commander of the Loyalist unit, the Queen's Rangers, in the American Revolution, Simcoe had earned a reputation as one of Britain's best North American officers.

Simcoe wanted to make Upper Canada a centre of British power in North America. To him, "democracy" and "republicanism" were wicked words. Believing that many in the new republic to the south remained actively loyal to England, he attempted to win Americans back to their old allegiance. He believed that a new colony with "a free, honourable British Government" would remind Americans of what they had lost in leaving the Empire and of the benefits they would reap by returning to it. Free grants of land, he reasoned, might also attract them.

Lasting evidence of Simcoe's plan to transform Upper Canada into a "little England" can be seen in his choice of place names. In 1793 the governor travelled through the colony, liberally choosing new designations. He went as far west as Detroit, confirming en route his choice of a site for the future capital at the place the Anishinabeg called "Ko-te-quo-gong" (At the Forks), at the headwaters of the Ashkahnesebe (Horn or Antler) River. The governor changed the name Kotequogong to London. The river that the Anishinabeg had named Ashkahnesebe because its branches reminded them of a deer's antlers became the Thames. Simcoe changed the name Toronto (an Iroquoian name) to York, and renamed two major rivers in the Toronto area the "Humber" and the "Don," after two rivers in northeastern England. When asked what he thought of John Graves Simcoe's contribution to the colony, Joseph Brant replied, "General Simcoe has done a great deal for this province; he has changed the name of every place in it."

207

The governor firmly believed in the established Church of England. The Anglican church alone would enjoy the right of performing marriages in the colony. Only reluctantly did Simcoe agree that justices of the peace in remote areas might conduct marriage ceremonies, provided they followed the Anglican ritual. Only in 1798 was the right to solemnize marriages extended to Lutheran, Calvinist, and Church of Scotland ministers. Methodists were excluded until 1831. The Upper Canadian administration regarded the Methodists, who had strong links until 1828 with their American parent church, as a dangerous American denomination.

Legislating a Colony into Existence

Simcoe also placed the new colony on a firm military footing. War with the Americans threatened to break out in the early 1780s over the British-held "western posts" (see Chapter 10). By the peace treaty of 1783, Britain and the United States had agreed to an international boundary that ran through the upper St. Lawrence and the Great Lakes to the lands claimed by Spain in the Mississippi and Missouri river basins. By the same treaty, the Americans had promised to allow the Loyalists to return to their homes and collect their legitimate debts, but they failed to honour that promise.

Seizing upon this violation, Britain initially refused to vacate the "western posts" of Oswego, Niagara, Detroit, and Michilimackinac. The British government allowed Simcoe to raise an infantry corps of some 425 officers and men, the Queen's Rangers (the name of his old Loyalist regiment in the revolution). Simcoe also had the Upper Canada Assembly pass a militia bill in 1793 requiring all able-bodied men from sixteen to fifty years of age to enrol and to attend parade drill for their local companies two to four times a year. By 1794 more than five thousand officers and men served in the militia. Only in that year did Britain agree to sign Jay's Treaty, which led to its withdrawal from the western posts by June 1, 1796.

208 THE ADMINISTRATION OF UPPER CANADA

Simcoe carefully structured his administration. Once he had established temporary headquarters at Newark (now Niagara-on-the-Lake), on the west bank of the Niagara River opposite Fort Niagara, he called for elections to the Legislative Assembly. Very much an English squire, Simcoe had personal reservations about the social background of the elected members of the Assembly. Once he described them as men "of a Lower Order, who kept but one Table, that is, who dined in Common with their Servants." Nevertheless, he was pleased that they supported his plans to fashion Upper Canada into a truly British province.

The legislature created a judicial system. The new governor selected William Osgoode, a respected English lawyer, as chief justice. Under his jurisdiction stood the Court of King's Bench, the new superior court of civil and criminal jurisdiction. Within each district surrogate courts and a provincial court of probate were established. At a lower level, meetings for the courts of quarter sessions were organized. The justices of the peace presided over these and performed as well a wide range of administrative and judicial duties. At the township level the justices of the peace enjoyed considerable power, trying court cases, supervising road and bridge construction contracts, and issuing various licenses, including one for taverns. Township officials in Upper Canada were appointed, not elected as they were in New England.

THE SLAVERY QUESTION

The legislature of Upper Canada addressed the issue of slavery. While the majority of black Loyalists and black slaves had gone to Nova Scotia after the revolution, some black slaves were brought to Upper Canada. Joseph Brant, the Iroquois war chief, for example, had black slaves, as did John

Stuart, the first Anglican missionary at Kingston. By 1792 the Niagara district alone had an estimated three hundred slaves. Slavery, however, proved to be an expensive proposition in a northern area such as Upper Canada. The short Canadian growing season ruled out such crops as cotton, which required a cheap, plentiful labour force. Furthermore, owners had to feed, clothe, and house slaves throughout a long and unproductive winter. Finally, there were those, including Simcoe, who found slavery abhorrent.

Under the governor's direction, an Assembly member moved that slavery gradually be abolished in the province, and the Assembly adopted the motion. Slaves already in Upper Canada had to remain slaves until they died, but all children born to slaves in the colony were to be freed at the age of twenty-five. Furthermore, no additional slaves could be brought to Upper Canada. With this new legislation in place, slavery declined steadily in Upper Canada.

209

LAND GRANTS

Although anxious to eliminate the slave class, the lowest rung of society, Simcoe sought to create in Upper Canada what he considered the highest class: an aristocracy. He believed that he could legislate such an elite into existence through generous land grants. He allowed members of the Executive and Legislative councils to receive large grants of 1200–2000 ha; these grants were equivalent to those given the highest-ranked military officers. Their children, often quite numerous, could obtain 480 ha. His idea, however, rebounded on the colony. The recipients had no intention of becoming country squires, preferring instead to sell their estates profitably in the future. These grants locked up much valuable land and, to the resentment of many ordinary settlers, kept it out of their hands.

Upper Canada really had two systems of land tenure. The first applied to the "official" settlers who obtained land on account of their past service to the Crown, or their social position. The second system consisted of immigrants' obtaining grants of 80 ha of land on the promise that they would develop it. Once these individuals built their homes and fenced and cleared the road allowance, they could gain title. This system involved mostly the so-called "late Loyalists," who arrived in the 1790s in search of free land.

The "late Loyalists" came to the north shore of Lake Ontario, as it lay on the advancing American settlement frontier. Southeastern Upper Canada, in fact, was located directly on the natural east–west migration route to northern Ohio. Many of these settlers were not interested in Simcoe's plan for an elite British colony; indeed, in future years hostilities would arise in the colony between the "official" and the "immigrant" settlers.

COMMUNICATIONS

Simcoe contributed to the improvement of communications in the colony. He decided in 1793 to build a military road from Burlington Bay to the Thames, which he named Dundas Street after Henry Dundas, then a secretary of state in the English cabinet. Simcoe believed that a second military road should be built from York to Lac aux Claies (which he renamed Lake Simcoe in honour of his father), to ensure rapid communication with the upper lakes. The Governor called this road Yonge Street after Sir George Yonge, the British Secretary of War.

These two military highways, Yonge and Dundas streets, became the principal pathways for future generations of settlers. Both roads allowed settlers to begin farms inland at a time when most people clung tenaciously to the navigable waterways.

210

SIMCOE'S LEGACY

John Graves Simcoe left Upper Canada in mid-1796. He served briefly in 1797 as the British governor of Saint-Domingue (Haiti). There, by a bizarre twist of fate, the dedicated abolitionist found himself nominally protecting the human property of French Royalist plantation owners against the brilliant Toussaint L'Ouverture, an ex-slave who led a revolt to liberate all the slaves on the island. In 1806 Simcoe was made commander-in-chief in India, but he died before taking up the post.

While in Upper Canada Simcoe experienced many disappointments. He may have considered the colony as something approaching the centre of the universe, but London did not. The home government turned down his schemes to build up the colony economically and militarily. His proposal to create a provincial university also received little support in London, as did his attempt to establish the Church of England in the colony under a bishop's tutelage. In addition, the hierarchical society he tried to construct did not materialize. But he did, at least, succeed in establishing a community. As historian Gerald Craig wrote, "Simcoe had helped to nurse a new province into being, but its inhabitants, busy with their own projects and their own local affairs, showed only a tepid interest in the goals he had set for them."[2]

For her part, Elizabeth Simcoe, the governor's wife, left behind a lasting legacy in the form of a diary and drawings and watercolours of Upper Canadian scenes in the mid-1790s. This well-educated Englishwoman, with her sharp eye for detail and with the leisure and talent required to record the unfamiliar scenes around her, left a fascinating record of life in the province two centuries ago.

LOYALIST WOMEN IN EARLY UPPER CANADA

Thanks largely to her diary, historians today remember Elizabeth Simcoe; regrettably, though, they have tended in the past to ignore her female Loyalist contemporaries. Yet these women played heroic roles. During the American Revolution, they had taken charge of their families and farms during their husbands' absences. Many had been harassed or persecuted. They had seen their property stolen by the insurgents, and their homes seized. Some had been jailed. They had been forced to flee through the wilderness to British refugee camps. But, as historian Janice Potter writes, once behind British lines, "They had to fit once again into a patriarchal power structure in which their inferiority and dependence were assumed." No one, then or now, has fully recognized their accomplishments; as Potter notes, "the memories of the travails and victories of the eastern Ontario Loyalist women died with them."[3]

Few accounts even mention Molly Brant, the Loyalist woman whose intervention did so much to prevent the Americans from gaining control of the entire Great Lakes area during the revolution. Brant, the sister of Mohawk chief Joseph Brant, lived in Kingston from 1783 to her death in 1796. As a clan mother, she wielded considerable influence among the Six Nations, and she used that influence to keep her people loyal to the British Crown. As an Indian Department official put it, "One word from her goes farther with [the Indians] than a thousand from any white Man without Exception."

The Indians of Upper Canada: A Displaced People

By the time of Simcoe's departure in 1796, the Indians were beginning to understand what the early land purchases meant to the British: the whites were denying them a right of way across their cleared fields, and if they camped on the white settlers' lands, the farmers shot their dogs. The tribal elders told the young people, such as Kahkewaquonaby (Sacred Feathers, known in English as Peter Jones), that when the British first came, they "asked for a small piece of land on which they might pitch their tents; the request was cheerfully granted. By and by they begged for more, and more was given them. In this way they have continued to ask, or have obtained by force or fraud, the fairest portions of our territory." Between 1805 and 1818 the Crown successfully pressured the Mississaugas to sell their last remaining tract, between Toronto and the head of the lake; in two separate agreements the British acquired the desired land.

Other tragedies followed. Between the 1790s and the 1820s, smallpox, tuberculosis, and measles killed almost two-thirds of the Mississaugas at the western end of the lake. The band's population in that area dropped to two hundred in the 1820s, down from more than five hundred a generation earlier. The Iroquois also experienced difficult times in the 1790s and 1800s, as land sales eliminated a great deal of their reserve on the Grand River. Joseph Brant wanted white farmers to settle among the Iroquois on the Grand River and to teach them European agricultural techniques. The Iroquois war chief realized that with European ploughs the Indians could produce more on the available land. Yet not all the Grand River Iroquois agreed with Brant. They objected to the presence of the white people on their land and to the fact that by 1798 the white settlers had gained control of two-thirds of the Six Nations' original grant on the Grand River.

Growth of Settlement

Upper Canada's non-Indian population increased dramatically at the turn of the century. Many of the influx of settlers were "late Loyalists" in search of cheap land. By 1812 this peaceful American invasion had put settlers on all the vacant townships along the north shore of Lake Ontario. Several townships developed on Lake Erie as well. Although roads remained very few in number, communication and transportation along waterways allowed for the dispersal of settlement along an 800 km front in a period of less than twenty years.

THE PLAIN FOLK

Among the new immigrants were members of sects commonly called the "Plain Folk"—Quakers, Mennonites, Dunkards, and Moravians. These religious sects opposed war, objected to taking oaths, and believed in a plain religion and plain dress. In most instances the Quakers were English in origin and the other groups were largely German. These pacifist groups had remained neutral during the American Revolution.

The lure of good land, the prospect of stability, and the promise of religious tolerance attracted the Plain Folk. Simcoe himself had welcomed Quakers to the province and declared that they would be exempt from bearing arms.

By 1800 large numbers of Plain Folk had settled in Upper Canada, many having trekked north using heavy, broad-wheeled Conestoga wagons. Perhaps the greatest number selected the Niagara peninsula, because of the easy access it afforded to the Quaker, Mennonite, and Dunkard settlements in Pennsylvania. The Bay of Quinte became another favourite area for religious minorities, as did Yonge Street, particularly in Markham and Vaughan townships.

The newcomers from Pennsylvania and New York made ideal farmers. Historian G. Elmore Reaman has noted their three great strengths: "They

Royal Ontario Museum, Toronto, Canada.

Old Fort Erie with the Migrations of the Wild-Pigeon in Spring, April 12, 1804, by Edward Walsh (1766–1832). In her diary entry for November 1, 1793, Elizabeth Simcoe commented that passenger pigeons were so numerous in Upper Canada in the spring and autumn that, at times, they darkened the entire sky. The pioneers put a stop to that. On both sides of the border, settlers trapped, clubbed, and shot the pigeons by the millions. The last recorded sighting of passenger pigeons in Ontario was in 1902. The last passenger pigeon in North America died in 1914 in a zoo in Cincinnati, Ohio.

were physically equipped both in knowledge of what to do in the wilderness and the strength to do it; they came with money and equipment; and they aided one another, whether Quaker, Huguenot, Lutheran, or Mennonite."[4]

The Mennonites' largest settlement was in the difficult-to-reach Waterloo County, on land originally belonging to the Six Nations Reserve. The last area to receive settlers from Pennsylvania, Waterloo is the only locality in Ontario to retain the ethnic characteristics of its early European settlers nearly two centuries later. The migration of the Amish directly from Germany in 1824 did much to strengthen the German character of the area, as did the later arrival of German Lutherans and Roman Catholics from Europe.

On the eve of the War of 1812 the population of Upper Canada reached seventy-five thousand. Scattered along the St. Lawrence and Lakes Ontario, Erie, and St. Clair, the settled areas rarely extended more than a few kilometres into the interior.

The work of establishing farms and clearing new land took much of the settlers' time, leaving little opportunity for politics. No clear-cut alignments existed in the Assembly and, apart from one newspaper at Niagara, no opposition press existed. The newcomers from the United States outnumbered the Loyalists and the British immigrants four to one. Like the Acadians of Nova Scotia a century earlier, these Americans lived within a British colony without really belonging to it. The War of 1812 would press them to choose sides—as the Seven Years' War did the Acadians.

UPPER CANADA AND THE UNITED STATES, 1791–1812

As long as Britain retained the western posts, war with the United States seemed inevitable. Simcoe, in fact, had hoped that the Indians south of the Great Lakes would defeat the Americans. In 1791, it appeared that they might. In that year they did win a major encounter with General Arthur St. Clair, the governor of the American Northwest Territory, killing six hundred Americans and forcing another fourteen hundred to flee for their lives across the Ohio. The Americans, however, responded by sending more soldiers to the borders of the Ohio country. In 1794 the American general "Mad" Anthony Wayne defeated the Ohio Indians at the Battle of Fallen Timbers and put an end to Simcoe's dream of an Indian buffer state.

International developments also contributed to Britain's decision to hand over the western posts. As a result of war with France, Britain needed to ease tension with the United States. In 1794 the two countries signed Jay's Treaty, named for John Jay, the American chief justice who negotiated the treaty with the British. By its terms, Britain agreed to evacuate the forts on the south shores of the Great Lakes in 1796. With Britain's imminent withdrawal, the Ohio Indians made peace with the Americans and, in the Treaty of Greenville (1795), ceded their claims to most of the present-day state of Ohio. But the Indians' resistance to the American settlers' march westward continued.

CAUSES OF THE WAR OF 1812

In the first decade of the century, Tecumseh, a Shawnee chief, and his brother, a religious leader, assembled a formidable Indian confederacy. In 1811 Tecumseh was in open war with the Americans. Many Ohioans, Tennesseeans, and Kentuckians suspected—incorrectly—that the British continued to encourage and finance the Indian raids. Many aggressive and intensely patriotic Americans judged it time to attack the British in the Canadas. At the same time, the American "war hawks," anxious to begin a war with Britain, argued that the United States could use the opportunity to seize the fertile peninsula of Upper Canada.

Two direct provocations by Britain led many Americans, including President James Madison, to support the pro-war party. In 1812 Napoleon's continental system closed all of western Europe, except Portugal, to British goods. Britain retaliated by imposing a naval blockade on France, preventing all ships, including American vessels, from trading with France. Officially neutral in the struggle, the Americans called for freedom of the seas. What right had England to board American ships on the high seas and prevent them from trading with countries on the continent? Madison considered this act the first provocation.

Britain also began to search American ships for British deserters who had gone over to American vessels to obtain higher wages, better food, and better working conditions. Without regard for neutral rights, British cruisers stopped American ships on the North Atlantic and seized thousands of sailors, alleging that they were British deserters. If a man produced his easily obtained certificate of American naturalization, the English ignored it, as their government did not recognize the right of a British subject to transfer allegiance to another country.

"Free Trade and Sailors' Rights" became the cry of many Americans. Forced, as he put it, to choose between war and degradation, Madison sent a message of war to Congress on June 1, 1812. Congress agreed and declared war against Britain.

UPPER CANADA'S SUCCESS IN 1812

Fortunately for the Canadas, the Americans had a faulty strategy of attack. Canada's key strategic points, in order of importance, were Quebec, Montreal, Kingston, Niagara, and the Detroit River, but the Americans chose to attack the Upper Canadians east of the Detroit River first, and then to strike at Niagara. In hindsight, it would have been wiser for them to cut the supply lines between Montreal and Kingston first; that way, Upper Canada would have fallen quickly. Throughout the first year of the war, however, the Americans believed incorrectly that Upper Canada's American population would welcome them as an army of liberation. Thomas Jefferson himself had assured Americans that the conquest of Upper Canada would be a "mere matter of marching." Moreover, the Americans had underestimated the strength of the British regular troops and their Amerindian allies.

Much of the credit for Upper Canada's success in 1812 is due to Major General Isaac Brock who had fought in the French wars in Europe and had then been stationed in North America. Realizing the strategy that must be followed, Brock built up the province's fortifications, trained the provincial militia, and maintained good relations with the Indians. He knew that, as soon as war broke out, Upper Canada would have to take the offensive in order to check the mood of defeatism in the colony—most people believed that the Americans, with their overwhelming superiority in numbers, would win.

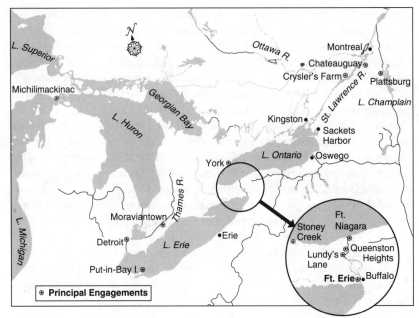

Principal Engagements in the War of 1812.

The Indians' military contribution best explains Brock's subsequent success. For the Great Lakes Indians, war did not break out in 1812; they had been fighting American frontiersmen for generations. Welcoming the outbreak of the second Anglo-American War in 1812, Tecumseh and hundreds of warriors joined the British in Upper Canada. The Indians helped a small British force take Michilimackinac, the leading fur-trading post in the Upper Great Lakes; then Tecumseh and his warriors cut off the Americans' lines of communication with Detroit, and effectively won that fort for the British.

Only a few weeks earlier William Hull, the American commander at Detroit, had crossed the border near Windsor to issue a proclamation to the Upper Canadians: "You will be emancipated from tyranny and oppression and restored to the dignified station of freedom ... I come prepared for every contingency. I have a force which will look down all opposition. ..." Despite all his bluster, once he believed that Brock had five thousand Indians with him (he really had only about six hundred), General Hull surrendered without a fight. The fall of Detroit led to the loss of all the American territory west of Lake Erie.

Brock's unexpected victory at Detroit changed British fortunes overnight. He had proved that Upper Canada could be defended. He did so again in October at Queenston Heights, but this time at the cost of his life: he was shot as he led a charge up the face of the heights. The attack, however, succeeded. Five hundred Iroquois joined one thousand British regulars and six hundred militia in retaking the strategic heights. They captured nine hundred American prisoners. Having lost one army at Detroit, the Americans lost another on the Niagara peninsula.

After the war, it was popularly believed that the civilian soldiers had won the contests at Detroit, Queenston Heights, and other battlegrounds. In reality, this is quite false. Regular soldiers constituted the first line of Britain's defence of Upper Canada, supplying the leadership and doing most of the fighting themselves. Throughout the war, the Upper Canadian militia proved quite unreliable. Zeal for the fight always declined at harvest time or whenever news arrived of danger to the men's families from raiding parties. The British regulars remained the backbone of Upper Canada's resistance in 1812 and for the next two years of the war.

The Campaigns of 1813 and 1814   *217*

The darkest moment of the war for the Upper Canadians came in the summer of 1813. The Americans briefly occupied York and launched a second invasion of the Niagara peninsula, forcing the British to withdraw to Burlington Heights at the head of the lake. Desertions from the militia grew, and two members of the Upper Canada Assembly actually joined the Americans. Only a surprise attack by British regular troops at Stoney Creek, immediately south of Burlington Heights, dislodged the Americans and saved Upper Canada. A second battle followed at Beaver Dams, where Iroquois from the Montreal area and from the Six Nations territory at the Grand River ambushed the Americans. The attackers benefited from vital information about the location of the American troops received from Laura Secord, a 37-year-old settler. Shortly after the Indian victory at Beaver Dams, the American invaders withdrew from the peninsula.

The Americans fared better in the west, especially after American captain Oliver Perry defeated the British in an important naval battle on Lake Erie, which became in effect, an American possession, totally controlled for the remainder of the war by their naval forces. The British then withdrew from Detroit. At Moraviantown on the Thames River, the Americans defeated the British regulars, the Upper Canadian militia, and the Indians. The Americans held on to southwestern Upper Canada until the end of the war.

Tecumseh was killed at Moraviantown on October 5, 1813. With his death, his confederacy collapsed. Never again in the Lower Great Lakes area did the Indians constitute a serious military threat.

After Moraviantown the battle lines consolidated for the remainder of the war. In July 1814 the British defeated the Americans' last great attempt to capture Upper Canada, at Lundy's Lane in the Niagara peninsula. Outside Upper Canada, the British unsuccessfully took the offensive on

Lake Champlain. In August 1814 a British expedition took Washington, burning the Capitol and the President's House (which, when rebuilt, was called the White House because the walls were whitewashed to hide the fire marks). The Americans halted the victorious British, however, at Baltimore. The only other major battle of the war (at New Orleans) took place after the peace treaty had been signed.

The War of 1812 did not change geography. The peace treaty essentially confirmed the status quo. But, in one respect, the war had a very profound effect on Upper Canada: the unsuccessful and destructive attacks of 1812–14 engendered anti-American sentiment among many non-Loyalist settlers. Ironically, the American invasion contributed to the work that Simcoe had begun—the promotion of a loyalty to the colony. In the words of Canadian historian A.R.M. Lower, "Upper Canada emerged from the War of 1812 a community, its people no longer Americans nor solely British subjects, but Upper Canadians."[5]

218

NOTES

[1]Kenneth Norrie and Douglas Owram, *A History of the Canadian Economy* (Toronto, 1991), 161.
[2]Gerald M. Craig, *Upper Canada: The Formative Years, 1784–1841* (Toronto, 1963), 41.
[3]Janice Potter, "Patriarchy and Paternalism: The Case of the Eastern Ontario Loyalist Women," *Ontario History* 81 (1989): 20.
[4]G. Elmore Reaman, *The Trail of the Black Walnut* (Toronto, 1957), 147.
[5]A.R.M. Lower, *Colony to Nation* (Toronto, 1957; first published 1946), 179.

Related Readings

The following essay in R. Douglas Francis and Donald B. Smith, *Readings in Canadian History: Pre-Confederation*, 3d ed. (Toronto, 1990) is of value to this topic: W.G. Shelton, "The United Empire Loyalists: A Reconsideration," 234–43.

BIBLIOGRAPHY

For an understanding of early Upper Canada, Gerald M. Craig's *Upper Canada: The Formative Years, 1784–1841* (Toronto, 1963) is essential. The period immediately before the establishment of Upper Canada is reviewed by A.L. Burt in "The Loyalists," Ch. 15 of *The Old Province of Quebec*, 2 vols. (Toronto, 1968; first published 1933), 2:76–115. Other sources on the Loyalists who settled in Upper Canada include Bruce Wilson, *As She Began: An Illustrated Introduction to Loyalist Ontario* (Toronto, 1981); James J. Talman, ed., *Loyalist Narratives from Upper Canada* (Toronto, 1946); Janice Potter, "Patriarchy and Paternalism: The Case of the Eastern Ontario Loyalist Women," *Ontario History* 81 (1989): 3–24; and W. Stewart Wallace, *The United Empire Loyalists* (Toronto, 1922). An interesting account is that of R. Louis Gentilcore, "The Beginnings of Settlement in the Niagara Peninsula (1782–1792)," *Canadian Geographer* 7 (1962): 72–82. Robert S. Allen's *Loyalist Literature: An Annotated Bibliographic Guide to the Writings on the Loyalists of the American Revolution* (Toronto, 1982) is a useful guide to the subject.

Simcoe's years in Upper Canada are reviewed in Stanley R. Mealing, "John Graves Simcoe," in *Our Living Tradition*, edited by Robert L. McDougall (Toronto, 1962), 57–76; and "John Graves Simcoe," in the *Dictionary of Canadian Biography*, vol. 5, *1801–1820* (Toronto, 1985), 754–59. Malcolm Macleod examines Simcoe's defence policy in "Fortress Ontario or Forlorn Hope? Simcoe and the Defence of Upper Canada," *Canadian Historical Review* 53 (1972): 149–78. Simcoe's founding of Toronto is the subject of Carl Benn's article "The Military Context of the Founding of Toronto," *Ontario History* 81 (1989): 303–322. For those interested in the early social history of Upper Canada, Mrs. Elizabeth Simcoe's diary is invaluable. John Ross Robertson's fully annotated version appeared as *The Diary of Mrs. John Graves Simcoe, Wife of the First Lieutenant-Governor of the Province of Upper Canada, 1792–6* (Toronto, 1911; reprinted Toronto, 1973). Mary Quayle Innis has edited an abridged version, *Mrs. Simcoe's Diary* (Toronto, 1965), and Mary Beacock Fryer has written a biography, *Elizabeth Posthuma Simcoe, 1762–1850* (Toronto, 1989). For information on Molly Brant, see Barbara Graymont's sketch in the *Dictionary of Canadian Biography*, vol. 4, *1771–1800* (Toronto, 1979), 416–19.

219

For the early history of Upper Canadian politics, see Jane Errington, *The Lion, the Eagle and Upper Canada: A Developing Colonial Ideology* (Kingston and Montreal, 1987), and David Mills, *The Idea of Loyalty in Upper Canada, 1784–1850* (Kingston and Montreal, 1988). Economic issues are examined in Ch. 6 ("Upper Canada") of Kenneth Norrie's and Douglas Owram's *A History of the Canadian Economy* (Toronto, 1991), 160–74. Consult also Douglas McCalla, "The 'Loyalist' Economy of Upper Canada," *Histoire Sociale/Social History* 16, 32 (November 1983): 279–304, and Bruce G. Wilson, *The Enterprises of Robert Hamilton: A Study of Wealth and Influence in Early Upper Canada, 1776–1812* (Don Mills, Ont., 1983). An interesting review of York just before the War of 1812 is Eric Wilfrid Hounsom's *Toronto in 1810* (Toronto, 1970).

The experience of the Six Nations in early Upper Canada is reviewed in Isabel Thompson Kelsay, *Joseph Brant, 1743–1807: Man of Two Worlds* (Syracuse, 1984), and Charles M. Johnston, ed., *The Valley of the Six Nations: A Collection of Documents on the Indian Lands of the Grand River* (Toronto, 1964). For a discussion of the Ojibwas, see Peter Schmalz, *The Ojibwa of Southern Ontario* (Toronto, 1991), and Donald B. Smith, *Sacred Feathers: The Reverend Peter Jones (Kahkewaquonaby) and the Mississauga Indians* (Toronto, 1987). Colin Calloway looks at the Great Lakes Indians in this time period in *Crown and Calumet: British–Indian Relations,*

1783–1815 (Norman, Oklahoma, 1987). Robert J. Surtees reviews the early treaties in *Indian Land Surrenders in Ontario, 1763–1867* (Ottawa, 1984). Daniel G. Hill's *The Freedom-Seekers: Blacks in Early Canada* (Agincourt, Ont., 1981) is a popular summary of the history of blacks in Upper Canada and in all of British North America. In *The Trail of the Black Walnut* (Toronto, 1957), G. Elmore Reaman tells the story of the "Plain Folk" and their arrival in Upper Canada.

A short summary of the War of 1812 appears in C.P. Stacey's essay, "The War of 1812 in Canadian History," in *The Defended Border: Upper Canada and the War of 1812*, edited by Morris Zaslow (Toronto, 1964), 331–38. Pierre Berton has written two very readable accounts of the conflict: *The Invasion of Canada, 1812–1813* (Toronto, 1980), and *Flames Across the Border, 1813–1814* (Toronto, 1981). George F.G. Stanley provides the best scholarly account in *The War of 1812: Land Operations* (Ottawa, 1983).

220 For early maps of Upper Canada, see *Ontario's History in Maps*, edited by R. Louis Gentilcore and C. Grant Head (Toronto, 1984). For the natural history of early Upper Canada, consult W. Fraser Sandercombe's *Nothing Gold Can Stay: The Wildlife of Upper Canada* (Erin, Ont., 1985). Valuable portraits of early Upper Canadian figures are in the *Dictionary of Canadian Biography*, vol. 4, *1770–1800*; vol. 5, *1800–1820*; and vol. 6, *1821–1835* (Toronto, 1979, 1985, 1987).

Upper Canada, 1815–1840: An Immigrant Society

The period from 1815 to 1840 was one of growth and consolidation for Upper Canada. During this quarter-century, the population expanded rapidly, from less than one hundred thousand in 1815 to more than four hundred thousand in 1840. Immigration accounted for much of this expansion. Some of the new immigrants were from the United States, but most were from the British Isles: Protestants from the north of Ireland, Roman Catholics from the south, Lowland and Highland Scots, Welsh and English. These immigrants brought British customs and attitudes that eventually mixed with those of the people already there to create a unique British North American character. The newcomers settled the land; established and refined political, social, and educational institutions; contributed to the colony's economic growth; and participated in its political movements. The British immigrants did much to inculcate a sense of loyalty to Britain and thus to distinguish Upper Canada from the American republic to the south even more.

Immigration and Settlement

After the War of 1812 the British government made every effort to encourage British immigration and to discourage American immigration to Upper Canada. New laws pertaining to "aliens" prevented Americans from obtaining grants of land until they had resided in the province for seven years. Nevertheless, some Americans did come, including fugitive black slaves from the South and free blacks from the northern states. Most blacks homesteaded along the border, with the exception of 150 who settled in Oro township on the western shore of Lake Simcoe. Some American immigrants became part of the general westward movement of the American frontier that carried immigrants beyond Upper Canada to the newly opened lands in the Mississippi Valley.

After 1815 the British settlers that Simcoe had so desperately wanted in the early years of the province finally arrived. Two factors account for the migration: peace and hard times. The end of the Napoleonic wars brought economic depression and unemployment to Great Britain, drastically reduced the army's demand for manpower, and made overseas travel less dangerous. For many people in crowded, postwar Britain, emigration seemed the answer to their problems. From the British government's perspective, it would reduce population, provide relief from social unrest, and facilitate expansion and control of its Empire.

The British government initially assisted the exodus with generous aid, similar to that first given the Loyalists. The assistance included the cost of transportation to the colony, free grants of land to each family head, rations for eight months or until established, agricultural supplies at cost, and a minister and school teacher on government salary for each settlement. At first, this program was intended mainly for demobilized soldiers and half-pay officers (those no longer in active service).

222

By October 1816 more than fourteen hundred people had taken advantage of the offer to settle in Upper Canada, chiefly in the Lanark area in the eastern part of the colony. The government then extended aid to unemployed Scottish weavers and their families, who were being uprooted by the land enclosure system in Scotland. In 1820 two thousand government-assisted Scots settled in the Rideau district south of present-day Ottawa. Worse off than the Scots, however, were the Irish, forced from their land by high rents and taxes. In the 1820s, some three thousand Irish immigrants under government sponsorship came to settle in the Peterborough area. A significant number from North Tipperary, Ireland, also settled in the Ottawa area and, later, around London, attracted by next of kin who had gone before them and had succeeded in acquiring land for their children.

In the mid-1820s the British government stopped aiding emigrants. The program was considered too expensive and also unnecessary, since private charitable associations, and landowners anxious to rid their estates of impoverished tenants, were providing at least some minimal assistance. Many immigrants were also willing to come on their own, without government assistance in order simply to escape the wretched conditions at home. This was especially true of the victims of the Irish potato famine. A certain number of these immigrants ended up as paupers in Upper Canada, a development that eventually led to the proliferation of workhouses for the care of the destitute.

Upper Canadian landowners also provided assistance to immigrants in the hope of profiting from government incentives for settlement and land development. Few were as successful as Col. Thomas Talbot, who secured 2000 ha near St. Thomas in southwestern Upper Canada. He subsequently

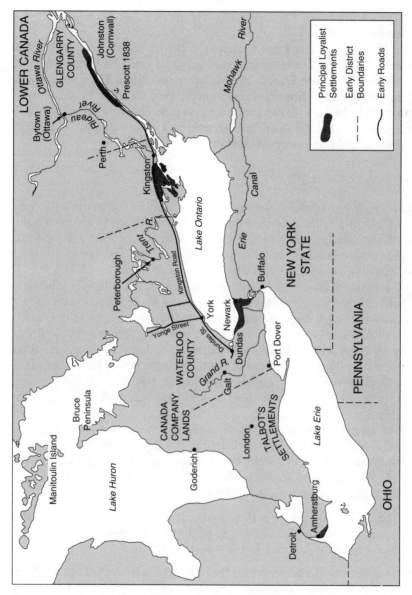

Source: Adapted from P.G. Cornell, J. Hamelin, F. Ouellet, and M. Trudel, *Canada: Unity in Diversity* (Toronto, 1967), 189.

Upper Canada in the early nineteenth century.

received 81 ha of adjoining land for each colonist he settled on a 20 ha lot of the original grant. Talbot eventually accumulated an estate of 8100 ha, making him one of the largest landholders in Upper Canada. In return, he settled more than 200 000 ha of forest for farmland, consisting of 3000 lots in southwestern Upper Canada. He also created an extensive road system in the area.

In 1826 the Canada Land Company, a British-based company headed by John Galt, began to settle approximately half a million hectares of land on the shores of Lake Huron. In addition to the Huron Tract, the Canada Company obtained from the government, for a nominal price, another half-million hectares elsewhere in the province. On the Huron Tract, the company founded the town of Goderich, and on another parcel of land east of the tract, the town of Guelph.

THE VOYAGE OVERSEAS

Most immigrants came at their own expense. Only a few of the well-to-do could afford £30 for first-class accommodation on an American frigate, which included a cabin with one or two bunks, a sofa, a window, and full meals. The remainder had to share bunks in the steerage of crowded passenger ships or in the dank holds of timber ships.

Most immigrants never forgot their crossing of the Atlantic to the New World in a timber ship. Makeshift two-metre-square bunks stacked two or three tiers high lined the sides and ran down the middle of the vessel. The shipowners packed as many as 250 immigrants into a space 28.5 m long by 7.5 m wide and little more than 1.5 m high. Four people, often complete strangers, were crowded into a single berth. Food was often rancid, clean water and clean air non-existent. Not surprisingly, sickness was rampant. There were few doctors, and medical supplies were inadequate.

The immigrants endured these intolerable conditions for up to six weeks—and sometimes longer, if sailing conditions were poor. Many of them had already spent a week or two waiting at dockside for the ship to sail. In his first novel, *Redburn*, Herman Melville describes how the emigrants talked of soon seeing America:

> The agent had told them that twenty days would be an unusually long voyage. Suddenly there was a cry of 'Land', and emigrants crowded a deck expecting America, but it was only Ireland.

Some never saw the New World; they died and were buried at sea. Many more arrived sick and debilitated, especially in the 1830s and 1840s, when cholera and typhoid spread through Britain and central Europe. One of every twenty-eight immigrants to Quebec died on board ship during these two decades. The wretched and bewildered immigrants who survived the trip and remained healthy were met by unscrupulous "runners," or profiteers, eager to take advantage of them. Finally, they had to face the arduous overland journey to their new homes.

Nonetheless, for the strong, the new land carried a blessing. The constant need for labour in Upper Canada gave even penniless immigrants an opportunity to earn a living, to adjust to a freer society, and to save for farms of their own. It took a lifetime for the average immigrant, lacking capital or labour, to clear a twenty-hectare farm and live comfortably. But in Upper Canada a landless labourer could become a landed proprietor—something nearly impossible in Britain.

THE NATIVE PEOPLES

The land came from the Native peoples, a group who, by 1815, were already outnumbered ten to one by non-Natives. After the War of 1812 the Indians of Upper Canada made seven major land surrenders, opening up much of present-day southern Ontario. In 1818 the government of Upper Canada had changed the method of purchasing the land, offering to pay the Indians annual payments or annuities in perpetuity, an arrangement that was preferable to a simple one-time payment. Although the Indians had by now come to realize that these land-sale agreements were final and irrevers- *225* ible, their numbers were too small to allow them to turn down the proposed cessions. In addition, settled areas now divided the bands from one another, which deterred a united response. Finally, many of the Indians' lands near the settlements had been ruined for hunting by the immigrant farmers. Apart from Governor Francis Bond Head's attempt in 1836-37 to relocate the Anishinabeg of southern Ontario (the Ojibwas, Odawas [Ottawas], and Potawatomis) on Manitoulin Island on the north shore of Lake Huron (a proposal they vigorously opposed), the Upper Canadian Indians were allowed to stay in their old hunting territories, but only on reserves. Here, they were taught to farm as part of an official British government program intended to "civilize" and Christianize them. During the time when the Upper Canadian Indians were losing control of their land, Indian migrants came north to settle in Upper Canada. They came to escape the American government's decrees in the 1830s legislating that Indians east of the Mississippi must move west of the river. Several thousand Anishinabeg took up residence in Upper Canada in the 1830s and 1840s. Most of the Oneida, one of the Iroquois tribes remaining in New York state after the American Revolution, also immigrated around 1840 and purchased land on the Thames River west of London.

Colonial Oligarchy: The Family Compact

During the years 1815 to 1840, Upper Canada came under the political control of a small, tightly knit elite popularly known as the "Family Compact." Through political domination of the Executive Council—the governor's "cabinet"—and the Legislative Council (the upper house of the government), its members decided government policy and controlled the government's day-to-day operations. Through political patronage they appointed like-minded people (who wielded considerable power of their own) to the local centres, thus creating smaller oligarchies throughout the province. By the 1830s, these local officials would challenge the policies of the administrative elite in Toronto.

At the centre of the Family Compact stood John Strachan, cleric and educator. For more than two decades he acted as a leading adviser to the governors of Upper Canada. A story circulated in the colony about Strachan's son: One day someone asked him, "Who governs Upper Canada?" "I do," he replied. When asked to explain, he answered, "I govern my mother, my mother governs my father, my father governs Upper Canada."

Around Strachan gathered a group of whom many were his former pupils. Members of this "old boy's network" had strikingly similar backgrounds and views. About half of the Compact consisted of descendants of the original Loyalist families. The other half included those who had come out from Britain as immigrants in the early years of the colony, like Strachan himself. Their role in the defence of the province during the War of 1812 heightened their determination to keep the province firmly within the British Empire. They believed that Upper Canada's strength came from its imperial connection and that the colony would weaken its position by becoming an independent nation or by forming part of a larger North American union. They believed that power had to remain in the hands of the governor and his appointed advisers. They agreed with Strachan that the colony needed the established Church of England to give a "moral underpinning to society." Finally, this elite believed in the economic progress of the province—to be directed by themselves—through commerce, canal building, settlement schemes, and banks.

Sir Peregrine Maitland, lieutenant governor from 1818 to 1828, reinforced the Family Compact's views of Upper Canada. He, too, favoured government through an appointed elite and readily allied himself with the members of the Executive Council. The governor and the Family Compact strengthened their hold on the colony through the Crown reserves.

By the 1820s, due to increased settlement during the immigration boom, the wealth from the Crown reserves had become substantial. These payments went directly to the governor and his Executive Council, much to the resentment of an emerging reform group in the elected Assembly.

The Clergy reserves became an even more contentious issue. In 1791 the British government had set aside one-seventh of the land in each township for the support of a "Protestant clergy" (see Chapter 11). John Strachan argued against the claims of the non-Anglican sects for a portion of these "Protestant reserves," maintaining that the Constitutional Act of 1791 had meant by the phrase "Protestant clergy" the Anglican church alone.

Religious Disputes

The first challenge to the Anglicans' ecclesiastical monopoly came from the Presbyterians. As the established Church of Scotland and a major Protestant denomination, they demanded a share of the revenues from the Clergy reserves. In 1829 the Colonial Office authorized the sharing of the revenues.

The Methodists, however, were denied a share of the revenues. This popular religious movement gained strength in Upper Canada with the influx of American immigrants. Its popularity rested on its appeal to a poor, backwoods frontier community. Through hymns, campfire meetings, and fervent preaching, Methodist preachers reached out to a population untouched by the more aloof and elitist Anglican church. Historian Fred Landon describes their camp meetings:

> Sometimes a wave of excitement would sweep over a gathering of this kind and as if moved by one impulse scores would rush to the altar, throwing themselves down, sobbing or groaning. This was the objective of the preaching and far into the night the ministers would move from group to group praying and exhorting the penitents.[1]

227

Using effective Native preachers such as Mississauga Indian Peter Jones, the Methodists converted two thousand Indians in Upper Canada to Christianity in the late 1820s. Indian and white Methodists built missions for Ojibwa-speaking converts at the Credit River, twenty kilometres west of York, and at Grape Island in the Bay of Quinte.

The growth of Methodism led to confrontation with the Anglicans. In 1825, Archdeacon John Strachan used the occasion of a funeral eulogy for Bishop Jacob Mountain of the Quebec Anglican diocese to make a vicious attack on certain "uneducated itinerant preachers" of the Methodist church. He described them as ignorant, incapable, idle, and, above all, disloyal, because of their emotionally charged and "republican" views.

The Methodists counterattacked through Egerton Ryerson, a twenty-three-year-old preacher who wrote a thundering reply, 12 000 words in length, in 1826. Raised in a prominent Anglican family but converted to Methodism, Ryerson asserted the educated quality of the itinerant preachers, denied that Methodists held republican views, and challenged the legality of Strachan's position that the Church of England was the established church in the province. So began the public career of Egerton Ryerson, to become a leading figure in education and politics for a half century in Upper Canada.

Other Protestant denominations and sects appeared in the province. Baptists, Quakers, Dunkards, Millerites, Campbellites, Christian Universalists, Mormons, and German-speaking Mennonites entered Upper Canada, creating greater religious pluralism. With the immigration of Irish Catholics, the Roman Catholic church strengthened its position, too.

Source: From Egerton Ryerson, *The Story of My Life*, edited by J. George Hodgins (Toronto, 1883), 59.

The Mississauga Indian village on the Credit River during the winter of 1826–27. The houses, just built, were dressed log cottages with two rooms, of the type erected as a second house by settlers who had been on their farms five to ten years. Two Indian families occupied each of these homes, each family having its own room. Originally twenty of these two-family houses were built.

Education

Religious disputes extended to education. Prior to 1815, schooling was very informal and frequently occurred in the home, conducted by parents, governesses, or tutors. Sunday schools began as a means of educating children who had to work the other six days of the week. A few grammar schools, or district schools, existed for the training of boys from well-to-do families who were destined for the professions. Girls fortunate enough to be educated were generally taught at home. In 1816 a committee of the Assembly introduced the Common School Act, which allotted £6000 annually to state-supported, common primary schools intended, at least in theory, for all children. Responsibility for building and maintaining the schools was to rest in the hands of local boards.

Strachan wanted these common schools under clerical control to counteract dangerous American tendencies, such as the use of American textbooks and American-trained teachers. But the Assembly successfully opposed the idea in favour of non-sectarian schools. It was a modest victory, however, since financial constraints reduced the annual appropriation for maintaining these schools to only £2500 in 1820.

Lack of local funds kept the number of schools to a minimum. J.G. Hodgins, the late-nineteenth-century historian of education in Ontario, noted that the proportion of Upper Canadian children in the 1830s who received an elementary education was about one in twenty-four.[2] Only after the Act of Union was implemented in 1841 was a proper, province-wide, non-sectarian educational system established, organized by the same young man who had confronted John Strachan in 1826—Egerton Ryerson.

Thwarted in his efforts for sectarian education in the common schools, Strachan directed his energy toward the grammar schools. These elite institutions, he believed, could offset the "Americanized" common schools. In 1819 he introduced legislation that required both an annual examination of all the grammar schools in the province and an annual report to the lieutenant governor. He also tried to introduce Andrew Bell's monitorial schools, an English system based on the teaching of Church of England doctrines, but the Assembly voted down the suggestion.

In an attempt to connect higher education with the Church of England, Strachan, in 1827, helped draw up a royal charter to establish King's College, a provincial university, in the capital town of York. The university was to be closely affiliated with the Church of England through the hiring of Anglican professors and through a divinity school for training Anglican clergy.

229

Once again, the Assembly opposed these "sectarian tendencies" and refused to support the provincial university. Strachan had to be content with a good preparatory school, modelled on the English classical schools and later known as Upper Canada College. King's College would not come into existence until 1843. By that time, the Methodists had already established their own university, Victoria College, in Cobourg, and the Presbyterians had Queen's College in Kingston.

Social and Humanitarian Concerns

With the large influx of immigrants, many of whom were destitute, into Upper Canada after 1815 came a concern for relief for the poor. Previously, relief had been granted to people in distress only on the recommendation of a magistrate. In 1817 the first major public-welfare agency, the Society for the Relief of Strangers, was established at York. Modelled on a similar society in London, England, this voluntary organization was created "to serve the wants and alleviate the misery" of destitute immigrants. In 1828 the society changed its name to "the Society for the Relief of the Sick and Destitute." The altered name reflected a change in attitude about social assistance: only individuals who were both sick and destitute would be eligible for relief. Able-bodied but unemployed individuals had to work in return for assistance. The assumptions were that work was available for everyone and that able-bodied people who did not work were lazy. What they needed was a moral lesson in frugality, hard work, and self-discipline. "Houses of Industry" were established in 1837 to provide work for all "fit and able inmates." Anyone who refused to conform was imprisoned and punished in order to instil fear and to create "a terror to evil-doers." More-hardened criminals were seen as being beyond reform.

Reformers also linked unemployment to crime, social unrest, and drunkenness. The first temperance societies in Upper Canada appeared in the Niagara peninsula. Drunkenness was a serious social problem contributing to family break-ups, poor work habits, and low productivity. Alcohol abuse also led to increased violence as well as social and political upheaval.

By the 1830s district temperance societies existed throughout the province, usually connected with the Methodist, Presbyterian, or Baptist churches. In 1839 the Upper Canadian temperance societies affiliated with the American Temperance Union. The temperance movement aimed at abstinence through self-restraint rather than through government legislation, in the belief that drunkenness was a personal problem requiring a personal solution.

Cholera, which entered the Canadas in the early 1830s with the British immigrants, posed an immediate and pressing social problem (see Chapter 13). Near-panic prevailed in the summer of 1832, when the board of health recorded 273 deaths from the dread disease in York alone. In the province as a whole, at least 550 people died that summer. The disease became most people's primary concern; as one Upper Canadian complained, "Nothing is to be heard but the 'cholera.' " The disease ran its course, only to return in 1834 to cause another nearly 350 deaths in Upper Canada. The first major medical breakthrough occurred only in the early 1850s: cholera was finally linked to contaminated water.

Economic Developments

The mass immigration of 1815–40 contributed to economic growth. During this period, Upper Canada became a thriving, complex, and viable society based on an exchange economy, both export and domestic, and financed by both capital and credit. The expansion rested primarily on wheat farming, and agriculture thus became the backbone of the Upper Canadian economy. Historian John McCallum notes that "close to three-quarters of the cash income of Ontario farmers was derived from wheat, and wheat and flour made up well over half of all exports from Ontario until the early 1860s."[3]

Successful farming required the collaborative effort of husband, wife, and children. Farm wives and daughters often took charge of barnyard chores and tended to gardens and fruit growing in addition to their household tasks, thereby freeing the men and boys to work in the fields. Many women also produced such goods as spun wool, woven goods, and butter and cheese both for home use and for sale. Revenues from such selling accumulated and often made the difference between lucrative and subsistence farming.

Only timber rivalled wheat as the major export staple of Upper Canada. The timber trade was a by-product of farming, since settlers had to clear the forests before being able to farm the land. No one thought in terms of conservation at the time. Trees had no inherent value beyond the price they brought as timber. In fact, the settlers often saw trees as their enemy. They recklessly cut down forested areas at the headwaters of rivers. The soil erosion that resulted caused tonnes of silt to pour into streams flowing into Lake Ontario. This, in turn, destroyed the Atlantic salmon's spawning grounds. By the mid-nineteenth century, the Atlantic salmon no longer migrated in vast numbers up the St. Lawrence to Lake Ontario. The last Atlantic salmon were caught in Ontario in the 1890s. (A century later, in 1988, the Ontario Ministry of Natural Resources began re-introducing the fish to Lake Ontario.)

231

Only in the Ottawa Valley, with its rich forests of pine and oak and the easy access it afforded to the St. Lawrence, did lumbering outstrip agriculture as the primary industry. Here, tensions between French Canadian and Irish lumbermen surfaced in the 1830s. The Irish lumbermen, or "Shiners," as they were called, were a boisterous and rugged group who terrorized the logging communities in the Ottawa Valley. Under the leadership of Peter Aylen, a millionaire who wanted to control the timber trade in the valley, the Shiners picked fights with the French Canadians over economic, ethnic, and religious issues. Their actions reflected their own uncomfortable position as Irish Catholics in a predominantly English Protestant society, and they lashed out at another minority. The Shiners' War, as it became known, gave Bytown (renamed Ottawa in 1855) a rough-hewn image.

Wheat and timber required transportation networks. Roads were built by the Canada Company, the Talbot settlers south of London, and the military settlers in the Ottawa Valley and the Kingston area. Around York, a road system was developed to link the capital to outlying regions that were dependent on it for trade.

In the 1820s the first regular stagecoach line was established between York and Kingston. The service was erratic at first, since the coaches required from two to four days to complete a one-way trip. By the 1830s, however, daily service was available all year round. At the same time, coach lines along Yonge Street began to service the towns, villages, hamlets, and farming communities north of York (or Toronto, as it was named again in 1834).

CANAL BUILDING

The Great Lakes–St. Lawrence natural waterway provided an effective alternative means of transportation, but only if natural obstacles, notably Niagara Falls and the rapids at Lachine near Montreal, could be overcome. Canals offered a solution, and in 1825 the first canal was completed around the Lachine rapids. Canals also enabled small naval vessels to enter the heart of North America to defend against possible American aggressors. Trade and military protection thus provided an incentive for canal building.

The British and Upper Canadian governments largely paid for the province's first two megaprojects constructed in the 1820s and 1830s— the Rideau Canal and the Welland Canal. The British government wanted the Rideau Canal to link Bytown (Ottawa) with Kingston for defence purposes. It put up the money for the entire cost of construction, which in the end amounted to one million pounds, making it the costliest military work undertaken until then by the British government in defence of North America. The British also provided the engineering expertise for the enterprise.

Lt.-Col. John By of the Royal Engineers arrived in 1826 to oversee the Rideau Canal project. Over a six-year period, By supervised a force of four thousand who worked with shovel and wheelbarrow, sometimes sixteen hours a day, six days a week. Swarms of mosquitoes and blackflies plagued the workers all spring and summer. In the swamps and marshes, swamp fever and malaria were rampant. A heavy, noxious mist arose from the decaying vegetable matter excavated after stagnant water had been drained off. Trees were cut back in an effort to provide freer air circulation at the work sites, in keeping with the prevailing medical belief that malaria was caused by foul air (*mal aria*). More than five hundred men lost their lives in the work camps.

When completed in 1832, the waterway, threading through a series of lakes, was more than 210 km in length and contained forty-seven locks. (The original locks are still in operation today.) It had been an ambitious undertaking to meet an American attack that never materialized; nonetheless, it helped boost the economy of the eastern part of the province.

The incentive behind construction of the Welland Canal was strictly commercial. But, once again, the impetus for action came from the United States. Although a political boundary existed between the two countries after 1783, there was no economic boundary. Montreal and New York merchants competed for the monopoly of inland trade. In 1825 the Americans completed the Erie Canal, which linked the Great Lakes by water with the Hudson River and the ice-free port of New York. The new canal attracted much of the trade from the American West and from Upper Canada. Great Lakes farmers found it cheaper and faster to ship via New York to Britain. New York rose to economic primacy in North America, with a population by the early 1830s of a quarter-million—roughly the size of Upper Canada's entire population. A young St. Catharines merchant and second-generation Loyalist, William Hamilton Merritt, dreamed of building a canal to by-pass Niagara Falls and thus make the St. Lawrence– Great Lakes waterway system an effective rival to the Erie Canal. The British government agreed to underwrite one-ninth of the cost of construction in return for the right of government ships to pass through the canal toll-free. John B. Yates, an American investor from Oswego, New York, became the largest shareholder in Merritt's Welland Canal Company, while the government of Upper Canada offered a land grant and a loan of £25 000. In the end, Merritt's private project became the biggest publicly financed project of its time. In 1829 Merritt completed the first Welland canal to join Lakes Ontario and Erie, by-passing Niagara Falls.

233

EARLY BANKS IN UPPER CANADA

These major projects required large amounts of capital, which, in turn, created a need for banks. Banks did not appear in Upper Canada until after the War of 1812. The early ones were branches of the Bank of Montreal, which soon proved inadequate for Upper Canadian merchants, who wanted their own banks. In 1819 the merchants of Kingston applied to the government to charter a provincial bank. Much to their dismay and anger, their appeal was denied in favour of a more recent one from prominent York merchants.

This York bank, known as the Bank of Upper Canada, came to be dominated by the government. Nine of its fifteen directors belonged to Upper Canada's Executive or Legislative councils, while the government supplied more than one-quarter of the bank's stock. As historian Gerald Craig concluded, "It is no exaggeration to say that the Bank of Upper Canada was a creature of the emerging Family Compact."[4]

The establishment of the first Upper Canadian bank at York rather than at Kingston indicated York's dominant position as the provincial capital, a position it had held since 1797, when the seat of government was transferred from Niagara-on-the-Lake for security reasons. Through control of the wholesale trade to towns and rural areas within its radius of influence, York had become the most influential community in central Upper Canada. In population, York went from twelve hundred in 1820 to more than nine thousand in 1834, the year of its incorporation as the city of Toronto. Economic growth in the 1840s and 1850s would further strengthen Toronto's dominance in Upper Canada. The areas immediately adjacent to the city, such as the Home and Gore districts, were largely under its control. In 1840, when the Canadas were united, one in five Upper Canadians lived within 125 km of Toronto.

Rise of a Reform Movement

The 1820s were a time of political polarization into conservative and reform camps. Led by the Family Compact, the conservatives favoured British monarchical association, appointed legislative and executive councils, and a stable and hierarchical society free of any political opposition. Their ideology was the Upper Canadian equivalent of the British "court" ideology that was premised on a strong central government. Economically, they endorsed enterprises such as building canals and establishing banks, which they believed would advance the commercial well-being of the province. The conservatives obtained strong support from the newly arrived middle- and upper-class British immigrants.

The Reform members of the Assembly opposed Conservative policies and called for political change. They tended to be "late Loyalists" or recent British immigrants who favoured an elected Legislative Council, or upper house, and an Executive Council that was responsible to the Assembly rather than the Governor. Economically, the Reformers favoured policies to promote agriculture, since, in large part, they represented the farmers of the central and western areas of the province. They often opposed commercial enterprises such as canal building and banks, which they saw as being either expensive or of no benefit to farmers.

Thus, there developed in the province a situation roughly parallel to that in Lower Canada (see Chapter 13). In both provinces, many of the conservatives could be considered "reactionary" politically but "progressive" economically, while the Reformers were "radical" politically but "reactionary" economically.

GOURLAY AND MACKENZIE

Robert Gourlay, a Scottish immigrant who arrived in Upper Canada in 1817, initiated the first serious criticism of the Family Compact. Soon after his arrival, he complained about the tiny elite's control of the appointed Legislative Council. He favoured township meetings similar to those in New England, where people could express their grievances. Gourlay also advocated more power for the elected Assembly. These radical views, along with his attempt to stir up discontent, led to his prosecution (under a wartime act dating from 1804 that regulated the conduct of immigrants) and his subsequent expulsion from Upper Canada in 1819.

This "banished Briton" left a legacy of political protest. Before his arrest, he circulated a questionnaire asking people to indicate what they believed to be the major problems in Upper Canada. He received a litany of complaints. Settlers thought the roads were in bad shape. They complained about the Clergy reserves and the Crown reserves. They opposed restrictions on American immigration. These and other complaints continued to be heard throughout the 1820s, especially among members of the Assembly who

National Archives of Canada/C-12632.

The road between York and Kingston, Upper Canada, 1830. A watercolour by James Pattison Cockburn (1779–1847), a British Army officer.

called themselves "Gourlayites" and who attempted to carry on their leader's agitation. A Reform party began to take shape in the Assembly in 1824.

William Lyon Mackenzie, who arrived in Upper Canada from Scotland in 1820, continued Gourlay's cause. In 1824, at Queenston, he started a newspaper, *The Colonial Advocate*, dedicated to the Reform cause. He relocated the newspaper to York in 1825, and the following year his editorial attacks on leading Upper Canadians led some young Family Compact members to break into his office and throw his typesetting equipment into Lake Ontario. Such acts only helped to make Mackenzie a hero to the Reformers and strengthened his determination to continue his campaign. The Scottish immigrant won a seat in the Assembly in the election of 1828.

That election returned the first Reform majority to the Assembly. Reformers such as John Rolph, Marshall Spring Bidwell (whose father, Barnabas Bidwell, had been expelled from the Assembly in 1821 under the Alien Act as an American), and William and Robert Baldwin (father and son) led the new group. But the election of 1830 saw the Reformers lose their majority in the Assembly. This defeat did not dampen their enthusiasm, however. They saw themselves as accomplishing for Upper Canada what like-minded Reformers in Britain and in the United States were doing for their countries. In Britain, the Whig government of Lord Grey was agitating for reform and in 1832 introduced the Great Reform Bill, which broadened the franchise to include people with a moderate amount of wealth, and not only those who possessed property. In the United States, President Andrew Jackson led a democratic movement based on universal suffrage and the right of anyone to hold public office. So the Upper Canadian Reformers believed that they were part of a greater progressive movement that would ultimately triumph.

236

Move to Rebellion

In the early 1830s William Lyon Mackenzie shifted to a radical reform position, chiefly as a result of a visit to the United States. In 1829 he had met President Andrew Jackson and had observed Jacksonian democracy— an attempt to make government responsive to the needs of the people— in practice. He returned to Upper Canada committed to the same ideals. Thwarted in his aspirations, he renewed his attacks on the political elite to the point that he was expelled from the Assembly, only to be re-elected and expelled three more times. In 1832 he visited England and met such British Reformers as Jeremy Bentham, Richard Cobden, and John Bright. In London the fiery newspaper editor presented the complaints of the Upper Canadian Reformers, as he saw them, to a sympathetic and receptive British government, which mistakenly believed that Mackenzie's views represented those of the majority of Upper Canadians.

Mackenzie's views were not even representative of the majority of Reformers. A rift occurred by the mid-1830s between a moderate wing led by Robert Baldwin and supported by Egerton Ryerson and a radical wing under Mackenzie and John Rolph. The moderates did not want the American form of elective government that Mackenzie advocated. Instead, they favoured the British plan of responsible government—that is, a government responsible to the Assembly.

After the Reformers regained control of the Assembly in 1834, the radical Reformers began taking action on their own. Mackenzie, just chosen as Toronto's first mayor as well as an Assembly member, was selected chairman of an Assembly grievance committee that produced the famous Seventh Report on Grievances in 1835. It contained a wide-ranging attack on the existing system of colonial government and demanded an elected Legislative Council, an Executive Council responsible to the Assembly, and severe limitations on the lieutenant governor's control of patronage.

The new governor, Sir Francis Bond Head, appointed in 1836, unexpectedly made a positive gesture to the Reformers by appointing two of their members, Robert Baldwin and John Rolph, to the Executive Council. *237* Then he proceeded to ignore the Council's advice, prompting Reformers on the Council to resign. They persuaded their fellow members to follow suit. The Assembly censured the governor and then blocked the granting of supplies, preventing the government from spending money. Head retaliated by refusing to approve any money bills. Then Bond Head dissolved the legislature and called an election for the early summer. He actively campaigned in the election for the Conservatives, warning that the battle was between American republicanism and the British connection.

The Tories won the election conclusively. Their success could be attributed in part to Head's intervention in the campaign and to his appeal to the loyalty of recent British immigrants. A large number in the colony sided with the governor and the Family Compact, fearing that the Reformers were dangerously radical and "republican." The Conservatives also used questionable tactics to influence the election: bribery, corruption, the careful selection of polling places, and the rapid enfranchisement of new British immigrants. This convinced Mackenzie and the radical Reformers that fair elections and peaceful reform were impossible. They overestimated, however, the popular mood for an armed rebellion.

In his newspaper, *The Constitution*, begun symbolically on July 4, 1836, Mackenzie cited the American Revolution as justification for direct action. A group of his followers issued a Toronto Declaration closely modelled on that of the American Declaration of Independence. It read in part:

Government is founded on the authority and is instituted for the benefit of a people; when, therefore, any Government long and systematically ceases to answer the great ends of its foundation, the people have a natural right given them by their Creator to seek after and establish such institutions as will yield the greatest quantity of happiness to the greatest number.

Economic and social forces had contributed to unrest in the province. In 1836 an economic downturn occurred in the Western world. In Upper Canada this recession led to tight bank credit and even a recall of loans, which hit farmers especially hard. Such action intensified Mackenzie's already deep distrust of banks. Along with hard financial times came a series of crop failures in 1835–37 that made a number of farmers in the region north of Toronto prepared to follow Mackenzie into rebellion.

In the western region of the province, around London, a separate group led by Dr. Charles Duncombe prepared to join them. News of the uprising of Lower Canadian Patriotes under Louis-Joseph Papineau (see Chapter 13) further encouraged rebellion.

238

The Upper Canadian Rebellion of 1837

Mackenzie set the date of the uprising for Thursday, December 7. The previous Friday, December 1, he had printed a leaflet urging people to prepare to arm. Meanwhile, John Rolph claimed that the Toronto authorities knew of the rebels' plans and proposed an earlier date of December 4, before government preparations were complete.

During the evening and night of December 4, about five hundred ill-clad and poorly armed rebels gathered at Montgomery's Tavern on Yonge Street (just north of present-day Eglinton Avenue) for the attack. The next day they marched down Yonge Street under the command of Mackenzie. A truce party, which included Robert Baldwin among others, met them, and Mackenzie explained the rebels' demands.

It was not until later in the afternoon that he led his followers farther down Yonge Street toward the city. The rest was tragicomedy. Mackenzie's forces met a party of twenty government men. Mackenzie's front rank fired, then dropped to the ground to let the next rank fire over their heads. Those behind thought their front-rank men had been killed, and they fled in panic.

That same night reinforcements for the government side arrived from Hamilton. By Thursday, December 7, the Loyalist forces were 1500 strong. They marched up Yonge Street to attack Mackenzie's force stationed at Montgomery's Tavern. During the second battle the rebels were routed within half an hour. The Loyalist forces then burned the tavern and marched back to Toronto.

Mackenzie's ill-conceived and ill-fated rebellion was over. He escaped to the United States while some of his followers were captured. Among them were two leaders, Samuel Lount and Peter Mathews, who were later

WHERE HISTORIANS DISAGREE

The Causes of the Rebellion of 1837 in Upper Canada

Amateur historians were the first to write about the rebellion of 1837 in Upper Canada. They were both partisan and emotional in their approach because of their closeness to the incident in both time and circumstance. Charles Lindsey, the son-in-law of William Lyon Mackenzie, the leader of the rebellion, blamed the Family Compact's refusal to compromise for driving the moderate Mackenzie to rebellion. In his two-volume work on the rebellion, *The Story of Upper Canadian Rebellion* (2 vols., Toronto, 1885), journalist cum historian J.M. Dent challenged Lindsey's view and depicted a diabolical and extreme Mackenzie who led the colony to an unnecessary struggle. These amateur historians all believed that the cause of the rebellion was political—a classic struggle between "democracy" and "privilege." This was the Liberal interpretation of history that held sway in the late nineteenth and the early twentieth centuries. During the 1920s, when Canada was moving toward autonomy, a nationalist school of historical writing saw the rebellion as an attempt to gain independence from Britain. The rebellion became an important event on the road from "colony to nation."

In the midst of the economic upheaval of the Great Depression of the 1930s, an economic interpretation of the rebellion appeared. Historian Donald Creighton depicted the rebellion in Upper Canada as a struggle between agrarian interests, represented by Mackenzie and his followers, and commercial interests, which controlled the appointed Executive and Legislative councils. "The rebellions were," Creighton wrote in *The Commercial Empire of the St. Lawrence* (Toronto, 1937), "the

final expression of that hatred of the rural community for the commercialism of the St. Lawrence" (p. 316). Creighton bolstered his economic argument by pointing out that the rebellions broke out in Upper Canada after a succession of crop failures that had brought farmers to the point of starvation and bankruptcy.

Intellectual historians depicted Mackenzie as a man of ideas, who drew his inspiration and his direction from Reform movements in both Britain and the United States. They saw the rebellion in Upper Canada as part of a general Reform impulse that swept western Europe and North America. In "The Political Ideas of William Lyon Mackenzie" in *Canadian Journal of Economics and Political Science* 3(1937):1–22, R.A. MacKay noted: "Few public men in Canadian history have so represented the spirit of their age as did William Lyon Mackenzie, and particularly during the pre-Rebellion stage of his career. This was the age of Catholic Emancipation and the Great Reform Bill, the age of Bentham and Byron, of Cobbett and Edinburgh Reviewers, of O'Connell and Huskisson; the age when the bourgeois monarchy of Louis Philippe triumphed over the last of the Bourbons at Paris, and when 'King' Andrew Jackson succeeded the Adams dynasty at Washington. On both sides of the Atlantic the new wine of liberty and democracy was bursting the old bottles of restriction and privilege.... In the 1820's and 1830's William Lyon Mackenzie was the principal purveyor of these wines of liberty to the backwoods colony of Upper Canada" (p.1).

In the 1960s social historians questioned whether the rebellion in Upper Canada was a class struggle.

Marxist historian Stanley Ryerson interpreted the rebellion as a bourgeois-democratic revolution caused by oppression and led by men who were fighting for the cause of popular liberty. "Workers . . . made up nearly half, and farmers over 40 per cent of the victims of oppression: a significant indication of the social forces that were engaged in action," Ryerson wrote in *Unequal Union: Confederation and the Roots of Conflict in the Canadas, 1815–1873* (Toronto, 1968), p. 131. Fellow Marxist historian Leo Johnson in "Land Policy, Population Growth and Social Structure in Home District, 1793–1851" *Ontario History*, 63(1971):41–60, saw the roots of the rebellion in an inequitable system of land grants designed from the time of Governor Simcoe to create a landed gentry class at the expense of the ordinary farmer. The rebellion was a fight between two different views of land ownership by two different classes of people.

Recently, historian Colin Read has challenged the image of the Upper Canadian rebellion as a "people's revolution," in *The Rising in Western Upper Canada* (Toronto, 1980). Using the less-known Duncombe uprising in the London area, Read has concluded: "There is no basis for arguing that the rebels comprised a clearly disadvantaged sector of society and hence were driven to arms by economic despair or the prospect of plunder" (p. 207). What did distinguish rebels from loyalists, according to Read, was the large number of rebels who were either American-born or born to American parents and who "retained or adopted the deep American dislike of Britain and have been more willing to rebel, hoping to sever the provincial ties to Great Britain" (p.208). This ideological split was the real cause of the rebellion.

The debate continues, with no interpretation emerging as the definitive one. The net result, however, is a richer and deeper understanding of the decade of the 1830s in Upper Canada, out of which the rebellion of 1837 arose.

tried and hanged. In the western region of the province, Duncombe had gathered five hundred troops by December 13. Allan MacNab, a businessman, land speculator, and Loyalist leader, led an opposing group of five hundred Loyalists. Upon hearing of Mackenzie's defeat, Duncombe's men began to desert the camp. When MacNab attacked on the morning of December 14, he found only a few rebels. Most, including Duncombe, had escaped to the United States.

COUNTERATTACKS FROM THE UNITED STATES

From across the border the rebel leaders planned further attacks on the government of Upper Canada. They found eager support in the United States among those who saw the rebellion either as a Canadian version of the American Revolution—an attempt to end British tyranny—or as an opportunity to annex Upper Canada to the United States. Some American supporters simply saw it as an opportunity for looting.

Mackenzie gathered together a motley band of supporters who occupied Navy Island on the Canadian side of the Niagara River, where they proclaimed a provisional government. Upper Canadian officials retaliated by burning the *Caroline*, an American ship used to ferry men and supplies from the American side to Navy Island.

Mackenzie's supporters and American sympathizers crossed the border throughout 1838. The largest incident was the Battle of the Windmill near Prescott, Ontario, in November, in which two hundred invaders barricaded themselves in an old windmill until they were forced to surrender. Thirty men were killed and the rest taken prisoner. The government hanged eleven for instigating and taking part in the battle. In the end, more than one thousand people in the province were jailed on suspicion of treason as a result of the rebellion.

Durham's Report

241

The Rebellion of 1837 in Upper Canada was a minor affair from a military standpoint, but together with the more extensive uprising in Lower Canada, it convinced Britain of the need for change. (These were the only British colonies that had resorted to violence to achieve responsible government.) The British cabinet responded by relieving Head of his post in early 1838 and sending out one of its most gifted politicians, Lord Durham, or "Radical Jack," as he was nicknamed, to inquire into the affairs of the colony and report back to the British government. The prime minister gave Durham broader powers than any of his predecessors, making him governor general of all the British North American colonies. He arrived in May 1838.

Durham spent most of his five months in Lower Canada, but he made one short visit to Upper Canada, where he consulted with Robert Baldwin, one of the Upper Canadian Reform leaders. Despite the brevity of his stay in the Canadas, the time spent was very important, for on it was based one of the most important documents in Canadian history—his famous *Report on the Affairs of British North America*, better known as *Durham's Report*.

In his report Durham made three main proposals. First, he recommended greater colonial self-government. He said that local affairs should be colonial matters, and only the larger issues such as constitutional concerns, foreign relations, trade with Britain and other British colonies, and disposal of public lands should be reserved by the mother country. Durham also believed that the colonial governor should choose his closest advisers, the members of the Executive Council, from the majority party in the Assembly and that the governor should abide by the wishes of these elected representatives. Although Durham did not call this "responsible government," it nonetheless came to be known as such.

Finally, Durham recommended a union of the two colonies of Upper and Lower Canada. Such a union was designed primarily to benefit Upper

Canada, since it would improve trade for the inland colony and force Lower Canadians to assume part of the debt incurred by Upper Canadians during the building of the canals. He saw such a union as the nucleus of an eventual larger union of all the British North American colonies, which he highly favoured, and as a necessary precursor to the assimilation of the French Canadians.

Lord Sydenham, Durham's successor, implemented the recommendation for a union of the Canadas in 1840–41. Before it came into effect Sydenham resolved a long-standing disagreement in Upper Canada. He worked out an arrangement by which the two leading Protestant denominations—the Church of England (Anglican) and the Church of Scotland (Presbyterian)—would share half the proceeds of future sales of Clergy reserves while the other half would be divided among the other denominations, according to their numbers.

By the terms of the Act of Union of 1840, the capital of the new province became Kingston. English was to be the only official language of the Assembly, the united colony would assume Upper Canada's debt, and the Assembly would consist of eighty-four members—forty-two from Upper Canada and forty-two from Lower Canada. Upper Canada officially ceased to exist. Instead, the area became known as Canada West and formed part of a larger union of English and French Canadians.

A new era began in the history of the province, one that ultimately led to a wider union of all the British North American colonies, as Durham had envisioned.

242

NOTES

[1]Fred Landon, *Western Ontario and the American Frontier*, (Toronto, 1967; first published 1941), 125.
[2]J.G. Hodgins, ed., *Documentary History of Education*, vol. 4 (Toronto, 1897), 160, cited in Hazel Mathews, *Oakville and the Sixteen* (Toronto, 1953), 107.
[3]John McCallum, *Unequal Beginnings: Agriculture and Economic Development in Quebec and Ontario Until 1870* (Toronto, 1980), 4.
[4]Gerald M. Craig, *Upper Canada: The Formative Years, 1784–1841* (Toronto, 1963), 162.

Related Readings

A useful article on this topic is contained in R. Douglas Francis and Donald B. Smith, *Readings in Canadian History: Pre-Confederation*, 3d ed. (Toronto, 1990): John Leslie, "Buried Hatchet: The Origins of Indian Reserves in 19th-Century Ontario," 379–85.

BIBLIOGRAPHY

The best overview of Upper Canadian society in 1815–40 is Gerald M. Craig, *Upper Canada: The Formative Years, 1784–1841* (Toronto, 1963). Gordon T. Stewart's *The Origins of Canadian Politics: A Comparative*

Approach (Vancouver, 1986) is a short interpretative study focussing on Upper Canada and looking at politics from an American-British-Canadian perspective. Also useful are the relevant chapters in J.M.S. Careless, ed., *Colonists and Canadians, 1760–1867* (Toronto, 1971): Michael Cross, "The 1820s," 149–72, and G.M. Craig, "The 1830s," 173–99. J.K. Johnson and Bruce G. Wilson, eds., *Historical Essays on Upper Canada: New Perspectives* (Ottawa, 1989): 593–604, contains an extensive annotated bibliography on topics in Upper Canadian history. The experience of immigrating to British North America is best described in Helen Cowan, *British Emigration to British North America: The First Hundred Years*, rev. and enlarged ed. (Toronto, 1961). A shorter version is Helen Cowan, *British Immigration Before Confederation*, a Canadian Historical Association booklet (Ottawa, 1968). Also useful are H.J.M. Johnston, "British Immigration to British North America, 1815–1860," the Canadian Museum of Civilization, Canada's Visual History Series, vol. 8 (Ottawa, 1974), and Edwin C. Guillet, *The Great Migration: The Atlantic Crossing by Sailing Ship since 1770*, 2d ed. (Toronto, 1963). Recent studies on Irish immigration and settlement in Upper Canada are D.H. Akenson, *The Irish in Ontario: A Study in Rural History* (Montreal, 1984), and Bruce S. Elliott, *Irish Migrants in the Canadas: A New Approach* (Kingston, 1988).

243

On the Family Compact, see Robert E. Saunders, "What Was the Family Compact?" *Ontario History* 49 (1957): 165–78, and reprinted in J.K. Johnson, *Historical Essays on Upper Canada* (Toronto, 1975), 122–40. The origins of an Upper Canadian elite and its change over time is the subject of S.J.R. Noel's *Patrons, Clients, Brokers: Ontario Society and Politics, 1791–1896* (Toronto, 1990). On conservatism in Upper Canada, see Jane Errington, *The Lion, the Eagle, and Upper Canada: A Developing Colonial Ideology* (Montreal, 1987), and David Mills, *The Idea of Loyalty in Upper Canada, 1784–1850* (Montreal, 1988). For the treatment of religion in the context of American immigration and political reform, see Fred Landon, *Western Ontario and the American Frontier* (Toronto, 1967; first published 1941). William Westfall's *Two Worlds: The Protestant Culture of Nineteenth Century Ontario* (Montreal, 1989) examines the different world views that emerged out of the two dominant religious strains—Anglican and Methodist—in mid-nineteenth century Upper Canada. An interesting survey is John Webster Grant's *A Profusion of Spires: Religion in Nineteenth-Century Ontario* (Toronto, 1988). On education, see S. Houston and A. Prentice, *Schooling and Scholars in Nineteenth-Century Ontario* (Toronto, 1988), and J. Donald Wilson, "Education in Upper Canada: Sixty Years of Change," in *Canadian Education: A History*, edited by J.D. Wilson, R.M. Stamp, and L.-P. Audet (Toronto, 1970), 190–213.

The importance of the wheat economy for Upper Canada is discussed in John McCallum, *Unequal Beginnings: Agriculture and Economic Development in Quebec and Ontario until 1870* (Toronto, 1980). On other aspects of the Upper Canadian economy, see D. McCalla's "The Internal Economy of Upper Canada: New Evidence on Agricultural Marketing Before 1850," in *Historical Essays on Upper Canada*, edited by Johnson and Wilson, 237–60, and his "Forest Products and Upper Canadian Development, 1815–46," *Canadian Historical Review* 68, 2 (June 1987): 159–98. Transportation developments and canal building in particular are briefly described in Gerald Tulchinsky, *Transportation Changes in the St. Lawrence–Great Lakes Region, 1828–1860*, Canada's Visual History Series, vol. 11 (Ottawa, 1974). Peter Baskerville reviews the history of banking in Upper Canada in his introduction to his edited work, *The Bank of Upper Canada: A Collection of Documents* (Toronto, 1987).

On early social assistance in Upper Canada, see Rainer Boehre, "Paupers and Poor Relief in Upper Canada," in *Historical Essays on Upper Canada*, edited by Johnson and Wilson, 305–40, and Stephen Speisman, "Munificent Parsons and Municipal Parsimony: Voluntary vs. Public Poor Relief in Nineteenth-Century Toronto," in *A History of Ontario: Selected Readings* edited by M.J. Piva (Toronto, 1988), 55–70. On early prisons in Upper Canada, see Peter Oliver, " 'A Terror to Evil-Doers': The Central Prison and the 'Criminal Class' in Late Nineteenth-Century Ontario," in *Patterns of the Past: Interpreting Ontario's History*, edited by R. Hall et al., (Toronto, 1988), 206–37. On the Shiners' War, see Michael Cross, "The Shiners' War: Social Violence in the Ottawa Valley in the 1830s," *Canadian Historical Review* 54 (March 1973): 1–26.

On the Reform movement, besides Craig, *Upper Canada*, and Landon, *Western Ontario* (both cited above), see Aileen Dunham, *Political Unrest in Upper Canada, 1815–1836* (Toronto, 1963; first published 1927). William Kilbourn's biography of William Lyon Mackenzie, *The Firebrand* (Toronto, 1956) is a lively account. On the discontent in western Upper Canada, see Colin Read's *The Rising in Western Upper Canada, 1837–38: The Duncombe Revolt and After* (Toronto, 1982) and, for the rebellion in general, Colin Read and Ron Stagg, eds., *The Rebellion of 1837 in Upper Canada* (Ottawa, 1985). The best short account of Egerton Ryerson is by Clara Thomas, *Ryerson of Upper Canada* (Toronto, 1969).

The standard work on Lord Durham remains C. New, *Lord Durham's Mission to Canada*, with an introduction by H.W. McCready (Toronto, 1963). Gerald Craig has edited and introduced an abridged version of Durham's Report in *Lord Durham's Report* (Toronto, 1963). A recent account is Janet Ajzenstat, *The Political Thought of Lord Durham* (Montreal, 1988). A valuable collection of articles, united under the title "Durham and His Ideas" appeared as a special issue of the *Journal of Canadian Studies* 25, 1 (Spring 1990).

A good overview of women in Upper Canada (and throughout North America) during this period is Alison Prentice et al., "Carders of Wool, Drawers of Water: Women's Work in British North America," ch. 3 in *Canadian Women: A History* (Toronto, 1988), 65–84. For bibliographical references to this topic, see Beth Light and Veronica Strong-Boag, *True*

Daughters of the North. Canadian Women's History: An Annotated Bibliography (Toronto, 1980). Jane Errington has written about Upper Canadian women in the early nineteenth century in " 'Woman . . . Is a Very Interesting Creature.' Some Women's Experiences in Early Upper Canada," *Historic Kingston* 38 (1990): 16–35. Recently, Elizabeth Gillan Muir published *Petticoats in the Pulpit: The Story of Early Nineteenth-Century Methodist Women Preachers in Upper Canada* (Toronto, 1991).

The Amerindian history of the period is reviewed for the Iroquois in Charles M. Johnston, ed. *The Valley of the Six Nations: A Collection of Documents on the Indian Lands of the Grand River* (Toronto, 1964), and for the Mississaugas and other Algonquian groups in Donald B. Smith, *Sacred Feathers: The Reverend Peter Jones (Kahkewaquonaby) and the Mississauga Indians* (Toronto, 1987); Peter S. Schmalz, *The Ojibwa of Southern Ontario* (Toronto, 1990); and James A. Clifton, *A Place of Refuge for All Time: Migration of the American Potawatomi into Canada, 1830 to 1850* (Ottawa, 1975). In his essay, "Native Limited Identities and Newcomer Metropolitanism in Upper Canada, 1814–1867," in *Old Ontario Essays in Honour of J.M.S. Careless,* edited by David Keane and Colin Read (Toronto, 1990): 148–173, Tony Hall reviews both the Iroquoian and Algonquian history of Upper Canada in the early nineteenth century. Ian A.L. Getty and Antoine S. Lussier, eds., *As Long as the Sun Shines and Water Flows* (Vancouver, 1983) contains several articles on the Indians of Upper Canada. On environmental destruction, see W. Fraser Sandercombe, *Nothing Gold Can Stay: The Wildlife of Upper Canada* (Erin, Ont., 1985).

245

Time Line: 1783–1864

1783–1818 — The Mississauga Indians surrender large tracts of land on the north shore of Lake Ontario and in the Niagara peninsula to the British.

1791 — The colony of Upper Canada is officially established.

1792 — John Graves Simcoe arrives as the first lieutenant governor of Upper Canada.
— The first legislature of Lower Canada is established.

1793 — Simcoe founds York (Toronto) which becomes Upper Canada's capital in 1796.

1794 — Signing of Jay's Treaty, which leads to the surrender of the western posts in 1796.

1806 — The timber trade undergoes dramatic expansion.
— The French Canadian newspaper, *Le Canadien*, is founded.

1812–1814 — War of 1812.

1812 — General Brock is killed at the battle of Queenston Heights.

1813 — Tecumseh, the great Amerindian leader, dies at the Battle of Moraviantown.
— An American invasion force is turned back at Châteauguay.

1817 — Canada's first chartered bank, the Bank of Montreal, is established.

1819 — Political activist Robert Gourlay is banished from Upper Canada.

1821 — With the union of the North West Company and the Hudson's Bay Company, Montreal ceases to be the centre of the fur trade.

1829 — Welland Canal opens for navigation between Lakes Ontario and Erie.

1832 — Rideau Canal is completed.
— The first of a series of cholera epidemics sweeps Lower Canada.

1834 — The Patriotes' Ninety-Two Resolutions of Grievances are adopted by the Assembly.

1837 — William Lyon Mackenzie leads an unsuccessful rebellion against British rule.
— The Patriotes are defeated at St-Charles and St-Eustache, after a Patriote victory at St-Denis.

1839 — In his *Report*, Lord Durham recommends the union of Upper and Lower Canada.

1840	—The Act of Union uniting Lower and Upper Canada is passed.
1841	—The Union of the Canadas comes into effect.
1845	—Publication of the first volume of François-Xavier Garneau's *Histoire du Canada*.
1846	—Britain introduces free trade and ends colonial timber and wheat preferences.
1848	—The Reform alliance of Robert Baldwin and Louis-Hippolyte La Fontaine secures responsible government in the Canadas.
1849	—Annexation Manifesto prepared in Montreal.
1852	—Susanna Moodie's *Roughing It in the Bush* is published.
1854	—British North America enters into a reciprocity agreement with the United States.
1857	—Queen Victoria chooses Ottawa as the future capital of Canada.
1858	—Octave Crémazie publishes his romantic historical poem, *Le Drapeau de Carillon*.
1859	—The Grand Trunk Railway, 1760 km long, is completed.
1861	—Outbreak of the American Civil War.
1864	—The "Great Coalition" is formed to work for British North American federation.

Rebellion on the St. Lawrence

The half-century between the partition of Quebec in 1791 and the union of the two Canadas in 1841 is usually remembered for the political and military events of the late 1830s. Certainly, the rebellion that broke out in Lower Canada at the end of 1837 and flared up again in late 1838 stands out as the most dramatic occurrence of this period. The Patriotes—that is, the rebels—shouted revolutionary rhetoric at mass meetings, laid plans to overthrow their British rulers, and took up arms. British troops intervened and brutally crushed the revolts. In the aftermath, the colonial authorities hanged, imprisoned, or exiled many Patriotes; hundreds more fled. The uprisings in Lower Canada were much more widespread and violent than those in Upper Canada.

Despite these dramatic events the real revolution taking place in Lower Canada lay in the transformation of the colony's economy, politics, society, and institutions. These profound changes had some positive effects, but they also contributed to the discontent that underlay the outbreak of violence in 1837–38.

Economic Revolution

At the close of the eighteenth century, Quebec entered a period of intense, if uneven, economic growth, as Britain's industrialization and urbanization created new markets for the colony's foodstuffs and resources. As the fur-trade era drew to a close, profits slumped because of declining demand overseas and ruinous competition at home. Yet some Montreal fur-trading firms succeeded in diversifying their interests, and prospered. Fur trader Peter McGill, for example, also became a timber exporter, a shipowner, a forwarder of goods to Upper Canada, a banker, and a railway promoter.

The decline of the fur trade was more than offset by the rise of the timber industry. Britain needed wood, especially to build ships. Napoleon's control of northern Europe from 1808 to 1810 cut Great Britain off from its traditional Baltic suppliers. As a result, Britain's imports of timber from Lower Canada and other North American colonies increased significantly. Then shipowners, working through the English Board of Trade, pressured the British government into doubling import duties on foreign timber. This effectively guaranteed a highly profitable monopoly to colonial suppliers even if the Baltic ports reopened. William Price, who came to Lower Canada in 1810, was one of several entrepreneurs who made his fortune selling timber. The company he founded would become a pioneer in the development of the pulp and paper industry nearly a century later.

Other sectors of the economy underwent significant, though less spectacular, development. Ships were built at nearly eighty localities along the St. Lawrence. Quebec City had the biggest shipyards, and much of its production went overseas to Britain. Sawmills, candle and soap manufacturers, textile factories, flour mills, and an expanding construction industry all participated in this growth. Beginning with the Bank of Montreal in 1817, banks were established to supply credit to new enterprises and commercial ventures.

Urban Life

The labour needed for resource exploitation and manufacturing was supplied by immigrants and by Lower Canada's rapidly growing population. Thanks to a birth rate that hovered slightly above 50 per 1000 throughout the period, the population quadrupled, rising from about 160 000 in 1790 to 650 000 in 1850. As early as the 1830s, French Canadians began emigrating to the United States in search of the land or work they could not find at home.

Lower Canada's cities developed rapidly as centres of both wealth and poverty. In the early 1800s, Quebec City grew at an annual rate of more than 5 percent, with the poor settling in the Lower Town suburb of St-Roch (much of which was destroyed by fire in May 1845. The next month, the Upper Town quarter of St-Jean-Baptiste was similarly ravaged by fire.) Most inhabitants had to pay seigneurial dues on their lots, and in hard times they often accumulated debts. Though faced with vehement opposition, the government occasionally attempted to force payment of these debts. During one of these periodic crises, in the fall of 1838, rumours circulated that the workers of St-Roch intended to sneak up to Quebec's Upper Town to strangle the bourgeois while they slept. Barrels of gunpow-

250

The Fire in the Saint-Jean Quarter, Seen Looking Westward, 1845, a painting by Joseph Légaré (1795–1855). Fire was a constant danger in communities with buildings constructed largely of wood. In June 1845, a fire broke out in Quebec's Upper Town, where it destroyed 1300 houses in the prosperous St-Jean quarter, leaving 10 000 people homeless. Only one month earlier a fire in Quebec's working class district of St-Roch in the Lower Town had demolished 1650 houses leaving 12 000 people homeless.

der and stocks of ammunition were discovered, and for some time thereafter the anxious burghers kept the city gates locked day and night.

Montreal also grew quickly. British North America's premier city had 22 500 residents in 1825. The merchants, who were mostly English speaking, dominated the city. Formerly involved in the fur trade, some diversified into grain and timber; others set up shops to manufacture products such as leather goods, clothing, barrels, and beer. To supply his Montreal brewery with locally grown barley, industrialist John Molson brought seed barley from England and distributed it among farmers. He also owned the first steamer on the St. Lawrence (which he acquired in 1809), sat in the Assembly and the Legislative Council, and was president of the Bank of Montreal.

Most workers were unskilled. Many labourers were forced to spend 60 percent of their earnings simply to feed their families. There were no unions, and legislation passed in 1802 authorized fines and prison sentences for striking workers.

Young women often found jobs as domestics. Some women took in boarders and were paid to provide meals and wash laundry. Convents began to train a few women as teachers.

Charitable institutions attempted to alleviate some of the problems associated with poverty. Roman Catholic nuns and Protestant philanthropists founded orphanages that took in the children of unwed, penniless, and even imprisoned women. Religious orders and lay associations also assisted destitute or sick women, as well as unmarried mothers.

Smallpox and Cholera Epidemics

In the early decades of the nineteenth century, disease posed a serious threat to public health. This was particularly true in the towns, with their unhealthy living conditions and relatively concentrated populations.

In 1815 Lower Canada's Assembly provided for public vaccination against smallpox. The method proved controversial, and public apathy and distrust kept many people away. In addition, politics intervened to undermine the credibility of the Vaccine Board: the government appointed as president of the board a doctor favoured by the British establishment rather than the highly respected Dr. François Blanchet, a senior physician and prominent member of the Assembly. Disputes over regulations and payment of doctors helped seal the fate of the program, which was ended in 1823, with very serious consequences. Smallpox continued to be a major source of death in the St. Lawrence Valley for many years: the last major outbreak, in 1885, killed three thousand people in Montreal.

251

In 1832 the first of a series of cholera epidemics provoked a wave of panic among Canadians. The disease, transmitted mainly through contaminated water supplies, had spread from the delta of the Ganges River across Europe to Britain. Its attacks were sudden, extremely painful, and very often fatal; death came within forty-eight hours, a result of complete dehydration of the victim's body. There was no known cure; in fact, treatment must often have hastened death. Patients were bled, even when they were in a state of collapse. Doctors administered laxatives, although the patients were suffering from uncontrollable diarrhea. Leeches and blisters were applied to the stomach. Fortunately for the victims of both the disease and the proposed remedies, physicians commonly prescribed opium as a pain-killer.

The arrival in Canada of large numbers of immigrants, very often indigents from the British Isles, caused much concern. They had been migrating in large numbers to Lower Canada since 1815, although most went on to Upper Canada or the United States. Some fifty thousand arrived in 1831. Many were steerage passengers who had spent weeks on the boats, in filthy conditions, and often near starvation. Worried about the threat these immigrants posed to public health, the government of Lower Canada established a quarantine station on Grosse Île, a small island in the

St. Lawrence below Quebec. The measure proved ineffective since regulations could not be enforced and medical services were totally inadequate.

Among those who perished in Lower Canada, perhaps on Grosse Île, was the wife of an Irish farmer named John Ford, who himself escaped illness. Ford went on to Detroit, where he began to farm. He was the grandfather of Henry Ford, the founder of the modern automobile industry.

Conditions in Lower Canadian towns enormously assisted the spread of infection. Many houses were dirty and overcrowded, yards and streets were piled with refuse, and towns had open sewers. Slaughterhouses, often located in residential districts, simply dumped their waste into open water. In early spring, 1832, the health board in Quebec City tried to force a general clean-up of streets, houses, and yards. Regulations that required homeowners to "scrape, wash and cleanse their premises and carry away all filth" proved to be unenforceable in the face of public indifference, if not outright hostility. In Montreal, city authorities had no choice but to sit back and wait for the expected attack of disease.

Cholera struck Quebec City at the end of the first week in June 1832. Hospitals overflowed with victims, while hundreds more lay in tents on the Plains of Abraham. Many panic-stricken residents fled to rural areas, often carrying the disease with them. To prevent despair, church bells were no longer rung for the dead after June 14. Police had to be called to enforce rapid burial of the deceased. By the end of October, seventy-five hundred residents of Quebec and Montreal—more than one-tenth of the population of each city—had died.

The disease had important political, as well as economic and social, consequences. French Canadians, particularly in nationalist circles, hotly debated immigration policy; many, including the mayor of Quebec, blamed the British authorities for doing nothing to control the merchants and shipowners who profited by transporting immigrants. They also vigorously censured Governor Aylmer's administration for its inaction.

During a second, less severe, outbreak of cholera in Quebec City in 1834, Lord Aylmer fled to Sorel, and most of the Executive Council took up more healthy residence in the country. Even the rich, however, were not spared. Perhaps out of self-interest more than concern for the poor, they began to lobby for the public-health measures that, decades later, would dramatically reduce the incidence of deadly diseases.

Rural Quebec

Nineteen out of twenty French Canadians in the early nineteenth century lived in rural areas, where they practised subsistence farming. Yet rural Quebec also underwent change. Thanks to the good harvests and high

252

wheat prices of the 1790s and early 1800s, many habitants accumulated small surpluses of wheat that they sold to grain merchants for export abroad. For a short time, habitants saw their living conditions improve.

But yields varied enormously, and after 1815, crop failures were more frequent. The productivity of even the best lands tended to drop after decades of cultivation without fertilization. New lands that had been opened up for colonization, especially those near the Canadian Shield, proved rocky and infertile. Crop diseases and insects were a constant threat: the wheat midge, for example, almost completely destroyed the harvests of 1834–36. While Upper Canada boosted its production, Lower Canada had to buy wheat from its western competitor to meet its own needs.

Farmers also had to contend with the effects of events abroad. The War of 1812 severely disrupted the grain trade, and depression in Britain in 1815–20 caused prices to fall dramatically. Tariff barriers, such as Britain's Corn Laws of 1815, blocked the entry of colonial grain when the British price fell below a certain level.

253

Historians agree that the 1830s witnessed a rapid deterioration of economic conditions, with famine reported in 1837. Some, like Fernand Ouellet, have blamed the habitant for failing to adopt more modern agricultural techniques such as crop rotation and for depleting soil nutrients while doing nothing to restore them. Others, like Jean-Pierre Wallot and John McCallum, contend that the habitants' alleged backwardness was the consequence, not than the cause, of their economic plight, and that farmers in Upper Canada and in the northeastern United States were no better versed in sound agricultural methods. Climatic factors and disease, as well as overpopulation, also seem to have played a part. Lacking the capital to invest in commercial substitutes for wheat, habitants turned more and more to peas, potatoes, and barley in order to avoid starvation. In despair, many of them supported the organizers of rebellion in 1837.

Alexis de Tocqueville, the French social philosopher, confirmed the existence of rural unrest during a visit to Lower Canada in the late summer of 1831. The Superior of the Sulpicians in Montreal assured him that there were no "happier people in the world than the French Canadians," and that they paid trifling rents and acquitted their dues to the church "ungrudgingly and easily." But when de Tocqueville rode into the countryside around Beauport, near Quebec City, and spoke with the habitants, he found them worried about immigration, resentful of the seigneurs, and envious of the wealth that the tithe placed in the hands of some clergy.

The habitants had annual seigneurial dues to discharge, although the dues were notoriously difficult to collect. Those who bought land had to pay a heavy mutation fine (transfer fee) to the seigneur. They were also obliged to grind their grain at the seigneur's mills—a lucrative privilege for the landed gentry. Historian Allan Greer asserts that this "feudal burden," while generally not crushing, made it difficult for the habitants to accumulate capital.[1] But in the crisis years of the 1830s, as the habitants' crops dwindled and their standard of living fell, their obligations must have weighed more heavily on them.

The Church

During this period, two groups vied to obtain influence and prestige among the habitants. On the one hand stood the Roman Catholic church, struggling to secure its independence from government dictates and implacably hostile to republican and liberal ideals. On the other was a new professional elite composed of notaries, lawyers, and doctors. They endorsed increasingly nationalistic ideas, particularly on political issues, and tended to be critical of the church; their forum was the colony's Assembly.

254

At the turn of the century, the church's position in Lower Canada was far from assured. In spite of what has been written by clerical historians about the habitants' profound religiosity, Canada was not a theocratic society, and the clergy were neither very influential nor dominant. Contemporary accounts detail the spread of religious indifference and even of anticlericalism, particulary among the bourgeoisie. Liberals read the works of philosophers such as Rousseau and Voltaire. As for the habitants, they did not challenge official dogma, although many were probably more superstitious and comformist than pious and fervent. They were also strong-minded and independent; they continually attempted to avoid paying tithes and other religious contributions and they feuded over pews, the location of new churches, and other matters of a material nature.

For its part, the clergy often complained of disorders and immorality, although that, admittedly, was their duty. Travellers reported frequently that the *Canadiens* danced, gorged themselves, got drunk to prepare themselves for Lent (which they scrupulously observed), then feasted again and got drunk to celebrate its passing. The church was even obliged to abolish several feast-days because of excesses, thus pleasing the British merchants who did not approve of these kinds of pleasures nor of the loss of time that they entailed.

To increase its influence within French Canadian society, the church needed more priests. Indeed, at this time, it faced a veritable crisis: the number of priests declined from about 200 in 1760 to only 150 in 1790 and then increased to somewhat more than 300 by the time of the rebellion—but the population had mushroomed from 70 000 to 500 000 in the same period. Bishop Ignace Bourget, who became Bishop of Montreal, complained that "there are not enough workers to help us cultivate the vine." During his tenure as Bishop of Quebec from 1806 to 1825, Monseigneur Joseph-Octave Plessis encouraged the establishment of classical colleges and succeeded in increasing the number of vocations.

The church, however, entertained serious doubts about the value of universal primary schooling. Many *curés* did not want to spend parish money on schools and some saw education as dangerous. Jean-Jacques Lartigue, named first bishop of the new diocese of Montreal in 1836, said of the habitants: "It is better for them not to have a literary education than to risk a bad moral education." As schools cost money and many habitants did not want to contribute to them, they agreed.

Some liberal French-speaking members of the Assembly saw education in a more positive light. So did the government, which in 1801 founded the Royal Institution for the Advancement of Learning (RIAL), a system of voluntary public education. The church, led by Plessis, was suspicious of the RIAL schools, since they were established by a Protestant government that still hoped for the assimilation and Protestantization of the habitants; the church, therefore, chose to ignore the schools and very few were established. *255*

When in 1818 the Assembly set up a board of trustees to oversee education, Plessis refused to participate in this essentially English-speaking Protestant body. The board, however, did authorize separate religious worship, visits to the schools by priests, and French-language textbooks. It also appointed French-speaking Roman Catholic teachers in French-speaking areas of the province. Still, the local priests regarded the schools at best with indifference and sometimes with outright hostility. Many refused to become visitors, often on Plessis's orders.

In an effort to remodel educational legislation to make it more satisfactory to the church, the Assembly authorized the church to build its own schools, to be financed and directed by parish *fabriques* or councils. In the Legislative Council, Plessis urged state financing, but the government replied that, because of the Assembly's obstruction, no money was available. It was becoming more apparent, however, that French-speaking liberals favourable to non-confessional schools constituted as much a threat to clerical ambitions as did Anglo-Protestant government officials. Indeed, in 1829, the liberals supported a bill that gave control of schools to the Assembly and to local officials (syndics).

Within three years, many state-supported schools were built, leading to disputes between parish priests and town officials over their operation. Finally in 1836, in the face of church pressure, the Assembly abrogated the Elementary Schools Act. The way was now open for clerical control of education.

THE CHURCH'S RELATIONS WITH GOVERNMENT

The church's major triumph in these years was the achievement of real independence from government dictates. Until the 1830s, the government continued to interfere with the nomination of bishops, but with decreasing success. When Bishop Bailly de Messein died in 1794, the governor gave the new bishop, Jean-François Hubert, a list of three names from which to choose a new coadjutor. But in 1825, the process was reversed: it was Bernard Claude Panet, the new bishop, who submitted a list of three names to the governor, Lord Dalhousie. Furthermore, only one of the candidates had indicated that he would accept the position. A somewhat humbled Dalhousie finally agreed to the only choice. By 1840, ecclesiastical nominations became purely a church matter.

On the issue of parish appointments, church and state also clashed. Here again the government sought to affirm its supremacy, examining lists of nominees and interfering occasionally, but aggressively, with the placement of priests. With the Constitutional Act of 1791, colonial administrators wanted amenable local clergy who could intervene to favour the election of pro-government candidates. Sir Robert Milnes, sent to the colony in 1799 as the new lieutenant governor, prevented the entry into Lower Canada of French priests whose loyalty he doubted in these years of war. Ultimately, though, the church's use of its only weapon—passive resistance—brought it success.

The church also prevailed on the question of the division of the large diocese of Quebec when, in 1836, Lord Gosford finally agreed to the establishment of the diocese of Montreal. A grateful Bishop Lartigue later wrote to Gosford to request his portrait "as a monument to your good deeds in this country."

The colonial government's principal administrators in the early nineteenth century made plans to subvert the Catholic church. Herman Ryland, Governor Robert Prescott's profoundly anti-French and anti-Catholic secretary, hoped to undermine its influence through a reform of the educational system. Jacob Mountain, the Anglican Lord Bishop of Quebec, sought to raise the prestige of his church by increasing its power while at the same time decreasing that of the Roman church. Attorney General (later, Chief Justice) Jonathan Sewell, more moderate and more patient, wanted to diminish gradually the powers of the Catholic bishops and, by giving Plessis and his coadjutor pensions and seats in the councils, make them obedient government servants. But by the time Sir George Prevost became governor in 1812, a good part of the momentum had gone out of these ambitious but dangerous projects. Plessis made it clear that an independent church could be a powerful ally during renewed war with the Americans.

TOWARD VICTORY

Undoubtedly, the local situation contributed to the church's ultimate victory in its long war with the state. Some governors were more willing to be flexible, and, in that, were perhaps more realistic, than others. For their part, many church leaders were skilful diplomats who exploited every opportunity to assert the church's independence while at the same time giving the government full co-operation and assuring British authorities of their unbending loyalty. In addition, the English rulers' hopes for converting the habitants were fading. Groups such as the Methodists, who used Swiss French-speaking agents, vainly attempted to proselytize. Indeed, Protestants often appeared preoccupied mainly with their own denominational rivalries. Anglican Bishop Mountain, for example, tolerated Presbyterian and Lutheran ministers, but the Methodist clergy he disdained as "a set of ignorant enthusiasts whose preaching is calculated only to perplex the understanding and corrupt the morals, to relax the nerves of industry and dissolve the bonds of society."

International events afforded the church new opportunities to demonstrate its loyalty. The clergy vigorously opposed the liberal ideals of the "anti-Christian" French Revolution that broke out with the storming of the Bastille prison in Paris on July 14, 1789. Horrified by the Reign of Terror that soon set in (among whose victims was King Louis XVI), Canadian prelates issued strong condemnations. These must have been all the more pleasing to the British authorities because war between Britain and France broke out in 1793. Then, while Napoleon's military campaigns provoked new suspicions of all things French, the War of 1812 gave the church a welcome opportunity to preach loyalty through pastoral letters and sermons. Led by the clergy, loyal French Canadians praised the exploits of Charles-Michel de Salaberry and his militia, who forced a numerically far superior American force to retreat at the battle of Châteauguay in 1813. Here were French-speaking troops winning a glorious victory for the British—undeniable proof of loyalty. Governor Prevost could well declare, "The Catholic clergy are my firmest supports." As for the events of 1837, except in some parishes where the Patriotes were well organized, they provoked additional manifestations of loyalty to the Crown, this time in the face of internal revolution.

The rise of the church in the early years of the nineteenth century took place partly at the expense of the colonial government, and partly at the expense of the new professional elite. This latter group was the church's only serious rival in the struggle for support and influence within the French-speaking population. The Rebellion of 1837 brought this conflict to a head and decided its outcome in the church's favour. By 1840 French Canada's clerical elite was poised to enter a golden age.

The Professional Elite

The new professional class was not so fortunate. Many of its members were sons of small farmers and, as such, could scarcely base their social

257

aspirations upon family wealth. Politics became an outlet for this group's ambitions. Espousing liberal, democratic, and, ultimately, republican ideals, it sought government reform through enlarging the powers of the lower house and curtailing those of the executive. The group was well aware of Lower Canada's colonial status and of French Canadians' lesser role in the economy and in government. These professionals thus aimed to become champions of national values, and they easily associated the interests of French Canada with those of their own class. Not surprisingly, they framed their declarations of battle in the name of the French Canadian nation.

This new middle class aspired to replace the seigneurs and, to a degree, compete with the clergy as leaders of French Canada. Many of its members viewed the seigneurs as exploiting the habitants when they raised seigneurial *rentes*, especially when the growing population in the seigneurial zone and better prices for timber enhanced the value of the seigneuries, more than half of which had passed to British owners. The French-speaking seigneurs also appeared as collaborators who bowed to the British to gain lucrative appointments and pensions. Many notaries and lawyers also condemned the church for its support of Britain. Some were openly anticlerical, espousing the ideals of the French Revolution and American democracy. Bishop Plessis had denounced these radicals as early as 1809, accusing them of "tending to annihilate all principles of subordination and to set fire to the province."

Understandably, the French-speaking professionals who formed the backbone of the Parti canadien (later called the Parti patriote) had increasingly hostile relations with the British merchants. Well represented in the governor's inner councils, the really wealthy merchants numbered only a few hundred but, as historian Donald Creighton noted, they were "the most self-conscious, purposeful and assertive of all the Canadian social classes."[2] The merchants wanted to control Lower Canada's political institutions in order to introduce new laws to promote economic growth, commerce, and transportation. Some even demanded the abolition of the seigneurial system. Naturally, they accused the Assembly's French-speaking majority of systematically blocking necessary change.

Members of the liberal professions anchored in rural Quebec had a very different view of Lower Canada's needs. Despite their political radicalism they were economic conservatives. While critical of many aspects of the seigneurial system they did see it as a rampart against English-speaking farmers (anxious to gain freehold title to their lands) replacing the habitant in the St. Lawrence Valley. The professionals defended traditional agriculture and denounced the threat of commercial capitalism, but, as political radicals, they called for greater autonomy for the colony and some even favoured rebellion.

Lower Canadian liberals were in tune with reformers elsewhere in British North America and in Britain itself on the issue of women's suffrage: they wanted to deny women the right to vote. In the early decades of the nineteenth century, women appear to have voted in numerous instances. In 1809 Louis-Joseph Papineau's mother was allowed to cast her vote for her son, whom she proudly described as "a good and faithful subject." But in 1820, after numerous complaints about voting by the wives of male property holders, the Assembly passed a resolution disenfranchising married women. Then, in 1832, it acted to end all female suffrage. Papineau and his party explained that electoral violence had attained such a point that "the public interest, decency, and the natural modesty of the sex" required that women not witness such scenes; also, it was alleged that the Patriotes did not always like the way that women voted!

Assembly versus Governor   259

The Rebellion of 1837 marked the failure of the Constitutional Act as a system of government for Lower Canada. Actually, the act's weaknesses had been apparent for at least a generation. Since the turn of the century, the increasingly French and Parti canadien–dominated Assembly had sought to strengthen the elective part of government and to weaken the all-powerful executive whose members were appointed in London and in Quebec.

The causes of the Rebellion of 1837 in Lower Canada were more complex than those in Upper Canada because of the colony's ethnic division. In part, this struggle pitted the English against the French, since Lower Canada's tiny English-speaking minority dominated the Executive Council and the Assembly represented the province's French-speaking majority. Yet the deterioration of French–English relations in the colony and the increasingly violent rhetoric on both sides did not prevent a small group of English-speaking Quebeckers from supporting the Patriotes. Some were Irish Catholics who had an intense hatred of England. Others, such as brothers Wolfred and Robert Nelson, both supporters of reform, endorsed Patriote demands for an executive that would be responsible to the Assembly.

The uprising was also, in many ways, a struggle between the haves and the have-nots. Hortense Globensky, daughter of a Polish immigrant, belonged to a wealthy French-speaking family and, like her soldier brother, Maximilien, cast her lot openly with the British. (Later, in the days of growing violence that preceded the rebellion, she calmly picked up a pistol, and drove off a threatening group of Patriotes.) Like the Globensky family, most defenders of authority, tradition, and wealth, including Roman Catholic prelates and seigneurs, opposed the reformers and disputed their claim to represent the French Canadian nation and the majority of the population. Yet, even this generalization needs qualification as the wealthy English-speaking merchants constantly attacked the economic status quo and lobbied for the economic reforms they judged beneficial to the colony's commercial development. At the same time, as members of a small minority, they obviously felt threatened by the French majority. Although they had previously been devoted advocates of an elected assembly, they now defended their positions on the appointed executive and legislative councils. They could not countenance political changes that would challenge their own economic dominance.

FINANCIAL QUESTIONS

In an effort to strengthen its role in government, the Assembly had for three decades sought greater control of the colony's finances. Constitutionally, it alone could initiate money bills concerning taxes and expenditures, but the executive itself also possessed revenues from Crown lands, from the military budget, and even from London, which enabled it to distribute patronage in the form of positions, salaries, and pensions to its supporters. Moreover, the appointed Legislative Council could—and often did—refuse legislation that reached it from the Assembly. As a last resort, the governor possessed extensive veto powers. If the Legislative Council were elective, the governor would no longer be able to fill it with his own people; popular control would thus be enhanced.

The Assembly's disagreements with the governor on these basic issues were frequent and heated. As early as 1805, for example, a bill designed to raise money to build prisons provoked a debate that showed the intensity of growing English–French conflict. French members favoured higher import duties, while British merchants wanted to tax the land. Agriculture was arrayed against commerce, French against English. When the Assembly voted for import duties, the merchants appealed first to the Legislative Council, then to the governor, and finally to London. "If the [French] Canadians succeed in building so many churches, why couldn't they pay for the construction of prisons?" they argued. During this confrontation, a French-language newspaper, *Le Canadien*, was founded in November 1806. Edited by four members of the Parti canadien, it was intended to enable French Canadians to assert "the loyalty of their character and defy the designs of the opposition [British] party."

Relations between the Assembly and the governor deteriorated further during the mandate of Sir James Craig (1807–11). In the face of *Le Canadien*'s vitriolic attacks on the beneficiaries of patronage and government land policies, and influenced by advisers such as the anti-Catholic Herman Ryland, Craig embarked upon a "reign of terror." When vocal Parti canadien members annoyed him, he dissolved the Assembly. When the election returned an almost identical body, he dissolved it again and went out campaigning. After *Le Canadien* denounced him, he had the paper's presses seized and its editors thrown in jail on charges of treason. When the second election brought back a reinforced Parti canadien, he attempted to frighten it into behaving, and he largely succeeded. As a long-term solution to the problem, he recommended assimilation through a union of the provinces, large-scale British immigration, the subordination of the Roman Catholic church, and the abolition of "the representative part of government." Craig then left the province, to the relief of the French Canadian populace.

The question of provincial revenues had produced a deadlock in relations between the Assembly and the governor by the 1820s. Louis-Joseph Papineau piloted the attack. Foremost among the leaders of the Parti canadien (called the Parti patriote after 1826), Papineau entered the Assembly in 1809 and became its speaker in 1815. As one who had been brought up on a seigneurie, and was himself a seigneur, Papineau defended the values of tradition, nation, and family. Yet his education and political career had acquainted him with liberal thought. As the political crisis deepened after 1830, Papineau's early esteem for British institutions evolved into admiration for republicanism and American-style democracy. Liberal in his religious views, he nevertheless viewed the Roman Catholic church as an important national institution, and he attended mass to set an example for his tenants. Here, indeed, was a "divided soul," as historian Fernand Ouellet has portrayed him.[3]

261

In 1828, believing that London would be more conciliatory once informed of the discontent in Lower Canada, the Assembly sent a petition bearing nearly 90 000 signatures and asking for curbs on the powers of the executive. But British politicians were convinced that a governor shorn of his powers would be unable to fulfil his constitutional obligations of responsibility to London.

Without saying as much, the Patriotes were apparently pushing for independence. At a time when the Empire still formed a single tariff unit, London refused to consider the idea. Worse, perhaps, an independent Lower Canada might slide under the domination of the United States and risk pulling the rest of British North America along with it. Moreover, Britain's great interest in the emigration of its surplus population also made it imperative to retain the colony. In any case, the English population of Lower Canada did not want independence. As the *Quebec Gazette* warned in 1833, "Colonies biting the apple of independence will awake like Adam and Eve and find themselves naked."

RADICALIZATION

The British Parliament adopted what it hoped would be perceived as a compromise solution. It gave the Assembly control of all expenditures on the condition that it agree to pay the civil list each year—that is, to pay for the civil administration of the colony, including the salaries of civil servants. But the mood among the Patriotes was uncompromising. In 1834 they drew up the Ninety-two Resolutions, a veritable manifesto that the governor, Lord Aylmer, interpreted as nothing less than a declaration of independence. To help resolve the executive's financial problems, London established the British American Land Company and granted it more than 400 000 ha of land, in return for a commitment to build roads and make annual payments to the Crown. The company, however, showed little interest in colonization and much interest in speculation.

Internal political problems made the Lower Canadian question a very low priority for British politicians. The Whigs, then in power, opposed further concessions to Lower Canada's assembly; at the same time, they wanted to appear conciliatory. Procrastination in the form of an investigation seemed the wisest policy. Unimpressed, the London *Times* in 1835 viewed this commission, headed by the Earl of Gosford, as "a frivolous and toad-eating embassy . . ., a temporizing mission, a bribe to the Radicals in the British Parliament to tolerate the Whig ministry."

Then, in March 1837, with the Ten Resolutions prepared by Lord John Russell, government leader in the British House of Commons, the Whigs announced an end to conciliation. The Colonial Office refused all of the Assembly's ninety-two resolutions. The government of Lower Canada would be able to pay its administrative costs from the tax revenues without needing the Assembly's approval. There would be no elective Legislative Council. The English-speaking minority's political influence would thus be preserved. The Executive Council, representing wealth and enterprise, would, as before, continue to be responsible to the governor alone, not to the Assembly.

Papineau and his party thus failed to gain control over executive powers. So-called responsible government, which would oblige the governor to choose his ministers from the majority in the Assembly, could not be reconciled with the colonial relationship; after all, the governor had to answer to London, not to the local assembly. Momentarily, Canadian considerations were forgotten by Britain; the events of November and December of that same year, however, abruptly brought them back to the floor of the British Parliament.

The Lower Canadian Rebellions of 1837–38

When they received news of Russell's resolutions, the Patriotes altered their tactics, since Britain apparently was not going to yield. For some, the time for revolt had arrived. More moderate views prevailed, though, and the plan agreed upon called for legal agitation that would bring the government to reconsider its positions. Revolution would be the ultimate recourse if this policy failed.

National Archives of Canada/C-17937.

This drawing of a Patriote in the Rebellions of 1837–38 by Henri Julien would be reproduced and distributed in millions of copies during the October Crisis in Quebec in 1970.

Throughout the tense days of summer and autumn 1837, the Patriote leaders worked on organization. They staged assemblies and collected funds. Patriote women established an association whose objective was "to assist, insofar as the weakness of their sex made it possible, in the triumph of the patriot cause."[4] They organized boycotts of imported goods in an attempt to strike at British merchants. In September an association with military sections, the Fils de la liberté, was founded. At a public assembly at St-Charles on the Richelieu River east of Montreal, attended by perhaps four thousand people, Patriote orators called for revolt. The meeting adopted resolutions that included a declaration of independence. Plans were developed to take Montreal and move on to Quebec.

When the government issued warrants for their arrest, the principal Patriote leaders, Papineau included, fled to the countryside south of Montreal. The prospective urban uprising was suppressed.

After an initial skirmish at St-Denis on November 23, which the Patriotes won, more British troops were called up. The fierce combat that ensued at neighbouring St-Charles was catastrophic for the rebels, led by Wolfred Nelson.

Having pacified the Richelieu Valley, Sir John Colborne, the former governor of Upper Canada who had just become commander-in-chief of all British troops in the Canadas, turned his attention to the area north of Montreal where Amury Girod, a Swiss immigrant, and Dr. Jean-Olivier Chénier headed the resistance movement. News of the Patriotes' defeat at St-Charles only hardened Chénier in his determination to "die fighting rather than surrender."

When Colborne approached St-Eustache in December 1837, Girod fled while Chénier and several insurgents took refuge in the church and other buildings. Some seventy Patriotes, including Chénier, died by gunfire or were burned to death. The village was then put to the torch, as was nearby St-Benoît, which had offered no resistance. One newspaper, which was usually favourable to the British, reported as follows: "For a radius of 15 miles around St-Eustache, not a building escaped being ravaged and pillaged by these new vandals" who displayed "no feelings of humanity."

By the time news of the insurrection reached London, just before Christmas, many of the rebel leaders had found asylum in the United States, where they attempted to muster support and regroup. Indeed, in February 1838, Robert Nelson led an incursion across the border. As provisional president of Lower Canada, he declared Canada's independence from Britain before fleeing back to safety on the American side.

In November 1838, revolt broke out anew, this time southwest of Montreal. Colborne responded by proclaiming martial law, and his troops once again intervened. The rebellion was suppressed, but Colborne—nicknamed *"le vieux brûlot"* ("the Old Firebrand")—was to be long remembered for his ruthlessness. After the rebellion, a grateful British government raised Colborne to the peerage as Lord Seaton—only many French Canadians chose to pronounce his new title "Lord Satan."

Intense historical controversy has surrounded the principal actors in this drama. Conservative clerical historians lauded the role of clergy such as Bishop Lartigue, who attempted to calm violent sentiment before it got out of hand. Others condemned the church for collaborating with the

Interpretations of the Rebellions of 1837–38 in Lower Canada

What were the causes of the uprisings of 1837–38 in Lower Canada? Despite decades of debate and discussion on the subject, no consensus on the causes of the insurrections has emerged yet.

Early-twentieth-century historians such as Thomas Chapais portrayed the rebellions that broke out in Lower Canada in 1837 as the outcome of bitter political conflict between the British colonial governor and the Patriote-dominated elected Assembly. Chapais, in his *Cours d'histoire du Canada*, vol. 4, *1833–1841* (Québec, 1923), judged the insurrection to be "regrettable and unjustifiable," an "overreaction when weighed against our grievances" (p. 226). Abbé Lionel Groulx, writing at about the same time, was torn by his various allegiances. As a conservative-minded priest, he reproved the Patriotes for their anti-clericalism and for their demagogic championing of "doctrinal fads" such as democracy and popular sovereignty. But, as a nationalist, he also saw in the events of 1837 "something extremely stimulating and healthy" (*Notre maître le passé*, vol. 2 [Québec, 1977], 86–87). Later, nationalists such as Maurice Séguin interpreted the insurrections as a struggle for liberation, led by "the most advanced French Canadian nationalists against British domination" (*L'idée d'indépendance au Québec: genèse et historique* [Trois-Rivières, 1971], 33).*

By the 1960s, historians were casting their nets more widely in search of the underlying causes of the rebellions. Although they did not deny the existence of serious political quarrels, they asked other questions that enlarged the debate: Who were the Patriotes and what were their ambitions? How did the habitants react to the appeals of the rebels, and what explains their reaction? Was the rebellion really an English–French conflict or was it mainly a struggle between classes?

Marxist historian Stanley B. Ryerson noted in *Unequal Union: Confederation and the Roots of Conflict in the Canadas, 1815–1873* (Toronto, 1968) that "acute class and national conflicts" came into play as a "native capitalist industry" saw its progress blocked by "landlordism and colonialism." He concluded: "The brazen handing over of huge expanses of unsettled land to companies of London speculators became one of the prime causes of revolt" (pp. 29–31). More recently, political scientist Daniel Salée has underlined the "revolutionary character" of the rebellions in an article entitled "Revolutionary Political Thought, the Persistence of the Old Order, and the Problem of Power in an Ancien Régime Colonial Society: Ideological Perspectives of Lower Canada, 1827–1838" (*British Journal of Canadian Studies* 3, 1 [1988]: 52). The Patriotes were "bourgeois liberals" whose language placed them solidly within a broad current of opinion that was becoming increasingly influential throughout the Western world at that time. Their economic program and their denunciations of the abuses of the seigneurial system enabled them to mobilize substantial support among the habitants.

In *Lower Canada, 1791–1840: Social Change and Nationalism* (Toronto, 1980), historian Fernand Ouellet meticulously traced the development of a severe agricultural crisis in Lower Canada in the early nineteenth century. He maintained that deteriorating economic condi-

265

tions—and the fear that they bred—served to "unite the French Canadian lower and middle classes in a single nationalist movement" whose objective was the overthrow of the British colonial authority (p. 135). Ouellet also sought to show that the Patriotes comprised a growing professional elite ambitious for political power and social prestige.

In contrast, some historians such as Jean-Pierre Wallot have questioned the very existence of the agricultural crisis. In a study completed with Gilles Paquet, Wallot and Paquet propose instead "a dynamic and entrepreneurial view of Lower Canada at the turn of the nineteenth century," (*Lower Canada at the Turn of the Nineteenth Century: Restructuring and Modernization,* Canadian Historical Association Historical Booklet No. 45 [Ottawa, 1988], 3).

Historian Allan Greer has studied conditions in the Lower Richelieu, a centre of Patriote activity and the scene of two important armed confrontations. He saw no precipitous decline in habitant wheat production there, and concluded that this region simply did not "fit easily" into Ouellet's chronology (*Peasant, Lord and Merchant: Rural Society in Three Quebec Parishes, 1740–1840* [Toronto, 1985], 211). Monographies focussing on other regions of the province could shed further light on the question of the existence of an agricultural crisis. Unfortunately, such monographies depend upon statistical series that are often incomplete and unreliable.

*Translations from the French in this paragraph are by Richard Jones.

National Archives of Canada/C-3653.

This scene, painted by M.A. Hayes, a British officer, shows British troops with Patriote prisoners captured during the Rebellion of 1837.

enemy. The Patriotes, too, have been the subject of differing judgements. Modern-day nationalists have seen them as heroes who struggled for Quebec's independence. Others, such as historian Fernand Ouellet, have described them as members of an ambitious professional elite, who sought political power and social prestige and were often very conservative despite their revolutionary appearance. For example, Papineau was a conservative landowner, seigneur of Montebello, who nonetheless spoke fervently about American democracy. But his revolutionary rhetoric became more ambivalent over time and he denied with vehemence that he wanted revolution. Half an hour after the beginning of the Battle of St-Denis, he fled to the American border.

It is clear that the Patriote leaders, who were French-speaking merchants and professionals, had ambitions as a group, and that they saw the welfare of the masses as a function of their own interests. Church leaders also had ambitions. So did seigneurs such as Pierre de Boucherville, who calculated that he would have lost an annual revenue of five hundred *louis* (gold coin pieces) if the revolution had succeeded. So did the English-speaking merchants, who, although a small minority, largely controlled the colony's economy. So did the British administrators, who believed that power should be entrusted to appointed officials, most of them English-speaking. So did the British Parliament, which still felt that colonies should be, and could be, useful to the mother country. And so, finally, did the habitants, who had many ideas of what was wrong with their situation and of what might better their lot, and who constituted the great majority—perhaps 95 percent—of the insurrection's active sympathizers.

267

Consequences of the Rebellions

London chose to address the Canadian problem by forming a royal commission to visit both Lower and Upper Canada. The future historian François-Xavier Garneau appealed to the commissioner on his arrival in Quebec: "Durham, close your ears to the counsels of vengeance; take upon yourself the defense of a helpless people." But Lord Durham was listening to other advice. Before he even left England, he had been lobbied by Canadian and British merchant groups who emphasized the ethnic aspect of the conflict; they urged union of the Canadas to save themselves from "the designs of the French faction, madly bent upon [the] destruction" of the rights, the interests, and the property of Lower Canada's British population.

Durham's concern for economic development made him sympathetic to the merchants' views. In his report he drew attention to the "deadly animosity" between French and English: "I found two nations warring in the bosom of a single state; I found a struggle, not of principles, but of races." A union of the two Canadas would yield a slight English majority, which immigration would further reinforce. As for the French, whom he viewed as innately inferior, Durham was convinced that "once placed, by the legitimate course of events and the working of natural causes, in a minority, [they] would abandon their vain hopes of nationality." Union with Upper Canada would thus assure the assimilation of the French— the ultimate solution to ethnic conflict in Lower Canada.

The rebellion, then, brought Lower Canada to its knees and made it easy to overlook the enormous changes that the colony had undergone at virtually all levels since 1791. The colony lost its own government and was to be joined to Upper Canada in a union that the great majority of the French Canadians did not want. Moreover, the avowed purpose of this union, as expressed by Durham, by British parliamentarians, and by Lower Canadian merchants, was to break the power of French Canada and eventually to assimilate it. But like the proponents of the Constitutional Act a half-century earlier, the advocates of union proved to be poor prophets. So, too, did the French Canadians who viewed the prospect of union so darkly.

268

NOTES

[1]Allan Greer, *Peasant, Lord, and Merchant: Rural Society in Three Quebec Parishes, 1740–1840* (Toronto, 1985), 122–39.
[2]Donald Creighton, *The Commercial Empire of the St. Lawrence, 1760–1850* (Toronto, 1937), 23, quoted in Gilles Paquet et Jean-Pierre Wallot, "Groupes sociaux et pouvoir: le cas canadien au tournant du XIXe siècle," *Revue d'histoire de l'Amérique française 27 (1974)*: 539.
[3]Fernand Ouellet, *Louis-Joseph Papineau: A Divided Soul* (Ottawa, 1960).
[4]The original French text reads, " . . . concourir, autant que la faiblesse de leur sexe peut le leur permettre, à faire réussir la cause patriotique." Quoted in Micheline Dumont et al., *L'histoire des femmes au Québec depuis quatre siècles* (Montréal, 1982), 145.

Related Readings

Fernand Ouellet provides an important overview of the Rebellions of 1837–38 in "The Insurrections," in *Readings in Canadian History: Pre-Confederation*, 3d ed., edited by R. Douglas Francis and Donald B. Smith (Toronto, 1990), 322–35. See also the essays by Gerald M. Craig, "Lord Durham's Report," 312–21, and Elinor Kyte Senior, "Suppressing Rebellion in Lower Canada: British Military Policy and Practice, 1837–1838," 336–46.

BIBLIOGRAPHY

Fernand Ouellet's *Lower Canada, 1791–1840: Social Change and Nationalism* (Toronto, 1979) is very useful for this period. His *Economic and Social History of Quebec, 1760–1850* (Toronto, 1980) and his *Economy, Class, and Nation in Quebec*, edited and translated by Jacques A. Barbier (Mississauga,

1991) should also be consulted. Jean-Pierre Wallot's and Gilles Paquet's research on social, economic and political history has often led them to criticize Ouellet's interpretations and to provide a contrary view on several issues. See, for example, "The Agricultural Crisis in Lower Canada, 1802–12; *mise au point*. A Response to T.J.A. Le Goff," *Canadian Historical Review* 56(1975): 133–61; "Stratégie foncière de l'habitant: Québec (1790–1835)," *Revue d'histoire de l'Amérique française* 39 (1985/1986): 551–81; and the Canadian Historical Association booklet, *Lower Canada at the Turn of the Nineteenth Century* (Ottawa, 1988). Allan Greer, *Peasant, Lord, and Merchant: Rural Society in Three Quebec Parishes, 1740–1840* (Toronto, 1985) suggests new insights. John McCallum's *Unequal Beginnings: Agriculture and Economic Development in Quebec and Ontario until 1870* (Toronto, 1980) and Michael Bliss's *Northern Enterprise: Five Centuries of Canadian Business* (Toronto, 1987) are also helpful.

Useful historiographical studies are Gérald Bernier and Daniel Salée, "Les insurrections de 1837–1838 au Québec; remarques critiques et théo- **269** riques en marge de l'historiographie," *Canadian Review of Studies in Nationalism/Revue canadienne des études sur le nationalisme*, 13 (1986): 13–30 and Fernand Ouellet, "La tradition révolutionnaire au Canada. A propos de l'historiographie des insurrections de 1837–1838 dans le Bas-Canada," *Revue de l'Université d'Ottawa/University of Ottawa Quarterly*, 60(1985): 91–124.

James Lambert has made a notable contribution to social and religious history in his doctoral thesis, "Monseigneur, the Catholic Bishop. Joseph-Octave Plessis, Church, State, and Society in Lower Canada: Historiography and Analysis," 3 vols. Ph.D. thesis, Université Laval, 1980. The impact of the French Revolution is discussed in Pierre Boulle and Richard Lebrun, *Le Canada et la révolution française* (Montréal, 1989) as well as in Louis-Georges Harvey and Mark V. Olsen, "French Revolutionary Forms in French-Canadian Political Language," *Canadian Historical Review*, 68(1987): 374–92. Alexis de Tocqueville's Canadian journal offers a contemporary portrait of Lower Canada in the early 1830s; see Jacques Vallée, ed., *Tocqueville au Bas-Canada* (Montréal, 1973) as well as Stéphane Dion, "La pensée de Tocqueville—L'épreuve du Canada français," *Revue d'histoire de l'Amérique française*, 41 (1987/1988), 537–52. The cholera epidemics are presented in Geoffrey Bilson, *A Darkened House: Cholera in Nineteenth-Century Canada* (Toronto, 1980). Barbara Tunis discusses the question of smallpox vaccination in an article, "Public Vaccination in Lower Canada, 1815–1823: Controversy and a Dilemma," *Historical Reflections* 9 (1982): 267–76. Jean-Marie Fecteau looks at crime and punishment in "Régulation sociale et repression de la déviance au Bas-Canada au tournant du 19e siècle (1791–1815)," *Revue d'histoire de l'Amérique française* 38 (1984/1985): 495–521.

For the events of 1837 and their origins, see Joseph Schull, *Rebellion: The Rising in French Canada, 1837* (Toronto, 1971) and Jean-Paul Bernard,

Les rébellions de 1838–1838 (Montréal, 1983). Jacques Monet, *The Last Cannon Shot: A Study of French Canadian Nationalism, 1837–1850* (Toronto, 1969) has useful material on both the rebellion and its aftermath. Relations between Britain and Canada are analyzed in Peter Burroughs, *The Canadian Crisis and British Colonial Policy, 1828–1841* (Toronto, 1972); Ged Martin, *The Durham Report and British Policy: A Critical Essay* (Cambridge, 1972); Phillip Buckner, "The Colonial Office and British North America, 1801–50," *Dictionary of Canadian Biography*, vol. 8, *1851–1860* (Toronto, 1985), xxiii–xxxvii; and James Sturgis, "Anglicisation as a Theme in Lower Canadian History, 1807–1843," *British Journal of Canadian Studies* 3 (1988): 210–29. Janet Ajzenstat sees Durham as a mainstream liberal but not as a cultural chauvinist in *The Political Thought of Lord Durham* (Montreal, 1988). The Spring 1990 issue of the *Journal of Canadian Studies* is a special issue devoted to Lord Durham, entitled "Durham and His Ideas." For material pertaining to women in Lower Canada in the early nineteenth century, see Micheline Dumont et al., *Quebec Women: A History* (Toronto, 1987) and Allan Greer, "La République des hommes: Les patriotes de 1837 face aux femmes," *Revue d'histoire de l'Amérique française* 44 (1990/91): 507–28. Aboriginal issues are reviewed by Daniel Francis in *A History of the Native Peoples of Quebec, 1760–1867* (Ottawa, 1983). Individuals mentioned in this chapter are also studied in various volumes of the *Dictionary of Canadian Biography;* see in particular Fernand Ouellet's article on Papineau in vol. 10, *1871–1880* (Toronto, 1972), 564–78.

The Union of the Canadas: Political Developments, 1840–1864

The Act of Union adopted in July 1840 joined the two Canadas, now rebaptized Canada East and Canada West. This act of the British Parliament gave the old province of Quebec its fourth constitution since the Conquest. The union had a short but stormy life. Indeed, many latter-day observers have seen it as simply a prelude to Confederation. After all, by 1864 perennial deadlock in the united province's Legislative Assembly led most of its members to agree to work toward the realization of a larger British North American Confederation.

Although ultimately a failure, the union could boast some political successes. As railway fever swept the nation's business community in the 1850s, solicitous politicians oversaw a multitude of costly and often competing construction projects. They fostered increased trade relations with the United States by negotiating a Treaty of Reciprocity covering natural products, which, it was said, was floated through on champagne by Canada's suave governor general, Lord Elgin. They tried to stimulate industrial growth by instituting a protective tariff on manufactured goods. In 1854 they finally abolished the seigneurial system in Canada East and even found a solution to the contentious Clergy reserves question in Canada West.

The union years also saw the resolution of another source of constant feuding between the Assembly and the governor. Within ten years after the failure of the rebellions, London accepted the principles of responsible government. Henceforth, the governor governed less; his ministers, who were responsible to the Assembly, made decisions in his place.

Most significantly, French- and English-speaking politicians found common ground on which to co-operate in solving many major political questions. The need to construct a *modus vivendi* also helped restrain ethnic and religious bigotry. French Canada again escaped assimilation. In many respects, Canada East, like Canada West, led a separate existence and this separateness became more pronounced as the years passed.

French–English Relations

The Colonial Office in London originally intended to use union to punish the French and assure their subjugation, if not their eventual demise, as a linguistic group. Certainly the conditions of union constituted a severe blow for Lower Canada in general and for the French Canadians in particular. English became the sole official language of parliamentary documents. The elective Assembly had an equal number of representatives from both halves of the colony, even though the largely French-speaking Canada East had 670 000 inhabitants and English-speaking Canada West had only 480 000.

The Act of Union also created "one consolidated revenue fund," making Upper Canada's heavy debt burden the responsibility of the Province of Canada as a whole. Upper Canada could no longer by itself finance costly transportation facilities like roads and canals. It had already borrowed heavily in London, and only union with the much less debt-ridden Lower Canada could strengthen its position.

British financial houses operating in Canada, worried about a series of bankrupticies, regarded union as imperative. It would bring in higher revenues since the United Canadas could raise tariffs, a measure that Lower Canada, where most goods from Europe entered, could no longer block. It would also recognize that the two Canadas formed a common economic bloc.

Charles Poulett Thomson, Lord Durham's successor as governor general of Canada, had spent eight years on the Board of Trade. This hard-headed administrator wanted Canada to be put on a sound financial footing to attract development capital. Investment would assure progress and make the appeal of the United States a little less enticing, thus warding off the constant threat of annexation. He also hoped that substantial British immigration would diminish the political and economic influence of French Canadians.

When the vain and strong-willed Thomson arrived in Canada in the autumn of 1839, his first task was to convince Upper Canada to agree unconditionally to the proposal for political union. He did not have to convince Lower Canada, which would have no say in the matter. As British prime minister Lord Melbourne had written to Colonial Secretary Lord John Russell to explain his policy, "We feel that we cannot impose this union upon Upper Canada without her consent, and therefore we give her a choice. We give Lower Canada no choice, but we impose it upon her during the suspension of her constitution."

The union was officially inaugurated at the Château de Ramezay in Montreal on February 10, 1841. Thomson, now Baron Sydenham, declared: "Inhabitants of the Province of Canada: henceforth may you be united in sentiment as you are from this day in name!" Most French Canadians, though, were defiant and bitter. Pierre-Joseph-Oliver

272

Chauveau, a future Quebec prime minister, condemned the British bankers whom he saw as the force behind union and prophesied: "Today a weeping people is beaten, tomorrow a people will be up in arms, today the forfeit, tomorrow the vengeance."

The French certainly had no reason to trust the assurances of the anti-French Sydenham. Moreover, the union simply had too many elements that they found objectionable. Augustin-Norbert Morin, a Patriote of 1837 and reform leader Louis-Hippolyte La Fontaine's lieutenant in Quebec City, commented frankly in a letter to Toronto politician Francis Hincks: "I am against the Union and against the main features, as I think every honest Lower Canadian should be." John Neilson, an urbane bilingual Scot who owned the *Quebec Gazette*, formed a committee in the fall of 1840 to work for the election of representatives opposed to union in order to express by non-violent means "our reprobation of this injustice which is done to this Province." Unyielding opposition appeared to be the only path open to the French.

Sydenham, however, soon proved himself a master strategist, as capable as he was unscrupulous. Indeed, he won over most of Canada West to "his" party, with the exception of a few Family Compact Tories such as Sir Allan MacNab (who judged the governor too sympathetic to the doctrine of responsible government), as well as some "Ultra Reformers" (who perceived him as too equivocal in his support of the same doctrine).

In Canada East, *le poulet* (the chicken), as the French disdainfully called Poulett Thomson, laboured under no illusions. He knew the French were hostile to him and would not support his candidates. Apart from areas with important English-speaking populations, he admitted: "We shall not have a man returned who does not hate British connexion, British rule, British improvements, and everything which has a taint of British feeling." This master political manipulator thus worked to assure the election of a maximum number of English-speaking members. He gerrymandered riding boundaries to eliminate French votes from certain districts and staged polls in English localities situated far from French-speaking towns. As returning officers for the polls he chose partisans, and he used British troops as well as Irish construction labourers to intimidate voters in the open voting (Canada obtained the secret ballot only in 1874). In La Fontaine's own district, thugs hired by the British candidate took possession of the polling place. Bitterly denouncing Sydenham's "law of the bludgeon," La Fontaine withdrew from the contest to avoid bloodshed and certain defeat. Not surprisingly, the governor won a comfortable working majority in United Canada's first legislature.

TOWARD FRENCH CANADIAN ACCEPTANCE OF UNION

Sydenham's heavy-handed tactics actually improved the chances for fruitful collaboration between reformers in Canada East and Canada West.

Since 1839 Francis Hincks, a pragmatic and ambitious Irish Protestant immigrant with a passion for journalism, business, and responsible government, assiduously cultivated good relations with La Fontaine. Hincks repeatedly assured the former Patriote that, in return for co-operation in working toward responsible government, his followers would assist French Canadian efforts to rid the union of objectionable features such as official English unilingualism. Hincks concluded: "You want our help as much as we do yours." At first suspicious, La Fontaine finally concluded that French Canada could obtain more by accepting union than by continuing to oppose it.

The particularities of politics in each section of the province created the conditions that brought most French Canadian leaders to work within the union. The threat represented by the imposed link with Canada West made it necessary for the French to practise a great degree of electoral cohesiveness. After 1850, when a few extreme liberals from Canada East took their places in the Assembly, tensions between the left and the right increased among the French. Nevertheless, this potential threat to the unity of the French *bloc* was successfully contained.

THE RISE OF A REFORM COALITION

Canada West's political spectrum was broad, featuring almost all shades of opinion, from Compact Tories on the right to Ultra Reformers on the left. Theoretically, in the early 1840s the French could have aligned with some of Upper Canada's extreme conservatives, Tories such as Sir Allan MacNab. Like the French, they opposed union, but mutual animosities precluded even a *mariage de convenance*. An alliance between Reformers and French seemed far more natural, in view of the political goals of both groups throughout the 1820s and 1830s. And since then, the rebellion had weakened the Reform movement and Lord Sydenham's ambiguous overtures had divided it.

It took time to establish this common front, however. Many so-called Reformers did not want to oppose the government, as the French had done, for fear of compromising the public-works projects promised for their districts by Sydenham and obviously desired by the voters. Hincks, at least until he, too, defected to the government side, and especially the more principled Toronto Reform leader Robert Baldwin, were virtually alone. Baldwin, for example, never succeeded in bringing Sydenham to appoint French-speaking members to the Executive Council. Essentially, then, when the governor died of lockjaw in September 1841 (caused by an injury, the result of a fall from his horse), the French were quite isolated.

But they could not long be ignored. As disappointed Reformers from Canada West abandoned the new governor, Sir Charles Bagot, and returned to Baldwin's leadership, Bagot, a highly successful diplomat, lobbied for French support to bolster his tottering government. Bagot's successor, Sir

Charles Metcalfe, was likewise convinced that the anti-French assimila-tionist policies of the union were impractical, although he, too, believed that Anglicization was an appropriate long-term policy.

These governors walked a tightrope in trying to govern without the aid of representatives of the French Canadians, who formed nearly half the united province's population. Yet they were conservatives and strong believers in the British connection, and, in trying to appease the suppos-edly disloyal and rebellious French, they risked losing support among the English-speaking of both Canadas.

In addition, the governors had difficulty persuading the British govern-ment to renounce at least any immediate hopes for assimilation. Bagot reported to Colonial Secretary Lord Stanley that it was all very well to wait for immigration to "hem in and overwhelm French Population and French Power"; in the meantime, he had to solve pressing political prob-lems by giving positions to French members and making other "conces-sions." When Bagot made good his threat and brought Baldwin and La Fontaine into his government, Lord Stanley was dismayed. On his deathbed, Bagot justified his conduct to his critics in London: "I had no choice in regard to [my measures] if the Union was to be maintained."

On the highly charged question of giving official status to the French language, Governor Metcalfe wanted to act before La Fontaine forced him to do so. Again, Lord Stanley vehemently disagreed since the Act of Union was designed "to promote the amalgamation of the French and English races" and to authorize bilingualism would be to abandon this goal. Only in 1848, three years after Metcalfe's request, did the British Parliament amend the Act of Union to end the proscription of the French language.

The achievement of responsible government did not curtail close co-operation between French- and English-speaking politicians. It did signify the need to build new alliances. In the turbulent early 1850s, when the loosely organized Reform group split into moderate and radical factions, most French-speaking members of the Assembly, members of the moder-ate Parti Bleu, began to co-operate with Conservatives from Canada West to form governments. This coalition, symbolized by the close association of John A. Macdonald and George-Étienne Cartier, carried over into the post-Confederation period.

The Arrival of Responsible Government

The most important single factor in bridging the ethnic gulf during the 1840s was the arduous, but ultimately successful, struggle for responsible government. In 1840, recognition of this principle still appeared far off. The Act of Union concentrated enormous power in the hands of the colonial governor, appointed by London. The governor appointed for life

The Impact of the Union of the Canadas

By the end of the 1840s, the position of the French appeared much stronger than it had just after union in 1841. For historian Mason Wade, this evolution represented an unqualified triumph: "Faced with the prospect of national extinction, the French Canadians closed their ranks and won the peaceful victory which insured their national survival" (*The French Canadians, 1760–1967*, vol. 1 [Toronto, 1968], 220). Moreover, their co-operation with anglophone politicians could be seen, Wade points out, as the first hesitant but positive steps toward "Canadian duality."

Other historians have been more critical in their judgements of union. For them, merely avoiding the worst possible outcome—assimilation—hardly constituted victory. There could be no real victory without equality, and union condemned the French to permanent inequality. Maurice Séguin, for example, viewed the union as a "second conquest" that the French had no choice but to accept *L'idée d'indépendance au Québec: genèse et historique* [Trois-Rivières, 1971], 36. It created a political entity in which the French, despite their large numbers constituted proportionally a minority. The French were also faced with political inferiority within institutions of government that were largely English-speaking. In addition, economic domination was a painful reality. Few leaders of industry or important merchants were French-speaking.

Historians supportive of federalism have replied that, despite its original design, the union benefited both French- and English-speaking Canada. As historian Jacques Monet argued in *The Last Cannon Shot: A Study of French Canadian Nationalism, 1837–1850* (Toronto, 1969), the union proved that "both French and English Canadians could live together within the bosom of a single state" (p. 6). Similarly, J.M.S. Careless has written that "The union had bound them [French- and English-speaking peoples] together, compelling them to work out new adjustments that were at least as significant as the strains so evident between them. . . . The union of the Canadas evolved the dual French–English political party, with dual ministerial leadership, and brought the two peoples to self-government in partnership. The major features of institutional growth under the union were produced by their joint efforts—as well as by their inability to escape the one really fundamental Canadian fact, that they had to live together" (*The Union of the Canadas: The Growth of Canadian Institutions, 1841–1857* [Toronto, 1967], xii).

As Canadians continue to debate the future of the country in terms of the relationship between English- and French-speaking Canadians a study of the first union in the 1840s becomes increasingly relevant.

the members of the upper house, or Legislative Council. He could also reward his supporters, since he had the right to name a host of public officials. In Parliament he chose his advisers, dismissing and replacing them at will. He also held broad veto powers over bills adopted by the

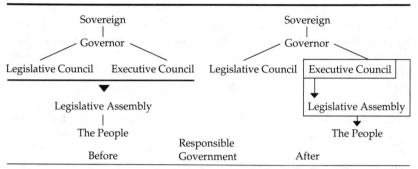

Source: Adapted from P.G. Cornell, M. Hamelin, F. Ouellet, and M. Trudel, *Canada: Unity in Diversity* (Toronto, 1967): 143.

Before responsible government was introduced, the legislative assembly had no effective control over the Executive Council, on whose advice the governor was required to act. With the coming of responsible government, the Executive Council could remain in office only as long as it had the Legislative Assembly's support. **277**

Legislature. Yet, over the course of the union's first decade, the governor's powers were radically curtailed.

Responsible government came only after dramatic battles. The Colonial Office urged Canada's governors to avoid concessions lest things get out of hand and Canada agitate for independence. On his deathbed, Sydenham considered the issue favourably resolved, but his reign of "harmony" implied an active, and often unscrupulous, participation of the governor in politics. In contrast, Bagot, a conciliator, was willing to risk appointing an Executive Council that would have the support of a majority in the Assembly. Taking into account the growing power of the French bloc in the Assembly, he invited La Fontaine to join his council. When the latter shrewdly demanded that Baldwin, too, have a place, the unhappy Bagot again yielded.

London was dismayed. The Duke of Wellington, Bagot's own uncle, called him "a fool." Colonial administrators expressed the strongest regrets—to which the governor replied that, had he acted otherwise, "Canada would have again become the theatre of a widespread rebellion, and perhaps the ungrateful separatist or the rejected outcast from British dominion." Despite Bagot's apparent recognition of the principle that he could only choose ministers who commanded the support of a majority of the members of the Assembly, there was still no guarantee that the governor might not some day replace his advisers if he disagreed with them. Moreover, Bagot's government, consisting of a wide variety of personalities of various political hues, did not really constitute a ministry. Party government had not yet come to the province.

More responsible for this outcome was Sir Charles Metcalfe, who arrived in Canada as governor in March 1843, determined to work to maintain the British connection. He had succeeded in pacifying Jamaica; now London hoped that he might do equally well in Canada. As the Queen's representative, he did not intend to submit to La Fontaine, and he would certainly not commit himself to taking his advice. The Reformers' distribution of patronage, and their unseemly rush for jobs for their people, greatly disturbed the governor. Metcalfe assured Colonial Secretary Lord Stanley that he would strive to get a majority in Parliament, and that if he failed he would dissolve the Assembly and try again, "and that if I fail then, still I cannot submit, for that would be to surrender the Queen's government into the hands of rebels, and to become myself their ignominious tool." Metcalfe proved every bit as steadfast as his confession of faith seemed to indicate. In the rancorous election of 1844, he did obtain a slim majority by inflicting a decisive defeat on the overconfident and "disloyal" Upper Canadian Reformers. He was, however, spectacularly unsuccessful in Lower Canada, where La Fontaine had built up an effective political machine.

278

The moderate regime that governed the colony from 1844 until 1847, led by the eloquent Conservative "Sweet William" Henry Draper as attorney general for Canada West and virtual prime minister, succeeded in adopting several important pieces of legislation, including school acts for both Canadas, legal reform, a revamped land-grant system that would lessen speculation, and a permanent civil list of salaried officials. True responsible government did not yet exist, because, although the Executive Council did have the confidence of the Assembly, the governor's powers remained very broad. Indeed, Conservatives hoped that if the governor's administrative measures were popular, responsible government would lose its appeal. Moreover, Draper's attempts to build significant French support failed utterly. The old Patriote Denis-Benjamin Viger agreed to work with him but was unsuccessful in gaining the backing of influential French Canadians.

The pace of events quickened with the arrival of Lord Elgin, the new governor general, in 1847. By this time, as historian Ged Martin has shown, the British Crown had ceased to play an active part in politics. Moreover, with the British move toward laissez-faire liberalism and the adoption of free trade, it became less imperative for London to control the colonies. Indeed, the British government was now convinced that only colonial autonomy could hold the empire together and it instructed Elgin to accept this principle and to behave in a strictly neutral fashion. The elections of 1848 produced a strong majority for La Fontaine's group in Canada East and a significant majority for Baldwin's Reform movement in Canada West.

The Reformers' victory achieved, Lord Elgin called on La Fontaine and Baldwin to form a government. Henceforth, the governor assented to legislation adopted by Parliament, unless he judged it contrary to the interests of Great Britain. Elgin proved as much in 1849 when he agreed to sign, despite personal reservations, the bitterly controversial Rebellion Losses Bill, which compensated all those (including rebels) who had lost property during the Rebellions of 1837–38.

Responsible government thus moved Canada forward along the road to democracy and political autonomy. The voters, through their elected representatives, would now do the governing—or at least the male portion would, for in 1849 the Reformers amended the election law to exclude women from the franchise. In spite of the common-law prohibition against female suffrage, a few women had voted. They had even helped a Tory win in 1844—an incident that the Reformers had not forgotten.

Ironically, after their hard fight to achieve responsible government and greater self-government from Britain, Canadian politicians imposed even tighter control over the Indian population of the Canadas. The government had established and surveyed reserves, but under the legislation adopted in the 1850s and 1860s, the Indians were given little opportunity to administer their remaining lands themselves.

One group, the Indians at Kanesatake (Oka), did not receive a reserve. During the Rebellions of 1837–38, the Sulpicians, who were the seigneurs at the Lake of the Two Mountains, had stood loyally by the British. The religious order encouraged Roman Catholics to enlist in British Militia units, and contributed money to support those units. Immediately after the uprisings, in 1840, the governor's appointed Special Council issued an ordinance that gave title to the land to the Sulpicians.

279

The Annexation Movement

Following the achievement of responsible government, the years 1848–54 saw feverish political activity. When Lord Elgin sanctioned the Rebellion Losses Bill on April 25, 1849, the fury of Montreal's Tories exploded. A mob invaded the House of Parliament and put it to the torch, then stoned Elgin's carriage, ransacked La Fontaine's house, and rampaged through the town.

Canada West experienced considerable unrest, too. Baldwin and William Lyon Mackenzie were burned in effigy, and Lord Elgin met a similar fiery condemnation from a Toronto mob. The Tories staged protest meetings to denounce the rewarding of "rebels" and "pardoned traitors," and thousands signed petitions demanding Elgin's recall. Said the *Brockville Statesman* of Her Majesty's representative: "Without peace there can be no prosperity, and that peace cannot be procured so long as his hated foot presses the free soil, or his lying lungs breathe the pure air of Canada."

For many Tories, this was French domination at its worst, and the British were bowing to it. At the same time, London's move toward free trade signified an end to imperial preferences. Exporters in the British

McCord Museum, Montreal.

This painting by Joseph Légaré depicts the burning of the Canadian
Parliament building in Montreal on the night of April 25, 1849. It is believed
that rioters protesting the passage of the Rebellion Losses Bill smashed the gas
mains, then set fire to the escaping gas. Earlier that day, crowds of English-
speaking protesters had thrown stones and rotten eggs at Lord Elgin's carriage,
because the governor general had sanctioned the bill. The riots lasted two days.
Subsequently, it was decided that Montreal should no longer be the seat of
government, and the capital alternated between Quebec City and Toronto.

North American colonies rapidly lost their relative advantage in British
markets over other nations to which higher tariffs had previously applied.
Britain's new trade policies thus helped to push large sectors of Canadian
commerce into depression. Shipping activity at Montreal declined by
more than 40 percent between 1847 and 1849. Finding none of the much-
vaunted benefits of the British connection, some Tories who had hitherto
proclaimed their loyalty and condemned traitors and rebels, now began
to campaign for annexation to the United States.

In Montreal, the hotbed of annexationist sentiment, the English-language press published in October 1849 the manifesto of the Annexation
Association. It was signed by 325 citizens, many of them notable business-
people, such as William Molson and John Redpath. Early in 1850 the
formation of the Toronto Annexation Association, supposedly embracing
"a large number of the most respectable merchants and inhabitants of this
city, of all parties and creeds," was announced.

Even French Canada displayed some interest in annexation, though obviously for entirely different reasons. Louis-Joseph Papineau, who had returned to Canada after having been granted amnesty in 1844, was well known for his admiration of American democratic institutions and his hatred of the Canadian union. Radical young intellectuals belonging to the Institut canadien, a literary and debating society in Montreal, or who wrote for the newspaper *L'Avenir*, took up the annexationist cause. They declared that they preferred "Brother Jonathan" (a personification of the United States), with his egalitarian principles, to John Bull (a personification of England), with his haughty and aristocratic airs. A naive but sincere Louis-Antoine Dessaulles, Papineau's nephew, expressed his ardent desire that French Canada imitate Louisiana, with its large French-speaking population, in order to obtain the advantages both of a separate state and of American prosperity and democracy. Dessaulles, journalist Jean-Baptiste-Éric Dorion (appropriately nicknamed *"l'enfant terrible"*), and their friends, however, constituted but a tiny group. Their movement had no popular base, and other elites in French Canada vociferously condemned annexation. George-Étienne Cartier echoed conservative sentiment when he warned that American democracy signified that "the dominant power was the will of the crowd, of the masses." The Roman Catholic clergy, for its part, feared that annexation would put an end to the liberty that it enjoyed under British rule.

281

In English-speaking Canada West, annexationism, though noisy, made little headway. Newspapers frequently published citizens' statements lauding the benefits of the relationship with Britain. John Strachan, now Anglican Bishop of Toronto, roundly denounced annexation as being opposed to "the plainest and most solemn declarations of the revealed will of God," for it signified union with republicans who sanctioned slavery. Opponents of annexation published their own manifestoes in the press.

In July 1849 Tories frustrated by the Reform government and by so-called French domination gathered at Kingston to launch the British–American League. Future prime minister John A. Macdonald apparently played an active behind-the-scenes role in its organization, but the Toronto *Globe*, edited by George Brown, Macdonald's great political opponent, reported that Macdonald "said little in the convention and indeed he never says much anywhere except in barrooms. . . ." Patriotic delegates overwhelmingly rejected a resolution favourable to annexation. One delegate declared passionately, "It was never intended by Providence that the American, or Gallic, eagles should ever build their nests in the branches of the British oak, or soar over her prostrate lion."

A later convention, held in Toronto in November, voiced support for a union of the British North American colonies, which many delegates viewed as a means of escaping from French domination. Macdonald judged this scheme "premature and impractical for the moment."

With the revival of prosperity in the early 1850s, annexationist sentiment receded rapidly. Although union with the United States had been
much discussed, it had little popular support. Also, the Americans' unre-
sponsiveness to annexationist tendencies north of the border hastened the
movement's decline.

New Political Alliances

While English-speaking Conservatives attempted to find a new basis for
unified action, the Reform movement began to splinter. By 1850, with
responsible government a reality, tensions were developing between moderates and radicals on issues such as political reform, railway policy,
financial affairs, and church–state relations. The radical Reformers, whose
stronghold was the area west of Toronto, denounced Montreal business
interests, actively promoted agrarian democracy, and announced that they
were seeking out "only men who are Clear Grit," *grit* being American slang
for firmness of character.[1] Under journalist George Brown's leadership,
the Clear Grits became vocal champions of "rep by pop," or representation
according to population, the implication being that Canada West, with its
larger and rapidly increasing population, deserved a greater number of
seats—and, therefore, a preponderant influence over government policy—
than did francophone Canada East.

282

At the same time, with Louis-Joseph Papineau's political revival, the
French Canadian Parti rouge made a modest appearance in the Assembly
in 1848. The *rouges* gained ground in the elections of 1851 and 1854,
especially in the Montreal region. These radical reformers inherited the
traditions of the Parti patriote. They tended to be somewhat anticlerical,
republican, strongly nationalistic, and highly critical of the close links
between government and business, notably as manifested in matters pertaining to the railways. Thus, in addition to its usual arch-Tory adversar-
ies, the governing coalition faced mounting pressures from the *rouges*
and the Clear Grits, particularly after the retirement of Baldwin and La
Fontaine in 1851. After initial attempts to attract Clear Grit support, the
government sought the endorsement of the Conservatives and of Hincks's
moderate Reformers. By the mid-1850s, the so-called Liberal–Conservative alliance emerged, soon to be led jointly by Macdonald and Cartier.

A Capital Is Chosen

In the 1850s, politics seemed to be largely divorced from the everyday
concerns of common people. The difficulty of choosing a capital for the

united province symbolized this apparent detachment. Indeed, between 1841 and 1859, the Legislative Assembly voted no fewer than 218 times on this seemingly straightforward matter. Political, ethnic, and geographical rivalries transformed the issue into one of the most divisive confronting the union. In 1841 the British government chose the small town of Kingston as the first capital, because it judged both Toronto and Montreal difficult to defend in the event of American attack; moreover, Toronto was too far west. Quebec, with its largely French-speaking population, was not acceptable either. But according to Lord Sydenham, a capital somewhere in Upper Canada would be good for French members because it "would instil English ideas into their minds, [and] destroy the immediate influence upon their actions of the host of little lawyers, notaries and doctors."

Many liberal-minded members soon found Kingston too deeply permeated by Orangeism and Toryism. The government therefore moved its seat to Montreal. But in 1849, the burning of the Parliament there again necessitated a move, and the seat of government migrated to Toronto. After stormy debate, the legislators agreed that the capital would remain on the humid shores of Lake Ontario for two years, after which it would alternate every four years between Quebec City and Toronto. Citizens of both cities were reluctant to see the capital depart, but Protestant or Catholic, English or French, the members of this so-called "log-rolling compact" preferred relinquishing the seat temporarily to seeing it settle on a permanent basis in some other city.

283

Eventually, the Assembly appealed to Queen Victoria to choose a capital. After receiving memorials from all appropriate Canadian towns (and from some less appropriate ones as well), the British government selected Bytown, which had recently been rebaptized "Ottawa." Quebeckers were dismayed. The Toronto *Globe* was outraged by this choice of a city in which more than 60 percent of the population was Roman Catholic and half was French Canadian. After more bickering, the Assembly finally deferred to the Queen's decision and, in 1865, Ottawa became the capital of the Canadas.

Politics and Business

Economic progress and, especially after 1845, railway development most engaged the attention of the legislators. Railways required extensive government financial assistance through tax concessions, guarantees, bonds, the assumption of bad debts, and outright grants when private capital subscribed was insufficient, as it always was (see Chapter 15).

At the time, many politicians had close links with business enterprises and exhibited few scruples about combining personal and state interests.

Sir Allan MacNab, co-prime minister in the MacNab–Morin and MacNab–Taché administrations from 1854 to 1856, was one. He affirmed candidly, after consuming "one or two bottles of good port," that "all my politics are railroads." The great reformer, Francis Hincks, an unabashed defender of railway schemes, was another. A parliamentary committee studied his conduct but found no evidence of corruption, although the former premier had obviously been in situations involving conflicts of interest. Alexander T. Galt of Sherbrooke, named Minister of Finance in the Cartier–Macdonald ministry in 1858, was also a very pragmatic businessman. He was a leading force behind, a large shareholder in, and eventually president of, the St. Lawrence and Atlantic Railway that linked Montreal to Portland, Maine, by way of Sherbrooke. The Grand Trunk Railway absorbed the line shortly after its completion in 1853. Galt also sat on the board of directors of the Grand Trunk and, in politics, sought to expand Montreal's influence westward.

284   None of today's conflict-of-interest legislation existed at that time. George-Étienne Cartier, for instance, actively concerned himself with Montreal business while serving as the director of a host of banking, insurance, transportation, and mining companies. Railways, though, were his main activity. Over many years, he held positions as cabinet minister, chairman of the Legislative Assembly's Railway Committee, and solicitor for the Grand Trunk Railway. Cartier guided the Grand Trunk's charter through the Assembly in 1854 and was prouder of that than of any other action in his life. Hugh Allan, a banker, shipping magnate, and railway promoter, made large contributions to Cartier's election campaigns. In return for the donations he received railway charters, favourable legislation, and the repeal of laws he disliked.

Politics and business were thus closely entwined. Hugh Allan's lawyer, for example, later testified before the Railway Committee: "On every one of these subjects—steamships, railways, canals—the Government had a policy which was favourable to his [Allan's] views, and in my opinion three times the sum would have been well spent had it been necessary to keep a government in power which had . . . the improvement of the country so deeply at heart as this Government appears to." Cartier, who reportedly said that Irish voters could be bought for a "barrel of flour apiece and some salt fish thrown in for the leaders," was obviously able to make good use of Hugh Allan's money.

The politicians themselves usually waged fierce verbal battles in committee and on the floor of the Assembly over any business-related decisions that the government made. Representatives from Quebec City, for example, such as Commissioner of Crown Lands Joseph Cauchon and Mayor Hector Langevin, protested vehemently that their pet project, the North Shore Railway to Quebec, was sabotaged by the Grand Trunk and its Montreal political allies Cartier and Galt, who had no intention of allowing trade to be diverted downstream.

"Rep by Pop"

As time passed, dissatisfaction with the legislative union grew, particularly in Canada West. Some representatives of both Canadas advocated the double majority vote. This notion implied that government ministers from each section of the colony needed the support of the majority of their section's members and, as a corollary, that controversial legislation could not be imposed upon one section of the colony by a majority composed largely of members from the other. Yet the government frequently had a difficult time building a simple majority, let alone finding majority support in both Canadas. In the 1840s, many measures were indeed imposed on Canada East as a result of majorities in Canada West. After 1850, the shoe was often on the other foot, as large numbers of *bleus* helped adopt laws that were approved by only a minority of members from the upper section. One such law was the Scott Act of 1863, which gave added privileges to Canada West's Roman Catholic schools. The double majority principle was simply unworkable. Only separation of the two sections, albeit within a federal system, could permit development according to each section's special needs and interests.

285

In the early 1850s, Canada West's population surpassed that of Canada East. The Clear Grits now took up as their campaign slogan "rep by pop." By 1857 it was the foremost plank in the Reform platform. To this demand, most inhabitants of Canada East responded with a resounding "no." Union had instituted equality of representation in 1841; both languages had official status; governments were headed by co-premiers, one from each of the Canadas; and each section of the province had its own attorney general and solicitor general, its own educational legislation, and its own deputy superintendent of education. Even the old pre-union names— Upper and Lower Canada—remained in common use. Some semblance of equality, indeed a crude sort of federalism, had been achieved in spite of the original intentions of the architects of union. Representation by population, it was feared, would only destroy this working system.

Toward Confederation

At the Reform party's convention in Toronto in November 1859, George Brown began to promote the idea, already advocated by the *rouges* of Canada East, of transforming the legislative union into a highly decentralized federative union of the two Canadas. The Conservatives, however, who governed only because of their large block of French support from Canada East, were opposed. Moreover, they countered with suggestions for a wider British North American union. Alexander Galt entered the ministry only after extracting from the Conservatives a promise to work toward Confederation, but initially the idea aroused only perfunctory interest. The Montreal *Gazette* believed that the proposal had possibilities and suggested forming a new English-speaking province that would join portions of eastern Upper Canada with Montreal and the Eastern Townships. Then the French-speaking East could "stand still as long as it likes" and the West could "rush frantically forward," while the centre enjoyed "that gradual, sure, true progress which is the best indication of material prosperity."

The Reformers were understandably suspicious of any Conservative proposal. After all, they had just witnessed Macdonald's political manoeuvres of 1858 that had permitted him to regain power only a few hours after it had been lost to a Brown–Dorion Reform–Parti rouge coalition, aptly termed the "Short Administration."

Confederation projects were discussed throughout the early 1860s. Many Upper Canadians were angry at having to pay for the expenditures voted by majorities built on eastern support. At last, a century after the Conquest, as George Brown said in the Canadian legislature, the representatives of the British population might aspire to justice without having to wait while "the representatives of the French population [sit here] discussing in the French tongue whether we shall have it." At the same time, Lower Canadians protested, as the newspaper *L'Ordre* put it, that without Lower Canadian help to pay Upper Canadian debts, Upper Canada today would be "nothing more or less than a forest put up for auction by British capitalists to repay their investments."

The deteriorating external situation seemed to instil a sense of urgency in resolving the political deadlock. Across the border, the Civil War raged and Britain's relations with the soon-to-be-victorious North were strained. Canadians began to fear that the Americans might decide to seek revenge on the British by attacking Canada. In addition, trade relations, which had been greatly stimulated by the Treaty of Reciprocity of 1854 as well as by the North's needs during the Civil War, continued to be endangered.

The deadlock that virtually paralyzed the union government provided the necessary push for change. In May 1862, the Cartier–Macdonald ministry resigned when, in the face of *bleu* defections over the issue of conscription, the legislature defeated its Militia Bill, much to the chagrin of the British government and "Little Englanders," who wished to shift more of the burden of Canadian defence away from British taxpayers. John A. Macdonald, the minister responsible for militia affairs, was inebriated and unavailable during most of the debate. A Liberal administration under John Sandfield Macdonald and Louis-Victor Sicotte, a moderate liberal, or *"mauve,"* took office, but the following year it failed to survive a vote of confidence and went to the people.

The 1863 elections saw the Liberals strengthened in Canada West, while in the East, the *bleus* at least avoided a rout. The Liberal camp, however, was weakened by internal division, and in 1864 Sandfield Macdonald gave up the hopeless task of governing. The Étienne–Pascal Taché–John A. Macdonald regime that replaced it was defeated in June 1864, after barely a few weeks in office. Now that opposing forces were almost evenly balanced, Canada became ungovernable.

Any evaluation of the rather brief union period must be qualified. Certainly there was progress in many areas. The coming of responsible government represented a significant milestone in the movement toward democracy and autonomy. For the French, in particular, the dire prophecies of assimilation made at the birth of union did not materialize, though ethnic and religious prejudice remained rampant throughout the era. Chronic political instability sealed the fate of the union. By 1864, Canada was thus once again in the throes of constitutional change.

NOTE

[1]John Robert Colombo, "Grit," *The Canadian Encyclopedia*, 2d ed., vol. 2 (Edmonton, 1988), 940. Grit is fine sand or gravel, which is often valued for its abrasive quality. The Clear Grits characterized themselves as "all sand and no dirt, clear grit all the way through."

Related Readings

R. Douglas Francis and Donald B. Smith, *Readings in Canadian History: Pre-Confederation*, 3d ed. (Toronto, 1990) contains one article on this topic: Gerald M. Craig, "Lord Durham's Report," 312–21.

BIBLIOGRAPHY

The union years are examined in J.M.S. Careless, *The Union of the Canadas: The Growth of Canadian Institutions, 1841–1857* (Toronto, 1967) and in W.L. Morton, *The Critical Years: The Union of British North America, 1857–1873* (Toronto, 1964). Maurice Séguin defends his thesis in *L'idée d'indépendance au Québec: genèse et historique* (Trois-Rivières, 1968). Paul G. Cornell, in *The Alignment of Political Groups in Canada, 1841–1867* (Toronto, 1962), treats the rather complex development of party groupings. R.C. Brown, ed., *Upper Canadian Politics in the 1850s* (Toronto, 1967) contains several helpful articles, while J.M.S. Careless, ed., *The Pre-Confederation Premiers: Ontario Government Leaders, 1841–67* (Toronto, 1980), constitutes a valuable addition to political history of the period. For biographies of Canada West's two leading politicians, see Donald G. Creighton, *John A.Macdonald: The Young Politician* (Toronto, 1956) and J.M.S. Careless, *Brown of the Globe*, 2 vols. (Toronto, 1959, 1963). The role of Conservative politicians of the era is studied in Carol Wilton-Siegel, "Administrative Reform: A Conservative Alternative to Responsible Government," *Ontario History* 78 (1986): 105–25, and Donald R. Beer, "Toryism in Transition: Upper Canadian Conservative Leaders, 1836–1854," *Ontario History* 80 (1988): 207–25.

Several other works also elaborate on the political developments of the period. On responsible government, see George Metcalf's essay "Draper Conservatism and Responsible Government in the Canadas, 1836–1847," *Canadian Historical Review* 42 (1961): 300–324. A useful article on the annexation movement in Upper Canada is Gerald A. Hallowell's "The Reaction of the Upper Canadian Tories to the Adversity of 1849: Annexation and the British American League," *Ontario History* 62 (1970): 41–56. Annexationist sentiment in French Canada is described in Jean-Paul Bernard, *Les rouges: libéralisme, nationalisme et anticléricalisme au milieu du XIXe siècle* (Montréal, 1971), 61–73. The conflict over the choice of a capital is recounted in all its intricacies in David R. Knight, *A Capital for Canada: Conflict and Compromise in the 19th Century* (Chicago, 1977).

British policy toward Canada is discussed in William Ormsby, *The Emergence of the Federal Concept in Canada, 1839–1845* (Toronto, 1969); Peter Burroughs, *British Attitudes towards Canada* (Toronto, 1971); Phillip Buckner, *The Transition to Responsible Government: British Policy in British North America, 1815–1850* (Westport, Conn., 1985); and Ged Martin, "Britain and the Future of British North America, 1841–1850," *British Journal of Canadian Studies* 2 (June 1987): 74–96. On French Canada in particular, see Jacques Monet's *The Last Cannon Shot: A Study of French Canadian Nationalism, 1837–1850* (Toronto, 1969). It should also be noted that biographies of the public figures of this age—including La Fontaine, Baldwin, Hincks, Cartier, and Morin—appear in various volumes of the *Dictionary of Canadian Biography*.

For the Indian policy of the union period, see John S. Milloy, "The Early Indian Acts: Developmental Strategy and Constitutional Change," in *As long as the Sun Shines and Water Flows: A Reader in Canadian Native Studies*, edited by Ian A.L. Getty and Antoine S. Lussier (Vancouver, 1983); J.E. Hodgetts's chapter, "Indian Affairs: The White Man's Albatross," in *Pioneer Public Service: An Administrative History of the United Canadas, 1841–1867* (Toronto, 1955), 205–25; and John F. Leslie, *Commissions of Inquiry into Indian Affairs in the Canadas, 1828–1858: Evolving a Corporate Memory for the Indian Department* (Ottawa, 1985). Tony Hall reviews developments in Canada West in "Native Limited Identities and Newcomer Metropolitanism in Upper Canada, 1814–1867," in *Old Ontario: Essays in Honour of J.M.S. Careless*, edited by David Keane and Colin Read (Toronto, 1990): 148–173.

Union of the Canadas: Economic and Social Developments, 1840–1864

Great economic and social transformation accompanied political change in the two Canadas in the mid-nineteenth century. In the late 1840s Britain adopted free trade, an event that led, with the signing of a reciprocity treaty with the United States in 1854, to a new north–south orientation to the Canadas' trade. The United Canadas also in the 1850s obtained a railway system that greatly transformed the agricultural, commercial, and urban character of the province. Large-scale immigration to Canada West and emigration from Canada East altered social and cultural life at mid-century. Education, especially in Canada West, became a much-debated social issue.

289

Commercial Empire of the St. Lawrence

Canadian historian Donald Creighton developed the Laurentian interpretation of Canadian history; that is, whoever controlled the St. Lawrence could dominate the economic life of the continent.[1] The American Revolution and the Treaty of 1783 created an artificial political boundary along the St. Lawrence and the Great Lakes, dividing the northern portion of the North American continent into two political units. But the political boundary did not immediately become an economic one. Throughout the early nineteenth century, the merchants of Montreal vied with those of New York for dominance of the commercial trade of the interior of North America.

Up to the mid-1840s, the merchants of Montreal competed successfully against their American counterparts, thanks to the highly favourable mercantile system of trade that the British North American colonies had with Britain. The British desired two staples that were readily available in the United Canadas: timber and wheat.

Archives of Ontario/11778-4

The timber industry in the Canadas. This photograph illustrates the process called "squaring the timber,"—that is, cutting the sides to make the round log into a square. After squaring the logs with heavy, razor-sharp axes called broadaxes, the shantymen would haul them to the river, where they tied them into rafts. The wasteful squaring practice left behind about a quarter of the log, which was left to rot on the ground. The logs were squared to allow them to be fitted tightly into the hold of the ships that transported timber to Britain.

Square-hewed timber, made from Canadian white and red pine, continued to be in demand for the masts of sailing ships. In addition, lumber for construction found a lucrative market in Britain. Wood thus became British North America's most valuable export commodity, making up nearly two-thirds of the value of all the colonies' exports to Britain by the 1840s. But the lumber industry was a vulnerable and volatile one, subject to fluctuating demand in Britain, low tariffs after 1842, and overproduction—all of which caused many businesses to go bankrupt during the 1840s and 1850s. Without preferential treatment in Britain, it was difficult for Canadian lumber merchants to compete with lumber exports from Europe, where transportation costs were considerably lower.

Within the United Canadas a second commodity—wheat, in the form of either coarse grain or ground flour—rivalled timber. Canada West was the greatest producer of wheat in British North America. After 1840 a combination of good weather and increased acreage due to rapid settlement of the rich farmland of Canada West greatly increased total production. The average farmer's export of wheat rose from 45 bushels in the 1840s to 80 in the 1850s, and to as high as 135 bushels in the 1860s. Improved

290

Notman Photographic Archives, McCord Museum of Canadian History.

The Anse-au-Foulon timber cove. Quebec City lived by the timber trade in the first half of the nineteenth century. Timber was stocked for kilometres along the shore near the city. Large rafts coming from the Ottawa River were beached at places such as the Anse-au-Foulon timber cove and shipyard. Here, the dockworkers loaded the square timber, or "deals" (planks 7.5 cm wide that could be sawed in England to the desired size), onto the timber ships. Anse-au-Foulon has another name in English—"Wolfe's Cove." It is here that a break in the cliff on the north shore of the St. Lawrence leads from the river to the Plains of Abraham. Wolfe and his invasion army took this route in the early morning of September 13, 1759.

transportation on the St. Lawrence–Great Lakes with the completion of the canal system lowered transport costs and reduced insurance rates. This helped to increase Canadian exports, making Canada West one of the chief suppliers of wheat to feed the growing urban population of industrial Britain.

TRANSPORTATION

Exporting bulky staples such as wheat and timber required a sophisticated transportation system. Roads were needed to get wheat to urban centres for local marketing or export. In the 1840s a series of roads, some of which were little more than dirt paths, crisscrossed the United Canadas. More important for transportation was the canal system linking Lake Erie with Montreal and the Atlantic Ocean. During the 1840s the government of the Canadas widened and deepened existing canals such as the Welland

and the Lachine. It built new canals between Montreal and Prescott, where rapids and shallows impeded shipping, and at Beauharnois, Cornwall, and Williamsburg. By 1848 a chain of first-class canals enabled the St. Lawrence–Great Lakes route to rival the Erie–Hudson River route, and Montreal to compete with New York as the major exporting and importing centre for the North American continent.

New York, however, had considerable advantages. It was a larger city, with a heavily populated hinterland based on a diverse economy and, unlike Montreal, with a year-round ice-free port. Shipping rates from New York to Liverpool were also considerably lower than those from Montreal to Liverpool. In addition, in 1845–46 the American government passed the Drawback Acts, which allowed Canadian exports and imports to pass in bond through American waterways duty free, thus making it profitable for Canada West farmers and timber merchants to ship via the United States. Finally, New York had the advantage of being linked to the growing American Midwest by an extensive railway system.

Advent of British Free Trade and Repercussions for the United Canadas

In 1846 the British government under Prime Minister Robert Peel made an important decision that had far-reaching implications for the British North American colonies: it adopted free-trade measures (for the political repercussions of this decision, see Chapter 14). Pressure on the British government to end the old colonial mercantile system came chiefly from factory owners who wanted reduced tariffs to enable Britain to compete in a world market. They also sought the repeal of the Corn Laws (British protective tariffs on grain), arguing that repeal of the laws would mean cheaper food for the working class, and hence an opportunity for employers to lower wages.

Liberal economists such as Richard Cobden disproved traditional mercantile theories by pointing out the costs, economic and military, of keeping colonies. They argued persuasively in favour of *laissez-faire* economics and free trade as benefiting all Britons. Historian J.M.S. Careless has summarized their argument: "When the whole world was its domain for markets and supplies, what reason was there to guide and husband overseas possessions that cost much more to maintain than they could ever return?"[2]

These free-trade lobbyists formed the Anti-Corn Law League, which convinced the Peel government to repeal the Corn Laws in 1846. Other free-trade measures included the lowering of the timber preference in 1842, when the duty on foreign imports was cut in half. Further reductions followed in 1845, 1846, 1848, and 1851. Then, in 1849, Britain ended the Navigation Laws, which had forbidden the colonies from accepting trade goods unless they were shipped in British or colonial vessels and listed the ports to which British ships could sail and the markets in which they could sell their produce. Britain wanted to purchase raw materials at the lowest possible price and to sell manufactured goods wherever it desired. The United States, in turn, obtained access to the Canadian–British trade and to all the Great Lakes trade.

Britain's move to free trade initially had a catastrophic impact on the Canadas. Exports via the St. Lawrence fell from £2.7 million in 1845 to a low of £1.7 million in 1848. The economic and political life of the British North American colonists rested on their relationship to England. They had lived in a protected trading system, with a privileged access to British markets. Now it appeared as though they had been set adrift by an indifferent mother country. They reacted with resentment, especially the Montreal merchants who, with the arrival of free trade, saw the demise of their dream of the commercial empire of the St. Lawrence. The current world depression added to the city's problems as bankruptcies spread. A movement to solve the problem by gaining access to the large American market began to take shape. Annexation manifestos circulated throughout the Canadas (see Chapter 14).

293

From Transatlantic to Transcontinental Trade

With the advent of British free trade the Canadas neither collapsed nor joined the United States. Commerce revived as British North Americans adjusted to meet the new challenges, and set new economic priorities. This process of adjustment first involved increased trade with the United States and, second, a new emphasis on railways as the major means of transportation. These two goals were complementary. Just as the waterways had been the best means of facilitating east–west trade across the continent and ultimately with Britain, railways best linked the Canadas with the United States for the north–south trade.

This transition came swiftly and dramatically. By 1850 the world depression was lifting and prosperity was returning through increased trade. Whereas industrialism in Britain had led indirectly to a temporary *decrease* in trade for the British North American colonies, industrialism in the United States led directly to an initial *increase* in markets for the Canadian staple products—timber and wheat. The rapidly growing cities of the eastern seaboard and of the American Midwest needed lumber, the universal building material at the time, to construct houses and commercial buildings, and wheat to feed the growing urban population. American consumption of British North American products was still much smaller than was British consumption, but it was growing. The trend from transatlantic to transcontinental trade was under way.

The era of the 1850s inaugurated what one historian, A.R.M. Lower, has described as "the North American assault on the Canadian forest."[3] Demand for Canadian lumber increased, and American lumber firms and sawmill owners established themselves in Canadian forest areas, especially the Ottawa Valley.

Equally, Canadian timber found a rising market in Canada West with its growing immigrant population. Pioneer settlers were as much consumers as producers. Saw and planing mills, sash and shingle factories, and cabinet-making firms served this market. Britain also increased its demand for Canadian lumber in the prosperous years of the 1850s. Despite the move to free trade, Britain remained, in relative terms, the most lucrative market for Canadian timber until into the 1860s, still accounting for approximately 80 percent of wood exports.

294

Canadian wheat did equally well during the prosperous 1850s. Clearly, the removal of the Corn Laws had little effect on Canada's ability to compete in British markets. A wheat boom developed during the Crimean War of 1854–56, when Britain prohibited the importation of Russian grain. Americans also purchased quantities of Canadian wheat to feed their growing urban population. Exports of Canadian wheat and flour via the St. Lawrence more than doubled, rising from 4.5 million bushels in 1845 to 12 million bushels in 1856—a figure not surpassed until the next decade. Furthermore, prices tripled in the same period. As a result, agriculture surpassed timber as the major staple of Canadian—indeed of all British North American—trade in the 1850s.

Farmers in Canada West benefited the most from this increased demand for wheat. Good prices along with high yields provided them with capital to increase their acreage and to diversify their farming. In addition to wheat, they exported wool, meat, eggs, butter, and cheese, especially to the United States.

Their compatriots in Canada East did not fare as well. Unlike Canada West, where new fertile land remained available until the mid-1850s, a shortage of good agricultural land along with problems of climate and fertility led to serious farm problems. Farmers in Canada East produced little wheat for export, although they did export such other grains as oats and barley, along with dairy products in limited quantities.

Reciprocity with the United States

To secure this lucrative trade with the United States, the government of the Canadas wanted a reciprocal trade agreement. Negotiations continued for eight years due to strong American protectionist sentiment. When the

Americans finally became receptive to the idea in the early 1850s, Canadians were less enthusiastic because they were then enjoying active trade with the Americans without an agreement. But, as J.M.S. Careless notes, "The emerging economic pattern of the early fifties indicated that if Canada could do without reciprocity, she could do much better with it."[4] The British government endorsed the idea, too, seeing closer economic ties between the United States and the United Canadas as a means of easing tensions and reducing Canadian dependence on the mother country.

Before agreement could be reached, however, two contentious issues needed to be settled. One, internal to the United States, was the slavery issue, because it affected the entry of new territories into the union. The divisions between the slave South and the free North affected all aspects of American development at the time, including economic relations with the British North American colonies. By the early 1850s a delicate balance had been achieved, and both sides feared that the incorporation of new states would offset this balance in favour of the other side. Northern senators favoured free trade because they believed it was a prelude to annexing the Canadas, which would lead to a preponderance of free states in the union. Southern senators opposed it for the same reason, until Lord Elgin, who went to Washington in May 1854 to persuade these senators to endorse free trade, convinced them that a prosperous Canada through free trade would be more likely to want independence from, rather than annexation to, the United States.

295

The other issue in dispute concerned Maritime fisheries. Britain and the United States had different interpretations of the territorial waters from which American fishermen were excluded under the Convention of 1818. New England fishermen claimed a right to fish in waters three miles (five kilometres) out from shore and following the shoreline. Nova Scotian and other Maritime fishermen claimed a boundary three miles from headland to headland, thus leaving most of the bays and inlets as exclusive British territory. Neither side wanted an armed conflict, and Britain was willing to use the fisheries issue as a negotiating tool for free trade of colonial natural products in the United States. In the end, Britain threatened to withdraw its patrol boats (which prevented American encroachment), unless Nova Scotia agreed to the treaty.

THE RECIPROCITY TREATY

The Reciprocity Treaty of 1854, approved by the American Senate and ratified by the colonial legislatures, allowed for the following: free trade of major natural products, such as timber, grain, coal, livestock, and fish, between the British North American colonies and the United States; mutually free navigation on the American-controlled Lake Michigan and the Canadian-controlled St. Lawrence; and joint access to all coastal fisheries north of the 36th parallel. The agreement ran for a ten-year period commencing in 1855 and was subject to renewal or termination.

For Canadians, this reciprocity agreement bolstered the prosperity that had already begun. After 1854 Canadians had one foot in the British market and the other in the American market. They moved closer to their future role as a partner in the North Atlantic triangle, a reciprocal trade relationship among Britain, the United States, and Canada.

The Railway Era

Closer economic ties with the United States coincided with the railway-building era in the Canadas. Suddenly constructing canals seemed old-fashioned. Increased Canadian–American trade provided the incentive, rationale, and prosperity for railway building; in turn, the railways provided the means for greater continental economic integration.

Railway building proceeded at a rapid pace in the 1850s. At the beginning of the decade, there were only 105 km of track in all British North America; by the end of the decade, there were 2880 km in the Canadas alone. Such expansion came as a result of the combination of popular interest, public and private financial support, and private promotion.

Governments eagerly courted railways. Railways required large expenditures of public funds and brought governments to the brink of bankruptcy, but they were believed to be worth the price. Since Canadians arrived late in the competition for railways (compared to Britain and the United States) and the country was as yet hardly industrialized, most of the capital for railway building had to come from outside the country, usually first from Britain and then from the United States.

As the governments in British North America had insufficient credit ratings to borrow vast sums abroad, they inevitably became involved in railway financing. But unlike canal building, in which the government often took control through public ownership, private corporations built railways with extensive government financial assistance. This partnership between government and private business built railways, but at the same time it led to waste, duplication of services, and an excessive drain on the public treasury (in the form of debt). Most of all, though, it led to corruption through the bribery of politicians for railway contracts (see Chapter 14). In 1849 the government of the Canadas introduced the Railway Guarantee Act, which was, in effect, an offer by the government to pay half the cost of railways more than 120 km in length.

Private companies built four key railway lines in the United Canadas in the 1850s. Begun in 1850 and completed in 1853, the St. Lawrence and Atlantic line between Montreal and Portland, Maine, gave Montreal access to a year-round ice-free port on the Atlantic. This rail link once more made Montreal competitive with New York in continental trade. The second line, the Great Western Railway, completed in 1855, went from Niagara Falls via Hamilton and London to Windsor. In the east, the line joined the New York network of railways, while in the west it connected with the Michigan Central. Ultimately, it was intended to capture the trade of the American Midwest by offering a quick route from Chicago through to New York by way of the Canadas. Presided over by Sir Allan MacNab and backed by British and American capital, this 575 km railway made a profit from the start. The third major line, the Northern Railway, went from Toronto, on Lake Ontario, to Collingwood, on Georgian Bay— a distance of roughly 160 km. The Northern serviced the rich farmland north of Toronto, opened up the forested area of the Georgian Bay and Muskoka regions, and provided access to the upper lakes. The fourth and most ambitious railway scheme of the decade was the Grand Trunk.

THE GRAND TRUNK RAILWAY   *297*

Chartered by Parliament in 1853, the Grand Trunk, when completed, was to extend from Windsor, Canada West, to Halifax, Nova Scotia, thus linking the interior of British North America with an ice-free Atlantic port. The railway's name came from its investors' original intention to have several smaller rail lines connect up to one main line, just as the branches of a tree join up to its trunk. When plans to build the Maritime section failed, the company purchased the St. Lawrence and Atlantic line, which ran between Montreal and ice-free Portland, Maine. The scheme proved costly, though, because the St. Lawrence and Atlantic track needed major repairs. Equally expensive was the Grand Trunk directorate's decision, when it failed in its attempt to purchase the Great Western, to build a competing line through the heart of Canada West from Toronto to Sarnia. As a result, the two railways often ran parallel to each other, and serviced the same area.

In 1859, the final year of construction, the Grand Trunk completed the world-famous Victoria Bridge, one of the great engineering feats of the century. This 2700 m bridge spanned the St. Lawrence from its south shore to the island of Montreal, and thus allowed for continuous rail connections between Sarnia and Portland.

When completed, the Grand Trunk Railway, at 1760 km, was the longest railway in the world. This distinction came at great cost to the Canadian public. From the beginning, the company ran into financial trouble. Difficulty on construction plus strong competition and inflationary labour costs made the railway too costly an undertaking for London bankers Thomas Baring and George Glyn, the railway's British investors. The railway company had to come to the provincial government for relief. The government felt obligated to bail it out, especially since six of the railway company's twelve directors belonged to the Canadian cabinet.

THE CANADAS: RAILWAYS AND CANALS
BEFORE CONFEDERATION

PRINCIPAL RAILWAYS
PRINCIPAL CANALS

N.R.   NORTHERN RAILWAY
G.T.R. GRAND TRUNK RAILWAY
G.W.   GREAT WESTERN RAILWAY

Source: Adapted from P.G. Cornell, J. Hamelin, F. Ouellet, and M. Trudel, *Canada: Unity in Diversity* (Toronto, 1967), 239.

Canadian railways and canals before Confederation.

By 1859, the Canadian government's debt exceeded $67 million, and the Grand Trunk Railway accounted for a large part of that debt. "This sum alone," economic historians Kenneth Norrie and Douglas Owram note, "was greater than all the money spent on public works—canals, bridges, roads, buildings—by the Province of the Canadas between the Act of Union in 1841 and Confederation."[5] To make matters worse, this trunk line, designed to tap American trade for the Canadas, had a 1.65 m track gauge—wider than that used in the United States. That meant American goods shipped via the Grand Trunk had to be reloaded at the border, causing the railway to lose most of the trade that it was built to capture! Throughout the pre-Confederation era, it never made a cent.

Urban and Commercial Development in the Canadas   *299*

The railways spurred commercial development. They brought in millions of dollars of foreign investment. They required thousands of workers to lay the track and then to maintain it. New railway-related industries sprang up across the province—engine foundries, car shops, rolling mills, and metalwork shops—and all needed skilled and unskilled workers. Many of these manufacturing businesses were owned by the railways themselves. By 1860 Canadian railways had 6600 people on their combined payrolls.

Along with canal building and shipbuilding, railways encouraged the development of a host of secondary industries: flour mills, saw mills, tanneries, boot and shoe factories, textile shops, breweries, distilleries, wagon and carriage manufacturers. Shipbuilders in Montreal and Quebec City built many of the steamboats that plied the St. Lawrence and Great Lakes after 1809, using timber from the Ottawa Valley. Ironworks were established in Hamilton because of the city's easy access to the American coal fields in Pennsylvania. Significant developments in the manufacturing of agricultural implements occurred, especially at Newcastle in Canada West, where Daniel and Hart Massey produced a combined rake, reaper, and mowing machine in 1855, marking the beginning of a lucrative Canadian business.

This industrial growth led to the creation of a host of towns, mainly along the rail lines, to service the prosperous agricultural hinterland. In Canada West the number of towns doubled to more than eighty between 1850 and 1870. Each provided a market centre for local produce and an import centre for manufactured goods. Fewer towns developed in the countryside of Canada East where little good agricultural land remained. On account of their lack of farmland and their inability to find work in Montreal and Quebec, a number of French Canadians emigrated to neighbouring New England, or to the American Midwest.

Eventually, a hierarchy of towns and cities developed in Canada West, with larger urban centres servicing the smaller towns and villages within their radius of influence. London became the major centre in southwestern Canada West. Its population tripled from five thousand in 1850 to fifteen thousand in 1856. The port of Hamilton dominated the hinterland to the west and south, extending its influence into the Niagara peninsula. Both London and Hamilton became supply depots and manufacturing centres. Hamilton also became an early industrial city.

RIVALRY OF TORONTO AND MONTREAL

Toronto became the dominant centre of Canada West, servicing a wealthy rural hinterland that extended roughly 20 km to the east, 20 km to the west, and 100 km to the north, to Lake Simcoe. Toronto had the advantage of good harbour facilities on Lake Ontario and, as the railway hub of Canada West, it had excellent rail service to various regions of the province. Import trade was its leading commerce, rising more than fivefold in value, from $1.2 million in 1849 to more than $6.6 million in 1856. Its export trade continued to be based on grain and wood to external markets, especially in the United States but also in Britain.

A new urban mercantile elite appeared in Toronto in the 1850s. Its members founded the Toronto Board of Trade as a means of dominating commerce in Canada West. In 1852 the Toronto Stock Exchange opened, and in 1856 the Bank of Montreal inaugurated its Toronto office. By the end of the decade the city had become the undisputable regional business centre of Canada West.

Toronto, however, could not replace Montreal as the largest city in British North America and the dominant metropolitan centre of the United Canadas. As one of the oldest centres in British North America, Montreal had an initial advantage that increased during the booming years of the mercantile system of trade. After a temporary setback in the late 1840s, the city surfaced again as a prosperous centre in the 1850s. Its important location on the St. Lawrence continued to benefit the city, especially since canal improvements in the 1840s made it cheaper and more efficient to ship goods by water than by rail.

Even in the competition for rail traffic, Montreal fared well once the Grand Trunk Railway was completed. The Portland, Maine, branch provided the city with an ice-free port on the Atlantic and access to the agricultural hinterland of Canada West and, to an extent, the American Midwest. Equally, Montreal served as an important import centre for the growing population of Canada West, rivalling Toronto for this lucrative market. Montreal also benefited from the Reciprocity Treaty of 1854, which helped it become a major export centre of Canadian timber and wheat for American markets.

301

City of Toronto Archives/SC498-2-N

King Street East, Toronto, 1856. Toronto had a reputation for the poor quality of its streets. Outside Toronto, a joke popular in the 1840s and 1850s went like this: A pedestrian walking along King Street one day spied a gentleman's hat on the muddy road. Reaching out from the wooden sidewalk, he picked it up from the mud and was startled to find a head underneath. In response to the offer of assistance, the head politely replied, "Don't worry about me, it's the horse that I'm riding who is in real trouble." Such are the tales of "muddy York," as some continued to call Toronto into the mid-nineteenth century (the name "York" had officially been changed to "Toronto" in 1834).

Service industries in Montreal grew in conjunction with increased trade. Footwear manufacturers, furriers, wood products manufacturers, distilleries, breweries, tobacco factories, brickyards, and sugar refineries opened their doors. Metal-based industries, such as the Victoria Iron Works (the largest industry, with 120 workers), also developed.

Social Developments in the United Canadas

Canadian society in the mid-nineteenth century was in a state of transition. Annually, 25 000–40 000 immigrants entered the province, especially into the western section. In 1851 the population of Canada West surpassed that of Canada East for the first time. Overall, the Canadas' population went from 1.1 million in 1841 to almost 2 million in 1851. A large number of

302

National Archives of Canada/C-9387.

Montreal Harbour from the Customs House, about 1870. Montreal, the largest city in British North America in the mid-nineteenth century, was more than two centuries old in the 1850s. The first buildings in Montreal were located at the point from which this photograph was taken. Montreal was founded in 1642.

new immigrants came from Ireland, part of the famine migration resulting from the failure of the potato crop.

Traditionally, historians have described these Irish as mainly impoverished Catholics from southern Ireland who lacked farming experience and money, and ended up in ghettos in the cities and towns. Recent research by historian Donald Akenson reveals, however, that by far the largest percentage (more than 75 percent) of Irish immigrants farmed on isolated homesteads in rural areas. Furthermore, more than two-thirds were Protestant.

American blacks came to the United Canadas. The passage of the Fugitive Slave Act in the United States in 1850 meant that thousands of presumably free blacks living in the northern states were liable to be captured and sent back into bondage. Canadian abolitionists organized the Canadian Anti-Slavery Society in 1851 to help these refugees escape. The largest number crossed at Detroit and settled near the border. Most went home after the passage of the Emancipation Act of 1863, having found temporary refuge but no more tolerance than they had experienced in the United States.

MIGRANT MOBILITY IN CANADA WEST

Within the province itself, people moved frequently. In a case study of rural Peel County, just west of Toronto, social historian David Gagan has shown that prior to 1840 the county had ample cheap land and a relatively self-sufficient population living off its own land and livestock. Two decades later, it had become a major wheat exporting region. Young people moved away from the now-overpopulated country areas, either to newer farming areas within the province, to the growing towns and cities of Canada West, or to other areas, such as the American Midwest. Those who stayed in Peel tended to be better off, with larger farms, a higher standard of living, and better-educated children than those who left. In general, people who did not move tended to be more prosperous than the transient in nineteenth-century North America.

Transiency also characterized the urban centres of Canada West. In a quantitative study of Hamilton, social historian Michael Katz noted that the city's population increased in five years (1846–50) by 150 percent and that individuals within this rapidly growing city moved frequently. More than one-third of those listed in the 1851 census could not be located for the 1861 census. This mobility was true of all social groups, from lower to upper class; people of all groups and all ages sought to improve their lot in life. And within the various occupational categories, the stable populations again tended to be more prosperous than those on the move.

303

URBAN SOCIAL STRUCTURE IN THE CANADAS

Within the city of Hamilton, as in the other towns and cities of Canada West, a fairly rigid social structure existed, with a small male elite dominating the social and political life of the community. Women were expected to stay at home, in what is now referred to as their "private sphere," where they performed domestic duties and reared children. A growing commercial middle class consisting of merchants, shopkeepers, and artisans had a prominent place. Equally evident in the towns and cities was a rising male professional class of clergymen, lawyers, doctors, and teachers. Increasingly, women were being hired as teachers (especially of girls at home), but they were still excluded from other professions.

Below the professional class stood the large class of wage labourers, made up mostly of immigrants, both male and female. Few, however, worked regularly for wages. Most often, wage-earning employment was temporary (as during a period of apprenticeship) or seasonal. This urban proletariat suffered from poor housing, inadequate sanitation, and seasonal unemployment. Most relied on their own ingenuity to survive, as virtually no help came from government. The prevailing ethos held that success came to those who worked hard; frustration and failure could only be the result of waste and a lack of individual initiative. Canada West thus remained a society modelled on the agrarian values of hardy "yeoman farmers" and robust, self-reliant pioneers.

The church reinforced that attitude in its parishioners. Religion played an important role in Upper Canadian society. The Church of England was the declared church of 22 percent of the population in 1840. The Presbyterians, at 20 percent, and the Methodists, at 17 percent (several schisms within the Methodist church had caused them to lose their position as the most numerous denomination in Canada West), were the next-largest denominations. The Baptists, Quakers, Lutherans, and Congregationalists together had 6 percent. The Roman Catholic population stood at 14 percent in 1841, most of it made up of Irish Catholic immigrants.

In Canada East people migrated as well, many to the United States. With a decline in agriculture and a sluggish timber trade (the two mainstays of the Quebec economy), hard economic times overtook the colony in the 1840s and 1850s. Existing land was depleted, new agricultural land was scarce, seigneuries were subdivided to the point where the habitants could no longer support their families, and unemployment was high in the urban centres. This crisis, along with continued high birth rates, a declining death rate, and increased British immigration, forced many French Canadians to move.

Some chose to settle in the Eastern Townships, where limited good agricultural land still existed, but most went to work in the New England factories. Others went to farm the virgin land of the American Midwest. As the Quebec historian Fernand Ouellet has noted: "between 1840 and 1850 French Canadian emigration to the United States acquired a magnitude hitherto unknown."[6] An estimated thirty thousand emigrants left during the decade.

The move of French Canadians to the cities and to the United States alarmed the Quebec clergy, who feared a loss of spiritual influence over their parishioners. After 1844 the Roman Catholic church became actively involved in the colonization movement designed to settle the northern areas of Quebec and, more important, to preserve the attributes of traditional family and religious life. "Let us take possession of the soil, it is the best means of preserving our nationality" became the rallying cry of the agrarian nationalism of the 1840s and 1850s. Yet for many French Canadians, the appeal went unheeded. They wanted to escape agriculture, and left for better economic conditions in "les États."

URBAN DEVELOPMENT IN QUEBEC

Some signs existed of increased urban growth in Canada East, but urban concentration took place only in a few centres. Even a long-established town such as Trois-Rivières had a population of only three thousand in the 1840s, while Sorel and Hull were virtually villages. The educated professional middle class of doctors, lawyers, and teachers constituted the elites in these communities. Sherbrooke was becoming the commercial centre for the predominantly English-speaking area of the Eastern Townships, but at mid-century it was still a village with a population of less than one thousand.

Only two urban centres could claim the title "city" in Canada East in the 1850s. The oldest of the two was Quebec, the centre of the timber trade. The majority of its commercial elite were English-speaking families associated with that trade in some respect. Many of the city's numerous labourers, who inhabited the Lower Town (*basse-ville*) of the city, also worked in the timber industry. Here, in overcrowded and dirty conditions, French Canadian and Irish workers intermingled. In contrast, the Upper Town, made up predominantly of the English, was considered "one of the cleanest cities in the world." In the northern section, around St. John Street (rue St. Jean), lived merchants, retail traders, artisans, and numerous tavern-keepers, while in the southern part resided officers and government officials.

Montreal was the largest and most socially advanced city in British North America. As factories were built in the 1840s and 1850s on the shores of the Lachine Canal in the west and closer to the centre of town, along the St. Lawrence in the neighbourhoods of Sainte-Marie and Hochelaga, the population grew rapidly. Employment prospects attracted workers from the countryside who might otherwise have emigrated to the United States. These French Canadians, along with the Irish immigrants, provided cheap labour for the new industries.

The city's sanitation system left much to be desired. Only in 1842 were the open sewers on Craig Street replaced by an underground system. No regular garbage pickup existed. Drinking water was often contaminated.

The eastern end of the city was overwhelmingly working class and predominantly French Canadian, while the west end was decidedly bourgeois and British. The English Canadian commercial entrepreneurs had begun to move "up the mountain" to build luxurious residences on Mount Royal. The Quebec historian, Paul-André Linteau, argues that "social divisions became so visible in Montreal's industrial sector that the city earned the fitting description 'City of wealth and death.' "[7]

305

A WORKING-CLASS CONSCIOUSNESS

A working-class consciousness began to develop in the Canadas by mid-century. A few, generally skilled, workers joined together in the 1830s to form local trade unions or self-help organizations such as the Ship Labourers' Benevolent Society. With a definite skill to offer employers, they enjoyed far more job security than did the labourers. Occasionally, when conditions became desperate, skilled and unskilled workers united to stage riots and strikes. Riots were a spontaneous means by which workers could express discontent with wages and working conditions. The majority of riots took place among railway workers.

Two early strikes were those called by labourers on the Lachine Canal in 1843 and on the Welland Canal in 1844–45. The workers laid down their tools to demand better working conditions and higher wages. In 1849, during the protests over free trade, shoemakers in Montreal ravaged a shoe factory and destroyed the sewing machines, in the tradition of the British Luddites, who opposed the mechanization of industry. By the 1860s strikes generally replaced riots as the main form of labour protest, despite the fact that they were illegal.

These expressions of working-class dissatisfaction were swiftly countered by the police or military personnel hired by employers or directed by government officials. The Rebellions of 1837–38 had shown the danger of letting unrest go unchecked.

In Canada East, one of the effects of a growing proletariat was the abandonment of children of poorer families to the Grey Nuns' Foundling Hospital. An estimated twelve thousand children became wards of the church between 1840 and 1870. The majority died at a young age as a result of their weakened condition upon arrival and the lack of pasteurized milk.

306

PROHIBITION MOVEMENT

The rise of an urban working class also had an impact on the prohibition movement throughout British North America. By the 1850s there was a noticeable shift in emphasis from temperance–abstinence through self-discipline–to prohibition–use of the power of the state to control and, it was hoped, eliminate alcohol. Social historian Graeme Decarie suggests that this shift in Canada West came about from a perceived threat to traditional Protestant middle-class values from the growing working class (often made up of Irish Catholics). Prohibition was a means for some middle-class Protestants to reassert their position of power and prominence. Furthermore, many rural inhabitants saw alcoholism as a predominantly urban phenomenon, another example of urban moral decay. "To them," Decarie notes, "a vote for prohibition was a vote for rural virtue and against urban decadence."[8]

Quebec's great "apostle of temperance" was Charles Chiniquy, a lively and eccentric Roman Catholic priest. He founded the Société de Tempérance in 1840 and by 1844 persuaded thousands to take the pledge of abstinence. "Everywhere his zeal goes, intemperance flies," the newspaper *Le Canadien* reported. His "zeal" took him to Kamouraska, Longueuil, and Montreal. His message, according to historian Jan Noel, could be summed up in one sentence: "the national survival of French Canada depends upon temperance. Giving up drinking might be unpleasant, but it was preferred to the decay and disappearance of a people."[9] The linking of temperance and nationalism was in keeping with some reform-minded members of the Roman Catholic church of the time, which felt threatened by an ever-increasing English-speaking population. (Later, Chiniquy was involved in a scandal and sent to Kankakee, Illinois. After his subsequent expulsion from the church, he married and converted to Protestantism).

Education and Culture in the United Canadas

In the mid-nineteenth century, education became a critical issue. Schools grew at a rapid rate to keep pace with the growing population, and the question of separate schools soon became a controversial one.

A move to non-sectarian education in Canada West took place in the 1840s and 1850s. State-supported schools under the sponsorship of the churches still existed, but they were on the defensive. In 1841 the government of the Canadas passed an Education Act extending the common schools throughout the western half of the united province. The act created the office of Superintendent of Education to oversee educational matters and established local boards of education with powers to tax inhabitants in each district to build and maintain schools. Opposition to the bill arose among those who argued for separate denominational schools to ensure that religion was an integral part of education. The government gave in to this pressure to introduce a separate school clause and to elect trustees responsible for establishing and maintaining separate schools. These separate schools received funding in proportion to the number of children in attendance.

At the heart of the separate-school controversy lay the question of the role of education. Roman Catholic leaders believed that education should have a religious component and that religious instruction should be in keeping with the teachings and beliefs of the Roman Catholic church. Catholic bishops argued that the common schools were non-religious or, at best, Protestant in orientation. They opposed teaching Catholic children from the Protestant Bible. Only separate schools, they felt, could ensure a proper Catholic and moral education. Furthermore, such church leaders as Armand Charbonnel, Bishop of Toronto, argued for the right of Catholic parents to direct the education of their own children.

Opponents of separate schools, such as Egerton Ryerson, the Methodist minister who served as superintendent of education for Canada West (Ontario) from 1844 to 1876, and George Brown, the influential political reformer and editor of the Toronto *Globe*, argued that education should be free, publicly funded, and non-sectarian. They believed that separate schools perpetuated sectarianism–an unhealthy development in education–and undermined the common school system. Brown further argued that separate schools would allow the church to undermine the educational

308

L'ABBÉ CHINIQUY
Apôtre de la Tempérance en Canada.

Archives nationales du Québec.

Sexual escapades and charges of embezzelement ended the priesthood of Charles Chiniquy, Lower Canada's greatest temperance speaker in the 1840s. After his excommunication in 1856, he became a Protestant and waged a war of slander against the Roman Catholic church until his death, at the age of eighty-nine, in 1899.

system and give the Pope undue influence in national affairs. The debate raged in the religiously intolerant atmosphere of the 1850s.

Separate and common schools proliferated in the 1850s and 1860s. By the School Act of 1853, a full-scale Catholic separate-school system came into being. The system had its own separate school board, with tax support coming from parents, who were exempt from paying common school taxes. A share of the provincial grant also paid expenses.

The final pre-Confederation education act, that of 1863, allowed separate schools to receive a share of both the provincial and municipal grants. Separate schools were also extended into rural areas. In return for these concessions, separate schools, like their common-school counterparts, submitted to provincial inspection, centralized control of curriculum and textbooks, and government control of all teacher training.

This was the system in effect when Canada West entered Confederation as the province of Ontario in 1867. It was also the system referred to in section 93 of the British North America (BNA) Act, which stated that nothing in any law relating to denominational schools "shall prejudicially affect any right or privilege . . . which any class of persons have by law in the province at the Union."

Common schools also came under greater centralized control as a result of Superintendent of Education Egerton Ryerson's efforts. By means of his Common School Act of 1846, he established a board of education (later the Council of Public Instruction) responsible for assisting the chief superintendent in establishing provincial standards, founded a normal school to train teachers, and held locally elected school boards responsible for operating the schools in their sections. These schools were expected to teach children good moral values—that is, Christian values—as well as to prepare them for work in an expanding and changing commercial economy. Ryerson believed a centralized and highly regulated system could best achieve these goals. Here lay the foundation of the modern Ontario school system.

309

In Canada West a similar process of secularism occurred in higher education. In 1849, under the direction of Ryerson, the government changed the Anglican-affiliated King's College into the non-sectarian University of Toronto. Once King's College had been transformed into the "godless" University of Toronto, John Strachan, Bishop of Toronto, founded the Anglican Trinity University in 1851. (At the turn of the century, Trinity, the Methodists' Victoria University, and St. Michael's, a Roman Catholic college founded in 1852, all became affiliates of the University of Toronto.)

EDUCATION IN QUEBEC

Canada East had Roman Catholic and Protestant schools, but the majority were Catholic. The Lower Canadian School Act of 1846 provided for the two state-aided school systems. Within each, the *curé* or minister had the right to veto the selection of teachers and textbooks, thus leaving only the task of financing the schools to the provincial authorities.

Not until 1851 did the legislature pass an act to establish a normal school to educate teachers, and then it took six years before it became operational. In 1859 the Council of Public Instruction was established. Consisting of fourteen members (ten Catholic and four Protestant) plus the superintendent of education, it was responsible for assisting the superintendent in making regulations for the normal school, for the organization and administration of common schools, and for the grading of schools and teachers.

At the university level, McGill University, chartered in 1821, became an influential institution. It admitted both English- and French- speaking students (although instruction was in English only) for advanced education in law, medicine, and the arts. Under the guidance of its able principal, William Dawson, appointed in 1855, McGill later acquired a distinguished reputation, especially in scientific research and medicine. In 1852 the Université Laval was established, having developed out of the Séminaire de Québec founded by Bishop Laval in 1663. Steeped in the French Catholic tradition, the first French Canadian university soon came to hold a position of respect in Canada East, with offerings in theology, civil law, medicine, and the arts.

CULTURE IN THE CANADAS

With the growth of towns and cities, the United Canadas witnessed a transformation of their society. This maturity was reflected in cultural developments. In Canada East, François-Xavier Garneau wrote a monumental history of French Canada. Octave Crémazie was the great French Canadian poet of the period, very popular for his nostalgic references to the happiness of New France and the miseries that followed after the British Conquest. Good-quality newspapers existed, such as Montreal's *La Minerve* and Quebec City's *Le Canadien*. French Canadian journalists and public figures gave well-attended lectures (many at Montreal's Institut canadien on popular topics of the day–education, national traits, and *la position de la femme*. In 1843 Ludger Duvernay, the editor of *La Minerve*, organized the Société Saint-Jean-Baptiste de Montréal. Many prominent French Canadians joined this patriotic organization, established to promote the interests of French Canada. In the larger centres of Montreal and Quebec, drama, art, and music flourished.

Canadian literature in English had a slow start. In fact, the earliest novel to be published in the Canadas and written by a British American-born author (Julia Catherine Beckwith's *St. Ursula's Convent*) appeared only in 1824, and the first anthology of poetry in English, in 1864. Throughout the 1860s, English-language poetry was popular in the Canadas. William Kirby described the migration of Loyalists to Niagara in his poem *The U.E.L.*, while Charles Sangster captured the beauty of the Canadian landscape in *The St. Lawrence and the Saguenay*. Other writers included Susanna Moodie and her sister Catharine Parr Traill, both of whom obtained publishers, and a readership, in Britain. There was no real publishing industry in the Canadas until the late nineteenth century. From 1847 to 1851, George Copway, an Ojibwa Indian from Rice Lake in Canada West, published four books in English in the United States, including the first autobiography by a Canadian Indian, and the first history of the Ojibwa Indians. Amateur historians, such as John Richardson (*The War of 1812*) and Robert Christie (*History of the Late Province of Lower Canada*), praised the early pioneers of the provinces.

In 1855 John McMullen, a journalist, produced the first history of English Canada, *The History of Canada from First Discovery to the Present Time*. While lacking François-Xavier Garneau's drive and flair, McMullen did have a justification for his history: "to infuse a spirit of Canadian nationality into the people generally–to mould the native born citizen, the Scotch, the English and the Irish emigrant into a compact whole." *311* Newspapers, among them Toronto's *Globe* and the *Leader*, helped cultivate a national feeling among English Canadians.

Between 1840 and 1864 the United Canadas underwent considerable economic and social change. Canadians adjusted to the end of the mercantile system of trade, to the advent of the railway age, and to rapidly changing social conditions in both rural and urban life. This was an age of transition from a British-oriented to an American-oriented economy and from a pioneer to a commercial society. The shift took decades to complete, but it saw its start in the period 1840–60.

NOTES

[1] See Donald Creighton, *The Commercial Empire of the St. Lawrence* (Toronto, 1937).
[2] J.M.S. Careless, *The Union of the Canadas: The Growth of Canadian Institutions, 1841–1857* (Toronto, 1967), 111.
[3] See A.R.M. Lower, *The North American Assault on the Canadian Forest* (Toronto, 1938).
[4] Careless, *Union of the Canadas*, 136.
[5] Kenneth Norrie and Douglas Owram, *A History of the Canadian Economy* (Toronto, 1990), 227.
[6] Fernand Ouellet, *Economic and Social History of Quebec, 1760–1850* (Toronto, 1980), 481.
[7] Paul-André Linteau, "Montreal–City of Pride," *Horizon Canada* 4 (1984): 88.
[8] Graeme Decarie, "Prohibition in Canada," *Canada's Visual History Series*, Canadian Museum of Civilization, vol. 29, 3.
[9] Jan Noel, "Dry Patriotism: The Chiniquy Crusade," *Canadian Historical Review* 71, 2 (June 1990): 200.

Related Readings

R. Douglas Francis and Donald B. Smith, eds., *Readings in Canadian History: Pre-Confederation*, 3d ed. (Toronto, 1990) contains the following articles related to this topic: John McCallum, "Urban and Commercial Development until 1850," 348–66; Gerald Tulchinsky, "Transportation Changes in the St. Lawrence–Great Lakes Region, 1828–1860," 367–76; and Michael Katz, "The People of a Canadian City: 1851–1852," 385–407.

BIBLIOGRAPHY

312

J.M.S. Careless provides an excellent survey in *The Union of the Canadas: The Growth of Canadian Institutions*, 1841–1857 (Toronto, 1967). Eric Ross reviews life in the Canadas in 1841 in *Full of Hope and Promise: The Canadas in 1841* (Montreal, 1991). For Canada East (Quebec), also consult the final chapters in Fernand Ouellet's *Economic and Social History of Quebec*, 1760–1850 (Toronto, 1980). Kenneth Norrie and Douglas Owram, *A History of the Canadian Economy* (Toronto, 1990) deals with the economy of the United Canadas. Donald Creighton develops the Laurentian thesis in *The Commercial Empire of the St. Lawrence*, 1760–1850 (Toronto, 1937). Economic questions are also addressed in Michael Bliss, *Northern Enterprise, Five Centuries of Canadian Business* (Toronto, 1987); R.T. Naylor, *Canada in the European Age: 1453–1919* (Vancouver, 1986); W.L. Marr and D.G. Patterson, *Canada: An Economic History* (Toronto, 1980); W.T. Easterbrook and H.G.J. Aitken, *Canadian Economic History* (Toronto, 1963); G.N. Tucker, *The Canadian Commercial Revolution 1845–1851* (Toronto, 1934; reprinted 1964); and D.C. Master, *The Reciprocity Treaty of 1854* (Toronto, 1963). P.J. Cain, *Economic Foundation of British Overseas Expansion, 1815–1914* (London, 1980) explains British economic policies in terms of imperial developments.

On agricultural developments in the Canadas, see John McCallum, *Unequal Beginnings: Agriculture and Economic Development in Quebec and Ontario Until 1870* (Toronto, 1980); for Canada East, see R.L. Jones, "Agriculture in the St. Lawrence Valley, 1815–1850," in *Approaches to Canadian Economic History*, edited by W.T. Easterbrook and M. Watkins (Toronto, 1967), 110–26, and Serge Courville and Normand Séguin, *Rural Life in Nineteenth-Century Quebec*, Canadian Historical Association, Historical Booklet No.47 (Ottawa, 1989); for Canada West, see R.L. Jones, *History of Agriculture in Ontario*, 1613–1880 (Toronto, 1977), and D. McCalla, "The Canadian Grain Trade in the 1840s: The Buchanan Case" and "The Wheat Staple and Upper Canadian Development," in the Canadian Historical Association, *Report* (1974), 95–114, and (1978) 34–46, respectively. On the timber trade, see A.R.M. Lower, *Great Britain's Woodyard: British America and the Timber Trade*, 1763–1867 (Montreal, 1973). On railway building in the 1850s, see G.P. de T. Glazebrook, *A History of Transportation in Canada*, vol. 1 (Toronto, 1964); for an appreciation of the excitement of railway building, see T.C. Keefer's *The Philosophy of Railroads* (1849), reprinted with an introduction by H.V. Nelles (Toronto, 1972).

Urban and commercial development in Canada West is discussed by Jacob Spelt, *Urban Development in South-Central Ontario* (Toronto, 1972; first published 1955); and Douglas McCalla, *The Upper Canada Trade, 1834–1872: A Study of the Buchanan's Business* (Toronto, 1979). For Canada East, see G. Tulchinsky, *The River Barons: Montreal Businessmen and the Growth of Industry and Transportation*, 1837–1853 (Montreal, 1977); Peter Baskerville reviews the history of the Bank of Upper Canada in his introduction to his edited work, *The Bank of Upper Canada: A Collection of Documents* (Toronto, 1987).

The chapters "Quebec in the Century After the Conquest," pp. 65–109, and "Ontario," pp. 110–68, in R.C. Harris and J. Warkentin, *Canada Before Confederation* (Toronto, 1974) provide an overview of social developments in the United Canadas. T.L. Cooper's "The Social Structure of Montreal in the 1850's," Canadian Historical Association, *Report* (1956): 63–73, examines the Canadas' largest city. Donald H. Akenson's *The Irish in Ontario: A Study in Rural History* (Montreal, 1984) is a valuable study. Two good quantitative studies to consult are David Gagan, *Hopeful Travellers: Families, Land and Social Change in Mid-Victorian Peel County, Canada West* (Toronto, 1981), and Michael Katz, *The People of Hamilton, Canada West: Family and Class in a Mid-Nineteenth Century City* (Cambridge, 1976). On French Canadian migration, see Bruno Ramirez, *On the Move: French-Canadian and Italian Migrants in the North Atlantic Economy, 1860–1914* (Toronto, 1991). Alison Prentice et al., *Canadian Women: A History* (Toronto, 1988) examines changes in the lives of women in the mid-nineteenth century, while Micheline Dumont et al., *Quebec Women: A History* (Toronto 1987) focusses on women in Lower Canada in the same time period.

The Amerindians' history in the the Canadas in the mid-nineteenth century is reviewed in several sources: Daniel Francis, *A History of the Native Peoples of Québec, 1760–1867* (Ottawa, 1983); Charles M. Johnston, ed. *The Valley of the Six Nations: A Collection of Documents on the Indian Lands of the Grand River* (Toronto, 1964); Peter S. Schmalz, *The Ojibwa of Southern Ontario* (Toronto, 1991); and Donald B. Smith, *Sacred Feathers: The Reverend Peter Jones (Kahkewaquonaby) and the Mississauga Indians* (Toronto, 1987). For an in-depth study of a reserve in Canada East, see Hélène Bédard, *Les Montagnais et la réserve de Betsiamites, 1850–1900* (Québec, 1988).

On the history of the working class in the United Canadas, consult M.S. Cross, ed., *The Workingman in the Nineteenth Century* (Toronto, 1974), and S. Langdon's pamphlet *The Emergence of the Working-Class Movement,*

1845–1875 (Toronto, 1975). On strikes, see H.C. Pentland, "The Lachine Strike of 1843," *Canadian Historical Review* 29 (1948): 255–77, and Ruth Bleasdale, "Class Conflict on the Canals of Upper Canada in the 1840s," *Labour/Le Travailleur* 7 (1981): 9–39 (reprinted in M.S. Cross and G.S. Kealey, eds., *Pre-Industrial Canada 1760–1849: Readings in Canadian Social History*, vol. 2 [Toronto, 1982]). On labour protest in general, consult Bryan Palmer, "Labour Protest and Organization in Nineteenth-Century Canada, 1820–1890," *Labour/Le Travail* 20 (1987): 61–84.

Educational questions are treated in J.D. Wilson, R.M. Stamp, and L.P. Audet, *Canadian Education: A History* (Toronto, 1970), 167–89 and 214–40. For Canada West, see also S. Houston and A. Prentice, *Schooling and Scholars in Nineteenth-Century Ontario* (Toronto, 1988), and Franklin A. Walker, *Catholic Education and Politics in Upper Canada*, vol. 1 (Toronto, 1976; first published 1955); for Canada East, see Claude Galarneau, *Les collèges classiques au Canada français* (Montreál, 1978). The best short biography of Egerton Ryerson remains Clara Thomas, *Ryerson of Upper Canada* (Toronto, 1969). On religion, see John S. Moir, *The Church in the British Era: From the British Conquest to Confederation* (Toronto, 1972); and John Webster Grant, *A Profusion of Spires: Religion in Nineteenth-Century Ontario* (Toronto, 1988). Cultural aspects of the era are reviewed in George Woodcock, *The Century That Made Us: Canada, 1814–1914* (Toronto, 1989). Musical developments are reviewed in Helmut Kallmann, *A History of Music in Canada, 1534–1914* (Toronto, 1960). For information on early newspapers in the Canadas, see Douglas Fetherling, *The Rise of the Canadian Newspaper* (Toronto, 1990).

Many portraits of the leading individuals in the Canadas between 1840 and 1864 appear in the *Dictionary of Canadian Biography*. Of particular interest is the sketch by Yves Roby of the colourful Charles Chiniquy (vol. 12, *1891–1900*, pp. 189–93). The biographical sketch of John A. Macdonald by J. K. Johnson and P. B. Waite also appears in vol. 12 (pp. 591–612).

The Maritime Colonies, 1785–1864

After the Loyalists' arrival, Atlantic British North America consisted of four separate colonies: Nova Scotia, New Brunswick, Prince Edward Island, and Cape Breton, the latter having been separated politically from the peninsula of Nova Scotia in 1784. Economically, the Maritime provinces depended on fishing and farming, but the full development of the land-based resources began only in the early nineteenth century. While Nova Scotia (to which Cape Breton was reattached in 1820) kept largely to fishing and trade, New Brunswick started to cut its extensive pine forests. On Saint John's Island (renamed Prince Edward Island in 1799 after Prince Edward, Duke of Kent, the future father of Queen Victoria), agriculture became the mainstay of the colonial economy. The Maritimes prospered when agriculture, the lumber industry, shipbuilding, and trade with the West Indies expanded. By the mid-nineteenth century, coal mining had also grown in importance. Politically, the Maritime colonies advanced from representative to responsible government in the period from 1785 to 1851.

By the 1850s, Nova Scotia, New Brunswick, and Prince Edward Island had reached maturity. They enjoyed responsible government and had healthy economies based on agriculture, fish, and forest products. Settled communities with churches and schools had been established. The Maritimes had become an area of several distinct regions and ethnic groups.

Economic Developments, 1785–1815

For more than a century before the American Revolution, trade linked New England with Britain and the West Indies. New England sold fish, lumber, and foodstuffs to the West Indies, which in turn supplied molasses to New England and sugar to Britain. The mother country provided

New England with manufactured goods. After the United States gained independence, Britain wanted the Maritime colonies to take over New England's function. This new trade relationship would bind the remaining colonies in the North Atlantic and the Caribbean to England. To help create such a system, Britain closed its West Indian ports to American ships.

TRADE WITH THE WEST INDIES

Initially, however, the Maritime colonies lacked the resources and the economic infrastructure needed to supply the British West Indies. They could supply only a limited amount of the islands' needs in fish and lumber. They could not meet their demand for other foodstuffs at all. Nova Scotia and New Brunswick even had to import American farm products. The Maritimes' expensive labour, its inadequate transportation system, and its land-granting system (which encouraged a general dispersal of the population) all contributed to the slow development of agriculture. Moreover, with cheap imported food from the United States, there was little incentive to begin full-time farming.

Direct trade between Nova Scotia and the West Indies actually decreased in the 1790s, when Britain met the planters' demands for cheap foodstuffs by allowing American shipping access to the West Indies. Maritime merchants now found it more profitable to sell their fish in New England for export to the West Indies in American ships than to export directly from Nova Scotia in British vessels.

THE BEGINNINGS OF REAL ECONOMIC GROWTH

Real economic growth in the Maritimes began with the outbreak of war between Britain and France in 1793 and, particularly, with the rise of Napoleon in the late 1790s. The British government spent lavishly on fortifications in Halifax, constructing public and military buildings. Halifax became the strongest fortress outside Europe.

After the beginning of the Napoleonic Wars, a flourishing timber industry developed in British North America (see Chapter 13). Britain required a safe supply of masts and spars for the Royal Navy, and it needed building timber. The imperial government put heavy tariff preferences for British American timber in place, and this led to a lumber boom in New Brunswick, the British Maritime colony with the greatest timber resources. Every winter, armies of lumberjacks cut down the trees and then, every spring, floated them down the Saint John, St. Croix, and Miramichi rivers tied into huge rafts. Heavily forested New Brunswick, being closer to Britain, was better situated than Canada for this trade.

Inadvertently, the United States also promoted the prosperity of the Maritimes. After France and Britain imposed blockades on each other in

1806, President Thomas Jefferson, in retaliation against both countries' restrictions on neutral trade, prohibited all commerce out of American ports in December 1807. The policy backfired, however, for by closing American ports, the president ruined New England's trade—and because Britain depended on American foodstuffs as much as the United States needed British manufactured goods, that trade continued through illegal channels. An active smuggling trade developed, with cargoes being transferred at sea or carried overland across the British–American frontier. In defiance of their government, American ship captains sailed into British ports, making the Maritime provinces in 1808 into a great clearinghouse for international trade. The Maritime colonies purchased American produce and goods and then re-exported them as if they were their own. Similarly, they sold British manufactured goods to the Americans.

This economic activity continued during the war of 1812 between Britain and the United States. The long-standing trade between the fish-exporting houses of Halifax and the British West Indies expanded in the early nineteenth century, at the time of the American embargo acts. Britain encouraged this by paying bounties on fish exported from Nova Scotia and New Brunswick to the West Indies. Convoy protection was provided, for after the British defeated the French navy at Trafalgar in 1805 there was no more danger of a French naval invasion of Britain, and the admiralty could spare ships for convoy duty. The shipping of American flour, beef, and dry goods to the West Indies via the Maritime provinces began.

317

Ironically, it was the continuance of strict American prohibitions against British trade that made Maritime harbours and towns among the busiest and most prosperous on the Atlantic seaboard. Nova Scotia's and New Brunswick's merchants and sea captains began to acquire the skill, experience, and self-confidence they needed to challenge New England's supremacy in West Indian markets.

The War of 1812 actually improved the highly favourable terms of trade enjoyed by New Brunswick and Nova Scotia. Throughout the war New England participated with great reluctance. The legislatures of the New England states openly condemned the war that had ruined their commerce. So much trade continued that the Halifax paper, the *Acadian Recorder*, wrote on May 14, 1814: "Happy state of Nova Scotia! amongst all this tumult we have lived in peace and security; invaded only by a numerous host of American doubloons and dollars, which have swept away the contents of our stores and shops like a torrent."

Political History, 1785 to the Mid-Nineteenth Century

Although the Maritime colonies experienced many economic changes during the thirty-year period after the American Revolution, they saw only two periods of political upheaval. The first was in New Brunswick, over the methods of raising and spending public monies, and the second centred on the same issue in Nova Scotia. In 1795 the opposition in the New Brunswick Assembly was focussed on James Glenie, a Scottish lumberman who had challenged the governor's financial controls over the Assembly. Governor Thomas Carleton, a younger brother of the more famous Sir Guy, believed that the opposition sought New Brunswick's independence and a revival of the principles of the American Revolution. For four years he resisted the Assembly's demands for greater control over money bills. Government ground to a halt. Finally, Glenie's coalition broke down, but only after Carleton conceded additional financial authority to the legislature. As historian W.G. Godfrey has written, "New Brunswick was witnessing the emergence of the assembly's 'political hegemony' as power passed to the elective branch of government."[1]

318

The authoritarian structure and operation of government remained in place longer in Nova Scotia than they did in New Brunswick. At first, a constitutional contest took place between the Loyalists and the English-speaking settlers, the planters, who had arrived before the revolution, but a wise distribution of patronage to both groups by Governor John Wentworth in the early 1790s cooled passions. Early in 1803, however, the firebrand Cottnam Tonge (pronounced "tongue") led a revolt in the Nova Scotia Assembly. Tonge became the champion of the townspeople and the farmers who wanted responsible government. Their opponents consisted of the governor and his officials, and the Halifax merchants.

Tonge's efforts failed, and he left the colony in 1808. But the Nova Scotia Assembly eventually succeeded: in the late 1840s, it obtained control over the spending of public funds raised by its own vote.

Prince Edward Island in these years still suffered the effects of its land-ownership system (see Chapter 8). In 1769 the island's proprietors had convinced the British government to establish a separate administration, which was eventually composed of a governor, a council, and an Assembly. The tenants gained control of the Assembly, but they could obtain no redress from the proprietors, many of whom were absentee owners who did not meet their colonizing obligations.

In the early nineteenth century a popular political movement emerged, one associated with the word *escheat*, which, to the tenants, meant the return to the Crown of all the lands of proprietors who failed to uphold their original agreements with the Crown. The Escheat movement was, in effect, the first agrarian protest movement in what would become present-day Canada. Once the British government, however, made it clear that it would not co-operate with the Escheaters, the movement declined in popularity. In London, proprietors such as Samuel Cunard, the owner of one-sixth of Prince Edward Island by the 1830s, had great influence. Well-protected in the British Parliament, the proprietors in the early nineteenth century successfully fended off the protests of the tenant-controlled Assembly.

Economic Developments, 1815–1864

The Maritimes continued to prosper for half a century after the War of 1812. As a result of the war, the Americans lost access to Maritime in-shore fisheries.

The peace treaty of 1783 had granted American citizens fishing privileges in the in-shore waters of the British North American colonies. However, at the Treaty of Ghent, which ended the War of 1812, the British argued that the Americans had abrogated this right by declaring war. Under the Convention of 1818, American fishermen lost the privilege of landing and drying their fish in the three Maritime colonies; they would now be permitted to do so only on unsettled shores in Newfoundland. American vessels could now enter Maritime harbours only to obtain water, purchase wood, or repair damages. Not until the signing of the Reciprocity Treaty in 1854 did the Americans regain access to the in-shore fisheries.

319

The Maritimers succeeded in improving their trade ties with the West Indies. After the war of 1812, Nova Scotia and New Brunswick successfully argued that the privilege of trading with the British West Indies rightly belonged only to loyal British colonies. Britain initially agreed and passed several measures favouring the shipping of goods between Saint John and Halifax and the West Indies, but in the face of subsequent American retaliatory measures, it backed down. The British West Indies also had complained about the higher cost of shipping American imports by the roundabout Maritime route. Finally, in 1830, Britain removed the restrictions on American trade to the islands but left duties on certain essential commodities. This arrangement allowed Nova Scotia and New Brunswick to import American produce duty free and then re-export it to the West Indies as their own. Colonial ships thus maintained much of their share of the trade.

AGRICULTURE

Improved trade relations with the West Indies strengthened the Maritime economy, as did the export of forest products. By 1825 New Brunswick supplied 40 percent of Britain's huge timber requirements. One sector of the Maritimes economy, however, remained weak—agriculture. While farming flourished on Prince Edward Island, in Nova Scotia's Annapolis Valley, and in New Brunswick's Saint John River valley, it did not do as well in other sectors of the provinces. Nova Scotia and New Brunswick as a whole continued to depend on American foodstuffs to feed their populations well into the nineteenth century. Commercial farming remained very limited, with only Prince Edward Island, the "Garden of the Gulf," exporting large amounts of farm produce. Lack of good roads, a scattered population, and the absence of protection against American imports accounted for the limited agricultural exports. Farming, though, remained the livelihood of more Maritimers than either logging or fishing, and a large number of those employed in logging and fishing worked on a part-time basis in agriculture to support their families.

An increase in immigration after 1815 added to the size of the local market and encouraged greater agricultural production. New Brunswick had roughly 75 000 inhabitants in 1824 and almost 200 000 by 1851. In the same period in Nova Scotia, the population rose from approximately 100 000 to 275 000. Prince Edward Island's population increased from 23 000 in 1827 to 72 000 in 1855. It became the most densely inhabited colony in British North America.

The Timber Industry and Shipbuilding

The exploitation of Maritime forests continued unabated after the War of 1812. Local entrepreneurs, many of them farmers and small merchants, began operations in settled or semi-settled areas of the Maritimes. The timber trade also brought into the colonies a new group of British traders and contractors interested in quick profits.

In his 1825 *History of New Brunswick*, Peter Fisher noted the heavy cost of the indiscriminate cutting down of the forests during the previous twenty years:

> The persons principally engaged in shipping the timber have been strangers who had taken no interest in the welfare of the country; but have merely occupied a spot to make what they could in the shortest possible time . . . Instead of seeing towns built, farms improved and the country cleared and stocked with the reasonable returns of so great a trade, the forests are stripped and nothing left in prospect, but the gloomy apprehension when the timber is gone, of sinking into insignificance and poverty.

Initially, timber companies simply went on Crown land and cut trees, even though the trees belonged to the government. But from the 1820s on, the New Brunswick government asserted itself against the timber barons. It sold timber licences and taxed output.

Forest revenues thus became vital to New Brunswick's economy. Already by 1826 three-quarters of the province's export revenues came from wood products—square timber, lumber, and ships. In mid-century one New Brunswick resident noted that the timber trade "has brought

National Archives of Canada/C-10103.

Lumbering and shipbuilding went together. Dorchester, New Brunswick, was one of a hundred shipbuilding villages on the Maritime coast.

321

foreign produce and foreign capital into the province, and has been the chief source of the money by which its roads, bridges and public buildings have been completed; its rivers and harbours made accessible; its natural resources discovered and made available; its provincial institutions kept up and its functionaries paid."

THE RISE OF SHIPBUILDING

The timber industry gave rise to shipbuilding. Square timber, a bulky commodity, had to be shipped in relatively large vessels, and as Britain could not meet the need for such ships in wartime, the Maritime shipbuilding industry expanded. The Maritimes soon supplied many of the new wooden ships being used to ferry timber to Britain. Shipbuilding became the first major manufacturing industry in the Maritime region.

From the 1820s onward, the Nova Scotia and New Brunswick fleets grew steadily. Maritime timber merchants found they could keep transportation costs low if they owned their own vessels. When prices for vessels rose, they made additional profits by selling the ship as well as its timber cargo. Other Maritime businessmen saw money to be made in owning ships involved in lucrative coastal trading, particularly in the West Indian trade.

By 1850 the region had gained a reputation as one of the leading centres of the North American shipping industry. In 1851 the James Smith shipyard at Saint John, New Brunswick, launched the *Marco Polo*, which became the colony's most famous ship. It cut a week off the previous record for the round trip from England to Australia, completing that trip in less than six months. The New Brunswick ship earned the title of the "Fastest Ship in the World." Generally speaking, however, Maritime shipbuilders built broad-beamed vessels designed to maximize carrying capacity, not speed. They increased sail capacity and improved ships' hulls. They extended the average life of Nova Scotia and New Brunswick vessels from a mere nine years in the 1820s to fifteen years by the end of the century. These shipbuilders also constructed their vessels cheaply. An iron steamer in Britain cost four or five times as much in the 1860s as did a wooden vessel from the Maritimes. The popularity of the steamers, however, grew rapidly, leaving only a tiny market for wooden ships at the end of the century. By 1900, most shippers preferred iron vessels.

In New Brunswick the major shipowners included many timber exporters, whereas in Nova Scotia the majority were fish exporters, West Indies traders, and import–export merchants. Samuel Cunard, the most famous of the Nova Scotia shipowners, had interests in the West Indies trade, a tea business, a bank, and the sale of imported goods. In 1840 he initiated the first regular steamship service across the Atlantic. Cunard was one of the first Nova Scotians to build a business empire.

A number of the shipowners in the 1850s entered new businesses. Thomas Killam of Yarmouth, like his contemporary Samuel Cunard, expanded his business enterprises dramatically. This small shipowner and West Indies trader of the 1830s had, before his death in 1868, expanded his operations to include a ship-outfitting business, a marine-insurance company, a telegraph company, a gas-lighting company, and a bank. He shifted capital from one industry to another, taking earnings from shipping and re-investing in industry. Enos Collins of Halifax had diversified his shipping interests after the War of 1812. When the old sea captain died in 1871 at the age of ninety-seven, he left behind an estate of six million dollars. Many Prince Edward Island shipowners sailed their vessels to Britain and sold them there.

Thousands of men and hundreds of women worked in the Maritime shipyards or in shops making materials for the ships. The sailors were most often in their twenties or early thirties. For most, seafaring was a short-term activity—a means of supplementing the family income, or a job when work was scarce on the main land.

It was a demanding job. No unions existed on board ship, where the jobs were arduous and often unsafe, the food was poor, and the working hours long. Desertion was one means of protection, and one-quarter of the crew usually deserted during a voyage. Until the sailing industry declined in the late 1870s, the numerous sailors in the ports of eastern Canada lived in what were called "sailortowns."

BANKING

The financial needs of the merchants involved in the timber industry and shipbuilding led to the rise of banks (see Chapter 15). In Britain, commercial banks developed in the eighteenth century, and in the 1790s scores of them opened in the United States. The banks dealt in foreign-exchange transactions, made loans, and circulated bank notes, on the understanding that the paper notes could always be redeemed, on demand, in real coinage. Depending on the risk the bankers were prepared to take, the banks could generally keep two to three times as many notes in circulation as they had gold or silver coins to redeem them. (The issuing of notes in place of coins allowed the banks to double or triple the amount of interest they collected.)

323

The Halifax Banking Company, the first bank in Nova Scotia, began trading in money in 1825. A group of merchants founded the Bank of Nova Scotia in 1832, and by 1840 it had branches in Windsor, Annapolis Royal, Pictou, Yarmouth, and Liverpool. New Brunswick's first bank, the Bank of New Brunswick, was founded in Saint John in 1820; the second, the Commercial Bank, in 1834. Prince Edward Island's first bank opened in the mid-1850s.

Urban Centres

Saint John, Halifax, and the much smaller Charlottetown became the dominant centres of the Maritimes, with lines of trade reaching into the outlying regions. Saint John, with a population larger than that of Halifax, was the third-largest city in British North America in the mid-nineteenth century (after Montreal and Quebec). In the 1850s Saint John controlled the timber trade of the Saint John River valley and was the natural market for the farmers and fishermen on both sides of the Bay of Fundy. Nearly half of the industrial output of New Brunswick was produced in and around Saint John. The great merchants of Saint John, however, delayed investing in manufacturing iron and steel, and concentrated instead on the traditional timber industries—shipbuilding, construction, and saw-milling. Their financial conservatism held back the development of a viable industrial base in New Brunswick by two decades, when the metal ship replaced the wooden sailing ship in the late nineteenth century.

In the 1850s Halifax also sought to become the commercial metropolis of the Maritimes. Although it had a large, secure, ice-free harbour and was situated very close to the major North Atlantic shipping lanes, Nova

Scotia's capital had no economic hinterland. Unlike Montreal and Saint John, it lacked a major waterway comparable to the St. Lawrence or the Saint John River, which extended more than 700 km into the interior. Halifax did, however, succeed in dominating the commerce of Prince Edward Island, Cape Breton Island, and the Miramichi country of eastern New Brunswick, but it lost the Bay of Fundy to Saint John. Reliant on imperial spending for much of its prosperity, Halifax also benefited from the Caribbean trade and from its role as the banking, judicial, and intellectual centre of Nova Scotia. It produced two of the wealthiest individuals in British North America: Enos Collins and Samuel Cunard.

In both Saint John and Halifax, there were charitable organizations to help penniless immigrants as well as the resident urban proletariat. Women organized and staffed voluntary organizations to help address the growing urban problems. In winter the poor faced cold, hunger, illness, and unemployment—or underemployment—until spring returned. The

seasonal nature of North Atlantic shipping meant that labourers, mill hands, seamen, carpenters, and other building-trades workers lost their jobs in the autumn. The voluntary charitable organizations run by churches and ethnic groups in Halifax and Saint John, however, had very limited means. Fortunately, in the 1860s, the colonial governments made a modest entry into the charitable field by establishing orphanages.

The Maritimes and Reciprocity

When Britain adopted free trade in the 1840s, many Maritimers came to favour the idea of continental reciprocity—the free admission into British North America and the United States of each other's natural resources. For New Brunswick, reciprocity was the key to gaining entry for its timber into the American market of twenty-three million people.

There was no hope of reciprocity until a border controversy between New Brunswick and Maine was settled in 1842. The Treaty of Paris in 1783 had set the boundary to run north from the St. Croix River to an undetermined height of land. In 1839, New Brunswick and Maine lumbermen almost caused a border war over which group had the right to cut in the no-man's land at the mouth of the Aroostook River, which was part of the disputed territory. Three years later Daniel Webster, the American secretary of state, and Lord Ashburton, the British envoy, resolved the controversy. The Webster–Ashburton Treaty of 1842 established the present-day New Brunswick–Maine boundary.

Reciprocity proposals also met with a favourable response in Nova Scotia (because of its fish for export) and Prince Edward Island (because of its farm produce). The Americans, for their part, wanted access to the Maritime in-shore fisheries from which they had been excluded in 1818.

The inclusion of the fisheries led the United States to sign a reciprocity agreement with the British North American colonies in 1854.

The treaty led to the desired increased trade with the United States. The Maritime colonies now bought one-quarter to one-half of their total imports from the Americans. New Brunswick shipped to the United States increased amounts of lumber; Prince Edward Island, more foodstuffs; and Nova Scotia, a slightly greater amount of fish. Certainly, the years of the reciprocity treaty proved prosperous, but not solely on account of the treaty. The great demand for the Maritimes' natural resources, brought about by the outbreak of the American Civil War, also helped. From 1860 to 1865, prices for the Maritimes' fish, timber, and foodstuffs doubled.

RAILWAYS

Railway construction in Nova Scotia and New Brunswick in the 1850s and 1860s also promoted the economic boom. From 1853 to 1866, New Brunswick built 350 km of railway. During the same period, the government of Nova Scotia constructed 235 km of track. Maritime promoters dreamed of continental expansion, of one day linking the ice-free Maritime ports with the St. Lawrence Valley and with the grain-producing American Midwest.

325

Merchants in Halifax and Saint John had visions of their respective cities serving as the focal point from which European commerce could be channelled into the continent and from which American and Canadian exports could be sent abroad. Yet railways were expensive to build and to operate. A single kilometre of track could cost as much as a sizable sailing vessel. To make money, the railway company owners needed both densely populated areas to provide local revenue and the shortest possible direct routes; neither Halifax nor even Saint John had such hinterlands. The larger communities in the interior were too distant, in contrast with those in the environs of Boston, New York, or Montreal, and the land routes passed through thinly populated territory.

Population of the Maritimes

In the nineteenth century, thousands of Scottish and Irish immigrants crossed the North Atlantic to British North America to escape the over-crowding, the famine, and the poverty of the British Isles. Successive waves of Scots and Irish joined the resident Maritimes: the Acadians, the blacks, Amerindians, and the descendants of the planters and the white Loyalists, as well as recent English immigrants. A number of the recent English settlers were public officials and merchants, who obtained good positions in the colonies' political and economic sectors.

THE ACADIANS

Just before the arrival of the Scots, the Irish, and the blacks, many Acadians had returned from exile. The Acadians clung tenaciously to the Roman Catholic church as the one institution that took an interest in their well-being. The church established elementary schools and, in 1864, the French-language Collège Saint-Joseph at Memramcook, New Brunswick. The college (which a century later became the nucleus of today's Université de Moncton) furnished the Acadian population with an educated professional elite from which the community drew many of its future political leaders and its sense of Acadian identity.

In the mid-nineteenth century the Acadians began to feel a new pride in their past. Undoubtedly influenced by Henry Wadsworth Longfellow's *Evangeline*, many Acadians became increasingly convinced that they belonged to a distinct people. In the late nineteenth century, the Acadian community in northeastern New Brunswick incorporated, through inter-marriage, many Irish, Scots, and English. Those individuals' modern-day descendants have British names like McGraw, Finn, McLaughlin, Ferguson, and Kerry, but their mother tongue is French and they consider themselves Acadian. French Canadian immigrants from Quebec, who arrived in the late nineteenth century, were also assimilated into these Acadian communities. In predominantly English-speaking areas, how-ever—on Prince Edward Island, for example—some Acadians themselves were assimilated into the English-speaking community. On Prince Edward Island, some Acadians Anglicized their names: Aucoin became Wedge, Poirier became Perry, Bourque became Burke.

THE SCOTS

Even though the journey from Scotland was perilous (on one ship that left in 1827, 20 percent of those aboard died), still the Gaelic-speaking Highlanders came, usually in groups or clans. (In the early nineteenth century, Gaelic was the third most common European language spoken in British North America.)

The promise of forty hectares of free land led thousands of landless Scots to immigrate to Nova Scotia. About forty thousand Scots came to Nova Scotia, in particular to Cape Breton Island, between 1815 and 1838. Although the magnificent hills and seacoast of Cape Breton reminded them of home, the Scots were ill prepared for clearing virgin forest and had many difficulties in starting up their farms. Some left, and some became fishermen and boat builders in coastal settlements. Many moved to Prince Edward Island.

THE IRISH

Scottish immigrants outnumbered Irish immigrants in Nova Scotia and Prince Edward Island, but the reverse was true in New Brunswick. No British American province was more Irish than New Brunswick in the nineteenth century. Ireland's depressed economy and its overpopulation forced many Roman Catholic and Protestant Irish to emigrate. The potato blight of the 1840s led to famine and drove nearly two million people out of Ireland.

Of the tens of thousands of Irish who boarded the timber ships headed for British North America, thousands died en route from cholera and typhoid. Nonetheless 8000 arrived in New Brunswick in 1842, 9000 in 1846, and 17 000 in 1847. Only in 1848 did the numbers fall below 4000. Although many Irish used New Brunswick as a stepping stone to the United States, a large number stayed. Those who were poverty-stricken congregated in the ports and lumber camps of eastern New Brunswick. The main areas of Irish settlement in New Brunswick before 1850 were the upper Saint John Valley, the Bay of Fundy, and the south shore of Chaleur Bay. Although the Loyalist settlers and their descendants, together with a number of recent English immigrants, controlled the colony's political life, in many communities the Irish outnumbered them.

327

THE BLACKS

Another group of newcomers arrived in two waves. The first post-Loyalist blacks to arrive were the Maroons, a group of runaway slaves from Jamaica. With a successful slave revolt then under way in neighbouring Haiti, the British grew anxious and arranged in 1796 to ship the Maroons to Nova Scotia. But the bitter winters and the unpalatable food made Nova Scotia unbearable for them. The British transported the Maroons and a number of the Loyalist blacks, at their own request, to Sierra Leone in West Africa.

The second wave came at the end of the War of 1812. These "refugee blacks," 3000–4000 strong, escaped from Chesapeake plantations during the British raids on Washington and Baltimore and asked to be taken to freedom. Unfortunately, they arrived when abundant, cheap white labour made it very difficult for them to find work. They also faced discrimination and prejudice in Nova Scotia and New Brunswick. Historian W.A. Spray has noted how poorly the four hundred black refugees were treated in comparison with the white settlers: "The policy in New Brunswick at this time was to give free grants of at least 100 acres to white settlers. . . . Yet the black refugees were to get only 50 acres, they were to pay for the surveys, and they were to receive licences of occupation for three years."[2] The black holders of these documents had no security of possession, as the government could simply refuse to reissue the licences after the three-year term had expired.

Provincial Archives of New Brunswick/P5-381.

Malecite Indians building a birchbark canoe, near Fredericton, New Brunswick around 1905.

THE AMERINDIANS

Amid the Scots, Irish, blacks, Acadians, descendants of the old American and Loyalist settlers, and recent English immigrants, the Maritimers with the longest residency in the area had the greatest difficulty in adjusting to the changing conditions. Unlike the Indians in Upper Canada after the Proclamation of 1763, the Maritime Indians did not sign treaties with the British government by which they surrendered their lands to the Crown. The Indians wanted payment, as Micmac chief Jean-Baptiste Cope told the British authorities in 1752: "[We] should be paid for the land the English had settled upon in this country." But the British and the Maritime governments held that the Micmacs' and the Malecites' title to the land had already been extinguished—first, by the fact that the French had occupied the area and, second, as a result of the Treaty of Utrecht in 1713. The British argued that the Treaty of Utrecht gave them sovereign title to Acadia.

The New Brunswick government set aside reserves for the Micmacs and the Malecites, but failed to protect them from encroachment by white settlers. The lack of proper legal descriptions and surveys of the reserve lands encouraged squatters to move into the areas that the Micmacs had not get settled and cultivated. A similar situation developed in Nova Scotia.

By the 1860s, the approximately 1000 Micmacs and 500 Malecites in New Brunswick officially had a land base of about 25 000 ha. In Nova Scotia the Micmacs, who numbered between 1400 and 1800, had only 8000 ha. But the Indians who faced perhaps the most difficult conditions were the several hundred Micmacs on Prince Edward Island. Until 1870, they had only a few campsites as reserve land. In that year, however, an English-based organization called the Aborigines' Protection Society arranged to buy Lennox Island for them, a small island off Prince Edward Island.

Political Change in the Mid-Nineteenth Century

In the mid-nineteenth century the Maritime colonies achieved the right to self-government. Britain's cutting of the last bonds of her old commercial empire in the late 1840s and early 1850s removed the rationale for close political control over the colonies' internal affairs. Throughout the 1830s and 1840s, the conviction had grown that government should be taken from the hands of the privileged and delivered into the hands of the people. In Nova Scotia the middle class began openly to oppose the small ruling clique, or, to use the Upper Canadian phrase, the Family Compact, in Halifax.

The Maritime assemblies in the early nineteenth century were small and elected by a limited provincial franchise. Women were barred by statute from voting in Prince Edward Island in 1836 and in New Brunswick in 1843. Only in Nova Scotia in the 1840s could women who met the property qualification vote—at least until 1851, when all women were disenfranchised.

Politics revolved around local personalities and interest groups. Standing as individuals, elected members represented local concerns in the Assembly, vigilantly seeing that their constituencies obtained their fair share of the provincial revenues. Yet, in Nova Scotia at least, two political groups, the Reformers and the Conservatives, had taken shape by the early 1840s, both co-ordinating their activities in the legislature.

THE REFORM MOVEMENT IN NOVA SCOTIA

In Nova Scotia the nucleus of the Reform party first developed in the mid-1830s under the leadership of Joseph Howe. Having purchased the *Novascotian*, a Halifax newspaper, Howe soon made it the most influential newspaper in the province. During each session of the Assembly, he personally reported on the debates. Howe's enemy became the Council of Twelve, or the governor's appointed Executive Council (cabinet), which conducted its meetings behind closed doors. An interrelated merchant oligarchy, largely from Halifax, controlled both the appointed Legislative Council (the upper house) and the Executive Council, and through these institutions dominated the political life of the province. Elected to the Nova Scotian Assembly in 1836, Howe led attacks against this privileged group, calling for an elected upper house and for the Assembly's control over Crown revenues.

The Assemblies elected in 1836 and 1840 favoured reform, of which Howe was a most influential advocate. In the election of 1847, the Reformers fought on the issue of responsible government, and finally won a majority. On February 2, 1848, the Colonial Office agreed that henceforth the Executive Council would have to collectively resign if it lost the Assembly's confidence. Nova Scotia became the first British North American colony to achieve responsible government and Howe boasted that the Reformers had achieved it peacefully, without "a blow struck or a pane of glass broken." Yet, he should have added that the rebellions in the Canadas in the 1830s had gone a long way in convincing Britain of the wisdom of conceding responsible government in British North America.

330

THE REFORM MOVEMENT IN NEW BRUNSWICK

In New Brunswick the political situation was somewhat different. Of all the British North American colonies, this province had always been among the easiest to rule. A relatively homogeneous group of Loyalists and their descendants had controlled the colony until the 1830s. Moreover, since Anglicans initially comprised a near majority of the population, the position of the Church of England as the established church caused less resentment among New Brunswick's English-speaking population than it did elsewhere. The New Brunswick Assembly in 1837 had even secured control of the revenues of Crown lands, including timber land revenues, in return for the provision of a civil list guaranteeing the salaries of officers of government. Nonetheless, the colony still lacked responsible government.

After 1837, two men, Charles Fisher and Lemuel Allan Wilmot, became the backbone of the New Brunswick Reform movements that worked toward responsible government. They made great advances. In practice, the Colonial Office—even before the official granting of responsible government in New Brunswick in 1848—made the Executive Council in the province responsible to the elected representatives in the Assembly.

Responsible government, however, opened up more than Executive Council seats to the Assembly; it gave the Assembly control over patronage—that is, the opportunity to make appointments to public office. Wilmot was one of the Reformers who took full advantage of the opportunity to benefit himself. C.M. Wallace, his biographer, has noted that "his pursuit of office, first on the Executive Council, then on the bench, and finally as lieutenant governor, might well be classed as rapacious."[3]

REFORM IN PRINCE EDWARD ISLAND

The winning of responsible government became an important issue in Prince Edward Island in the 1840s. Initially, the Colonial Office opposed granting internal self-government to such a small colony, but it eventually yielded. The Reformers on the Island, politicians such as George Coles and Edward Whelan, insisted on full equality with the mainland colonies. When they won the general election in 1850, they demanded cabinet government, which the Colonial Office granted in 1851. Immediately, the population hoped that the constitutional change would lead to a settlement of Prince Edward Island's land question. Two-thirds of the Island's inhabitants in the 1830s still lived on land owned by absentee owners, few of whom were descendants of the original grantees of 1767—indeed, most had purchased their lands on speculation. Samuel Cunard, the Halifax merchant, controlled an estate of 85 000 ha on the Island—an area more than twice as large as all the Amerindian reserve lands in the Maritimes.

331

The Colonial Office, however, refused to consider escheat and upheld the rights of private property. The Island's Executive and Legislative councils, both controlled by a small group of the leading families in Charlottetown, also protected the proprietors. To challenge this position, the Assembly set up an investigative commission to study the problem. It recommended in 1860 that tenants be allowed to purchase their land and that owners obtain a fair valuation of their property. Progress was slow. As late as 1873, only one-third of the Island was owned by the tenants.

Cultural Developments

The cultural life of Maritimers was enriched in the nineteenth century. Throughout the colonies, church choirs flourished. In the urban centres, the large Anglican and Roman Catholic churches often had organs and skilled musicians. Music societies existed in the cities; among the earliest in British North America were the New Union Singing Society of Halifax (1809) and the Philharmonic Society of Saint John (1824).

Throughout the nineteenth century, theatre was available to audiences in Maritime cities. At first, the Halifax garrison performed plays in makeshift theatres in taverns, but in 1789 it opened the New Grand Theatre. For the opening, the officers and men produced Shakespeare's *Merchant of Venice*. Charlottetown built its first theatre in 1800, and by 1809 Saint John had its own Drury Lane Theatre. Professional companies—and leading actors—from both the United States and Britain visited in the mid-nineteenth century.

The Maritimes produced one major North American literary figure in the mid-nineteenth century—Thomas Chandler Haliburton. From 1823 to 1860, the Nova Scotian judge wrote political pamphlets and many works on the history of the province, but it is for his fiction that he is best remembered. Haliburton's classic, *The Clockmaker; or, the Sayings and Doings of Samuel Slick of Slickville*, first appeared in 1836, and was followed by two more series of the same humorous stories about the shrewd Yankee peddler who crossed the province selling his poorly produced clocks to easily fooled Nova Scotians. As many as seventy editions of *The Clockmaker* have since appeared and the book has remained in print for more than 150 years. Haliburton was the first British North American writer to gain an international reputation.

Religion and Education in the Maritimes, 1785–1864

There was considerable religious diversity in the Maritimes. To introduce what they believed to be the correct religious principles, Nova Scotia's leaders appealed in 1787 to Charles Inglis, the former rector of Trinity Church in New York City, to become the colony's first bishop, with jurisdiction over the Province of Quebec, New Brunswick, and Newfoundland in addition to Nova Scotia. Inglis saw his task as that of securing the Anglican church's predominance in the Maritimes. Bishop Inglis succeeded in founding an Anglican college, King's College, at Windsor, in 1788. But he failed in his attempt to make the Church of England a dominant force in Maritime society.

RELIGIOUS DENOMINATIONS

The Anglicans quickly lost ground to the Baptists, the most active of the Protestant denominations. With their close-knit organizations and high degree of church discipline, the Baptists filled the religious void left in the rural areas of the Maritimes after Henry Alline's death in 1784. The Baptists became the largest Protestant denomination in New Brunswick. Next came the Methodists, who had succeeded by the 1820s in building up an influential following, including converts from the professional classes, taken largely from among the ranks of the evangelical Anglicans. Presbyterians came into their own with the large Scottish immigration to the Maritimes, and they settled throughout the Maritime colonies. Catholics could draw on the support of sizable numbers of Scots, Irish, Acadians, and Micmacs throughout Nova Scotia, and particularly in northern and eastern New Brunswick. In the 1860s almost half the population of Prince

Edward Island was Roman Catholic. Lutheranism was strong in Nova Scotia's Lunenburg county. Small Quaker and Jewish communities existed as well.

EDUCATION

As in the Canadas (see Chapter 15), religious conflicts spilled over into education. Only a quarter of Nova Scotia's school-aged children outside Halifax attended school in 1825. As a result, the provincial government intervened. The colonial legislatures in the other two Maritime colonies also made provision for public schools to complement the church-run or separate schools.

Maritime Roman Catholics sought state financial support for their church-run schools, whereas the Anglicans, Baptists, Methodists, and Presbyterians favoured publicly funded, state-run primary schools that taught Protestant moral values. Fearful of the electoral consequences among Protestant voters, none of the colonial governments gave separate schools formal legislative approval. Without legal status, denominational schools would not be guaranteed financial aid in any of the three colonies in the 1860s, on the eve of Confederation.

Higher education remained largely the churches' responsibility. King's College at Windsor excluded four-fifths of all possible candidates for degrees in the arts because they refused to swear an oath supporting the doctrines of the Church of England. Governor Dalhousie therefore founded the college that still bears his name, to provide an education to students of all religious denominations.

In the early nineteenth century, Presbyterians built Pictou Academy, while in 1828 Baptists established Horton Academy at Wolfville, Nova Scotia (ten years later, it became Acadia College). By mid-century, Roman Catholics had built St. Mary's College in Halifax. In 1853 Scottish Roman Catholics in eastern Nova Scotia opened Arichat Seminary, which moved to Antigonish in 1855 to become St. Francis Xavier University. Just across the border, Methodists established Wesleyan Academy—the forerunner of Mount Allison University—at Sackville, New Brunswick. Anglicans founded King's College at Fredericton in 1830; it would be reconstituted the non-sectarian University of New Brunswick in 1859. In Charlottetown, Roman Catholics established St. Dunstan's College in 1855; in 1969, it became part of the University of Prince Edward Island.

By the mid-nineteenth century, the three Maritime colonies had become recognizable economic and political units. Eight of every nine people in the region had been born there. But the inhabitants were far from homogenous. Religious, ethnic, and provincial divisions remained, and some groups such as the Micmacs and the blacks and, to a lesser extent, the Acadians, had been pushed to the margins of Maritime society. Regional

333

loyalties were also strong. Many Maritimers were skeptical of the possibility of Maritime union when politicians first seriously discussed the idea in the early 1860s. The idea of union with the Canadas seemed even more remote.

NOTES

[1] W.G. Godfrey, "Thomas Carleton," *Dictionary of Canadian Biography*, vol. 5, *1801–1820* (Toronto, 1983), 160.
[2] W.A. Spray, "The Settlement of the Black Refugees in New Brunswick, 1815–1836," in *The Acadiensis Reader, Atlantic Canada Before Confederation*, vol. 1, edited by P.A. Buckner and David Frank (Fredericton, 1985), 152–53.
[3] C.M. Wallace, "Lemuel Allan Wilmot," *Dictionary of Canadian Biography*, vol. 10, *1871–1880* (Toronto, 1972), 710.

Related Readings

R. Douglas Francis and Donald B. Smith, *Readings in Canadian History: Pre-Confederation*, 3d ed. (Toronto, 1990), has two articles on this topic: T.W. Acheson, "The Great Merchant and Economic Development in St. John, 1820–1850," 409–33, and Ian Ross Robertson, "The Prince Edward Island Commission of 1860," 433–42.

BIBLIOGRAPHY

The basic study of the Maritime history of this period remains W.S. MacNutt, *The Atlantic Provinces: The Emergence of Colonial Society, 1712–1857* (Toronto, 1965); for New Brunswick, see also his *New Brunswick: A History, 1784–1867* (Toronto, 1963), and Graeme Wynn, *Timber Colony: A Historical Geography of Early Nineteenth Century New Brunswick* (Toronto, 1981). A.H. Clark reviews Prince Edward Island's story in *Three Centuries and the Island* (Toronto, 1959). An up-to-date popular history of the Island is *Land of the Red Soil*, by Douglas Baldwin (Charlottetown, 1990). Kenneth Donovan's two edited books, *Cape Breton at 200: Historical Essays in Honour of the Island's Bicentennial, 1785–1985* (Sydney, N.S.; 1985), and *The Island: New Perspectives on Cape Breton's History, 1713–1990* (Fredericton, 1990), review Cape Breton's last two centuries. Two useful overviews of Maritime history are William Menzies Whitelaw, "The Atlantic Provinces and Their Neighbors," in his study *The Maritimes and Canada Before Confederation* (Toronto, 1966; first published 1934), 9–37, and John Warkentin, "The Atlantic Region," in *Canada Before Confederation*, edited by R. Cole Harris and John Warkentin (Toronto, 1974), 169–231. Michael Bliss reviews economic developments in *Northern Enterprise: Five Centuries of Canadian Business* (Toronto, 1987). Farley Mowat discusses environmental aspects of the nineteenth-century Maritimes in *Sea of Slaughter* (Toronto, 1984).

Economic and social questions receive attention in the following: "The Atlantic Colonies," Ch. 4 of Kenneth Norrie's and Douglas Owram's *A History of the Canadian Economy* (Toronto, 1991), 104–130; S.A. Saunders, "The Maritime Provinces and the Reciprocity Treaty," in *Historical Essays on the Atlantic Provinces*, edited by George A. Rawlyk (Toronto, 1967), 161–78; Eric W. Sager and Lewis R. Fischer, *Shipping and Shipbuilding in Atlantic Canada*, 1820–1914, Canadian Historical Association, Historical Booklet no. 42 (Ottawa: 1986); and Eric W. Sager with Gerald E. Panting, *Maritime Capital: The Shipping Industry in Maritime Canada, 1820–1914* (Montreal, 1990). *Atlantic Canada Before Confederation*, vol. 1, *The Acadiensis Reader*, edited by P.A. Buckner and David Frank (Fredericton, 1985), contains Judith Fingard's essay, "The Relief of the Unemployed Poor in Saint John, Halifax and St. John's, 1815–1860," 190–211. Fingard's "The Winter's Tale: The Seasonal Contours of Pre-industrial Poverty in British North America," appeared in the Canadian Historical Association's *Historical Papers* (1974), 65–94. Her *Jack in Port: Sailortowns of Eastern Canada* (Toronto, 1982) describes the life of merchant sailors in Saint John and Halifax, and her *Dark Side of Life in Victorian Halifax* (Porters Lake, N.S., 1989) focusses on the lives of nearly one hundred habitual offenders in Halifax in the mid-nineteenth century. Several essays in Philip Girard and Jim Phillips, eds., *Essays in the History of Canadian Law: The Nova Scotia Experience* (Toronto, 1990) examine aspects of the province's legal history in the nineteenth century. William B. Hamilton reviews the educational history of the three Maritime colonies in *Canadian Education: A History*, edited by J. Donald Wilson, Robert M. Stamp, and Louis-Philippe Audet (Scarborough, Ont., 1970), 86–125. For the early history of British American universities, see Patricia Jasen, "Cicero on the Frontier: Higher Learning in Pioneer Canada, Nova Scotia and New Brunswick," *The Beaver* 71, 2 (April/May 1991): 42–50. An entertaining popular account of Halifax is Thomas H. Raddall's *Halifax: Warden of the North*, rev. ed. (Toronto, 1971). Sport in Halifax is the subject of Robert D. Day's "The British Garrison at Halifax: Its Contribution to the Development of Sport in the Community," in *Sports in Canada: Historical Readings*, edited by Morris Mott (Toronto, 1989), 28–36. T.W. Acheson's *Saint John: The Making of a Colonial Urban Community* (Toronto, 1985) is an in-depth study of New Brunswick's largest city. A collection of materials relating to Maritime women has been edited by Margaret Conrad, Toni Laidlaw, and Donna Smyth: *No Place Like Home: Diaries and Letters of Nova Scotia Women, 1771–1938* (Halifax, 1988).

Maritime political developments are examined in Phillip A. Buckner, *The Transition to Responsible Government: British Policy in British North America, 1815–1850* (Westport, Conn., 1985). W.G. Godfrey reviews Thomas Carleton's career as governor of New Brunswick in the *Dictionary of Canadian Biography*, vol. 5, *1801–1820* (Toronto, 1983), 155–63. A short sketch of Joseph Howe appears in the *Dictionary of Canadian Biography*, vol. 10, *1871–1880* (Toronto, 1972), 362–70, by Murray Beck, who has also written the two-volume study *Joseph Howe* (Kingston, 1982). Carmen Miller reviews the 1860s in "The Restoration of Greater Nova Scotia," in *Canada and the Burden of Unity*, edited by David Jay Bercuson (Toronto, 1977), 44–59. Prince Edward Island's complicated land question is examined by Ian Ross Robertson in *The Prince Edward Island Commission of 1860* (Fredericton, 1988). Important portraits of Maritime political, economic, and cultural leaders appear in the volumes of the *Dictionary of Canadian Biography* devoted to the nineteenth century.

For an introduction to cultural developments in the Maritimes in the nineteenth century, see the following two short articles in *The Canadian Encyclopedia*, 2d ed. (Edmonton, 1988): Helmut Kallman, "Music History," 3:1415–19, and L.W. Conolly, "English-Language Theatre," 4:2136–44. Fred Cogswell has written an interesting biography of Thomas Chandler Haliburton in the *Dictionary of Canadian Biography*, vol. 9, *1861–1870* (Toronto, 1976), 348–57. The early press in Maritime Canada is reviewed by Douglas Fetherling in *The Rise of the Canadian Newspaper* (Toronto, 1990).

A useful study for reviewing the history of the Native peoples of the Maritimes is L.F.S. Upton, *Micmacs and Colonists: Indian–White Relations in the Maritimes, 1713–1867* (Vancouver, 1979). Ralph T. Pastore's "Native History in the Atlantic Region during the Colonial Period," *Acadiensis*, 20, 1 (Autumn 1990): 200–25, provides an overview of the most recent literature. G.F.G. Stanley, "The Flowering of the Acadian Renaissance," in *Eastern and Western Perspectives*, edited by David Jay Bercuson and Phillip A. Buckner (Toronto, 1981), 19–46, surveys the Acadians' history. Richard Wilbur outlines the Acadians' experience from the 1860s in *The Rise of French New Brunswick* (Halifax, 1989). For a study of the Acadians on Prince Edward Island, see Georges Arsenault's *The Island Acadians, 1720–1980* (Charlottetown, 1989). Charles Dunn's classic *Highland Settler: A Portrait of the Scottish Gael in Nova Scotia* (Toronto, 1953), and D. Campbell and R.A. MacLean, *Beyond the Atlantic Roar: A Study of the Nova Scotia Scots* (Toronto, 1974) deal with the Scots in Nova Scotia. A number of works have recently appeared on the history of the Irish in British North America. The popular account entitled *Flight from Famine: The Coming of the Irish to Canada* (Toronto, 1990) contains a number of Maritime references. A valuable case study is Terrence M. Punch, *Irish Halifax: The Immigrant Generation* (Halifax, 1981). For a discussion of the blacks in the Maritimes, consult Robin W. Winks, *The Blacks in Canada: A History* (New Haven, 1971), and see W.A. Spray's "The Settlement of the Black Refugees in New Brunswick, 1815–1836," in *Atlantic Canada Before Confederation*, vol. 1, *The Acadiensis Reader*, 148–64.

For maps of the Maritimes in the late eighteenth and nineteenth centuries, see Donald Lemon's *Theatre of Empire* (Saint John, 1987).

Time Line: 1785–1864

1785	—The incorporation of Parrtown, New Brunswick, as the city of Saint John.
1796	—The Maroons, a group of blacks from Jamaica, and some Loyalist blacks leave Nova Scotia to settle in Sierra Leone in West Africa.
1799	—Saint John's Island is renamed Prince Edward Island.
1812–1814	—War of 1812.
1815	—Population of Newfoundland reaches about 40 000.
1820	—Cape Breton Island is united with Nova Scotia as one colony.
1824	—Newfoundland recognized as a regular colony and naval government abolished.
1829	—Shawnadithit, the last known surviving Beothuk Indian, dies of tuberculosis.
1832	—Newfoundland obtains representative government.
1836	—Thomas Chandler Haliburton's novel, *The Clockmaker; or, The Sayings and Doings of Sam Slick of Slickville*, is published.
1842	—The Webster-Ashburton Treaty establishes the present-day New Brunswick–Maine boundary.
1840s	—Britain ends its special protection of the timber trade.
1848	—Responsible government is achieved in Nova Scotia, and later in Prince Edward Island (1851) and New Brunswick (1854).
1854	—The Reciprocity Treaty with the United States is signed.
1855	—Newfoundland acquires responsible government.
1858	—First transatlantic cable connects Newfoundland with Britain.
1864	—The governments of New Brunswick, Nova Scotia, and Prince Edward Island agree to meet in Charlottetown to discuss Maritime Union.

Newfoundland to the 1860s

338 In the sixteenth century the fleets of four nations—England, France, Spain, and Portugal—sailed to the Newfoundland banks and shared its deep, land-locked eastern harbours. The ships came to one of the world's greatest fishing grounds for the codfish, called "the beef of the sea," a staple food of Roman Catholic Europe.

England, and then France, tried to colonize the Avalon Peninsula of Newfoundland in the seventeenth century. These attempts led the Beothuks, the local Indians, to withdraw from the area. Unlike the Micmacs in the Maritimes, the tribe could not adjust to permanent European settlement. But by staying in the interior in order to avoid the newcomers, the Beothuks lost access to the valuable food supplies off the coast. They became greatly weakened by starvation and by tuberculosis, which the Europeans had inadvertently introduced. In the end, within two centuries of the Europeans' arrival, the Beothuks disappeared completely.

After a half-century of Anglo-French conflict, France ceded Newfoundland to England by the Treaty of Utrecht in 1713. Powerful English merchants, mostly from Devon and Dorset in England's West Country, sought exclusive rights to the fishing grounds and persuaded British monarchs and parliaments in the late seventeenth century to discourage additional permanent settlement on the island. In the eighteenth century the merchants' opposition ended, and the British government sanctioned settlement. Early in the nineteenth century the island had a permanent population of more than forty thousand people. Their livelihood depended on exporting fish and on trade with Britain, the Mediterranean countries, the West Indies, and, to a more limited extent, the rest of British North America.

By the mid-nineteenth century the spirit of political reform that swept through the other British North American colonies surfaced in Newfoundland and led to intense and bitter disputes. On the eve of Confederation,

Newfoundland was in many respects like the other British North American colonies and yet, in other ways, it was quite different.

Growth of the International Fishery

The success of the early Newfoundland cod fishery initially depended on the harvesting of salt left by the evaporation of sea water. This salt was better than the mineral variety for curing fish because it was more uniform in quality. France, Spain, and Portugal produced an abundance of "solar salt," but England, not as blessed with sunshine, did not. This hurt England in the age of the "green fishery," the term sailors used to describe a method of salting fish immediately upon catching them, then transporting them back to Europe for drying. To compensate for their lack of solar salt, the English developed "dry fishing"—drying their lightly salted fish before returning home.

England profited greatly by the decline of Spanish naval strength after the defeat of the Spanish Armada in 1588. It gained a market for its dried cod in southern Europe, including Spain. The English sold the firmest and whitest cod in the Mediterranean. They classified slightly damaged fish as second grade and also shipped it to overseas buyers. They packed the poorest grade fish in casks and sold it to slave owners in the West Indies.

English fishing expeditions to Newfoundland became an annual event. From December to February the English fishermen cleaned, overhauled, and completely fitted their ships. Then in March they left from the great ports in southwestern England—Plymouth, Poole, and Dartmouth—with sufficient provisions and stores for eight months. Estimates of the number of English ships involved in the Newfoundland expeditions around the year 1600 vary from 250 to 400, and the number of men, from six thousand to ten thousand. These expeditions made good England's claim to the Avalon Peninsula on Newfoundland's east coast, the location of the best English fishing and processing sites.

The English practised fishing methods that they had first used off the coast of Iceland. They fished from open boats or from barrels suspended over the ship's side. Before the fishing began, they searched for the most convenient "room"—that is, a tract of land on the waterfront of a cove or harbour adjacent to their fishery. There they constructed the sheds, drying racks ("flakes"), wharves ("stages"), and other facilities where they landed their boats and processed their catch. A large fishing room was called a "plantation," and its owner, if he lived permanently on it, a "planter." Most of the ships carried a crew of twenty, of whom a dozen fished while the rest cured the fish on shore. The fishing day was an arduous one. Up before dawn, the men fished until 4:00 P.M.. Then, at about 6:00 P.M., the

339

National Archives of Canada/C-3686.

A View of a Stage & also of ye manner of Fishing for, Curing, & Drying Cod at Newfoundland. An engraving on a map of North America prepared by Herman Moll and published in 1718.

first boat reached the staging to unload the catch. The men worked eighteen to twenty hours a day to take advantage of the run of fish. The method of curing involved splitting, lightly salting, and drying the cod, producing an excellent "stock" fish that did not spoil during the long voyages to the tropics.

On the high seas, many dangers awaited—fog, floating ice, and pirates. During the early seventeenth century the "Barbary Rovers" (North African Moslems who travelled the coasts of Europe) allied themselves with France and extended their operations as far as the English Channel. There they waited for the unarmed ships from Newfoundland to return. They sold into slavery any seamen who were not needed to work on the pirate ships. The town of Poole in Dorset, which sent out twenty ships annually to Newfoundland, lost twenty ships, or one-quarter of their fleet, over a four-year period. Only after an Anglo-Dutch mission bombarded the pirates' North African headquarters in the late seventeenth century did the danger to English shipping diminish.

The men and boys in the migratory fishing fleet usually came from their ship's home port and its surrounding area. They were farmers without enough land to support their families, tradespeople without sufficient work, and orphans. On board, they earned wages slightly higher than farm workers'.

Early Settlement in Newfoundland

England was anxious to secure a permanent foothold in Newfoundland, believing that whoever controlled settlement would hold the fisheries. Newfoundland ranked second only to Virginia as a chosen location for British settlement in North America. Between 1610 and 1661, private individuals made seven different attempts to establish settlements on the island. The French also established a colony in Newfoundland. In 1660 they began a settlement at Plaisance (Placentia) about 100 kilometres west of St. John's on the Avalon Peninsula. By the time the French commenced their colony, several of the earlier English settlements had already failed.

341

In 1610 a group of London and Bristol merchants formed the London and Bristol Company. That same year the merchants sent a governor, John Guy, and forty men to establish Newfoundland's first colony at Cupids on Conception Bay. The London and Bristol Company believed its men would have an advantage over the visiting fishermen by being there before the annual visitors arrived. But the visiting fishermen caught just as much fish as did the colonists, and it was just as good. Moreover, the settlers had to charge as high or higher prices for their fish to cover the colony's expenses. Finally, the settlement could not sustain itself. The rocky land had almost no agricultural potential, so settlers could not grow grain and their cattle died from lack of fodder. The failure to discover mineral resources and to begin a commercial trade in furs with the resident Beothuk Indians also contributed to the colony's demise.

Another drawback to colonization was the weather. Lord Baltimore, for example, founded Ferryland, south of St. John's, in 1621. But after wintering on the island in 1628–29, he wrote as follows of his wife and family: "I have sent them home after much sufferance in this wofull country, where with one intolerable wynter were we almost undone. It is not to be expressed with my pen what wee have endured." Lord Baltimore re-directed his colonizing efforts to Virginia, where just after his death in 1632 his son received a charter to what became known as Maryland. Some of the Newfoundland settlers remained behind after the colony disintegrated and became part of the continuing permanent population of Ferryland.

In spite of several unsuccessful colonization attempts, the permanent non-native population of the island grew slowly. By 1650 an estimated 500 English-speaking residents, including 350 women and children, lived in about forty settlements scattered along on the eastern coast, between Cape Bonavista and Trepassey. The population rose to an estimated 2000 by

1680 and consisted of two groups: the first included descendants of settlers brought out by colonizers such as John Guy and Lord Baltimore; the second consisted of "bye-boatmen" from England's West Country, who came out as passengers on the fishing ships and returned in the autumn. They worked for the settlers or merchants who owned the bye-boats, the small fishing boats left in Newfoundland harbours for use in the spring. As time went on, many of these skilled fishermen remained in Newfoundland during the winter and frequently stayed for several years. Some became permanent settlers.

Without any organized government on the island, the settlers and the bye-boatmen faced difficult times. They had to earn their living during the short season of cod fishing in the summer, for there was no employment in the winter. When the fishing fleet departed in September or early October it left the isolated communities on their own until the following spring. If food ran out, they starved. If illness occurred, no medical people could be called. No births, marriages, or burials could be legally registered, since no clergymen lived on the island between 1650 and 1702. The island had no law officers or courts because it had no official status as a colony.

The English government faced a difficult problem in the late seventeenth century. It wanted to prevent settlement on the island, as the Royal Navy relied on the annual fishing voyages to train seamen and to maintain ships. In addition, the British government feared that a Newfoundland resident fishery would put an end to the English migratory fishery, as had been the case in New England. Yet, if Newfoundland had no settlers or resident fishermen, France might seize it. According to historian Frederick W. Rowe, three-quarters of the island's 10 000-km-long coastline "was already, in effect, almost wholly under the control of the world's most powerful country. How long would it be before France would be occupying the entire Island of Newfoundland?"[1] England resolved this dilemma in 1699. It formally recognized the permanent settlers on the island, but forbade them to encroach on the fishing areas of the migratory fishermen. Moreover, the authorities announced that no government would be established on the island. The Act to Encourage Trade to Newfoundland, or the Newfoundland Act, the first English statute pertaining to the island, remained the only constitution Newfoundland would have for the next 125 years, until it became a British colony in 1824.

The Anglo-French Struggle for Newfoundland

Just when the English began settlements on Newfoundland's east coast (the eastern Avalon Peninsula), the French claimed Newfoundland's south shore. In 1662 the French fortified Plaisance (Placentia). The deep, ice-free harbour offered an excellent refuge for French ships. To build up

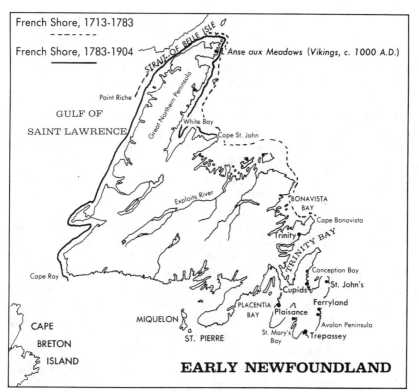

French Shore, 1713-1783

French Shore, 1783-1904

STRAIT OF BELLE ISLE

L'Anse aux Meadows (Vikings, c. 1000 A.D.)

Point Riche

Great Northern Peninsula

GULF OF
SAINT LAWRENCE

White Bay

Cape St. John

Exploits River

BONAVISTA
BAY

Cape Bonavista

Trinity

TRINITY BAY

Cape Ray

Conception Bay

Cupids

St. John's

Ferryland

PLACENTIA
BAY

Plaisance

MIQUELON

Avalon Peninsula

CAPE

ST. PIERRE

St. Mary's
Bay

Trepassey

BRETON

ISLAND

EARLY NEWFOUNDLAND

343

Source: Adapted from P.G. Cornell, J. Hamelin, F. Ouellet, and M. Trudel, *Canada: Unity in Diversity* (Toronto, 1967), 111.

Early Newfoundland.

settlement, the French government initially provided free passage and one year's financial support to settlers migrating to Plaisance. As in New France, however, large-scale French assistance ceased in the early 1670s. The colony grew very slowly after that, and its population, probably never exceeding nine hundred, remained much smaller than that of the English colony.

Conflict between the English and French settlements seemed inevitable. War broke out in 1689, and seven years later Pierre Le Moyne d'Iberville, New France's greatest soldier, with his troops, laid waste the English settlements, killing 200 people and taking 700 prisoners. The English retaliated when an expedition in 1697 recaptured all the settlements. From that point on, the English presence was secure, thanks largely to its superior naval power. But the devastation caused by the French did much to slow down the development of the permanent English settlements.

By the Treaty of Utrecht, England gained control of the entire island. The French ceded Plaisance and their claim to Newfoundland but retained the right to dry cod on what came to be known as the French Shore, between Cape Bonavista and Point Riche (in the northeastern bays and around Newfoundland's Great Northern Peninsula, to a point located about a quarter of the way down the west coast, an area including approximately one-third of Newfoundland's coastline).

By an Anglo-French agreement in 1783, Cape Ray, on the island's south western tip, was substituted for Point Riche and the eastern boundary moved from Cape Bonavista to Cape St. John. The French Shore now encompassed the entire west coast, the Great Northern Peninsula, and White Bay. British or Newfoundland fishermen were not allowed to interrupt the French fishery in that area and the French disputed their right to settle there. The question of the French Shore troubled Anglo-French relations for nearly two centuries, until England purchased French landing rights in 1904.

Although the French settlement at Plaisance became British, the French still held New France and the great fort of Louisbourg on Cape Breton Island. On account of France's naval strength, Newfoundland was in danger of a French naval attack until the 1760s. In 1762 the French actually took St. John's, although the English recaptured the town the following year. The first Treaty of Paris in 1763 had reaffirmed France's Newfoundland landing rights, and to compensate for the loss of French fishing bases in Cape Breton, Britain ceded the islands of St. Pierre and Miquelon off Newfoundland to France, "to serve as a shelter to the French fisherman." More than two centuries later (1977), the extentions of Canada's fishing zone to 220 kilometres, led to a French claim of exclusive rights around St. Pierre and Miquelon. In the 1980s, the failure to reach a common definition of the French fishing zone in the waters around the islands greatly troubled Franco-Canadian relations.

Law and Order in Eighteenth-Century Newfoundland

As early as the seventeenth century, competition for favourable harbours reached such a high level that the fishing fleets evolved their own crude system of administration. They worked out the "fishing admiral system," a rough-and-ready means of keeping some kind of order in the harbours. To the first ship in a port, regardless of nationality, went the right to take the best fishing room, or strip of beach. The first ship's captain became the "fishing admiral," with the customary responsibility to maintain law and order in each harbour. Much of the admiral's authority, however, rested on his strength. If he had a sizable and well-armed vessel and a large crew, then his will could be enforced.

In 1634 the English government had confirmed the admiral system in the First Western Charter, the first regulation issued on the Newfoundland fishery. The Newfoundland Act of 1699 again affirmed the rights and the authority of the fishing admirals. The system had several serious defects, however. First, the admirals stayed for only three or four months in the spring and summer; for the rest of the year, there was no one authorized to maintain law and order. Second, even when present, the admirals had no way of enforcing their rulings, and, as settlement grew, the problems they had to resolve became more complex. Third, the admirals received no payment for presiding over the courts and, since they had come primarily to fish, they had little interest in enforcing the law. Conditions on the island degenerated rapidly under the fishing admiral system. In the long period between the departure of the ships in the late summer and their return the next year, those guilty of murder, rape, and robbery had ample opportunity to escape.

Historian Keith Matthews has offered two explanations for England's delay in establishing a proper legal system.[2] One is that the establishment of law and other services on the island would have encouraged further permanent settlement, something the government sought to discourage. The other is that the placement of law enforcement officers in many different parts of the island would have involved enormous expenditures for the British government.

345

In 1729, Britain made a modest improvement in the system. The commander of the annual naval convoy to Newfoundland became the island's governor and commander-in-chief, but he lived on a ship and remained in Newfoundland only during the the summer fishing season. Whenever the governor deemed a local regulation desirable, he could issue a proclamation and his word became law. As governor, he also had the right to appoint magistrates from among the most respected local residents. While the fishing admirals retained, until the late eighteenth century, their authority under the Newfoundland Act of 1699 to rule in the summers on the fisheries and on related matters, the magistrates gained an increasing jurisdiction, both in terms of the nature of the cases they could hear and the time of year they would hear them.

The Beothuk Indians

The Beothuk Indians, Newfoundland's original inhabitants, suffered greatly from the presence of the newcomers. The Beothuks first encountered European fishermen in the sixteenth century. From their use of red ochre on their bodies, clothing, and utensils, the early Europeans called them "Red Indians"—an expression still used in Britain to describe the American Indians. The word *Beothuk* means "people," and it is the term that the aboriginal Newfoundlanders applied to themselves.

Unlike the Micmacs in the Maritimes, who adjusted to living near the French, the Beothuks habitually withdrew from the Europeans. With the increasing number of European fishers on the Newfoundland coast, it became difficult in the mid-seventeenth century for the Indians to gain access to their seaside summer campsites and, hence, to their food resources, particularly on the eastern and southern coasts. Starvation became a major problem.

The pressure on the Beothuks became even more intense in the early 1700s. Several factors contributed to increased European settlement in the northeast and in the interior: a salmon fishery developed near the mouths of the rivers of northeast Newfoundland; settlers began to trap fur-bearing animals in the interior; and the spring seal hunt, which was best operated from the northeast coast, was growing rapidly. The British settlers became seal hunters in the spring, salmon catchers in the summer, and trappers in the winter, thus depriving the Beothuks of their traditional sources of food and clothing.

When the Beothuks encountered the Europeans on the northeastern coast, violence often broke out. The settlers harassed them and raided their camps. George Cartwright, a prominent merchant in Labrador, issued a warning to the Colonial Office in 1784:

> Instead of a friendly intercourse with these Indians, our people dispossessed them from beaches and salmon rivers and it is now well known, that the poor Indians are put to the greatest difficulties to procure a scanty subsistance. If some effectual measures will not be taken, that unhappy race of mortals will soon be extirpated, to the disgrace of our Government, our country and our religion.

The Beothuks retaliated. According to contemporary reports and oral traditions, the Beothuks killed about a dozen settlers and wounded nearly as many more between 1750 and 1790. The settlers took their own revenge, killing and wounding Indians and destroying their wigwams. The Indians' lack of firearms weakened their ability to defend themselves.

Justice went undone. Neighbours and employers were reluctant to become involved in the prosecution of the British criminals, especially since it could mean missing out on the summer's fishing and having to pay for the return expenses from St. John's. The culprits remained at large, unpunished. Even when murder trials were held at St. John's in the mid-eighteenth century, the court made few convictions.

Several concerned naval officers and settlers in the late eighteenth and early nineteenth centuries worried about the Beothuks' fate. A number of attempts to reach the Beothuks failed, but one, in 1811, succeeded. After trekking for twelve days up the Exploits River (see page 343) in heavy snow and sub-zero temperatures, Captain David Buchan and his party of twenty-seven made contact with a band of about forty Beothuks. The Indians, though, remained suspicious and killed the two seamen who had been left with them as hostages.

Attempts made to locate the Indians the following summer failed. Many of the Beothuks apparently died, most likely from starvation and tuberculosis. From evidence accumulated by anthropologist Ingeborg Marshall, it appears that a few Beothuks joined the Micmacs in the southern part of the island, either voluntarily or because they were kidnapped.[3]

In 1823 three starving Beothuk women surrendered to a British settler. Both the mother and one of her two daughters died shortly afterward of tuberculosis. The second daughter, Shawnadithit, called Nancy, who was between sixteen and twenty years old, survived for six years. She lived at first as a servant in the household of a justice of the peace, but spent the last year of her life in St. John's, informing William Cormack, a champion of the Beothuk, about her people's culture, history, and language. Shawnadithit died in 1829. Apart from two or three of her people who may have lived with the Newfoundland Micmacs, no other members of her tribe are known to have survived.

347

Growth and Development

At the end of the eighteenth century Newfoundland's population grew rapidly. The number of permanent residents rose from approximately 2300 in 1720 to about 20 000 by 1800, and about 40 000 in 1815. As late as 1790, resident men outnumbered women five to one.

The environmental impact of the increased coastal population was striking. As the settlers built dwellings and warehouses and used increasing amounts of firewood, the forests rapidly disappeared. According to geographer Grant Head, the coastal forests were replaced by a "clutter of stages, flakes, boats, ships, warehouses, dwellings, vegetable patches, wandering cattle, and snaking trails."[4]

Much of the population growth came from a large influx of immigrants, chiefly Irish. The first potato famines in the 1720s and 1730s led thousands of Irish to seek refuge across the Atlantic, and Newfoundland was the first place in the New World to receive large numbers of Irish immigrants. By the 1750s Irish Catholics comprised probably half the Avalon Peninsula's total population, and by the 1830s they numbered half the entire island's population.

The Irish immigrants brought with them little love for England, which had invaded Ireland repeatedly, seized Irish lands, and then proscribed the Catholic religion. The Irish came with respect for, and strong loyalty to, their priests, but found that Roman Catholic priests were not allowed on the island. Not until 1784 did the governor grant religious freedom.

Mistrusting each other, the Irish and the English communities segregated themselves geographically. In the larger towns such as St. John's, English and Irish settlers tended to live in separate neighbourhoods. Even when the Roman Catholic Irish moved away from the Avalon Peninsula, they kept to themselves and settled in harbours not occupied by English Protestants.

As the population expanded, the economy became more diversified and the shore cod fishery was no longer the only industry. The development of salmon fishing, sealing, and the fur trade led to an expansion of settlement to the northern bays of the island. Settlers occupied hundreds of coves, harbours, and islands chosen for their proximity to the fishing grounds. The Avalon Peninsula's scattered pockets of fertile land were put under cultivation.

THE RISE OF ST. JOHN'S

In the late eighteenth century St. John's came into its own as the dominant urban centre on the island. The town's population rose from about 1000 in 1790 to more than 5000 in 1810. St. John's had become the island's capital in 1729, when the British naval convoy commander was made governor. A number of the town's settlers had left the fishery to open taverns and stores catering to the needs of the thousands of fishermen who came to the island annually. An English garrison was also located in the town. Already the administrative capital of the island, St. John's became its business centre in the late eighteenth century.

At first glance, St. John's, situated at the extreme eastern tip of the island, does not seem an obvious choice for the island's great commercial centre. In fact, however, it was located in Newfoundland's most densely populated area—the Avalon Peninsula, which is larger than Prince Edward Island. The peninsula itself was fortunately located, being almost equidistant between the chief ports of New and Old England. In historian William Menzies Whitelaw's words, it was "the natural stepping stone between the old world and the new."[5] In addition, the peninsula lay immediately west of the North Atlantic's best fishing grounds—the Grand Banks.

St. John's importance increased in the late eighteenth and early nineteenth centuries. The governor had made his headquarters there. The establishment of the Newfoundland Supreme Court in 1792 and of customs and naval offices further raised the town's standing. After the American Revolution, merchants involved in the Canada and West Indies trade established themselves in St. John's. The town's merchants and shipowners financed the fishing trade, marketed dry cod, and distributed foodstuffs and manufactured goods to the outports. The merchants at St. John's were in a position to control the island's affairs, and kept the smaller merchants in the island's outports indebted to them. Newfoundlanders originated a new word, the "fishocracy," to describe the powerful St. John's merchants who were involved in exporting cod and acting as suppliers to the smaller merchants and fishermen in the outports.

As the town's wealth grew, newspapers, health services, and schools were established. St. John's thus became the only community on the island with an educated and moderately wealthy middle class. The capital, though, could not escape its past, and continuing, livelihood. George Warburton, an Irish soldier and writer, visited St. John's in the mid-1840s on a tour of British North America. In his book, *Hochelaga; or, England in the New World* (1846), he provides a delightful sketch of St. John's, Newfoundland—the "fishiest" capital in the world.

In trying to describe St. John's there is some difficulty in applying to it an adjective sufficiently distinctive and appropriate. We find other cities coupled with epithets which at once give their predominant characteristic: London the richest, Paris the gayest, St. Petersburg the coldest. In one respect the chief town of Newfoundland has, I believe, no rival: we may therefore call it the fishiest of modern capitals. Round a great part of the harbour are sheds, acres in extent, roofed with cod split in half, laid on like slates, drying in the sun, or rather the air, for there is not much of the former to depend upon. Those ships, bearing nearly every flag in the world, are laden with cod; those stout weatherly boats crowding up to the wharves have just now returned from fishing for cod; those few scant fields of cultivation, with lean crops coaxed out of the barren soil, are manured with cod; those grim, snug-looking wooden houses, their handsome furniture, the piano and the musical skill of the young lady who plays it, the satin gown of the mother, the gold chain of the father, are all paid for in cod; the breezes from the shore, soft and warm on this bright August day, are rich not with the odours of a thousand flowers but of a thousand cod. Earth, sea and air are alike pervaded with this wonderful fish.

349

THE OUTPORTS

Life was harsher in the outports than in St. John's. Jacob Mountain, a young Anglican priest, discovered as much during his seven years of missionary work on Newfoundland's south coast. There is no such thing, he wrote in his posthumously published *Some Accounts of a Sowing Time on the Rugged Shores of Newfoundland* (1857), as a typical Newfoundland fishing village:

In one place you will find them clean, tidy, thriving; houses neatly and substantially built, and a certain air of sobriety and self-respect about the people; the children a picture of delight, with their beautiful eyes, well-formed faces, soft flaxen hair. In another close by, the very reverse of all this; houses, or rather hovels of studs, the crevices gaping wide or filled with moss, the roof covered with rinds of trees and sods, the entrance constructed by heaps of dirt, often nothing that deserved the name of door, the aperture so low that one must stoop to enter, the interior without any furniture but a low table and rough stool, scarcely raised three inches from the ground, the children wretchedly ragged and dirty, crouching round, or creeping into the smoky wood fire, an oil sail and a few more studs forming the only partition between the kitchen and sleeping-room, if such terms can be applied to such miserable dens.

Mountain died in 1856, after a protracted bout of fever "caught in his constant visiting in infected houses." He was only thirty-eight.

Scattered along ten thousand kilometres of coast, the population of almost all of Newfoundland's distant and remote coves and harbours grew without the benefit of clergy or schoolteachers. One result of this isolation was a rich and varied language. Numerous words survive today in Newfoundland that are found only—if anywhere—in dialects of the British Isles. Residents of various Newfoundland areas can still be distinguished from one another by their accents, which all hark back to western England or Ireland.

350

RELIGION AND EDUCATION

Organized religion came to the island in the eighteenth century. The Anglicans began their work in 1703 with the appointment of John Jackson as the first missionary in Newfoundland for the Society for the Propagation of the Gospel in Foreign Parts (SPG). During the 1700s two or three Anglican clergymen were stationed on the island. The Roman Catholic church was prohibited in Newfoundland by law at this time, although Roman Catholic priests had probably arrived and worked secretly on the island before freedom of worship was granted in 1784. After this date, Protestant groups such as the Methodists and the Congregationalists also organized churches on the island. On the Labrador coast, the Moravian missionaries began their work among the Inuit in 1771.

No school is known to have existed in Newfoundland until the eighteenth century, when the SPG established a few schools for the poor and underprivileged. Later, the Wesleyan Methodists and other groups opened schools as well. Most children, however, had no schooling and remained illiterate. The availability of education improved with the foundation of the Newfoundland School Society in 1823. The society, which was closely identified with the Church of England, operated forty schools in the decades to follow.

In the larger towns, particularly St. John's, the upper classes had private tutors and private schools and, in a few cases, sent their children off to be educated in England, since "respectable classes" did not want their children to attend the SPG or Methodist schools with the "lower orders." A rigid class structure existed in the capital.

The Migratory Fishery Becomes Resident

Both the American and the French revolutions and the subsequent Napoleonic Wars had a profound impact on Newfoundland's trade patterns.
With the departure of New England from the British Empire in 1783 and
Britain's subsequent exclusion of Americans from the Empire's carrying
trade, Newfoundland became the major supplier of fish to the British West
Indies. Fishery production expanded, creating new jobs and, in turn,
causing a sharp decline in emigration from Newfoundland to New
England. Newfoundland became an integral part of the triangular trade
linking it with Britain and the West Indies. A growing fleet of ships now
operated from Newfoundland ports. As it was now illegal for British
subjects to own American-built ships, the island began to construct its
own vessels.

The outbreak of the last and the longest of the wars with France, the
Napoleonic Wars (1793–1814), also contributed to the new prosperity
on the island. The price of dried fish rose substantially during the later
years of the war because the French had to abandon their Newfoundland
fishery. France simply could not protect its fishing fleet in wartime
when the country needed to mobilize all of its naval resources to fight
England.

351

During more than two decades of war between Britain and France,
Newfoundland's fishery underwent a major transformation. The three-
centuries-old migratory West Country–Newfoundland fishery came to an
end. Just as the French no longer came to fish off the French Shore, the
English vessels also stayed at home. Fears of press-gangs in England
forcefully seizing sailors for service in the Royal Navy also convinced
many of the bye-boatmen to remain on the island. The resident population,
and the fishery, grew. By 1815 residents owned almost the complete fishing
fleet and produced the entire yield of saltfish, whereas immediately before
the Napoleonic Wars the English migratory fishery produced more than
half the total English–Newfoundland catch.

During these prosperous years, shipowners, settlers, and St. John's entrepreneurs invested heavily in the fishery, creating a resident Newfoundland fleet. They began sending ships to less crowded parts of the coast,
to the northern part of the island, and on to Labrador. Each June, thousands of Newfoundland fishermen sailed for Labrador to catch cod.
Those who fished out of fixed locations with a "room" on shore became
known as the "stationers" (or "squatters" or "roomers"); those who
lived aboard their schooners and followed the fish were the "floaters" (or
"green fish catchers"); those who chose to settle permanently on the
Labrador coast became "the livyeres" (most likely a corruption of "live
here"). As the Labrador fishery expanded, Britain decided to re-attach
Labrador to Newfoundland, taking it out of Lower Canada's control in
1809.

Provincial Archives of Newfoundland and Labrador

Sealers "copying" the floes, ca. 1920. "Copying" in Newfoundland and Labrador means leaping from floe to floe.

THE RISE OF THE SEAL FISHERY

Seamen entered the waters off Labrador and Newfoundland's northern coasts to harvest the seal herds on the ice floes. Mammals and fish provided the bulk of the world's industrial oil in the early nineteenth century, and young seals had an excellent fat for fine-quality oil. Their skins could also be sold in England. The industry grew rapidly. Between 1831 and 1833, the seal fishery averaged between 30 and 40 percent of Newfoundland's total exports. Output reached more than six hundred thousand seals in 1831 alone, and by the 1850s, thirteen thousand men were employed annually in the seal hunt. In the 1860s, however, a decline due to overharvesting set in.

The lack of written records makes it difficult to re-create the sense of independence and the outlook of these hardy Newfoundlanders on the Labrador coast in the nineteenth century. Their spirit, though, echoes forth in one of their favourite chanteys (and one still popular in Newfoundland today), "Jack was every inch a sailor":

'Twas twenty-five or thirty years since Jack first saw the light.
He came into this world of woe one dark and stormy night.
He was born on board his father's ship as she was lying to.
'Bout twenty-five or thirty miles southeast of Bacalieu.

Chorus
Jack was every inch a sailor, five and twenty years a whaler,
Jack was every inch a sailor, he was born upon the bright blue sea.

When Jack grew up to be a man, he went to the Labrador.
He fished in Indian Harbour, where his father fished before.
On his returning in the fog, he met a heavy gale,
And Jack was swept into the sea and swallowed by a whale.
Repeat Chorus
The whale went straight for Baffin's Bay, about ninety knots an hour,
And every time he'd blow a spray he'd send it in a shower.
"O, now," says Jack unto himself, "I must see what he's about."
He caught the whale all by the tail and turned him inside out.
Repeat Chorus

353

Political Changes in the Nineteenth Century

Until 1832 Newfoundland's government differed from that of any other British North American colony. There was no legislature and the naval governor still had near-dictatorial powers. But by the early nineteenth century, the new mercantile and professional elite of St. John's led the struggle for social and political reform. Cut off from regular communication with the capital, the distant outports remained removed from the discussion, which really preoccupied only the Avalon Peninsula. The campaign for self-government was thus led by a group of first-generation arrivals who were anxious for political power but knew little about the island—except for what happened in St. John's.

A Scottish physician, William Carson, who had come to St. John's in 1808, led the Reform movement. In his first tract, written three years after his arrival, he argued against the system of naval governors and called for constitutional reform. The first advance came in 1817, when Newfoundland officially became more than a summer fishery. The Colonial Office decided that the governor should remain on the island all year and not just for two or three months in the summer. Then, in 1824, Britain recognized Newfoundland as a regular colony and abolished the naval government. It repealed the old fishing laws, an action that, among other things, allowed residents to hold clear title to land. In addition, in 1832 Britain instituted representative government. Parliament made provision for a Newfoundland legislature with elected and appointed chambers. Almost all of the male residents of the island gained the franchise.

Political reform increased internal dissension between Protestants and Roman Catholics (now almost evenly divided in number), between English and Irish, between radicals and conservatives, between merchants and fishermen, and between St. John's and the outports. In 1842 Britain suspended Newfoundland's constitution in order to end political deadlock. The Colonial Office then formed a new integrated legislature consisting of eleven elected members and ten Crown appointees. This reduced the Reformers to a small minority, at least until the two-chamber system was restored in 1848.

With William Carson's death in 1843, the Reform movement lost much of its momentum, but it revived in 1850 with a platform of obtaining responsible government. Carson's successors, such as John Kent, a fiery Reform politician, demanded that the island obtain cabinet, or responsible, government. This goal was achieved in 1855, finally ending direct British rule. The first premier, the Reform, or Liberal, leader Philip Francis Little, a Roman Catholic, tried to bridge the divisions between the two religious communities by inviting both Roman Catholics and Protestants into his cabinet, a goal that a Conservative successor, Frederick Carter, a Protestant, also pursued.

354

On the eve of the discussions for British North American federation, Newfoundland looked eastward toward Britain, not westward toward the mainland. Newfoundland was a North Atlantic country, with patterns of trade and settlement linking it to Europe, the West Indies, and the United States. The development of the western part of the island, which contained the land most suitable for agriculture, would have served as a bridge to Canada. Until 1904, however, the French held on to their treaty rights to dry fish on the western coastline.

Its geography and distinctive history placed Newfoundland very much apart from the Canadas and even from the three Maritime colonies. As historian William Menzies Whitelaw wrote of nineteenth-century Newfoundland, "In many ways it was an integral part of British North America, but in others it remained as remote as Bermuda had been from the thirteen colonies."[6]

NOTES

[1]Frederick W. Rowe, *A History of Newfoundland and Labrador* (Toronto, 1980), 109.
[2]See Keith Matthews's comments on the growth of law in Newfoundland in *Lectures on the History of Newfoundland, 1500–1830* (St. John's, 1973; reprinted 1988), 131–50.
[3]Ingeborg Marshall, personal communication, May 22, 1987.
[4]C. Grant Head, *Eighteenth Century Newfoundland: A Geographer's Perspective* (Toronto, 1976), 245.
[5]William Menzies Whitelaw, *The Maritimes and Canada before Confederation* (Toronto, 1966; first published 1934), 29.
[6]Whitelaw, *Maritimes*, 28.

Related Readings

For a short survey of early Newfoundland history, see Keith Matthews's "The Nature and the Framework of Newfoundland History," in *Readings in Canadian History: Pre-Confederation*, 3d ed., edited by R. Douglas Francis and Donald B. Smith (Toronto, 1990), 149–58. For a review of the colony's response to Confederation, consult James Hiller, "Confederation Defeated: The Newfoundland Election of 1869," 523–47.

BIBLIOGRAPHY

Frederick W. Rowe's *A History of Newfoundland and Labrador* (Toronto, 1980) is at the present time the most complete study of Newfoundland's history. Peter Neary and Patrick O'Flaherty provide a short introduction to the island's history in their popular work *Part of the Main: An Illustrated History of Newfoundland and Labrador* (St. John's, 1983). For several valuable maps of Newfoundland and the fisheries before 1800, see R. Cole Harris, ed., *Historical Atlas of Canada*, vol. 1, *From the Beginning to 1800* (Toronto, 1987). G.O. Rothney has written a short survey in the Canadian Historical Association booklet series, *Newfoundland: A History* (Ottawa, 1964). For a brief historical overview, Shannon Ryan's essay "The Fishing Station," *Horizon Canada* 8 (1985): 169–75, is useful, as is his article, "The Seal and Labrador Cod Fisheries of Newfoundland," in the Canadian Museum of Civilization's *Canada's Visual History Series*, vol. 26, pp. 1–8. Another valuable review is Patrick O'Flaherty, *The Rock Observed: Studies in the Literature of Newfoundland* (Toronto, 1979).

Studies on the history of Newfoundland in the pre-nineteenth century period include Gillian T. Cell, *English Enterprise in Newfoundland, 1577–1660* (Toronto, 1969), and Keith Matthews, *Lectures on the History of Newfoundland, 1500–1830* (St. John's, 1988). Specific information on Lord Baltimore's colony is contained in Luca Codignola's *The Coldest Harbour in the Land. Simon Stock and Lord Baltimore's Colony in Newfoundland, 1621–1649* (Montreal, 1987). W. Gordon Handcock reviews English settlement in Newfoundland in *Soe Longe as There Comes No Women* (St. John's, 1989). Several essays on early Newfoundland appear in G.M. Story, ed., *Early European Settlement and Exploitation in Atlantic Canada: Selected Papers* (St. John's, 1982). For the eighteenth century, see C. Grant Head, *Eighteenth Century Newfoundland: A Geographer's Perspective* (Toronto, 1976). Several sections of W.S. MacNutt's *The Atlantic Provinces: The Emergence of a Colonial Society, 1712–1857* (Toronto, 1965) refer to Newfoundland, as do portions of William Menzies Whitelaw's *The Maritimes and Canada before Confederation* (Toronto, 1966; first published 1934).

355

The complex question of the French Shore is reviewed in Frederic F. Thompson's *The French Shore Problem in Newfoundland* (Toronto, 1961).

The mid-nineteenth century political history of the island is reviewed in Keith Matthews, "The Class of '32: St. John's Reformers on the Eve of Representative Government," in *Atlantic Canada Before Confederation*, vol. 1, *The Acadiensis Reader*, edited by P.A. Buckner and David Frank (Fredericton, 1985), 212–26, and Gertrude E. Gunn, *The Political History of Newfoundland, 1832–1864* (Toronto, 1966). P.B. Waite has written a sketch of John Kent, the Reform politician, in the *Dictionary of Canadian Biography*, vol. 10, *1871–1880* (Toronto, 1972), 398–401. Other important biographies of prominent Newfoundlanders appear in this invaluable biographical series.

An entertaining collection of references to Newfoundland in the nineteenth century is R.G. Moyles's *"Complaints is many and various, but the odd Divil likes it"* (Toronto, 1975). James Hiller and Peter Neary have edited a collection of articles, *Newfoundland in the Nineteenth and Twentieth Centuries: Essays in Interpretation* (Toronto, 1980). Shannon Ryan reviews nineteenth-century economic developments in "Fishery to Colony: A Newfoundland Watershed, 1793–1815," in *Atlantic Canada Before Confederation*, 1:130–48. For the history of the Newfoundland seal hunt, consult James E. Candow, *Of Men and Seals* (Ottawa, 1989). A short introduction to Newfoundland dialects appears in Phillip W. Rogers, "The Dictionary of Newfoundland English," *Queen's Quarterly* 91 (1984): 832–37. A fascinating look at Newfoundland English is G.M. Story, W.J. Kirwin, and J.D.A. Widdowson's edited work, *Dictionary of Newfoundland English. Second Edition with Supplement* (Toronto, 1990).

A substantial literature exists on Newfoundland's Indian population. Book-length treatments include James P. Howley's *The Beothucks or Red Indians: The Aboriginal Inhabitants of Newfoundland* (Toronto, 1974; first published 1915), and Frederick W. Rowe, *Extinction: The Beothuks of Newfoundland* (Toronto, 1977). Valuable articles include L.F.S. Upton, "The Extermination of the Beothucks of Newfoundland," *Canadian Historical Review* 58 (1977): 133–53; Ingeborg Marshall, "Disease as a Factor in the Demise of the Beothuck Indians," *Culture* 1 (1981): 71–77, and her "The Beothuk," *Horizon Canada* 14 (1985): 326–31; and Francoy Raynauld, "Les pêcheurs et les colons anglais n'ont pas exterminé les Beothuks de Terre-Neuve," *Recherches amérindiennes au Québec* 14 (1984): 45–59. Ralph Pastore reviews the history of the Micmacs in Newfoundland in "Indian Summer: Newfoundland Micmacs in the Nineteenth Century," *Canadian Ethnology Society*, Papers from the Fourth Annual Congress, 1977 (Ottawa, 1978), 167–78. For the Micmacs' history, see also Dennis Bartels, *"Ktaqamkuk Ilnui Saqimawoutie:* Aboriginal Rights and the Myth of the Micmac Mercenaries in Newfoundland," in *Native People, Native Lands: Canadian Indians, Inuit and Metis*, edited by Bruce Alden Cox (Ottawa, 1988), 32–36. The most recent literature on both the Micmacs and the Beothuks is listed in Ralph Pastore's "Native History in the Atlantic Region during the Colonial Period," *Acadiensis*, 20, 1 (Autumn 1990), 200–25. Ralph Pastore and G.M. Storey's sketch of Shawnadithit, the last known survivor of the Beothuks, in the *Dictionary of Canadian Biography*, 6, 1821–1835 (Toronto, 1987): 706–709, is very valuable.

The North-West to the 1860s

The Blackfoot-speaking Indians occupied the rich buffalo ranges of present-day southern Alberta and northern Montana in the mid-eighteenth century. The horse, brought to Mexico by the Spanish, reached them about 1730, at about the same time that Cree middlemen brought them guns. Apart from possibly one or two "northern white men," as they later termed the English, the only Europeans they encountered on the northern plains in the 1740s and 1750s were French traders from Canada, whom they called "real white men."

After the fall of New France in 1760, hundreds of Europeans ventured into the interior from the north, the east, and the south. The best furs came from the North-West, and independent fur traders from Montreal came to buy them. In the early 1780s these Scottish and American fur traders formed the North West Company (whose agents came to be called Nor'Westers) to challenge the Hudson's Bay Company, already more than a century old. Thirty years of competition between the two companies ended with their merger in 1821. Even after the Métis broke the Hudson's Bay Company monopoly in the Red River in 1849, the company remained the leading commercial power in the North-West.

The establishment of a Red River settlement by Lord Selkirk in the early nineteenth century helped change the Europeans' perceptions of the country. Two expeditions in the late 1850s also contributed to that change. Once the Hind and Palliser scientific expeditions in the North-West reported on the agricultural potential of the Red River area and lands farther west, tens of thousands of landless British North Americans sought to settle there. No longer did British North Americans look upon the North-West as a vast fur preserve with a harsh climate.

359

Glenbow Museum, Calgary.

Indian Greeting White Man, a painting by famous American illustrator Frederic Remington (1861–1909). "Real White Man" is what the Blackfoot Indians of Alberta call the French in the Blackfoot language, probably because the French were the first Europeans to make contact with them.

The French and the English in the Interior

The French came west in search of a short route to China. Since Verrazzano's voyage in 1524, the French had believed in the existence of a gulf that cut deeply into the continent from the Pacific, like Hudson Bay or the Gulf of Mexico. Jean Nicollet de Belleborne, the first explorer charged with finding the "inland sea," left Quebec in 1634, taking with him a colourful flowered Chinese robe, so that he would be properly attired when he encountered the officials of the Chinese emperor. When René-Robert Cavelier de La Salle travelled inland in 1669 in search of China, his neighbours named his land grant on the south bank of Montreal Island "La Chine" (China), in recognition of his ambition to reach the Orient by way of "La Mer de l'Ouest" (the Western Sea). Half a century later, the French still hoped that somewhere between the 40th and 50th parallels of latitude they would find a navigable strait joining the Western Sea to the Pacific.

THE FRENCH SEARCH FOR THE "WESTERN SEA"

In 1717 the French Crown supported attempts to discover the Western Sea, but did not provide financing. Profits from fur-trade posts west of Lake Superior went to cover the exploration costs. Finally, in 1730, Lt.

Pierre Gaultier de Varennes et de La Vérendrye, commander of the fur-trading post of Kaministiquia (present-day Thunder Bay), offered to establish a post on Lake Winnipeg. He agreed to conduct explorations for the Western Sea from this base, at no expense to the Crown.

From Kaministiquia, La Vérendrye travelled westward in the 1730s, building fur-trading posts in the Lake of the Woods district and around Lakes Winnipeg and Winnipegosis. The Chevalier de La Corne, a successor, founded a fort farther west, near the forks of the north and south branches of the Saskatchewan River, in 1753. The French never found "La Mer de l'Ouest," but they did locate the key to the interior—the Saskatchewan River, whose twin branches flow through the central plain in a huge, wavering Y.

THE HUDSON'S BAY COMPANY'S INLAND EXPEDITIONS

The English had established trading posts in the late seventeenth century at the mouths of rivers emptying into Hudson Bay. From these forts they carried on a profitable trade with Cree and Assiniboine Indians, who, acting as middlemen, brought furs to them. These key middleman tribes came to dominate the exchange of furs. They charged the interior Indians a considerable markup on the European goods they obtained from the English and, until 1713, from the French.

A series of armed clashes occurred on Hudson Bay between the French and the English. By the Treaty of Utrecht in 1713, however, France recognized England's possession of the coastline of Hudson and James bays.

The English sponsored only two inland expeditions southwest of York Factory, their major post on Hudson Bay. In 1690–91 they sent Henry Kelsey, a young employee known to the Hudson's Bay Company's committee in London as "a very active lad, delighting much in Indians' company, being never more pleased than when he is travelling amongst them," to explore the interior. He travelled with a Cree band and reached the prairies, probably in present-day east–central Saskatchewan. But upon his return the company decided not to establish costly forts in the interior. As long as the Crees and the Assiniboines brought good furs to them, the English would stay on Hudson Bay.

More than half a century after Kelsey's journey, however, the English were feeling the effects of French competition through their trade along the Great Lakes–Lake of the Woods route. In 1754 they sent Anthony Henday to convince the Indians to give up their trade at the French posts and to come to the bay. In his journal, which is far more precise than Kelsey's, Henday identified the specific tribes in the interior and provided notes on their way of life. The young trader became the first Englishman to describe the buffalo hunt, in which the Indians, on horseback, used bows, arrows, and lances. Henday returned to York Factory with an Indian wife who had helped him immeasurably as an interpreter, an assistant, and a reliable source of information.

Impact of the Gun

Guns wrought great changes in the lives of the Native peoples in the North-West. The European musket became one of the most sought-after trade items by the Woodland Crees and the Assiniboines. The guns did have disadvantages: loading powder and shot was awkward; the gun barrels were always prone to explosion; the guns broke easily in the cold and required maintenance by European gunsmiths; and the Indians in the interior could not obtain ammunition easily, since the traders did not stock large supplies. For buffalo hunting, the Plains tribes preferred to use their sinew-backed bows with metal-tipped arrows, which did not make a noise that would prematurely stampede a herd. Moreover, experienced hunters could easily reload a bow on horseback. But in battle, the Indians used firearms for their obvious advantages there. Bullets went a longer distance than arrows and had greater killing power. Rawhide shields and armour offered little protection against a musket ball. In addition, in the context of warfare, the gun's loud report gave its user a psychological advantage.

361

TRIBAL MIGRATIONS

In the early eighteenth century, it appeared, the Chipewyan Indians moved into the woodlands immediately north of the Woodland Crees. Directly supplied by the English at Churchill, the Chipewyans sold European goods to interior tribes. Like the Crees, they became the traders' middlemen. In addition, the European gun gave them an advantage in their struggle with the Inuit to the north and the Crees to the southwest. In 1770–72 Samuel Hearne, a Hudson's Bay Company explorer, made an epic journey with a group of Chipewyans across the barren lands from Churchill to the Arctic Ocean. His account, *A Journey from Prince of Wales's Fort, in Hudson's Bay, to the Northern Ocean*, is still regarded as one of the classics of North American travel and provides an eyewitness account of eighteenth-century Chipewyan life.

Apparently, the Woodland Crees migrated westward along the North Saskatchewan River, until they entered the plains, and Blackfoot country. Their intrusion ended the initially friendly relations they had had with the "Prairie People."

Individual Cree bands travelled over the plains independently. No single chief co-ordinated the expansion. As historian Hugh Dempsey has written, the chiefs "did not order their people to move, they simply told them their own plans. A good chief had a faithful following, and they would go with him; but if for any reason his people disagreed with him, they were free to make their own decisions."[1]

THE ARRIVAL OF THE HORSE

The horse had an even greater impact on the Plains Indians than did the gun. With the acquisition of horses, many Blackfoot Indians used them for hunting buffalo. Horsemen replaced warriors on foot in driving and luring the animals into buffalo pounds or over cliffs (buffalo jumps). Mounted hunters began to rush straightaway into a herd, singling out an animal, riding beside it, and then killing it at close range with two or three arrows from their bows.

362

The Blackfoot sought five qualities in their buffalo horses: the ability to sustain a high speed over a distance of several kilometres; the ability to respond instantly to commands; the ability to move quickly alongside a buffalo and the ability to stay clear of it and its horns; the ability to run swiftly without stumbling over uneven ground; and finally, the ability to remain controlled in face of a stampeding buffalo. It took great patience to train a horse to run close alongside a buffalo, and a trained horse was worth several simple riding or pack animals.

The horse caused a cultural revolution on the Plains and became a standard of wealth among the Indians. Some rich tribesmen owned herds of seventy to one hundred horses. By giving away horses, or even by lending them, one could enhance one's prestige. Horses were borrowed for hunting and for war parties, with the borrower returning in payment a portion of the game killed or of the goods seized. The horse thus contributed to the development of a class structure among the Plains peoples, one based almost solely on the number of horses owned.

The introduction of the horse had other effects. It intensified intertribal warfare. Face-to-face combat on horseback with a bow and arrow, lance, war club, or knife—or a European gun—led to a great increase in casualties. The horse also enabled the Woodland Assiniboines and many of the Woodland Crees to hunt buffalo on the Plains, thus freeing them from their dependence on European guns and trade goods. In general, life became very mobile for the Plains Indians, particularly for the equestrian Blackfoot-speaking tribes. As historian Hugh Dempsey has written, "There were no clear-cut boundaries, and the bands moved according to their needs, often dictated by the location of buffalo herds, the availability of ripe berries in season, the replacing of worn tepee poles in the mountains, the danger of enemy incursions, and problems created by intertribal quarrels."[2]

The Fur Trade after the Fall of New France

After the fall of New France in 1760, the Hudson's Bay Company hoped to enjoy a trade monopoly in the North-West. But the company soon faced new rivals: aggressive Scottish and American traders operating out of Montreal (see Chapter 10). In the early 1770s these traders employed large numbers of voyageurs and sent large shipments of goods to the West.

The entry of so many European intruders onto the Plains led to clashes with the Indian population. In 1779 the Plains Cree attacked an independent trading post on the North Saskatchewan River, killing two traders. Other incidents occurred, including a battle at a post on the Assiniboine River in 1781, in which three traders and thirty Indians died. Only the outbreak of a smallpox epidemic in 1781–82 saved the traders from large-scale Indian retaliation.

In the early 1780s the Montreal traders combined their capital and established a large organization to look after long-distance trade. They formed the North West Company, which soon expanded beyond the limits of the French fur trade to the Peace, Mackenzie, and Columbia river districts.

363

THE EMERGENCE OF A NEW RIVAL: THE NORTH WEST COMPANY

On these expeditions into the interior, the North West company employed experienced French Canadian, Métis, and Iroquois canoemen, because they knew the fur country, the inland routes, and the Native peoples. These hardly voyageurs crossed half a continent. As a rule, they were not big men, as long legs were a definite disadvantage in a birchbark canoe, but they had great strength and endurance. The voyageurs could paddle from twelve to fifteen, even eighteen, hours a day, if they had to. With their light paddles and rapid strokes, they could make forty strokes a minute (one traveller reported counting sixty strokes a minute). They also carried loads of eighty kilograms on their backs over rocky portage trails.

The company underwent great expansion in the 1780s and 1790s. Fur trader Peter Pond led the way for the Montreal merchants in the Athabasca and Peace River country, rich with fur-bearing animals, in 1778. Alexander Mackenzie journeyed down the Mackenzie River in 1789 and reached the Pacific in 1793. The North West Company then opened up the Mackenzie Basin and, later, the Columbia River.

The cost of sending supplies, however, greatly curbed the company's profits. Its great handicap was its long supply line, which stretched from Montreal to Fort Chipewyan on Lake Athabasca (in present-day northern Alberta). The Nor'Wester organization, though, continued to grow and, in 1804, incorporated the XY Company (formed in the late 1790s by independent Montreal fur traders).

364

National Archives of Canada/C-3610.

Hudson's Bay Company employees with their stock and canoes. Voyageurs with a tumpline around their foreheads normally carried two of these forty-kilogram packages of furs or merchandise over a portage.

Rivalry with the North West Company forced the Hudson's Bay Company to go farther inland to obtain the best furs. The expansion of the

The Amerindians' Role in the Fur Trade

For years, many fur trade historians argued that the Amerindians were passive agents in the fur trade, which was quickly dominated by more dynamic European traders. E.E. Rich, for example, in *The Fur Trade and the Northwest to 1857* (Toronto, 1967), wrote that the Indians "Within a decade of their becoming acquainted with European goods, tribe after tribe became utterly dependent on regular European supplies. The bow and arrow went out of use, and the Indian starved if he did not own a serviceable gun, powder, and shot; and in his tribal wars he was even more dependent on European arms" (pp. 102–103). Then, in the 1970s and early 1980s scholars such as Arthur J. Ray, Robin Fisher, Daniel Francis, Toby Morantz, and Paul C. Thistle challenged this traditional interpretation. They underlined the independence of the Natives and their power in the trade. Historian Olive Dickason neatly summarized the new approach to fur-trade history in a review of Paul C. Thistle's *Indian–European Trade Relations in the Lower Saskatchewan River Region to 1840*: "Common to all of these works is the theme that Amerindians were as aware as Europeans in matters of self-interest, and during the early days of the fur trade at least, were able to manipulate matters to their own advantage. As long as they held the monopoly in fur production, they were also able to dictate the terms by which they were willing to trade. It was only when the exploitative nature of the fur trade began to affect the availability of resources, coupled with the widening technological gap that was a consequence of the Industrial Revolution, that

Europeans were able to gain the upper hand" (*Western Canadian Publications Project Newsletter* 21 [May 1987]: 2).

The attack on the old conventional history has corrected many false images, and has led to a new recognition of the importance of the Amerindians' role in the fur trade. Amerindians were partners and initiators, as well as consumers. They became involved in the trade by their own choice. As historian Robin Fisher, in fact, has written about the early maritime fur trade, "The Indians of the northwest coast exercised a great deal of control over the trading relationship and, as a consequence, remained in control of their culture during this early contact period," (*Contact and Conflict: Indian-European Relations in British Columbia, 1774–1890* [Vancouver, 1977], p. 1.). He goes on to add, "Even in these early years, the Indians were not passive objects of exploitation. Rather, they vigorously grew accustomed to the presence of the Europeans, they also became shrewder in trading with them" (p. 4).

The absence of Native peoples' own narratives and points of view remains the great weakness of research into the fur trade. Daniel Francis has suggested that this has perhaps led historians to overemphasize the importance of the trading exchanges. In his *Battle for the West: Fur Traders and the Birth of Western Canada* (Edmonton, 1982), he observes that "the two groups met briefly at the posts to exchange goods, each receiving from the other things it could not produce for itself. Then they parted, the Indians returning to a world the trader never entered or understood, a world with

365

its own patterns of trade, its own religion and social relations, its own wars and alliances ... for the most part traders were peripheral to the real concerns of the Indian people" (p. 62).

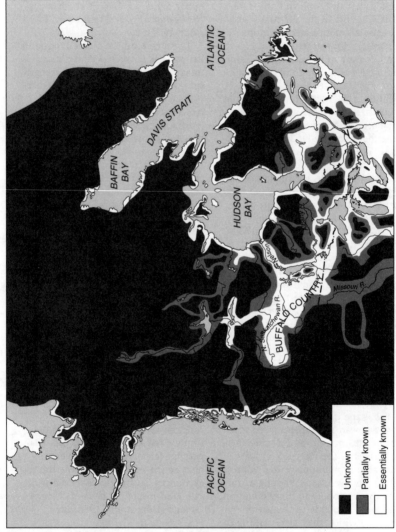

Source: Adapted from Richard I. Ruggles, *A Country So Interesting: The Hudson's Bay Company and Two Centuries of Mapping, 1670–1870* (Montreal and Kingston, 1991), 73.

Non-Natives' knowledge of the territory of present-day Canada in 1795.

European trading networks led to the elimination of the Cree and Assiniboine middlemen, as both the Nor'Westers and the Hudson's Bay Company established direct contact with the hunting bands. Many of the Woodlands Assiniboine and the Woodlands Cree bands moved out onto the Plains and became provisioners, supplying the two trading companies with pemmican (dried buffalo meat mixed with buffalo fat and berries). This highly concentrated food was easy to transport, kept well, and, even without any other supplements, provided a nutritious, balanced diet. The demands of both companies were enormous: a voyageur would consume nearly a kilogram of pemmican a day—the equivalent of approximately three kilograms of fresh meat.

Despite its opponent's great size, the Hudson's Bay Company had the advantage of a shorter, hence less expensive, transportation route, Hudson Bay being much closer than Montreal to the inland posts. The smaller company could take trade goods to the Athabasca country at one-half the cost. The Hudson's Bay Company's cumbersome York boats could also be used on the North Saskatchewan to carry greater amounts of trade goods in, and furs out, than could the Nor'Westers' canoes.

367

Rise of the Métis

French fur traders were well established in the Upper Great Lakes by the 1690s (see Chapter 9). As they intermarried with Indian women, a distinct group of "mixed-bloods," or Métis, appeared. Their culture was a unique blending of the Indians' ways and European customs. The number of mixed marriages grew steadily. After a generation or two, Métis settlements extended from the Upper Great Lakes west to the Red River and south through the Plains to the Arkansas River.

The French and the Métis voyageurs travelled throughout present-day western Canada and the United States. They introduced a number of French words to describe the new terrain: "coulee" (from *coulée*) for a deep gulch or ravine; "butte" for a flat-topped hill; and "prairie" (from *pré*) for meadow. The French also left a permanent record of their presence in the pronunciation of place names—for instance, in the silent terminal "s" of Arkansas and Illinois.

THE MÉTIS AT THE RED RIVER

In the early nineteenth century, encampments of the French and their mixed-blood descendants developed at the junction of the Red and the Assiniboine rivers (at present-day Winnipeg). Increasing numbers of inter-marriages furthered the growth of the "New Nation" of the Métis.

Like the mixed-bloods on the Upper Great Lakes, the Métis built homes of squared logs covered with bark roofs. These descendants of Europeans and Indians made a baking-powder biscuit called "bannock," which is still a staple food in Métis communities today. Although they did farm a little, growing peas and potatoes in small gardens behind their cabins, the early-nineteenth-century Métis lived essentially off the buffalo hunt.

They also adapted European technology to prairie life. In the early nineteenth century they introduced the small wagons used by the French Canadians in Quebec. These "Red River carts," built entirely of wood and tied together with leather, were easy to repair. Although the carts were extremely efficient, the constant rubbing of wood against wood made a terrible noise (one observer described it as the sound of a thousand fingernails being drawn across a thousand panes of glass at the same time) and they gave off clouds of dust that could be seen several kilometres away. To cross a river, one simply took off the wheels, some of which were two metres in diameter, strapped them underneath the cart, and used the vehicle as a raft. The Red River cart aided the Métis during the buffalo hunt. An ox-drawn cart could carry a load of four hundred kilograms more than thirty kilometres in a day. Several carts might be tied together in a caravan, and a driver could handle five oxen and carts. Soon the Red River cart trails running across the prairies rivalled the rivers as transportation routes.

The Métis' blending of French and Indian worlds was also manifested in the development of a new language—French Cree, or, as the Métis called it, "Michif." John C. Crawford, a linguist, has described the language as follows: "The extraordinary characteristic of Michif is the manner in which French and Cree components combine; the noun phrase is a French domain; verb structure is clearly and thoroughly Cree, and syntax is Cree with French and probably English influence."[3] Bungee, an entirely different tongue, evolved among the Amerindians who lived close to the Scottish settlement in the Red River. It was a dialect of English with a strong Cree and Ojibwa component.

By the late eighteenth and early nineteenth centuries, many servants of the North West and Hudson's Bay companies had taken Native wives. Besides companionship, such marriages offered voyageurs economic as well as emotional benefits: a union with the daughter of a leading hunter or chief brought to her new husband the trade of his new father-in-law, as well as of his less-immediate relations. Through the Native women, the men became acquainted with the customs and languages of the tribes, and the women acted as guides and interpreters for their husbands. Moreover, in order to survive, the fur traders needed someone to make pemmican, gather berries, fish, dress skins, and make moccasins and snowshoes. Some traders and voyageurs took several wives.

In the early 1800s marriage between Europeans and Indians was so common that the North West Company was sheltering approximately one thousand women and Métis children at its posts. The North West Company encouraged its labourers to marry the mixed-blood daughters of the older employees. In fact, it eventually forbade its workers to marry full-blood Indian women. The Company sought to reduce the number of dependants at its post, and thereby reduce the demands on it for assistance. Many of the young Métis women had the ideal background for life as wives at a fur-trading post. They were familiar with both the skills of their Indian ancestors and the domestic duties required at the post, including cleaning, planting, and harvesting.

The Métis were not yet considered a distinct community, but they were on the verge of such recognition.

The Selkirk Colony and the Fur Trade Wars

In 1811, Lord Douglas, the Fifth Earl of Selkirk, established an agricultural colony for evicted Scottish tenant farmers at the forks of the Red and the Assiniboine rivers. He had already settled eight hundred displaced Highlanders on Prince Edward Island and had begun a less successful settlement at Baldoon on Lake St. Clair in Upper Canada. After his family purchased control of the Hudson's Bay Company, Selkirk obtained from the company an enormous land grant of three hundred thousand square kilometres in the Red River Valley—an area five times the size of Scotland—that was named Assiniboia. The North West Company protested, because the founding of an agricultural colony in the heart of the Red River might lead to a curtailment of the North West Company's vital supply of Red River pemmican.

369

ESTABLISHMENT OF SELKIRK'S RED RIVER COLONY

The advance party of 18 of Selkirk's settlers reached the Red River from Hudson Bay in late August 1811, and another 120 joined them in late October. Miles Macdonell, Selkirk's choice as governor, established the settlers near the junction of the Red and the Assiniboine rivers (now downtown Winnipeg).

The idealistic but impractical Lord Selkirk had sent them off without ploughs, and they had only hoes and spades to use for cultivation. Their one line of communication stretched back more than a thousand kilometres to a tiny fort on Hudson Bay, visited once a year by ships from Britain. To survive the first winter, the newly arrived colonists had to camp near the Hudson's Bay Company post at Pembina, about 125 km to the south. As for their crops the following year, only the potatoes yielded well. The settlers were forced to spend another rugged Red River winter at Pembina in log huts. Only the generous assistance of the local Métis and North West Company traders allowed the Selkirk settlers to survive those first two years. Then the aggressive Macdonell foolishly antagonized his benefactors, who were already upset by the presence of the newcomers.

Macdonell's "pemmican proclamation" of early January 1814 placed an embargo on the export of pemmican from the Red River. As noted earlier, the North West Company depended on supplies of Red River pemmican to feed its voyageurs. It could not afford to provision its men with food-stuffs from the distant Canadas. The proclamation confirmed the Nor'Wes-ters' suspicions that the Hudson's Bay Company had indeed planted the Red River colony to ruin them. The North West Company retaliated first by approaching the Selkirk settlers and offering them free transport to new homes and better land in Upper Canada. Two-thirds of the two hundred settlers accepted the offer in 1815. After arresting Miles Macdo-nell and forcing the remaining settlers to withdraw, the Nor'Westers burned the settlement. Selkirk, meanwhile, sent more settlers to reoccupy the colony, along with a new governor, Robert Semple.

During the following year (1816), the rivalry between the North West Company and the Hudson's Bay Company intensified as the Nor'Westers plotted to see their rival expelled from the Red River. To achieve their goal they approached the French-speaking Red River Métis. They selected young Cuthbert Grant, then in his early twenties, and three French-speaking mixed-bloods as captains of the Red River Métis. Grant, the son of a Scottish Nor'Wester and a Cree mother, became the leader of an organized movement to drive out the Selkirk colony. Named Captain General of the Métis by the North West Company in 1816, he gathered his forces and then advanced toward the Red River colony. The mixed-bloods believed that they were defending their own identity and group interest in that they were fighting for their rights to the land in the Red River, which they believed they had inherited from their Indian ancestors.

On June 19, 1816, on a battlefield called Seven Oaks, Grant and his men met Governor Robert Semple and twenty-six colonists. Fighting broke out, and Semple and twenty of his men lost their lives. Only one of Grant's men was killed.

The Métis victory sealed the Métis' unity. It reinforced an identity that already existed among the French-speaking mixed-bloods in the Red River. Within hours, the conflict had been retold in a song by the Métis bard Pierre Falcon. That song became the French-speaking mixed-bloods' national anthem. Their collective memory of the victory gave the French-speaking Métis in the Red River a cohesion, and sense of a common identity, that the English-speaking mixed-bloods (called the Country-born) around the Hudson's Bay Company posts to the north, never really acquired.

The violence at Red River in the late 1810s, prompted the British government to suggest a compromise solution: the union of the Hudson's Bay and the North West companies. The consolidated company (to be called the Hudson's Bay Company) immediately abandoned the long canoe routes connecting the interior posts to Montreal in favour of the York boats from Hudson Bay. Under the direction of George Simpson, governor

370

of the vast Northern Department (bounded by Hudson Bay, the Arctic and Pacific oceans, and the Missouri Valley), other changes followed. "The Little Emperor," as his employees nicknamed the red-haired Scot, brought financial order to the new Hudson's Bay Company for the next forty years, until his death in 1860. He introduced strict conservation measures in areas that had been overtrapped, laid off hundreds of redundant employees, kept salaries down, and closed unnecessary posts.

Red River Society in the Mid-Nineteenth Century

The Red River Scottish colonists and mixed-blood farmers faced great environmental challenges. Grasshoppers destroyed their crops in 1818–19, and the great flood of 1826 levelled their settlement. Whenever the Red River overflowed its banks, the water spread quickly over huge areas because of the flatness of the valley. In 1826, in just one day, the flood waters rose nearly three metres, transforming the settlement into a lake. Houses were swept toward Lake Winnipeg. For shelter, the survivors dug cellars on the Plains, roofed them with sod, and lived underground through the winter. Floods would strike the Red River colony twice more during the century, in 1852 and 1882. Frosts destroyed the colony's crops totally or partially at least once every decade from 1810 to 1870.

371

By the 1840s, the settlement was a stable and prosperous community of 6000 inhabitants. It was divided at the junction of the Red and the Assiniboine rivers, with the Métis, who comprised about half the population, residing south and west of the forks of the two rivers. To the north, down the Red River toward Lake Winnipeg, lived the Country-born, the descendants of English-speaking fur traders and their Indian wives. They comprised about a third of the settlement, and their neighbours, the original Selkirk settlers, about a tenth. The Amerindians were also about a tenth of the Red River population.

THE COUNTRY-BORN

The English-speaking mixed-bloods or Country-born, came from Hudson Bay. Many of their European ancestors were from the Orkney Islands, northeast of Scotland. In fact, before 1800, the Hudson's Bay Company recruited more than 80 percent of their personnel there. Most of the employees were under age 21, and they worked as contract labourers for three or four years before returning home. Some, however, remained much longer; a few more than twenty years. These individuals fathered large families before leaving their Native wives and children to retire in the Orkneys or in Scotland. From their savings, a number of the men made provision for their "country wives" and Native children. With the establishment of the Selkirk settlement, however, old employees of the company could retire in the Red River on their savings, with their Native families. An increasing number did so in the 1820s and 1830s.

In the Red River the Hudson's Bay Company men's children, the Country-born, were introduced to farming and many joined the Anglican church. (John West, the colony's first Anglican minister, arrived in 1820.) A few obtained lower-ranked positions in the Hudson's Bay Company (which tended to employ Europeans in the higher-ranked, clerical-managerial posts). Although racial bonds united them with the French-speaking Métis, the Country-born did not mix a great deal with them. Although racial bonds and often the common use of the Cree or Ojibwa languages united them, religion and their place of residence in the Red River divided them.

THE FRENCH-SPEAKING MÉTIS

The French-speaking Métis created a cohesive community focussed, in particular, on their Roman Catholic faith. The arrival of the first French-speaking missionaries in the Red River settlement in 1818, and then the first sisters, the Grey Nuns, in the 1840s, strengthened the Métis' Christian faith as well as their knowledge of the language and culture of their French Canadian ancestors. The Métis also obtained a sense of community through participation in their expanding buffalo hunt.

In the 1840s the Métis went on two annual hunts from the Red River—in June and in September or October. These expeditions included more than a thousand people. The Métis elected ten captains by vote at a general council, one of whom they named "chief of the hunt," or "governor." Each captain had ten "soldiers" under his command who helped the governor of the hunt maintain order. After the election of the officers, regulations were drawn up and proclaimed by the crier to all those in the hunt. Such rules as "no person or party to run buffalo before the general order" show the discipline of the hunt. Discipline was necessary to prevent the premature stampede of the herds and to repulse raids by the Sioux.

THE SAYER TRIAL, 1849

The Métis, the largest group in the Red River colony, came to resent the Hudson's Bay Company's tight control over the settlement. The test case of the Métis' power in the Red River came during the trial of Pierre-Guillaume Sayer, a Métis trader arrested in 1849 on a charge of illegally trafficking in furs. The Hudson's Bay Company insisted that it had a monopoly over selling goods to the colonists and trading with the Indians and that Sayer had violated that monopoly. The Métis, who had not yet left on the spring hunt, organized an informal self-defence committee. Between two hundred and three hundred Métis gathered outside the courthouse. After hearing the evidence, the court found Sayer guilty as charged. The judge, however, imposed no sentence. It would have been difficult to do so, because the Métis hunters constituted the most powerful military force in the colony. When Sayer emerged from the courthouse a free man, the Métis knew that they had broken the Hudson's Bay Company's monopoly. "*Vive la liberté, le commerce est libre,*" they shouted.

THE BATTLE OF GRAND COTEAU, 1851

The second test of the Métis' power came in present-day North Dakota in 1851. As the Métis moved farther to the southwest to hunt buffalo, they came into conflict with the Sioux. The Métis–Sioux wars intensified in the 1840s and came to a head in 1851, at the battle of Grand Coteau ("big hillock"), southeast of present-day Minot, North Dakota. During the confrontation, in which the Métis fought from behind a circular barricade made with their carts, packs, and saddles, at least twenty of the Sioux, but only one Métis, died. The Métis' victory over a numerically larger party of Sioux demonstrated their growing military supremacy in the Red River and surrounding areas.

373

THE END OF THE RED RIVER'S ISOLATION

By the 1840s the Red River Métis had developed a largely self-sufficient economy based on the buffalo hunt, some small-scale farming, and seasonal labour for the Hudson's Bay Company. But it was in the 1850s that the colony's horizons grew enormously, mainly as a result of its more-frequent contacts with Minnesota to the south. From 1851 to 1869 the number of Red River carts journeying to St. Paul, Minnesota, to sell furs and to purchase supplies rose from 100 to 2500. Mail service to the Red River came through St. Paul after 1853, rather than by the slower and more cumbersome route through York Factory on Hudson Bay. A railway reached St. Paul in 1855, and within a year the Hudson's Bay Company used it to bring in supplies. The establishment of a regular steamboat connection with St. Paul and to the Red River in 1859 made the ties with Minnesota (population nearly 200 000 by 1860) all the more binding. Indeed, only the depression of 1857, the American Civil War in 1861–65, and the outbreak of war between the Americans and the Sioux in 1862–64 checked Minnesota's desire to annex the Red River country.

The river settlement changed rapidly in the 1860s. Louis Goulet, a Métis who grew up in the Red River valley during that decade, left a colourful account of the region and the Red River Métis immediately before union with Canada. "Everything had been improved, from transportation to food on the table. Craftsmanship was considerably improved, thanks to superior tools that could now be bought in almost any ordinary general store and at prices most people could afford." Most houses had floors, pane glass windows, and partitioned rooms. Spinning wheels and weaving looms were also present in many Métis homes.

Many Métis moved farther west in the early 1860s in search of buffalo. Those who spent the winter on the Plains to be nearer the herds became known as *hivernants* ("winterers"). The growing Métis involvement in the buffalo-robe trade led them to establish settlements at the forks of the Saskatchewan River, in the North Saskatchewan River valley, in the Cypress Hills area of present-day southwestern Saskatchewan, and at Lac Ste. Anne, about eighty kilometres northwest of Fort Edmonton. Lac Ste. Anne was the largest Métis settlement of the Red River until St. Albert (about fifteen kilometres northwest of Edmonton) was founded in 1862. By the mid-1860s the buffalo herds were so distant from present-day Manitoba that the Red River–based hunt had almost ended.

In 1871 approximately 2000–4000 mixed-bloods lived along the North Saskatchewan River between Red River and the Rockies, and about 11 000 at the junction of the Red and the Assiniboine rivers. The Métis and Country-born population of 13 000–15 000 was approximately one-half of the estimated number of Plains Indians (25 000) in British North America. The mixed-bloods' increasingly frequent intrusions into the Plains Indians' hunting grounds in search of buffalo bred resentment among the Indians.

374

The Plains Indians in the Mid-Nineteenth Century

While the Métis and Country-born population doubled in the Red River every fifteen to twenty years, that of the Plains Indians seriously declined in the mid-nineteenth century. In 1837–38 smallpox once again ravaged the Canadian Plains tribes, just as it had a half century earlier (in 1780–82). Diseases tended to be carried along the trade routes, via the drainage systems of the Missouri and the Saskatchewan rivers. Non-Native crewmen were the carriers of the smallpox viruses. The boat brigades' tight schedules often caused crews to be dispatched while the men were still infectious. They moved into the interior, where Indians were gathered in their large summer camps. Many of the Indians became infected and, in turn, carried the disease farther inland.

The Indians' way of life inadvertently contributed to the spread of the new diseases: as much for warmth as for friendship, they lived in close-knit family groups in very small living areas. The Indians had no idea of how these new diseases were transmitted. As one Peigan Indian told David Thompson, "We had no belief that one Man could give it to another, any more than a wounded Man could give his wound to another."

The idea of quarantine being foreign to them, the Indians insisted on visiting the sick and, in doing so, unknowingly spread the illness. The

Assiniboine population declined by two-thirds, as did that of the Black-foot. Thanks to the efforts of the Hudson's Bay Company traders, however, many of the Cree around the company's posts were saved.

The spread of the epidemic was checked by a smallpox vaccine discovered in Europe around 1800. The Hudson's Bay Company, seeing the Indians fleeing northward, began the first extensive vaccination program among the western Canadian Indians. The vaccinated population constituted an effective barrier, and the highly contagious disease spread no farther north than the Hudson's Bay Company posts on the northern fringes of the Plains. Saved from smallpox, the Cree became the most numerous Indian group on the Canadian Plains. After the epidemic had run its course, the Crees could more readily move farther onto the Plains, since the strength of the Blackfoot-speaking Indians had been so reduced.

Other infectious killer diseases were also rampant, for many Plains Indians had no immunity to the so-called "childhood diseases" of the Europeans. In 1864–65 a winter outbreak of scarlet fever killed more than a thousand Blackfoot-speaking Indians. An epidemic of measles hit the Cree. Influenza and whooping cough also took their toll. Smallpox carried away more than thirty-five hundred Indians, Métis, and Country-born on the Canadian Plains in 1870, because, at this time, little vaccine was on hand. A new disease—tuberculosis—arrived in the 1860s, brought by refugee Sioux from the United States and by Red River people moving west (both groups had already been exposed to the deadly bacteria).

375

ARRIVAL OF THE WHISKEY TRADERS

In the mid-1860s the Blackfoot-speaking tribes experienced another assault in addition to disease—that of the American whiskey traders. In the 1850s and the early 1860s the Blackfoot had traded with both the Hudson's Bay Company and the American Fur Company. At Fort Edmonton and Rocky Mountain House they exchanged pemmican and horses (as well as the few beaver furs they trapped) for British trade goods; they traded bulky buffalo hides and robes (which were difficult for the Hudson's Bay Company to transport profitably in their York boats) for American goods at Fort Benton in Montana. The hides made excellent coats and robes, and they could also be tanned into a very tough and durable leather suitable for making industrial machinery belts. The American Fur Company bought all that it could, shipping the furs down the Missouri by steamer to St. Louis.

The stability of the Missouri River fur trade suddenly ended, however, in 1864 with the collapse of the American Fur Company. Then, just after the end of the American Civil War in 1865, the discovery of gold brought a flood of prospectors and merchants to the mountains of Montana, and with them came a flourishing whiskey trade. After U.S. marshals began to enforce laws against the trade, many of the traders moved north to present-day southern Alberta and Saskatchewan to make their fortunes. Their arrival led to great social disruption among groups that had little acquaintance with alcohol and no social controls in place to deal with its consequences.

Canadians and the North-West

Until the late 1850s the fur traders and the early visitors to the North-West had all reported that the treeless prairies, which stretched as far as the eye could see, were unsuitable for farming. As Wreford Watson, an historical geographer, has noted, "There developed in the minds of Europeans an equation that went a follows: bareness equals barrenness equals infertility equals uselessness for agriculture."[4] This perception changed in the late 1850s, and by the 1860s, Canadians had come to covet the North-West. Good agricultural land was scarce in the United Canadas, and the western lands were most inviting. In the early 1860s both the Canadian and the British expeditions published their findings on their explorations west from Lake Superior to the Rocky Mountains. Of the two, the British-sponsored expedition led by John Palliser is the best known. Dispatched in 1857, it was commissioned to report on the possibilities for agricultural settlement. In the same year, the Canadians sent out an expedition with Henry Youle Hind, a professor of geology and chemistry at Trinity University in Toronto, as scientific observer.

Both expeditions reported that there were magnificent possibilities for European agriculture, particularly in the Red River area and the "fertile belt" of the North Saskatchewan River valley. Here was the incentive for the westward expansion of the eastern British North American colonies.

The fur trade first attracted the French to the North-West, and later the British. Two rival companies in the British period, the Hudson's Bay Company (founded in 1670) and the North West Company (established in the 1780s), vied for monopoly over the fur trade in the region. In 1821 the British government forced a merger of the two companies under the Hudson's Bay Company name. Settlement grew in the area, first at the junction of the Red and the Assiniboine rivers, and later, in the 1860s, farther west, nearer the diminishing buffalo grounds. The intermarriage of fur traders and Indians had led to the creation of two new peoples, the Métis and the Country-born. By the end of the 1860s, these two mixed-blood groups numbered 13 000–15000 in the British North-West, more than half the estimated Plains Indian population of 25 000. It was the Métis, with their group assuredness of constituting "a new nation," who would confront the Canadians when they tried to take control of the region in the late 1860s.

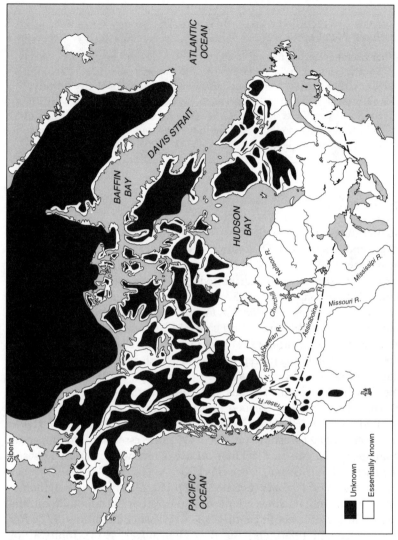

377

Source: Adapted from Richard I. Ruggles, *A Country So Interesting: The Hudson's Bay Company and Two Centuries of Mapping, 1670–1870* (Montreal and Kingston, 1991), 119.

Non-Natives' knowledge of the territory of present-day Canada in 1870.

NOTES

[1] Hugh A. Dempsey, *Big Bear* (Vancouver, 1984), 48.
[2] Hugh A. Dempsey, *Red Crow* (Saskatoon, 1980), 7.
[3] John C. Crawford, "What Is Michif?: Language in the Métis Tradition," in *The New Peoples: Being and Becoming Métis in North America*, edited by Jacqueline Peterson and Jennifer S.H. Brown (Winnipeg, 1985), 233.
[4] Wreford Watson, "The Role of Illusion in North American Geography: A Note on the Geography of North American Settlement," *The Canadian Geographer* 13 (Spring 1969): 16.

> *Related Readings*
>
> Four useful essays on this topic appear in R. Douglas Francis and Donald B. Smith, *Readings in Canadian History: Pre-Confederation*, 3d ed. (Toronto, 1990): Arthur J. Ray, "Fur Trade History as an Aspect of Native History," 51–63; Sylvia Van Kirk, " 'Women in Between': Indian Women in Fur Trade Society in Western Canada," 64–78; John C. Ewers, "Indian Views of the White Man Prior to 1850: An Interpretation," 444–57; and D.N. Sprague, "The Red River Settlement to 1869," 457–71.

BIBLIOGRAPHY

378

The literature on the North-West is voluminous. For the archaeological background, see Olive P. Dickason's "A Historical Reconstruction for the Northwestern Plains," *Prairie Forum* 5 (1980): 19–37, reprinted in *The Prairie West: Historical Readings*, edited by R. Douglas Francis and Howard Palmer (Edmonton, 1985), 39–57. A popular guide to the archaeological story is Liz Bryan's *The Buffalo People: Prehistoric Archaeology on the Canadian Plains* (Edmonton, 1991). Gerald Friesen's *The Canadian Prairies: A History* (Toronto, 1984) provides an excellent overview of the entire period. Changing perceptions of the North-West are reviewed by R. Douglas Francis in *Images of the West* (Saskatoon, 1989).

For information on the Indians in the eighteenth and nineteenth centuries, consult Arthur Ray, *Indians in the Fur Trade* (Toronto, 1974). John Ewers' history, *The Blackfeet* (Norman, 1958), and his *The Horse in Blackfoot Indian Culture* (Washington, D.C., 1955) are essential. The impact of the horse and the gun on Blackfoot culture is reviewed by Oscar Lewis in *The Effects of White Contact Upon Blackfoot Culture: With Special Reference to the Role of the Fur Trade* (Seattle, 1942). Hugh Dempsey's biographies of three Plains Indian chiefs offer a vivid portrait of Blackfoot, Blood, and Cree life in the nineteenth century: see *Crowfoot* (Edmonton, 1972), *Red Crow* (Saskatoon, 1980), and *Big Bear* (Vancouver, 1984). John Milloy reviews the history of the Cree from 1790 to 1870 in *The Plains Cree* (Winnipeg, 1987). In his provocative monograph, *Eighteen-Century Western Cree and their Neighbours* (Ottawa, 1991), Dale R. Russell questions the statement that the Cree and the Assiniboine only came out onto the Plains after their contact with the European fur traders. A fascinating eyewitness account of the Chipewyan is Samuel Hearne's famous *A Journey from Prince of Wales' Fort, in Hudson's Bay, to the Northern Ocean*, published in 1795; see the edition edited by Richard Glover (Toronto, 1958). The collection *Native Peoples: The Canadian Experience*, edited by R. Bruce Morrison and C. Roderick Wilson (Toronto, 1986), contains the following useful articles on the western Canadian Indian: Jennifer Brown, "Northern

Algonquians from Lake Superior and Hudson Bay to Manitoba in the Historical Period," 208–36, and Hugh A. Dempsey, "The Blackfoot Indians," 404–35. For information on the health of the Plains Indians, see G. Graham-Cumming, "Health of the Original Canadians, 1867–1967," *Medical Services Journal of Canada* 23, 2 (1967): 115–66.

E.E. Rich provides an overview of the fur trade in western Canada in *The Fur Trade and the North West to 1857* (Toronto, 1967), as does Frits Pannekoek, *The Fur Trade and Western Canadian Society, 1670–1870*, Canadian Historical Association, Historical Booklet no. 43 (Ottawa, 1987). For a review of the way of life of the fur trade's canoemen, see Grace Lee Nute, *The Voyageur* (New York, 1931). Glyndwr Williams has written a short survey, "The Hudson's Bay Company and the Fur Trade: 1670–1870," *The Beaver*, outfit 314:2 (Autumn 1983): 4–86. Another interesting survey is that by Dan Francis, *Battle for the West: Fur Traders and the Birth of Western Canada* (Edmonton, 1982). The French experience on the western Plains during the French regime is reviewed by W.J. Eccles in "La Mer de l'Ouest: Outpost of Empire," in *Essays on New France* (Toronto, 1987), 96–109. British contact is discussed in Arthur J. Ray, "The Northern Great Plains: Pantry of the Northeastern Fur Trade, 1774–1885," *Prairie Forum* 9, 2 (1984): 263–80. For short sketches of the most important European fur traders, see the essays on Kelsey, La Vérendrye, Henday, Hearne, Thompson, and others in the multivolume *Dictionary of Canadian Biography* (Toronto, 1966–). Studies of specific regions include Paul C. Thistle, *Indian–European Trade Relations in the Lower Saskatchewan River Region to 1840* (Toronto, 1986) and John Foster, "The Home Guard Cree and the Hudson's Bay Company: The First Hundred Years," in *Native People, Native Lands: Canadian Indians, Inuit and Métis*, edited by Bruce Alden Cox (Ottawa, 1988), 107–16.

The Métis are the subject of numerous studies. One popular work is D. Bruce Sealey and Antoine S. Lussier, *The Métis: Canada's Forgotten People* (Winnipeg, 1975). A helpful overview is that by John Foster, "The Plains Métis," in *Native Peoples: The Canadian Experience*, edited by Morrison and Wilson, 375–403. The edited work *Native People, Native Lands*, edited by Cox, contains two interesting articles on the Métis: Herman Sprenger's "The Métis Nation: Buffalo Hunting versus Agriculture in the Red River Settlement, 1810–1870," 120–35, and Jennifer S.H. Brown, "The Métis: Genesis and Rebirth," 136–47. George Woodcock has recently translated Marcel Giraud's Classic *Le Métis Canadien* (Paris, 1945) into English, under the title *The Métis in the Canadian West*, 2 vols. (Edmonton, 1986). Jacqueline Peterson and Jennifer S.H. Brown have edited *The New People: Being and Becoming Métis in North America* (Winnipeg, 1985). In *Cuthbert Grant of Grantown* (Toronto, 1963), M.A. MacLeod and W.L. Morton recount the life story of the first prominent leader among the Plains Métis. Guillaume Charette's *Vanishing Spaces: Memoirs of a Prairie Métis* (Winnipeg, 1980) contains the memoirs of Louis Goulet, who was born in the Red River valley in 1859. D.N. Sprague reviews Red River Métis history in his introduction to *The Genealogy of the First Métis Nation: The Development and Dispersal of the Red River Settlement, 1820–1900*, compiled by D.N. Sprague and R.P. Frye (Winnipeg, 1983), 11–28. Gerhard Ens reviews the movement of the Métis westward in "Dispossession or Adaptation? Migration and persistence of the Red River Metis, 1835–1890," Canadian Historical Association, *Historical Papers* (1988), 120–44.

Frits Pannekoek discusses Red River society in his essay "The Anglican Church and the Disintegration of Red River Society, 1818–1870," in *The West and the Nation: Essays in Honour of W.L. Morton*, edited by Carl Berger and Ramsay Cook (Toronto, 1976), 72–90, and, at greater length, in his *A Snug Little Flock: The Social Origins of the Riel Resistance, 1869–70* (Winnipeg, 1991). Contrary conclusions about Red River society are reached by Irene Spry in "The Métis and Mixed-Bloods of Rupert's Land before 1870," in *The New Peoples: Being and Becoming Métis in North America*, edited by Peterson and Brown, 95–118.

380

The subject of Native women and the fur trade is told by Jennifer S.H. Brown in *Strangers in Blood: Fur Trade Company Families in Indian Country* (Vancouver, 1980), and by Sylvia Van Kirk in *"Many Tender Ties": Women in Fur Trade Society in Western Canada* (Winnipeg, 1980). The first chapter, "The Founding Mothers," in Alison Prentice et al., *Canadian Women: A History* (Toronto, 1988): 17–40, provides a good overview.

For an introduction to the northernmost area of the North-West in this period consult Keith J. Crowe's *A History of the Original Peoples of Northern Canada* (revised edition, Montreal and Kingston, 1991). The story of Arctic exploration in the mid-nineteenth century is well-told in Hugh N. Wallace, *The Navy, the Company, and Richard King: British Exploration in the Canadian Arctic, 1829–1860* (Montreal, 1980). Valuable maps of the North-West appear in R. Cole Harris, ed. *Historical Atlas of Canada*, vol. 1, *From the Beginning to 1800* (Toronto, 1987); and in Richard I. Ruggles, *A Country So Interesting: The Hudson's Bay Company and Two Centuries of Mapping 1670–1870* (Montreal and Kingston, 1991).

Time Line: 1690–1867

1690 —Henry Kelsey, a Hudson's Bay Company employee, sets out on a journey into the interior of North America.

1730s —Pierre La Vérendrye establishes French posts around lakes Winnipeg and Winnipegosis.

1761 —French traders withdraw from the interior as a result of the French capitulation at Montreal.

1774 —The Spanish expedition led by Juan Pérez encounters the Haida off the Queen Charlotte Islands.

1778 —Captain Cook visits Nootka Sound on the west coast of Vancouver Island.

1780s —Formation of the North West Company.

1793 —The Pacific coastline mapped by George Vancouver for the Royal Navy.

—Fur trader Alexander Mackenzie becomes the first to cross the continent, from Lake Athabasca to the Pacific Ocean.

1811–1812 —Establishment of the Selkirk colony in the Red River.

1816 —Battle of Seven Oaks.

1818 —49th parallel becomes the boundary line between American and British claims from Lake Superior west to the Rockies.

1821 —Union of the Hudson's Bay Company and the North West Company.

1827 —Fort Langley is built by the Hudson's Bay Company near the mouth of the Fraser River.

1843 —The Hudson's Bay Company builds Fort Victoria on Vancouver Island.

1846 —Under the Oregon Treaty, the 49th parallel becomes the international boundary between British and American claims from the Rockies to the Pacific Ocean.

1849 —The colony of Vancouver Island is established by the Hudson's Bay Company on the request of the British Crown.

—Free trade obtained at the Red River.

1851	—Battle of Grand Coteau between the Métis and the Sioux.
1858	—The Fraser River gold rush leads to the establishment on the mainland of the colony of British Columbia, separate from the colony of Vancouver Island.
1862	—Construction of the Cariboo Road begins.
1866	—The two colonies of British Columbia and Vancouver Island are united.
1867	—The United States purchases Alaska from Russia.

CHAPTER NINETEEN

The Pacific Coast to the 1860s

The northwestern coast of North America remained unexplored by Europeans until the 1770s. The Indian population of present-day British Columbia lived alone along the major salmon rivers, at scattered village sites along the ocean, and inland along the Fraser, Bella Coola, Skeena, and Nass rivers.

Initially, Spain, Russia, Britain, and the United States competed for control of the North Pacific coast. Eventually, however, the sector between Russian Alaska and Spanish California was disputed by only Britain and the United States, which in 1818 agreed to joint occupancy of the area. In 1846 the two countries consented to extend the international border along the 49th parallel from the prairies to the Pacific, and to include Vancouver Island in Britain's jurisdiction.

Immigrants first settled at the southern tip of Vancouver Island in the 1840s and then at the mouth of the Fraser River during the gold rush of 1858. In the 1860s these immigrants claimed ownership of the entire coast and interior of British Columbia.

The Northwest Coast Indians

The Indians had been living on the Pacific Coast for thousands of years. One of the oldest archaeological sites in the Fraser River Canyon dates back at least 8500 years. The Indians probably arrived in successive waves, for five Native linguistic families are represented on the British Columbia coast today. Hemmed in by towering mountains, the narrow coastline was heavily populated. It is estimated that nearly half of the total Indian population of Canada lived in British Columbia at the moment of European contact. For these maritime people, salmon was the main food resource. Red cedar was used for the construction of their plank houses, canoes, containers, and carved masks, as well as of their most famous objects of all—totem poles.

NOTIONS OF PROPERTY

In several respects the Northwest Coast Indians' notion of property was similar to that of the Europeans. The primary unit of their society was a large group of kinsmen, or a lineage—a group of people who shared a common ancestor in the real or mythological past. One or several kin groups might occupy the same winter village, and these villages in turn constituted independent units within the larger tribe. Local kin groups claimed ownership of the fishing stations, berry patches, cedar groves, and stretches of beach. When they left their permanent winter villages for the salmon fisheries, they went to their own recognized stretches of the salmon rivers. When the Europeans came, the chiefs or leaders of the kin groups made them pay for the wood and even the fresh water they used.

384

THE POTLATCH AND SOCIAL STRUCTURE

Indian society had a hierarchical social structure. An elaborate stratification existed among the local Indian kin groups. At the bottom stood the slaves, acquired in war or by purchase, and then above them, in a very careful ranking, everyone else. Anthropologist Philip Drucker confirms that "each society consisted not of two or more social classes, but of a complex series of statuses graded relatively, one for each individual of the group."[1] The ranking existed for functions such as the potlatch, which involved a distribution of gifts according to each person's position.

European society had no direct equivalent for the potlatch. Anthropologist Wilson Duff has described it as "a large gathering to which important people were invited in order to witness some event, such as a young person assuming a new name or the completion of a new house and erection of a totem pole. On such an occasion the host would display his wealth and present gifts to his guests. The more he gave away, the more prestige he acquired."[2] Honour came in giving, not in receiving. In the late nineteenth century European missionaries succeeded in outlawing the potlatch ceremonies. They regarded them as an immoral squandering of wealth and a barrier to converting Indians to Christianity.

The Northwest Coast Indians had other unique traditions. Each local Indian kin group, for example, had identifiable privileges indicating its members' common origins. One lineage of the Nimpkish, a village group among the Kwakiutl, believed themselves descended from a giant halibut and a thunderbird that transformed themselves into men. This lineage had the right to display the thunderbird and the halibut as crests on their houses, dance blankets, and painted screens. Today, the Nimpkish can point out the rock where the thunderbird first landed.[3] The kin group also had the right to specific prerogatives in their intricate ceremonial system, such as the right to certain names, songs, and dances.

IMPRESSIONS OF THE EUROPEANS

Two centuries ago the Northwest Coast Indians were mystified by the white strangers' arrival. Well into the early twentieth century, the Squamish Indians of the Capilano reserve at Vancouver had an oral tradition about the first time their ancestors encountered the newcomers a century and a half earlier. As Chief Mathias told the story, the warriors hesitated for a long time about boarding the floating island with cobwebs hanging from the sticks growing on it, until, with great misgivings, the bravest climbed the rope ladder onto the deck. The pale-faced captain who looked like a corpse advanced with outstretched hand. Never having heard of the handshake, the chief thought they were being challenged to an Indian finger wrestling match. He therefore waved away the man with whom the captain was trying to shake hands and called for the Squamish strong-man to accept the challenge. Seeing he was misunderstood, the captain shrugged and approached the chief with outstretched hand. The chief then said to the strong-man, "He doesn't want you. He thinks you are not strong enough." With that, the chief refused to consider the captain's "challenge." The strangers' gifts also greatly puzzled Mathias's ancestors. It appeared to them that they had received snow in a sack (flour) and buttons (coins).

385

THE ARRIVAL OF THE SPANISH

Spain reached the Pacific before any other European power. Nevertheless, it took the Spanish two and a half centuries to advance northward from Mexico. In effect, their expansion ended after the conquest of Mexico and Central and South America—huge territories with great populations. Apostolos Valerianos, a Greek pilot who spent forty years in the Spanish service in the Americas, better known by his Spanish name of Juan de Fuca, allegedly sailed north along the Pacific coast and discovered, in 1590, a vast gulf or wide inlet between the 47th and 48th parallels that led into a broader sea with many islands. Fuca believed this to be the western outlet of the fabled Straits of Anian, a body of water that could provide a convenient, practical sea passage between Europe and Asia. But the Spanish took so little interest in the expedition they had sponsored that they failed to preserve any authentic record of it, and only Fuca's later statement that he made the voyage survives.

Crippled by depressions, epidemics, and defeats on European battlefields, Spain lost its pioneering spirit. Rival European empires had seized Spanish islands in the West Indies, but luckily for Spain, its European rivals seldom ventured to the Pacific, until the Russians arrived there in the eighteenth century.

RUSSIAN ACTIVITY IN THE NORTH PACIFIC

The first documented Russian voyage to Alaska was that of Vitus Bering, a Danish navigator in the Russian service. In 1728 he built a ship and sailed along the eastern coast of Siberia until he found the strait that now bears his name. On another voyage, in 1741, he reached North America and explored an area in present-day southeastern Alaska. His return, however, proved disastrous: the sixty-year-old mariner died of scurvy after having been shipwrecked on an island off the Siberian coast. It was this ill-fated voyage that first established Russia's claim to the Alaskan Panhandle.

Bering's last voyage led to Russian economic expansion in the Pacific. The survivors from Bering's ship brought with them to the mainland a cargo of nine hundred sea-otter pelts. In Chinese markets, these brought high prices, since the Chinese upper classes prized the furs for their warmth and their glossy beauty. Within a half-century, the highly profitable sea-otter trade led to an international rivalry among Russia, Spain, and later Britain and the United States.

Rumours of Russian activity prompted Spain to advance northward to protect Mexico. In 1767 the Spanish developed a major port at San Blas on Mexico's west coast and established settlements in California at San Diego, Monterey, and San Francisco. They also sponsored expeditions to investigate Russian advances along the northern coast and to assert Spanish sovereignty north of Mexico. Juan Pérez sailed from San Blas in late January 1774 to Alaska, but bad weather caused him to turn back in Alaskan waters just north of the Queen Charlotte Islands. Pérez met 150 Haida Indians off the Queen Charlottes, the first recorded meeting between Europeans and British Columbian Indians. The meeting was friendly, and the Spaniards traded small shipboard objects for Indian artifacts (which are now displayed in the Museo de América in Madrid).

THE ARRIVAL OF THE BRITISH

In place of the Russians, the British became the Spaniards' greatest threat in the late 1770s. Captain James Cook, already renowned for his discoveries in Australasia and Antarctica, visited the North Pacific Coast on his third expedition to the Pacific. As a young man, the distinguished naval officer had been present at the French surrender of Louisbourg in 1758 and had helped to guide the English armada to Quebec in 1759.

In the spring of 1778 Cook's two vessels, *Discovery* and *Resolution*, arrived at Nootka Sound, sighted by Pérez four years earlier. Here, Cook spent a month re-fitting his ships. Since no other European power knew

Collection: Museo de América 13.042.

A Haida artifact (43 mm in height, 69 mm in length) made from the tooth of a sperm whale. The duck's wings are folded and the feet drawn up. On the wings is a totemic figure. Juan Pérez encountered Haida Indians off the Queen Charlotte Islands in 1774. This was the first contact between the Amerindians of the Northwest Coast and the Europeans. Pérez acquired the artifact by trade from a Haida woman who was wearing the tiny ornament around her neck. It and other pieces were sent to the Spanish king. About half of the objects acquired during this encounter are now in the Museo de América in Madrid. (Our thanks to John Kendrick of Vancouver for his help in securing a copy of this illustration.)

of the Spaniards' previous visit, Cook (who was killed in January 1779 by natives in Hawaii) received credit as Nootka's discoverer, and the British claim to the North Pacific Coast received international recognition.

To strengthen their claim to the North Pacific, the Spanish in 1789 established a colony at Nootka Sound and maintained a garrison of 200–250 men there for six years, with only a brief absence during the winter of 1789–90. The Nootka Sound Controversy, as it became known, brought Spain and Britain to the brink of war. Spain argued that it had the exclusive right to trade and to control the coast, while Britain claimed that navigation was open to any nation. But in 1795 Spain agreed to share the northern ports and resources because it badly needed British assistance in its war against France. Thus ended Spain's attempts to exert a Spanish presence north of California. Today, about one hundred geographical names, such as "Valdes" and the "Galiano" Islands, remain to remind us of the early Spanish expeditions.

The Maritime and Inland Fur Trade

The publication in 1784 of the official account of James Cook's third voyage was a turning point in the international contest for the Northwest Coast. Captain James King, who had taken command shortly after the death of Cook, recounted in *A Voyage to the Pacific Ocean* (1784) how sea-otter pelts obtained in trade on the Northwest Coast had brought as much as $120 each at Canton, China. Other mariners saw their opportunity to make their fortunes. The first was the sea captain James Hanna, who sailed in a British vessel appropriately named *Sea Otter*. Several British and American ships followed. In 1784 the Russians had established a base at Three Saints Harbour on Kodiak Island in the Gulf of Alaska. North of the present-day Alaskan boundary the Russians encountered intense British and American competition for sea-otter pelts.

The withdrawal of Spain in the mid-1790s left the Northwest Coast open to three contenders: Russia, Britain, and the newly independent United States. The Russian traders, however, laboured under several major handicaps. In contrast to both the Americans and the English, they possessed fewer and poorer trade goods and inferior trading vessels. The Russian advance slowed down in the Alaskan Panhandle, where they faced strong competition from British and American traders and from the Tlingit Indians, who acted as middlemen, trading European goods to the interior bands in the present-day Yukon and northwestern British Columbia.

Britain strengthened its claim to the Northwest Coast with the dispatch of a three-year expedition under George Vancouver, a naval officer who had served with Cook's expedition in 1778. From 1792 to 1794 Vancouver methodically and painstakingly charted the intricate coastline from Oregon to Alaska. This thorough survey proved that Juan de Fuca Strait was not the entrance to the great inland sea that Fuca had reported. Vancouver later wrote in *Voyage of Discovery to the North Pacific Ocean*: "I trust the precision with which the survey ... has been carried into effect, will remove every doubt, and set aside every opinion of a *northwest passage*, or any water communication navigable for shipping, existing between the north pacific, and the interior of the American continent, within the limits of our researches."

Before leaving the Northwest Coast the navigator named the huge island now known as Vancouver Island "Quadra's and Vancouver's Island" (sharing the honour with his friend, Juan Francisco de la Bodega y Quadra, the Spanish Commander at Nootka Sound). Later, it became known simply as Vancouver's Island, and finally as Vancouver Island.

The outbreak of war between Britain and France in 1793, which lasted until 1815, curtailed British voyages to the Northwest Coast. As Britain withdrew seamen from its merchant ships for service in the Royal Navy, American entrepreneurs captured Britain's trade in the North Pacific.

After the mid-1790s, American traders dominated the coastal trade until the mid-1820s, by which time the sea otter was virtually extinct due to over-hunting.

THE INDIANS AND THE MARITIME FUR TRADERS

The Indians welcomed the Maritime fur traders with their iron trading goods. They wanted the metals out of which the European tools were made in order to construct their own. The Spanish, in fact, discovered that the Indians coveted iron so much that they even took off the metal strapping on the sides of the ships. Not even the rudder chains were safe. The Indians horrified the friars when they tore down a large cross to take out the nails that held it together.

In addition to iron goods, the Indians bought cloth, clothing, and blankets. They also developed a liking for rum, smoking tobacco, and molasses. In addition, they wanted muskets. The Indians paid careful attention to the quality of goods they purchased and refused iron that contained flaws or was too brittle.

389

Often the Indians whom the traders met were middlemen who added their own markup to the furs and goods they traded. Women traders also participated actively in the transactions with the white newcomers. Although the linguistic diversity of the Pacific Coast exceeded that of Europe, a single trade language called the Chinook jargon came into use along the west coast in the 1830s. It was spoken as well in the inland districts, and the middlemen knew that language. Indians on the coast traded European goods to interior groups at 200–300 percent markups. The coastal Indians initially exercised considerable control over the early European fur trade, preventing the Europeans from coming into contact with the inland groups. The entry around 1810 of the fur traders into the interior, however, took away much of the Indian middleman's trade.

The fur trade enriched the coastal Indians' culture. The tools they made from their new supplies of iron allowed them to produce better and more refined ceremonial headdresses, costumes, and masks for feasts and ceremonials. In addition to the new tools, new dyes and pigments became available through the traders. Although the Indian carvers favoured the traditional colours, weavers began to supplement the original pigments— red and yellow ochres, black and blue-green copper oxide—with the whole spectrum of European trade colours. Wood carving expanded. During these years the totem poles, which displayed individual families' genealogies, underwent much elaboration and were built to greater heights.

THE INLAND FUR TRADE

After European navigators had reached the Northwest Coast by sea, European fur traders arrived by land. Anxious to find a short supply line to the

Pacific, the North West Company searched for a new route westward from Lake Athabasca to the Pacific. The Nor'Wester Alexander Mackenzie, the first European to canoe the northern river that now bears his name and reach the Arctic Ocean, completed the first crossing of North America (north of Mexico) in 1793 by travelling down the Fraser River, then over to the Bella Coola River, and down to the Pacific. The arduous route proved useless for transporting furs, but the journey made the twenty-four-year-old Mackenzie's reputation as one of the most fearless and daring of trader-explorers.

Two other Nor'Westers worked to find a commercial route to the Pacific. In 1808, Simon Fraser, who had first opened up fur-trading posts in the interior of present-day British Columbia, travelled with a small party down the treacherous river that would be named after him. He succeeded, but the route was unnavigable.

Finally, in 1811, David Thompson, a partner of the North West Company, followed the Columbia River, and thereby connected the North West Company trade route from east of the Rockies to the Pacific Coast. Meanwhile, a sea expedition sent by John Jacob Astor's Pacific Fur Company had arrived in late March 1811, several months before Thompson. On the basis of having founded Fort Astoria, the Americans claimed the Oregon country.

JOINT OCCUPATION OF OREGON TERRITORY

As a temporary compromise, Britain and America agreed in 1818 to occupy the Columbia country jointly and to decide its fate later. The agreement left commerce open to both British and American traders between latitudes 42° and 54°40′ (from the northern boundary of California to the southern limits of Alaska).

With the merger of the North West Company and the Hudson's Bay Company in 1821, the new Hudson's Bay Company under the management of Sir George Simpson began to exploit the rich fur resources of the Northwest Coast. Having obtained from the British Crown a twenty-one-year lease to the trade in the "Indian Territory" (the lands between the Rocky Mountains and the Pacific), George Simpson located a Pacific depot at Fort Vancouver, 150 km up the Columbia River. Other forts followed. The three most important were Fort Langley, near the mouth of the Fraser River, built in 1827; Fort Simpson, on the boundary of the Russian territory to the north, in 1831; and Fort Victoria, strategically located on the southern tip of Vancouver Island, in 1843. The Hudson's Bay Company's energetic commercial activities thus established a strong British presence on the Pacific Coast.

American interest in the Columbia country mounted in the early 1840s. American adventurers began arriving in the 1830s and by 1843 numbered about one thousand. Over the next three years, another five thousand

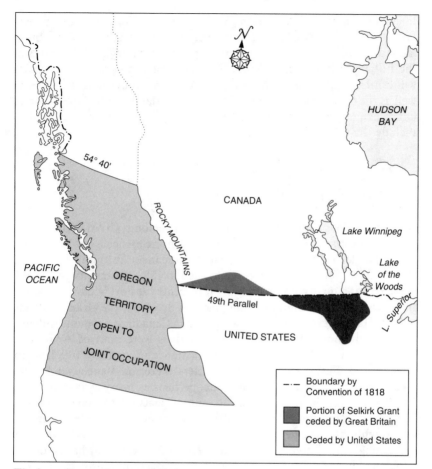

The boundary settlement of 1818.

settlers arrived in the Columbia River valley. But thanks to the Hudson's Bay Company's network of posts, inland trails, and shipping routes, Britain dominated north of the Columbia River. Nevertheless, American president James Polk, who came into office in 1845 with an electoral promise of "54°40' or fight," demanded all of "Oregon," up to the Russian border.

Fortunately for Britain's claim, however, the Americans began a war with Mexico in 1846 and Polk did not want a war on two fronts. An obliging Britain also retracted its claim to all the land south of the Columbia River. The Anglo-American treaty signed in June 1846 extended the 49th parallel (which had become the international border across the Plains in 1818) from the Rockies to the Pacific, and left all of Vancouver Island in British hands.

Anxious to counter the threat of American squatter settlement in its Pacific territory, the British government asked the Hudson's Bay Company to colonize, as well as to manage, Vancouver Island for ten years. A royal grant of 1849 stipulated that the company had to develop the island, make lands available to settlers at reasonable prices, and safeguard the rights of the Indians. By the end of 1849, Fort Victoria served as the company's western headquarters, its shipping depot, and its provisioning centre, as well as the capital of the colony of Vancouver Island. In 1852 the Colonial Office extended the jurisdiction of the governor of Vancouver Island to include the Queen Charlotte Islands.

On The Eve of the Gold Rushes

In the mid-1850s approximately one thousand colonists lived in the Pacific colony. The discovery of coal at Nanaimo on the east coast of Vancouver Island had led to the founding of a small permanent European settlement there. But until the Fraser River gold rush in 1858, the colony continued primarily as a fur-trading region, with its centre at Fort Victoria. The fur traders included immigrants from places as diverse as the Orkney Islands and the Hawaiian Islands, along with French Canadians, Iroquois Indians, and mixed-bloods. Many of the non-Natives were married to Indian, Country-born, or Métis women. The existence of virtually free land in Oregon and Washington attracted settlers there; on Vancouver Island, land had to be purchased. At the time, perhaps as many as two hundred Europeans lived in the various fur-trading posts on the mainland. On Vancouver Island and the mainland, the Indians outnumbered the Europeans roughly fifty to one.

Although the Native peoples of the Northwest Coast may have enjoyed a higher standard of living after European contact, they also began to die in large numbers. The absence of accurate statistics makes it difficult to provide even rough estimates of the casualties, but diseases such as measles, mumps, and, especially, smallpox and tuberculosis took their toll, as they did elsewhere in the Americas upon European contact. Anthropologist Wilson Duff estimates that the smallpox epidemic that started in Victoria in 1862 killed about one-third of the Native population within two years.[4] Some historians argue that no evidence exists to prove that the losses were this high, but they do not deny the actual occurrence of the epidemic or its catastrophic impact on Native society.

JAMES DOUGLAS AS GOVERNOR OF VANCOUVER ISLAND

James Douglas became governor of the colony of Vancouver Island in 1851, replacing Richard Blanchard, the first governor, who resigned one year after arriving in Fort Victoria. A "Scotch West Indian," Douglas was born in British Guiana, South America, the son of "a free coloured woman" and a Scottish merchant. Sent to Scotland for his schooling at the age of twelve, James later left school and joined the North West Company as an apprentice four years later. After the union of the two rival companies, he entered northern "Oregon," or New Caledonia, as the company called it. There, in 1828, he married Amelia Connolly, the Métis daughter of fur trader William Connolly and his Cree wife. In 1830 the company transferred James to Fort Vancouver, and nine years later the industrious and capable employee became chief factor. With his promotion to Victoria in 1849, he became the senior company officer west of the mountains.

JAMES DOUGLAS'S INDIAN POLICY

Douglas refused to intervene in quarrels among the Indians, but he did use his power, including the Royal Navy's gunboats, to settle disputes between Europeans and Indians. Shortly before he became governor, Douglas wrote that in all his dealings with Indians, he had "invariably acted on the principle that it is inexpedient and unjust to hold *tribes* responsible for the acts of *individuals*." The governor meted out stern discipline to individuals he perceived as warranting such treatment, but not to their communities. Unlike many of the early settlers on the island, Douglas tried to understand Indian society. Above all, he did not want the open warfare that had broken out between the American settlers and the Indians in Washington to spill over the border.

393

Anxious to avoid conflict between the Indians and the settlers, Douglas purchased the Indians' land before settlement occurred. Between 1850 and 1854, he made fourteen treaties with groups living in areas that Europeans wanted to settle. The governor purchased, in total, roughly one thousand square kilometres of land, or about 3 percent of the total area of Vancouver Island. Douglas allowed the Indians to select the land they wanted for their reserves and instructed the surveyors to meet the Indians' wishes:

> To include in each reserve the permanent Village sites, the fishing stations, and Burial grounds, cultivated land and all the favorite resorts of the Tribes, and in short to include every piece of ground to which they had acquired an equitable title through continuous occupation, tillage, or other investment of their labour.

In hindsight, Douglas was not terribly generous with the amount of land allotted to reserves on both Vancouver Island and later on the mainland. Just before he retired as governor of the mainland colony of British Columbia in 1864, he told the legislature, "The areas thus partially defined and set apart, in no case exceed the proportion of ten acres (4 ha) for each family concerned." On the Plains in the 1870s the Canadian standard would be 640 acres (256 ha) of reserve land per Amerindian family.

Some of the white settlers complained that although the governor might handle Indians well, he not handle the colonists properly. They protested that Douglas had not carried out his obligation to settle the island, that he ruled autocratically, and that he relied too heavily on the company's officials for advice. Most of all, they objected to his setting the price of land at £1 for one acre (two-fifths of a hectare) when land in the neighbouring American Pacific Northwest could be occupied at one quarter the price.

When settlement on Vancouver Island grew in the late 1850s, Douglas continued to make determined efforts to purchase the Indians' land and to set aside reserves in the areas the settlers were moving into. Want of funds, however, made the process more difficult. In 1858 the governor left the Hudson's Bay Company and no longer had access to the company's storehouses. Moreover, the Indians wanted larger payments for their lands, as they had come to realize its true value to the newcomers. The Vancouver Island House of Assembly, established in 1856, looked to Britain to loan it money for Indian land payments. The Colonial Office refused and replied that the funds should be raised locally. As the colonial legislature considered itself unable to buy out Indian title on Vancouver Island, they gave the Indians no compensation for their lands after 1859. The government of Vancouver Island (and later British Columbia) set aside Indian reserves without extinguishing the Indians' title to the land.

Gold Rushes

Repercussions from the discovery of gold on the lower Fraser River in 1858 worried James Douglas. When word of the new mining field reached California in the spring of 1858, the rush began. Nine years earlier, in 1849, eighty thousand people had flocked to the California gold fields in one year alone. By 1858, though, the California gold rush had lost its momentum, and the gold seekers headed north. Seemingly overnight, a tent town arose at Victoria. Many new businesses or branches of American firms, financed by San Francisco capital, were established. One witness counted 225 new commercial buildings in Victoria in 1858.

Once in Victoria, the miners faced the challenge of reaching the gold-fields. They needed boats in which to cross the Strait of Georgia to the mouth of the Fraser River. Lacking the requisite boat-building skills, many launched their own hastily made vessels and, not surprisingly, some swamped, and their owners drowned. Once the would-be prospectors reached the mouth of the Fraser, they faced a 250 km journey up the river to the first big strike, just south of Yale, an old trading post. In the last two weeks of May, ten thousand men travelled up the Fraser by canoe, sailboat, and raft. Another fifteen thousand arrived by the end of the year.

The entry of thousands of Americans on the mainland threatened British sovereignty and raised the danger of an Indian war. As the senior British official in the neighbourhood of the Fraser River, the governor of

Vancouver Island claimed the mainland and its minerals for the Crown. He drew up mining regulations, licensed miners, and hired constables. The Colonial Office praised Douglas for having taken the initiative, even though, strictly speaking, he lacked legal authority on the mainland. The British government then established a second colony on the mainland, separate from that of Vancouver Island. Queen Victoria named it British Columbia.

James Douglas became British Columbia's first governor while still serving as governor of Vancouver Island (which in 1859 also came under the direct control of the Colonial Office after the royal grant to the Hudson's Bay Company was terminated). Col. Richard Clement Moody, the first lieutenant governor of British Columbia, placed the site of the colony's new capital near the mouth of the Fraser River. Queen Victoria christened it New Westminster.

James Douglas, together with Matthew Baillie Begbie, British Columbia's first chief justice, established a uniform judicial system for the colony. Douglas and Begbie worked well together. Historian Margaret Ormsby has given us this portrait of Begbie: "A Cambridge graduate of considerable intellectual attainment, a man with a natural *hauteur*, an accomplished teller of anecdotes, and something of a musician, Begbie had the distinction of mind and manner so much admired by Douglas."[5]

395

Judge Begbie's circuit court tours established a frontier version of British law in the scattered mining camps. His and Douglas's efforts to establish a strong, centralized administration helped to ensure that the colony remained British.

In 1860 four thousand gold miners (the majority from California and Oregon, the rest from eastern Canada, Britain, Europe, and even China) proceeded eastward, pushing into the Thompson, Lillooet, and then the southern Cariboo regions. By 1861, with big strikes at Richfield, at Barkerville, and at Lightning on Williams Creek, the Cariboo had become the major mining field.

The gold resources in the interior could not be exploited without a road link to the coast. Using public funds, James Douglas built the 650 km Cariboo Road, completed in 1863, which connected the gold-towns of Yale and Barkerville.

JAMES DOUGLAS'S ACCOMPLISHMENTS

Douglas remained in office as governor of both British Columbia and Vancouver Island until 1864. The settlers had long complained about the veteran fur trader's autocratic ways and his "despotism," but in their haste to condemn the governor, they overlooked his accomplishments–the establishment of the basic industries of coal mining, lumbering, fishing, and farming. On the mainland, he had confronted the Americans and

National Archives of Canada/C-8077.

The Cariboo Road, connecting the gold-towns of Yale and Barkerville. When completed, the road was five metres wide and more than six hundred kilometres long. The photo shows the trail near Yale in 1867 or 1868. Yale was linked by the Fraser River to New Westminster on the coast.

firmly established British institutions. By building the Cariboo Road, he solved the problem of inland communication.

The governor's Indian policy constituted perhaps his greatest achievement. Thanks largely to him, Vancouver Island and British Columbia were spared the fierce wars between Indians and settlers that raged in the United States. The real test came in the Fraser River valley and the Cariboo country during the gold-rush days in the late 1850s and early 1860s. Apart from an attack in 1864 by Chilcotin Indians on a road-building crew who had entered their territory uninvited, no major acts of Indian armed resistance occurred. When he died in Victoria on August 2, 1877, James Douglas was already known as "The Father of British Columbia."[6]

British Columbia in the Mid-1860s

British Columbia experienced a post-gold-rush slump in the mid-1860s. Gold production fell and people left the colony. The region was rich in many natural resources, but high transportation costs ruled out their large-scale exploitation. High American tariffs reduced British Columbia's and

James Douglas's Contribution to British Columbia

In the historiography of British Columbia, James Douglas is a figure comparable to Champlain in Quebec and to Simcoe in Ontario. Few have been more laudatory of his contribution to British Columbia than historian Margaret Ormsby, who wrote of him as follows in a biographical sketch in 1972: "A man of iron nerve and physical prowess, great force of character, keen intelligence, and unusual resourcefulness, Douglas had had a notable career in the fur trade. As colonial governor his career was even more distinguished. Against overwhelming odds, with indifferent backing from the British government, the aid of a few Royal Navy ships, and a small force of Royal Engineers, he was able to establish British rule on the Pacific Coast and lay the foundation for Canada's extension to the Pacific seaboard. Single-handed in the midst of a gold-rush he had forged policies for land, mining, and water rights which were just and endurable" ("Sir James Douglas," *Dictionary of Canadian Biography*, vol. 10, *1871–1880* [Toronto, 1972], 248).

Recently, however, reassessments of Douglas have begun to appear, and his contribution, while still acknowledged as significant, is being summarized more critically. Historian Jean Barman, in her new study, *The West beyond the West: A History of British Columbia* (Toronto, 1991), has introduced several criticisms of Douglas's administration. She notes his "overbearing style of governing" (p. 80), and the fact that he readily extended his authority beyond his legitimate power. Moreover, "he alienated newcomers from Ontario and the Maritimes through his haughty demeanour and preference for Britons over Canadians"

(p. 97). His feverish road-building program, she adds, left the mainland colony of British Columbia burdened by debt.

Douglas's Amerindian policies have also been questioned. Political scientist Paul Tennant argues in *Aboriginal Peoples and Politics: The Indian Land Question in British Columbia, 1849–1989* (Vancouver, 1990) that the governor was far less generous to Amerindians than has formally been believed. Earlier commentators such as Robert Cail in *Land, Man and the Law: The Disposal of Crown Lands in British Columbia, 1871–1913* (Vancouver, 1974); Robin Fisher in *Contact and Conflict: Indian-European Relations in British Columbia, 1774–1890* (Vancouver, 1977); and Wilson Duff in *The Indian History of British Columbia. Volume 1. The Impact of the White Man* 2nd ed., (Victoria, 1969), p. 61, have regarded the governor's Native policies favourably. Anthropologist Wilson Duff, for instance, wrote in *The Indian History of British Columbia*, "As colonization progressed, his main concerns, in addition to maintaining law and order, were to purchase the Indian ownership rights to the land and to set aside adequate reserves for their use" (p. 61). Tennant himself does concede that, "at a time when aboriginal peoples elsewhere were routinely being forced from their lands and often actively exterminated, Douglas displayed a spirit of tolerance, compassion, and humane understanding" (p. 29). Nonetheless, with the exception of fourteen small treaties signed between 1850 and 1854 on Vancouver Island, he made no further attempts to negotiate the transfer of land title with the Indians. Moreover, the man who had complete control of the mainland from 1858 to 1864 made no treaties there at all. Instead, he spent large sums of money, principally on roads, to take miners in and out of the interior.

Tennant does acknowledge, however, that at least, inadvertently, James Douglas made an enormous contribution to the survival of aboriginal British Columbia. The governor's decision to set aside reserves for Amerindian communities at locations of their own choosing helped to protect these groups from cultural extinction. As Tennant writes, "The surviving members of traditional communities could thus remain resident on preferred sites within their ancestral homelands and so could retain a sense of communal unity and an active connection with historic places and communal memories. Confined to their small reserves, they could nurture a deepening sense of injustice as they witnessed the takeover of their surrounding traditional lands without regard to aboriginal title. Douglas's approach thus facilitated the retention of the communal and tribal group identities that he assumed would vanish" (p. 38).

Vancouver Island's trade with the United States, although Vancouver Island did sell some coal to San Francisco. Beginnings had been made in lumber and fishing as export industries, but mining was still the most important industry, despite its decline. Some farming had begun, with specialization in wheat in the upper Fraser region, and with dairy and market gardening under way on the island.

In the late 1860s, twelve thousand non-Natives lived in British Columbia and on Vancouver Island, more than half of them in the southwestern corner of the island. Between one thousand and two thousand lived in the lower Fraser Valley, with the remainder along the routes to the gold-fields or at fur-trading posts. Since most Americans had left by now, at least three-quarters were British or Canadians and, of these, males predominated. More than a thousand Chinese from California remained to work finds in the Cariboo.

Apart from doing some backpacking and some work at the diggings, the Indians, who were the largest ethnic group in the two colonies, had obtained little economic benefit from the gold rush. The newcomers clearly had no intention of sharing with the original inhabitants the area's rich lands and resources. Although James Douglas had allowed the Indians to chose the location of their reserves, he had made no treaties with them on the mainland. They had received no compensation for the expropriation of their lands. Moreover, the miners simply intruded on their village sites, fishing stations, and cultivated areas. The increased number of non-Indians also led to the outbreak of disease, such as the smallpox epidemic of 1862 that claimed the lives of many Indians living both along the coast and in the interior.

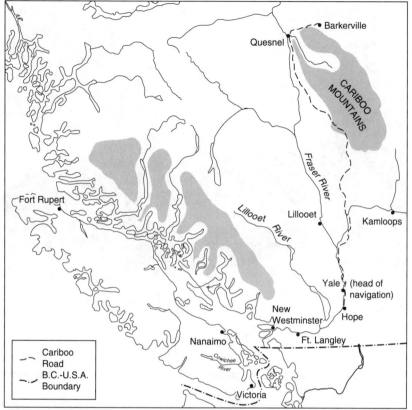

Source: Adapted from P.G. Cornell, J. Hamelin, F. Ouellet, and M. Trudel, *Canada: Unity in Diversity* (Toronto, 1967), 313.

Vancouver Island and British Columbia in the 1850s and 1860s.

CHRISTIAN MISSIONARIES AND THE INDIANS

The missionaries began outreach work to convert Indians to Christianity. William Duncan began his work at Fort Simpson in 1857 and continued it at neighbouring Metlakatla, where he built a model mission. Other Anglican missionaries followed. Methodists from Canada West also came, men like Thomas Crosby, who worked on Vancouver Island and along the northern coastline. In the late 1850s the Oblate Fathers established Roman Catholic missions along the south coast and in the Okanagan and the Fraser valleys. The missionaries tried to make the Indians into good Christian Europeans. This attempt was revealed in the early church architecture. Historian Robin Fisher writes that "in the main, the churches expressed the missionaries' overall intent to replace that which was Indian with that which was European."[7] In their zeal, the missionaries even banned totem poles. In 1900 the annual report of the Department of Indian

A Haida village on the Queen Charlotte Islands, July 1878.

Affairs noted that roughly 80 percent of British Columbia's Indians were reported to be Christians.

At the same time, the disruption to Indian culture can be overstated. Anthropologist Rolf Knight points out that many Indians near the settlements adjusted to the new economic conditions.[8] Independent of both mission and government direction, some Indians began to tend potato gardens in the 1850s, and in the decades to follow, they started mixed farming. As early as the mid-1850s independent Indian loggers delivered logs to sawmills. Many of the Hudson's Bay Company supply ships and several private trading schooners employed Amerindians as seamen throughout the nineteenth century. They worked as hunters and crewmen on European sealing ships and, on occasion, wintered in Japan. Indian-owned schooners began to appear in the 1870s, some of which the Indians themselves had constructed. From the 1870s on, Indians entered the commercial fishing and canning industry. Thus, under difficult circumstances, a number of Amerindians adjusted to the new conditions.

UNION OF THE TWO COLONIES

Major economic problems faced the two colonies of British Columbia and Vancouver Island in the mid-1860s. With the end of the gold rush, the economy was depressed and the two governments were nearly bankrupt.

Anxious to save money, Britain promoted union of the two colonies, which would allow substantial reductions in administrative costs. In 1866 the colonies joined together and New Westminster became the capital. (A vigorous lobby, however, led by John Sebastian Helmcken, James Douglas's son-in-law, convinced the governor to move the capital to Victoria in 1868.) Despite the political consolidation of the two colonies, the depression continued. In 1867 a new issue arose: the American purchase of Alaska. This put in doubt the independence of British Columbia. As Dr. Helmcken noted in his diary, the Americans "boasted they had sandwiched British Columbia and could eat her up at any time!"

In 1867 the new united colony of British Columbia, but one year old, was the youngest of all of Britain's North American colonies. With the exception of a handful of European fur traders, none of the approximately eight thousand Europeans in the colony had lived more than twenty-five years on Britain's North Pacific Coast. Thanks to the Hudson's Bay Company, Britain had retained this huge territory against Russian, and particularly against American, advances. But what now would be the province's fate? *401*

As the Canadas, New Brunswick, and Nova Scotia completed the final arrangements for their union, European British Columbians started to debate the options open to them. At no point did they consult the province's twenty-five thousand Amerindians; rather, they proceeded as if the original inhabitants did not exist. The options were three: Britain, the United States, or Canada. Emotionally, most favoured the province's continuation as a British colony. Those seeking to increase British Columbia's trade with its most important trading partner, though, endorsed annexation to the United States. Finally, many British Columbians who had been born in the Canadas and the Maritimes wanted union with Canada, as did those who saw Confederation as the best means of protecting British institutions on the North Pacific and of developing British Columbia's resources.

NOTES

[1]Philip Drucker, "Rank, Wealth, and Kinship in Northwest Coast Society," in *Indians of the North Pacific Coast*, edited by Tom McFeat (Toronto, 1966), 137.
[2]Wilson Duff, *The Indian History of British Columbia*, vol. 1, *The Impact of the White Man* (Victoria, 1964), 58.
[3]Peter L. Macnair, *The Legacy: Continuing Traditions of Canadian Northwest Coast Indian Art* (Victoria, 1980), 21.
[4]Duff, *Indian History*, 1:43.
[5]Margaret Ormsby, *British Columbia: A History* (Vancouver, 1958), 171.
[6]Margaret Ormsby, "James Douglas," *Dictionary of Canadian Biography*, vol. 10, *1871–1880* (Toronto, 1972), 248.
[7]Robin Fisher, "Missions to the Indians of British Columbia," in *British Columbia: Historical Readings*, edited by W. Peter Ward and Robert A.J. McDonald (Vancouver, 1981), 123.
[8]Rolf Knight, *Indians at Work: An Informal History of Native Indian Labour in British Columbia, 1858–1930* (Vancouver, 1978), 7–27.

Related Readings

Three articles in R. Douglas Francis and Donald B. Smith, eds. *Readings in Canadian History: Pre-Confederation*, 3d ed. (Toronto 1990), are useful for this topic: Robin Fisher, "Indian Control of the Maritime Fur Trade and the Northwest Coast," 79–92; J.M.S. Careless, "The Business Community in the Early Development of Victoria, British Columbia," 473–91; and Barry M. Gough, "The Character of the British Columbia Frontier," 492–503.

BIBLIOGRAPHY

The best overview of the history of the two Pacific colonies is Jean Barman's *The West beyond the West: A History of British Columbia* (Toronto, 1991). An older account, one still worth consulting, is Margaret Ormsby's *British Columbia: A History* (Toronto, 1958); however, the author's omission of a discussion of the Native peoples is a serious short-coming. A popularly written survey is George Woodcock's *British Columbia: A History of the Province* (Vancouver, 1990). R. Cole Harris provides a geographical overview in "British Columbia," in *Canada Before Confederation*, edited by R. Cole Harris and John Warkentin (Toronto, 1974), 289–311.

Reviews of British Columbia's Amerindian past appear in Wilson Duff, *The Indian History of British Columbia*, vol. 1, *The Impact of the White Man* (Victoria, 1965); Robin Fisher, *Contact and Conflict: Indian–European Relations in British Columbia, 1774–1890* (Vancouver, 1977); Robin Fisher, "Missions to the Indians of British Columbia," in *British Columbia: Historical Readings*, edited by W. Peter Ward and Robert A.J. McDonald (Vancouver, 1981), 113–26; and Rolf Knight, *Indians at Work: An Informal History of Native Indian Labour in British Columbia 1858–1930* (Vancouver, 1978). The new study by Paul Tennant, *Aboriginal Peoples and Politics: The Indian Land Question in British Columbia, 1849–1989* (Vancouver, 1990) is very useful. Four papers on the Pacific peoples are included in *Native People, Native Lands: Canadian Indians, Inuit and Métis*, edited by Bruce Alden Cox (Ottawa, 1987): Leland Donald, "Slave Raiding on the North Pacific Coast," 161–72; Loraine Littlefield, "Women Traders in the Maritime Fur Trade," 173–85; Jo-Anne Fiske, "Fishing Is Women's Business: Changing Economic Roles of Carrier Women and Men," 186–98; and James Andrew McDonald, "The Marginalization of the Tsimshian Cultural Ecology: The Seasonal Cycle," 199–218. Barry Gough has reviewed both American and British Indian policies in "The Indian Policies of Great Britain and the United States in the Pacific Northwest in the Mid-Nineteenth Century," *Canadian Journal of Native Studies* 2, 2 (1982): 321–37. For a study of an Amerindian group in the interior of British Columbia, see Joanne Drake-

Terry, *The Same as Yesterday: The Lillooet Chronicle the Theft of Their Lands and Resources* (Lillooet, B.C., 1989).

Amerindian statements include *The Spirit in the Land* (Gabriola, B.C., 1987), which provides a summary of the land claim of the Hereditary Chiefs of the Gitksan and Wet'suwet'en people to nearly sixty thousand square kilometres in Northwestern British Columbia. Native traditions on the Northwest Coast are reviewed in Ruth Kirk, *Wisdom of the Elders* (Vancouver, 1986). Chief Mathias Capilano presents a Squamish Indian version of the Europeans' arrival in "Strangers Appear on English Bay," in *Romance of Vancouver*, vol. 2 compiled by the Native Sons of British Columbia (n.p., 1926), 5–6. A beautifully illustrated introduction to Northwest Coast art is Peter L. Macnair et al., eds., *The Legacy: Continuing Traditions of Canadian Northwest Coast Indian Art*, (Victoria, 1980). Tom McFeat provides excerpts from important anthropological articles in his edited work, *Indians of the North Pacific Coast* (Toronto, 1966). A bibliographical guide has been compiled by Robert Steven Grumet, *Native Americans of the Northwest Coast* (Bloomington, Ind., 1979). *403*

Warren L. Cook's *Flood Tide of Empire: Spain and the Pacific Northwest, 1543–1819* (New Haven, 1973), and three articles by Christon Archer— "The Transient Presence: A Re-appraisal of Spanish Attitudes Toward the Northwest Coast in the Eighteenth Century," *B.C. Studies* 18 (1973): 3–32; "Spanish Exploration and Settlement of the Northwest Coast in the 18th Century," *Sound Heritage* 7, 1 (1978): 33–53; and "Cannibalism in the Early History of the Northwest Coast: Enduring Myths and Neglected Realities," *Canadian Historical Review* 61 (1980): 453–79—provide the background on Spanish activities. In *The Men with Wooden Feet: The Spanish Exploration of the Pacific Northwest* (Toronto, 1985), John Kendrick also reviews the Spanish experience. Alan Rayburn has recorded many of the North Pacific Spanish names in "Spanish Names Along Our West Coast," *Canadian Geographic* 105, 3 (June–July 1985): 86–87.

For a review of Russian and American activities in the North Pacific, see James R. Gibson's "Bostonians and Muscovites on the Northwest Coast, 1788–1841," in *British Columbia: Historical Readings*, edited by Ward and McDonald, 66–95; and, for the Russian presence, see Glynn Barratt, *Russia in Pacific Waters, 1715–1825* (Vancouver, 1981). Barry Gough has reviewed early British contact in *Distant Dominion: Britain and the Northwest Coast of North America, 1579–1809* (Vancouver, 1980); he has studied the later period in *Gunboat Frontier: British Maritime Authority and Northwest Coast Indians, 1846–90* (Vancouver, 1984). The *Dictionary of Canadian Biography*, vol. 4, *1771–1800* (Toronto, 1979) contains sketches of James Cook by Glyndwr Williams, pp. 162–67, and of George Vancouver by W. Kaye Lamb, pp. 743–48. Barbara Belyea has analyzed historians' treatments of David Thompson's exploration of the Columbia River in "The 'Columbian Enterprise' and A.S. Morton: A Historical Exemplum," *B.C. Studies* 86 (Summer 1990): 3–27. For a survey of the inland fur trade, see Theodore J. Karamanski, *Fur Trade and Exploration: Opening the Far Northwest 1821–1852* (Vancouver, 1983).

Other items can be cited for the nineteenth century. Margaret Ormsby concisely reviews the life of James Douglas in the *Dictionary of Canadian Biography*, vol. 10, *1871–1880* (Toronto, 1972), 239–49. *British Columbia: Historical Readings*, edited by Ward and McDonald, includes James E. Hendrickson's "The Constitutional Development of Colonial Vancouver Island and British Columbia," 245–74. David R. Williams has written a biography of Mathew Baillie Begbie, " . . . *The Man for a New Country*" (Sidney, B.C., 1977). Dorothy Blakey Smith provides a sketch of J.S. Helmcken in her introduction to *The Reminiscences of Doctor John Sebastien Helmcken* (Vancouver, 1975). An interesting look at early Victoria is provided by Peter A. Baskerville in *Beyond the Island: An Illustrated History of Victoria* (Burlington, Ontario, 1986).

Economic history is a growing field of research. A lively account of the *404* | British Columbian gold rushes is contained in Douglas Fetherling's *The Gold Crusades: A Social History of Gold Rushes, 1849–1929* (Toronto, 1988). John Douglas Belshaw has written two articles on coal mining on Vancouver Island, "Mining Technique and Social Division on Vancouver Island, 1848–1900," *British Journal of Canadian Studies* 1 (1986): 45–65, and "The Standard of Living of British Miners on Vancouver Island, 1848–1900," *B.C. Studies* 84 (Winter 1989/90): 37–64. Lynne Bowen has completed an interesting study of labour unrest on Vancouver Island in 1849: "Independent Colliers at Fort Rupert," *The Beaver* 69, 2 (April/May 1989): 25–31. Paul A. Phillips's essay, "Confederation and the Economy of British Columbia," in *British Columbia and Confederation*, edited by W. George Shelton (Victoria, 1967), 43–60, is very useful.

The Road to Confederation

Proposals for British North American union had been considered before the 1860s—indeed as far back as the time of the Loyalists' arrival—but they had always proved premature. As historian P.B. Waite aptly put it, "The Confederation movement followed Newton's first law of motion: all bodies continue in a state of rest or of uniform motion unless compelled by some force to change their state."[1] By the 1860s, however, several such "forces" were suddenly present. The danger of an American attack after the American Civil War drew the British North American colonies together. At the same time, Britain also pressured them to unite to defend themselves. In addition, internal problems in the colonies, such as public debt from extensive railway building and, in the case of the Canadas, political deadlock (and the desire to acquire the North-West), convinced both Canadians and Maritimers of the necessity of union. These unique circumstances, rather than a spirit of nationalism, prepared the way for Confederation.

Impact of the American Civil War

Fear of an American takeover during the Civil War was perhaps the leading cause of Canadian Confederation. As historian F.H. Underhill once wrote, "Somewhere on Parliament Hill in Ottawa ... there should be erected a monument to this American ogre who has so often performed the function of saving us from drift and indecision."[2]

Britain's proclamation of neutrality during the Civil War and its recognition of the South as a belligerent convinced many Unionists that it favoured the South. The British policy of allowing Confederate ships to be built and fitted out in British ports further antagonized the North. These armed cruisers, such as the *Alabama*, the most famous of all, inflicted great damage on the North's merchant marine. The American government argued that because Britain knew the uses to which the South put these ships, it was effectively a contributor to the war and should pay for damages caused by this policy. One proposal included all of Canada as part of the compensation.

Another incident heightened Anglo-American antagonism during the Civil War—the *Trent* affair. In November 1861 an American warship stopped the British steamer *Trent* and forcibly removed two Confederate agents on their way to England to secure assistance for the Southern cause. Tempers flared on both sides, with Britain threatening retaliation if these Confederate agents, seized in neutral waters, were not freed. Anxious to avoid war with Britain, President Abraham Lincoln released the prisoners on Christmas Day, 1861.

These hostilities inevitably affected the British North American colonies. Fear of an impending American attack led Britain to send fourteen thousand soldiers—the largest detachment of troops to be sent since the War of 1812. The resulting tension made Britain anxious to withdraw its expensive garrisons from North America as soon as it was possible to do so, and London encouraged the colonies to begin to shoulder the burden of their own defence.

The colonies realized that they had to assume more responsibility for defence. They also saw the need for a railway that would extend from an ice-free port on the Atlantic into the interior without leaving British North American territory. A federation of the British North American colonies could lead to the organization of a united colonial army and to the construction of an intercolonial railway. Militarily, British North America undoubtedly needed a rail link—the fourteen thousand British troops sent to protect the Canadas had had to travel overland through New Brunswick by sled in the middle of winter.

THE ST. ALBAN'S RAID

The *Trent* affair, the raids of the *Alabama* and other Confederate ships, and then the St. Alban's raid increased Anglo-American tension. As the Union army began its victorious march south, the Confederacy planned to launch attacks on the North via Canada. At St. Alban's, Vermont, on October 19, 1864, twenty-six Confederate sympathizers terrorized the town, robbed three banks of $200 000, set several fires, wounded two men and killed another, and then fled to Canada. The government arrested them, but a Montreal magistrate, Charles Joseph Coursol, released them (and even returned the money to them) on a technicality.

More than the raid itself, this act infuriated Americans. The Canadian government quickly condemned Coursol's action and in January 1865 passed a new Alien Act that provided for the deportation of aliens involved in acts against a friendly foreign state. Nevertheless, Canada once again became suspect. General John A. Dix, commander of the American military district in the east, threatened Canada with retaliation if it refused to turn Southern raiders over to American authorities immediately.

The Great Coalition

This was the atmosphere in which Canadian politicians tried to solve the problem of political deadlock in their Assembly. Neither the Conservatives nor the Reformers could form a stable government. Between 1861 and 1864, for example, there were two elections and three changes of administration in which neither side was able to command a majority of seats. On June 14, 1864, the most recent government, the Macdonald–Taché coalition, went down to defeat. Macdonald requested dissolution, but rather than accept his request, Governor General Monck urged the Conservative leader to open negotiations with George Brown, leader of the Clear Grit Reform party, with the possibility of forming a coalition. For two weeks, the two sides negotiated. On June 30, a jubilant House heard the announcement that Brown had agreed to enter a coalition cabinet along with two others from his Reform party, Oliver Mowat and William McDougall, and to work for federation. Thus was born the famous "Great Coalition of 1864."

Brown immediately made three demands in return for his support. First, he insisted that the coalition government work toward a federation of all the British North American colonies and, should this fail, toward a federation of the two Canadas alone. Second, he demanded representation by population, or "rep by pop," as it became popularly known. The Clear Grits, who followed the model of American democratic practices and who were well aware that Canada West's population was greater than Canada East's, believed that representation in the Assembly (or lower house) should be based on population distribution. After 1851, this meant that instead of an equality in the number of seats (see Chapter 14), Canada West would have more seats than Canada East.

Brown's third demand was for the incorporation of the North-West into Confederation. For George Brown, eastward expansion and incorporation of the Maritimes into a federal union had to be accompanied by westward expansion to the Pacific. Brown had a strong interest in the North-West. For nearly a decade, his newspaper, the Toronto *Globe*, had kept Upper Canadians informed about developments in the area. The *Globe* provided generous excerpts from the reports of the two scientific expeditions in the late 1850s—the British Palliser and the Canadian Hind expeditions. Brown's interest in the North-West lay in its potential for the development of Canada West. On January 22, 1863, for example, Brown outlined his imperial vision:

If Canada acquires this territory it will rise in a few years from a position of a small and weak province to be the greatest colony any country has ever possessed, able to take its place among the empires of the earth. The wealth of 400 000 square miles of territory will flow through our waters and be gathered by our merchants, manufacturers and agriculturists. Our sons will occupy the chief places of this vast territory, we will form its institutions, supply its rulers, teach its schools, fill its stores, run its mills, navigate its streams.

Charlottetown Conference

408   The Maritime colonies had long considered union among themselves. The Colonial Office strongly endorsed the idea, believing Maritime union would reduce the military and economic dependency of these colonies on Britain. Charles Tupper, the premier of Nova Scotia, and Leonard Tilley, his counterpart in New Brunswick, concurred, as did Premier John H. Gray of Prince Edward Island. Although all three governments had some reservations about the suggestion, they had agreed to meet. No date or place, though, had yet been set for the conference when, in July 1864, the Canadas, suddenly and surprisingly, asked permission to attend and to present a proposal for a wider British North American federal union. The Maritimers agreed and arranged the meeting for September 1, 1864, in Charlottetown.

At the conference, the Canadian delegation presented an impressive *tour de force*. John A. Macdonald and George-Étienne Cartier set out the arguments in favour of Confederation and the general terms of the Canadian proposal, particularly those aspects dealing with the division of powers between the central government and the provincial governments. Alexander Galt, the Minister of Finance in the Canadas, dealt with financial issues, while George Brown handled constitutional concerns. The main features of their proposal included continued loyalty to the British Crown through membership in the British Empire; a strong central government within a federal union in which the provinces retained control over their own local affairs; and representation in the lower house based on population and in the upper house, on regional representation. Thomas D'Arcy McGee, the gifted poet-politician, spoke in terms of the need for a national vision. Within four days, the Canadians had presented such a convincing case that the Maritime delegates abandoned their talk of Maritime union. Before the conference adjourned on September 7, the delegates agreed to meet again on October 10 at Quebec City to work out the final details of British North American federation.

National Archives of Canada/C-733.

A group of future Fathers of Confederation in front of the Prince Edward Island legislative building on the first day of the Charlottetown Conference, September 1, 1864. Photo by G.P. Roberts. John A. Macdonald is shown seated in the foreground, and George-Étienne Cartier is standing, facing him, on the left. Immediately between them is D'Arcy McGee, the Canadian Minister of Agriculture and Immigration. In rousing public speeches, McGee had called for a "new nationality" in Canada. In April 1868, he was assassinated in Ottawa. Immediately, the Fenians were suspected, because the Irish-born politician had strongly opposed the secret society, which called for an end to English rule in Ireland.

Quebec Conference

Within a month, the Canadian cabinet translated the broad general principles of Charlottetown into specific resolutions and presented them at Quebec in the form of seventy-two resolutions. For the next two weeks the Maritime and Canadian delegates refined and altered the resolutions, finally reaching agreement on the terms of what, with only a few minor alterations, became the British North America Act. The danger of an American attack, British encouragement of the union, and a desire for the North-West all combined to maintain the momentum of Charlottetown.

As in Charlottetown, the delegates at Quebec agreed in principle on federation, but strongly disagreed about the division of powers between the central and the provincial governments. The magnitude of what they attempted to do is impressive. Over a two-week period, they sought to establish the entire political framework for a future union of half a dozen

409

British North American colonies. Creatively, they adopted aspects of both the British unitary system and the American federal system.

Macdonald favoured a legislative union, arguing that the Civil War in the United States could be attributed to overly powerful state governments. Along with the Colonial Office in Britain, the Maritime governors agreed that all major decisions must be made by a single government, as was done in the United Kingdom. The Maritime delegates, however, feared a loss of their identity in a legislative union and opposed such a measure. They wanted their own legislatures. The French Canadians, through their spokesman, George-Étienne Cartier, insisted that the future Quebec retain control over language, religion, and civil law, all considered to be fundamental aspects of French Canada.

The delegates finally reached a compromise by granting the central government residuary powers (powers not specifically assigned to the provinces), and by including under the powers of the federal government such general and vague phrases as "to make laws for the peace, order and good government of Canada." The federal government also gained the power of disallowance—the right to reject provincial laws of which it did not approve.

DEBATE OVER THE SEVENTY-TWO RESOLUTIONS

The delegates confirmed their agreement at Charlottetown that the federation's central government would have a lower house based on representation by population, and an upper house based on regional representation. But they disagreed strongly on the number of representatives each region would have in the upper house, or the Senate. This issue almost destroyed the conference. The issue became contentious because the smaller Maritime provinces saw the Senate as a means of strengthening their regional representation to offset their numerical weakness in the lower house. They therefore objected to being considered one unit, and opposed the proportion of Senate seats allotted to them (twenty-four), which was the same number given to each of Ontario and Quebec. Debate also followed over the means of choosing senators. Only after discussing and eliminating a number of proposals did the delegates agree on appointment for life by the central government. (In hindsight, that decision destroyed the possibility of the Senate's becoming an effective voice for regional or provincial interests. Only on exceptional occasions has the appointed Senate challenged the views of the elected House of Commons.)

After considerable discussion, the delegates accepted the financial arrangement proposed by A.T. Galt. He had suggested that the new federal government assume the public debts—up to a specified maximum amount—of all the provinces that joined. In addition, the federal government would finance the Intercolonial Railway (under an agreement written directly into the future British North America Act).

Galt also argued successfully that the central government, with its heavy financial obligations, should control the main sources of revenue. The federal government would have unlimited taxing powers, including the collection of both direct taxes and indirect taxes, such as customs and excise duties, one of the main sources of revenue at the time. The provinces could levy only direct taxes. To compensate the provinces for the cost of education, roads, and other local obligations, Galt proposed that the federal government pay annual subsidies based on eighty cents per head of their population. The provinces could raise additional revenue by direct taxation or by selling their natural resources (public lands, minerals, and waterpower), which would remain in provincial hands.

Responses to the Confederation Proposals

When the Quebec Conference ended, the delegates returned to their respective provinces to secure approval for the resolutions. None of them could possibly have realized that the distribution of powers they had agreed upon would lead to federal–provincial disputes that would persist to the end of the twentieth century.

The Fathers of Confederation originally considered submitting the draft constitution for popular approval but later decided to follow the British procedure of ratification by the provincial legislatures. They worried about public opposition to the scheme. Afterall, the projected union was the work of a small but influential political elite.

In the legislatures of the Canadas, there was significant opposition when debate began in early February 1865. George Brown and his Reformers initially expressed concern about a wider union with the Maritimes, favouring instead a revised union of the Canadas as being more advantageous to Upper Canadians. Canada West's Reform leader also believed that the Intercolonial Railway would be another expensive publicly funded railway like the Grand Trunk. Still, Brown was willing to overlook both these reservations if federation were to be based on "rep by pop" and if it were to include the North-West. In general, however, Upper Canadian leaders tended to favour Confederation, realizing that they had the most to gain from the union.

DEBATE OVER CONFEDERATION IN CANADA EAST

Members of the Parti rouge, under the leadership of Antoine-Aimé Dorion, had serious reservations. Canada East's Reform leader argued that "It is not at all a confederation that is proposed to us, but quite simply a Legislative Union disguised under the name of a confederation. How could one accept as a federation a scheme ... that provided for disallowance of local legislation?"

Furthermore, he pointed out that in the proposed House of Commons the English Canadian representation from Canada West and the Maritimes greatly outnumbered the French Canadian. Dorion also emphasized that union of the British North American colonies would heighten rather than diminish tension with the United States, as the increased armed might of British North America would pose a greater threat. Finally, this nineteenth-century liberal denounced the Fathers of Confederation for refusing to allow the people to make their views known, either through a plebiscite or an election. In a prophetic statement, Dorion summarized his misgivings:

> I greatly fear that the day when this Confederation is adopted will be a dark day for Lower Canada ... I consider it one of the worst measures which could be submitted to us and if it happens that it is adopted, without the sanctions of the people of the province, the country will have more than one occasion to regret it.

George-Étienne Cartier countered Dorion's criticism with the argument that, in the new federal union, French Canadians would gain control of a provincial government and their own legislature, have their own local administration, and retain the French Civil Code. Furthermore, he argued, the French language would be official in the province of Quebec as well as in the federal administration, and the school rights of religious minorities would be recognized in all the provinces. On the question of English Canadian dominance, he pointed out that the "new nationality" would be a "political nationality" only, and not a "cultural nationality" requiring French Canadians to suppress their cultural differences for the sake of some common pan-Canadian nationalism. He also reminded his French Canadian compatriots of the importance of the British connection to offset the threat of American annexation and the loss of identity that would ensue. (Cartier had an almost morbid fear of the Americans and an equally strong dislike of republicanism.)

Finally, the practical politician Cartier presented Confederation to French Canadians as their best hope for cultural survival in a world of limited possibilities. The existing union, crippled by deadlock, could not go on; for French Canadians, union with the United States would be the worst possible fate. Only a larger federation of British North American colonies, Cartier concluded, offered French Canadians possibilities beyond their own provincial boundaries at the same time as it protected their affairs within their own province. Cartier's close association with the Grand Trunk Railway (as one of the company's directors) and his desire to play a larger role as a stateman on a national stage made him an enthusiastic advocate of union.

Cartier faced a difficult struggle promoting Confederation in Quebec and therefore enlisted the support of the clergy, despite his personal concerns about mixing politics and religion. But he could not count on unreserved support. Ignace Bourget of Montreal, the most powerful bishop, feared for the future of the church in a new political union with other English-speaking colonies with large Protestant populations. He kept silent about his misgivings, however, since the other Quebec bishops were more favourably disposed, at least in principle. For the church to have opposed Confederation would have put them in the camp of their arch-enemies, the *rouges*, who were strongly anticlerical.

The Confederation debates in the Canadas lasted just over a month, from February 3 to March 11, 1865. In a final vote, 91 favoured and 33 opposed Confederation. In the breakdown of votes in the two sections, 54 of the 62 members from Canada West favoured the proposal, as did 37 of the 62 members from Canada East. Of the 48 French Canadian members present, 27 voted for and 21 against. Overall, Confederation won overwhelmingly, but among French Canadians the victory was narrow, indicating serious reservations on their part.

413

NEW BRUNSWICK INITIALLY REJECTS CONFEDERATION

The struggle for Confederation in the Maritimes became as intense as it was among French Canadians in Canada East. In New Brunswick, Leonard Tilley, a Saint John druggist who had been premier of the province since 1857 and who had represented it at both the Charlottetown and Quebec conferences, tried to point out the advantages of Confederation for New Brunswickers. He stressed the need for a year-round ice-free port such as Saint John for the export of Canadian goods, and the lucrative market that would exist in central Canada for Maritime coal and manufactured goods. The promised rail link would make such trade possible. But Tilley faced a strong opposition. A.J. Smith, the opposition leader, argued that the terms of union with the Canadas (and, in particular, those contained in the Quebec Resolutions) offered few—if any—benefits to New Brunswick. There was no guarantee that the Intercolonial Railway would be constructed; and, if it were built, it was not clear where it would run and which area of the province (the north shore or the southern Saint John Valley) would benefit from it. One member of the Assembly asked derisively: "Mr. Tilley, will you stop your puffing and blowing and tell us which way the Railway is going?"

The opposition pointed out that New Brunswick's economic trade pattern, especially since the Reciprocity Treaty of 1854, had a north–south rather than an east–west orientation. Commercial interests in the province had no economic ties with the Canadas. Furthermore, union with Canada could lead to a flooding of the New Brunswick market by Canadian imports, and a high tariff structure. In addition, New Brunswickers would be forced to assume a portion of the heavy Canadian debt from canal and railway building. Smith also argued that Confederation would diminish New Brunswick's political power by giving the province representation of only 15 MPs in a House of 194 members. The Roman Catholic clergy in the province opposed Confederation as well, believing that a Canada dominated by Protestant extremists like George Brown would attack Roman Catholic schools and the church itself.

These arguments against Confederation found an effective forum in the election campaign in early 1865, fought chiefly on the issue of Confederation. New Brunswickers responded clearly and decisively—the Tilley pro-Confederation government lost heavily.

OPPOSITION IN NOVA SCOTIA

414 In Nova Scotia, Charles Tupper faced a challenge equal to Tilley's in New Brunswick. Opposition to the Quebec Resolutions and to Confederation transcended party lines and centred on Joseph Howe, now no longer a member of the Assembly but still the most powerful political figure in Nova Scotia. As the Father of Responsible Government, the "voice of Nova Scotia" saw Confederation as restricting the colony's potential by reducing it to a backwater province in an insignificant North American nation. If it accepted Confederation, Nova Scotia would lose its identity and cease to be an important colony in a great empire. Howe presented his position in a series of letters he entitled "The Botheration Letters." In Howe's opinion the province looked eastward to the Atlantic Ocean and Britain, rather than westward to the continent and the Canadas. As Howe vividly expressed it, "Take a Nova Scotian to Ottawa, away above tide-water, freeze him up for five months, where he cannot view the Atlantic, smell salt water, or see the sail of a ship, and the man will pine and die." Howe appealed to those areas of the colony that looked to the sea and depended on ocean trade, shipbuilding, and fishing for their livelihood. Tupper drew his main support from the interior, where the coal, steel, and railway interests saw greater economic benefits from transcontinental, as opposed to oceanic, trade.

Like Antoine Dorion, Howe also objected to Confederation's being imposed without consulting the electorate. In the winter of 1865–66 he went to England to present his case to the Colonial Secretary and the British Parliament. Dissent in the province against Tupper's School Act of 1864, which placed the cost of education on the localities themselves rather than on the provincial government, aided Howe in his anti-Confederation campaign. Knowing full well that he could not win an election on the Confederation and schools issues, Tupper pressured the other British American colonial leaders to conclude their union before he had to face an election in 1867.

REJECTION OF CONFEDERATION IN PRINCE EDWARD ISLAND

In Prince Edward Island, support for Confederation went from little to none. At the Charlottetown and Quebec conferences, the Island representatives had driven the hardest bargain, pressing for better terms on representation in the Senate and the House of Commons, and for better economic terms.

This solidarity and inspiration, however, had disappeared once the delegates returned home. Disagreement broke out across party lines, as personal feuds and in-party fighting erupted. Within the governing Conservative party, chaos occurred after Premier Gray resigned in mid-December 1864 over his own party's opposition to Confederation. He was replaced by an anti-Confederate, J.C. Pope, the provincial secretary. Ironically, the new premier's brother, W.H. Pope, the new provincial secretary, supported Confederation.

The real opposition, however, came from the Islanders themselves. Prosperous and content, many Prince Edward Islanders wanted nothing to do with Confederation. On December 30, 1864, the Charlottetown *Islander* wrote that "the majority of people appear to be wholly averse to Confederation.... We have done our duty. We have urged Confederation—the people have declared against it."

415

Islanders opposed Confederation for two reasons. One was the age-old issue of absentee landlordism. From the mid-eighteenth century onward, the Island had been controlled by absentee British landlords, much to the resentment of the local population. In 1860 a British commission appointed to investigate the question issued a report favourable to the Islanders, only to have it rejected by the proprietors and by the Colonial Office. Thus, when the Colonial Office pressured Prince Edward Islanders to adopt Confederation, they resisted. Also, many Islanders saw Confederation as simply replacing one set of distant landlords in Britain with another in Ottawa. In addition, Islanders believed that Confederation would give them very little. Union would mean higher taxes to support the enormous Intercolonial Railway project and higher tariffs to create interprovincial trade—neither of which would greatly benefit Prince Edward Island. They also disliked the proposed form of representation in the Senate and House of Commons, which would give them little, if any, power in distant Ottawa.

DEBATE OVER CONFEDERATION IN NEWFOUNDLAND

Newfoundland failed to support Confederation out of apathy, not opposition. Newfoundland had not participated in the Charlottetown Conference, but it had sent two representatives—Ambrose Shea, a liberal Catholic, and F.B.T. Carter, a conservative Protestant—to Quebec meetings at which both delegates had endorsed Confederation. They returned to a colony that was initially mildly interested but soon became largely indifferent. The initial enthusiasm came as a result of Newfoundland's destitute conditions. Fishing, the chief industry, was in decline throughout the 1860s. Agriculture and the timber trade, while distant seconds to fishing as commercial activities, also experienced hard times. Although Newfoundlanders initially hoped that Confederation might solve their economic ills, they lost faith simply because, for them (much more than for the three Maritime colonies), Canada seemed so far away. Essentially, the island continued to look eastward to Britain rather than westward to Canada.

The politicians never overcame the Newfoundlanders' indifference to Canada. Premier Hugh Hoyles, who had also been premier at the time of the Quebec Conference, favoured Confederation, as did most members from both parties in the Legislative Council and the Assembly, but few people outside government circles endorsed the idea. In April 1865 Hoyles retired, to be replaced by F.B.T. Carter. He allied with his political opponent, Ambrose Shea, to form a coalition government to persuade Newfoundland to join Confederation. They even had the enthusiastic support of the pro-Confederation governor, Anthony Musgrave. But even this impressive political coalition could not stir up interest in the subject. R.J. Pinsent, a representative of the Legislative Council, spoke for many Newfoundlanders when he noted, "There is little community of interest between Newfoundland and the Canadas. This is not a Continental Colony."

External Pressures

By the end of 1865 the idea of Confederation appeared to have insufficient support among the British North American colonies, except in Canada West. All four of the Atlantic colonies opposed it. Two developments, however, altered the situation: British intervention and the American threat.

Anxious to rid itself of the expense of defending British North America and seeking to ease the tensions in its relations with the United States, Britain now intervened directly to bring about a colonial federation. When a Canadian delegation arrived in London in the autumn of 1865, it was warmly welcomed. A counter-delegation from Nova Scotia under Joseph Howe received a cool reception. The British government replaced the governor of Nova Scotia with a new appointee, one more sympathetic to Confederation, and it ordered New Brunswick Governor Arthur Gordon to intervene in his province's politics to ensure the success of Confederation. Britain also agreed to guarantee the loan interest for the Intercolonial Railway, giving the Maritime provinces an additional incentive to unite with the Canadas.

While Britain applied pressure directly, the United States supplied it indirectly. When the Civil War ended in 1865, extremists now suggested that the Northern army be used to annex Canada. Moreover, influential American politicians in the Midwest—Senators Alexander Ramsey of Minnesota and Zachariah Chandler of Michigan—advocated annexation of the British North-West. Other American politicians, such as Congressman Nathaniel Banks, Senator Charles Sumner, and even the Secretary of State in Ulysses S. Grant's administration, Hamilton Fish, wanted all the British territory in North America.

At the same time, the American government moved to terminate the Reciprocity Treaty of 1854 (see Chapter 15). The treaty had come under pressure from American protectionist interests as early as 1862. American annexationists believed that the treaty's abrogation would lead the British colonies to welcome union with the United States, that the colonies would find it impossible to survive economically without American trade. In December 1865 Congress passed a motion to end the Reciprocity Treaty, with the law to come into effect in March 1866. Ironically, rather than forcing the British colonies into the arms of the United States as expected, the abrogation of reciprocity instead encouraged the colonies to form a new commerical union among themselves.

417

FENIAN RAIDS

A more direct American threat also furthered the cause of Canadian Confederation. The Fenians, fanatical republican Irishmen, formed a brotherhood in 1859 in the United States for the independence of Ireland. They devised a grandiose scheme to capture the British North American colonies and use them as ransom to negotiate with the British government for the liberation of Ireland. Their marching song was an explicit expression of their goals:

> We are the Fenian Brotherhood,
> skilled in the art of war,
> And we're going to fight for Ireland,
> the land that we adore,
> Many battles we have won, along with
> the boys in blue,
> And we'll go and capture Canada for
> we've nothing else to do.

The Fenians fully expected the sympathy and support of Irish Catholics in the British colonies to the north, but they were disappointed: prominent public figures such as Thomas D'Arcy McGee refused their support.

The Fenians posed little threat until the end of the American Civil War. In the summer of 1865 the Union army released thousands of Irish American soldiers, who were trained, idle, and receptive to mobilizing in defence of their native country. Furthermore, the Fenians met with little resistance and even muted support from an American government that sympathized with their anti-British sentiments. Many American politicians also feared alienating American Irish Catholic voters.

The Fenian threat tended to be more psychological than physical, with the actual military activities restricted to a few border skirmishes. But the Fenians made two concerted attacks that alarmed British North Americans. The first took place in New Brunswick. In April 1866 small bands of Fenians moved into the coastal towns of eastern Maine. New Brunswickers were alerted and volunteer soldiers called out to meet the challenge. This attack conveniently coincided with a hotly contested election on the issue of Confederation, and in the end the raid strengthened the Confederation cause in New Brunswick. The Fenians succeeded only in stealing the flag from a customs house before the New Brunswick militia and British regulars overwhelmed them, forcing them back across the border.

418

The second incident, at Fort Erie on the Niagara frontier, was more serious. On May 31, 1866, some fifteen hundred Fenians crossed the Niagara River into Canada West. For two days, sporadic fighting continued between the Fenian soldiers and the Canadian militia and British soldiers. The final battle took place at Ridgeway, near Fort Erie. On June 3 the Fenians withdrew across the border. This was the last serious attack by the Fenians, although they continued to threaten Canada until 1870. These Fenian raids contributed to the pro-Confederationists' electoral victory in New Brunswick in 1866, and to increased support for union in Canada West.

Confederation Opposed and Accepted

In New Brunswick the anti-Confederationist government of A.J. Smith that took office in 1865 ran into considerable difficulties shortly thereafter. Smith's government contained many conflicting interests and lacked internal unity.

The first blow came in the autumn of 1865, when R.D. Wilmot and T.W. Anglin, two of Smith's ablest cabinet ministers, resigned. Wilmot was converted to the support of Confederation during a visit to the Canadas in September 1865. Anglin left for another reason: he opposed his government's decision to assist a private company to build an important provincial railway. (He wanted the New Brunswick government itself to construct it). A second blow came in November when the Smith government lost an important by-election in York Country to Charles Fisher. The win in York was interpreted as a victory for the pro-Confederation forces, especially since the government of the Canadas had contributed handsomely to Fisher's campaign fund. Finally, Smith failed in his bid to persuade

Why Nova Scotia and New Brunswick Joined Confederation

Why did the two Maritime provinces of Nova Scotia and New Brunswick, which appeared to have so little to gain from union and in which opposition to Confederation was so pronounced, agree in the end to join with the Canadas? This question has generated considerable debate. In the 1920s, when separatist sentiments were strong in the region, Maritime historians focussed on the opposition to Confederation. They explained it in terms of the desire on the part of local communities to maintain the status quo and the absence among them of any feeling of identity with the distant communities of the Canadas. In other words, an inherent conservatism prevailed that worked against Confederation. How, then, did these historians account for Confederation? In "New Brunswick's Entrance into Confederation" (Canadian Historical Review, 9 [1928]: 4–24), George Wilson attributed the success of the pro-Confederationists in the election of 1866 to the Fenian raids (which led many New Brunswickers to fear for the security of their colony) and to the financial contribution of the Canadas to the election campaign. William Menzies Whitelaw stressed the manipulative tactics of the Canadian politicians at the Quebec Conference of 1864 that won Maritime leaders over to Confederation.

In the 1960s, historians believed that the greatest pressure for union came from Britain and the United States. In *The Idea of Continental Union* (Lexington, 1960), Donald Warner emphasized the American military threat along with British imperial pressure as the decisive factors in overcoming Maritime opposition to union. P.B. Waite argued

that Confederation was "imposed on British North America by ingenuity, luck, courage, and sheer force" (*The Life and Times of Confederation, 1864–1867* [Toronto, 1962], p 323).

Waite also added a new explanation. Writing on the eve of the Canadian centennial, he interpreted the Maritimers' support for Confederation as a desire to overcome parochialism by becoming part of a larger and greater transcontinental nation. In other words, he believed that a nascent Canadian nationalism was stirring. Kenneth Pryke later challenged this assumption. "Support for union ... did not always indicate a broadsighted vision," he wrote in *Nova Scotia and Confederation 1864–1871*, (Toronto, 1979), "nor did opposition to it necessarily indicate a reactionary sectionalism" (p. 6). Instead, Pryke argued, acceptance of Confederation in Nova Scotia was simply an acquiescence to colonial realities—it was an acceptance of the inevitable.

Del Muise shifted the debate from politics (and the pressures exerted on Maritime politicians) to economics ("The Federal Election of 1867 in Nova Scotia: An Economic Interpretation," *Nova Scotia Historical Society, Collections* [1968], pp. 327–51). He noted that the political divisions that arose in Nova Scotia over Confederation coincided with the economic divisions that existed in the province. Anti-Confederationists were proponents of the old maritime economy based on "wood, wind and sail"—those who looked to Britain and the ocean for their livelihood—and pro-Confederationists were proponents of a continental economy—they were a younger generation who saw a better future for the province in railways, coal, and

419

industrialization. With regard to New Brunswick, Alfred G. Bailey associated the main opposition to Confederation with the "business fraternity who had been endeavouring for a decade to integrate the commerce of the province more closely with that of the United States" ("The Basis and Persistence of Opposition to Confederation in New Brunswick," *Canadian Historical Review*, 23 [1942]: 382–83). By implication, the supporters of Confederation envisioned a brighter economic future for the province within a Canadian transcontinental economy.

Other historians have seen the division between the anti- and the pro-Confederationists as a cultural one between native-born and British-born Maritimers. Ethnic historians have found the greatest opposition to Confederation among Irish Catholics and Acadians, and the strongest support among the English elite. There are, however, sufficiently significant exceptions to these generalizations to put their validity in question.

More recently, historian Phillip Buckner has shifted the debate away from the subject of opposition and toward that of the union. He notes that, "if one turns the traditional question on its head and asks not why were so many Maritimers opposed to Confederation but why so many of them agreed so easily to a scheme of union that was clearly designed by Canadians to meet Canadian needs and to ensure Canadian dominance . . ., then the Maritime response to the Canadian initiative looks rather different" ("The Maritimes and Confederation: A Reassessment," *Canadian Historical Review*, 71 [1990], pp. 14–15). Buckner points out how weak and ineffective Maritime opposition to Confederation was. He also argues that it would have taken more than external pressure to push the Maritimes into a union they did not really want, and concludes that there had to have been internal support for the cause. Buckner suggests that such popular support was evident in "those who equated consolidation with material progress and modernization" (p. 22). Thus, he calls for studies of the "intellectual milieu in which literary figures and the growing number of professionals functioned, of clerical thought, and indeed of changing views of the role and function of the state held by entrepreneurs and by other groups in society" in order to see to what extent support for Confederation came from those groups seeking "the emergence of larger and more powerful institutional units of government" (p. 23). This is indeed an area of study that has been neglected in Maritime historiography to date and that might shed new light on the ongoing debate about the Maritimes and Confederation.

420

the American government to renew the Reciprocity Treaty of 1854. In addition to these setbacks, Smith had to fight Governor Arthur Gordon who, at the British government's insistence, encouraged New Brunswickers to support Confederation.

In exasperation, the Smith government resigned in April 1866. In the ensuing election, Leonard Tilley made a skilful presentation to the people of New Brunswick on what they could expect from Confederation: lower taxes, the Intercolonial Railway, a fair share in the running of the nation, a market for their raw materials and manufactured goods, and hence, material progress and modernization. He and the pro-Confederates argued that union "will open up and colonize immense tracts of fertile lands . . . lying unreclaimed and desolate. It will multiply the sources of industry and intensify the demand for labour. It will tend to keep our young men at home and allure those of other lands to our shores." Such views were in keeping with the more-cosmopolitan attitudes that were becoming evident in the Maritimes by the mid-1860s.

Both parties benefited from external funds, with the anti-Confederates receiving money from Nova Scotia and probably the United States, and the pro-Confederates from the government of the Canadas. "Give us funds," a desperate Tilley cabled Macdonald. "It will require some $40 000 or $50 000 to do the work in all our counties." John A. Macdonald agreed, because he wanted to ensure that Confederation did not go down to defeat in New Brunswick simply for lack of money. Direct British intervention and threatened Fenian raids also assisted Tilley.

In the end, these various pressures, along with an ineffective campaign on Smith's part (he had lost his only viable alternative to Confederation— reciprocity with the United States), resulted in a resounding victory for Tilley. The victory came as the delegates were meeting in London to finalize the Confederation agreement. Tilley had the New Brunswick legislature accept the proposal without reference to the voters.

THE LONDON CONFERENCE

In the autumn and winter of 1866, delegates from Nova Scotia, New Brunswick, and the United Canadas met in London to prepare the passage through the British Parliament of the British North America Act. At London, the Quebec Resolutions served as the starting point for this last round of negotiations, and they were accepted as the final resolutions except for a few minor but significant changes. Rather than a "federation," the union would be known as a "confederation." Subsidies to the provinces would be increased beyond the agreed eighty cents a head by a fixed grant from the federal government. The contentious issue of separate schools, which had been heatedly debated in the legislature of the Canadas in the spring of 1865, was settled by applying the Quebec clause on education (which safeguarded the Protestant separate schools in Quebec) to all other provinces in the union, or to new provinces that had separate schools "by law" at the time they joined Confederation. Furthermore, religious minorities had the right of appeal to the federal government should their school systems, as they existed before Confederation, be threatened by the actions of a provincial government.

Right up to the time of Confederation, opposition continued in Nova Scotia. While the delegates met in London to finalize the terms of Confederation, Joseph Howe contacted British officials to try to convince them to reject the union. He denounced British and Canadian politicians as

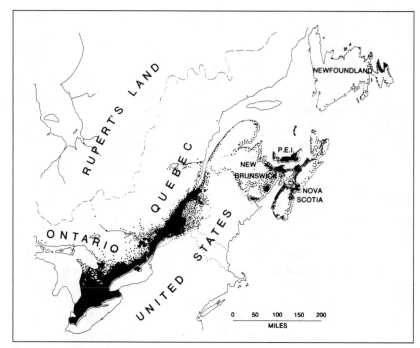

Source: Adapted from John Warkentin, *Canada: A Geographical Interpretation* (Toronto, 1968), 45.

The extent of settlement in Canada, 1867.

422

attempting to force Confederation against the popular will. The British government refused to retract its support, however, and when the British North America Act was signed on March 29, 1867, Howe returned to Nova Scotia cured "of a good deal of loyal enthusiasm" and embittered against the Canadians. He was not alone. Many Nova Scotians saw Confederation as the beginning of the end for Nova Scotia. Elsewhere, Confederation was accepted on July 1—although not with enthusiasm in Quebec.

The union became known as the Dominion of Canada. John A. Macdonald had preferred "Kingdom of Canada" to show a spirit of greater independence from Britain, but the British government vetoed the idea. Leonard Tilley had chanced upon the alternative title of "Dominion" as well as an appropriate motto for the new nation, *A Mari Usque Ad Mare* (From Sea to Sea), while reading Psalm 72:

> Let his dominion also be from sea to sea, and from river unto the world's end
> And blessed be the name of his majesty forever.

A new nation was born in North America.

NOTES

[1]P.B. Waite, "Confederation," in *The Canadian Encyclopedia*, 2d ed. (Edmonton, 1988), 1: 488.
[2]F.H. Underhill, *The Image of Confederation* (Toronto, 1964), 4.

Related Readings

R. Douglas Francis and Donald B. Smith, eds., *Readings in Canadian History: Pre-Confederation*, 3d ed. (Toronto, 1990) includes several important articles on the subject of Confederation: Jacques Monet, "True Blue, True Grit," 505–12; Del Muise, "Railroaded into Union," 512–17; Rosemarie Langhout, "About Face," 518–23; and James Hiller, "Confederation Defeated: The Newfoundland Election of 1869," 523–47.

BIBLIOGRAPHY

The three best general texts on Confederation are Donald Creighton, *The Road to Confederation: The Emergence of Canada, 1863–1867* (Toronto, 1964); W.L. Morton, *The Critical Years: The Union of British North America, 1857–1873* (Toronto, 1964); and P.B. Waite, *The Life and Times of Confederation, 1864–1867: Politics, Newspapers, and the Union of British North America* (Toronto, 1962). The Canadian Historical Association has issued a number of pamphlets on aspects of Confederation by leading scholars in their fields: J.M. Beck, *Joseph Howe: Anti-Confederate* (Ottawa, 1966); J.-C. Bonenfant, *The French Canadians and the Birth of Confederation* (Ottawa, 1966); P.G. Cornell, *The Great Coalition* (Ottawa, 1966); W.L. Morton, *The West and Confederation, 1857–1871* (Ottawa, 1962); P.B. Waite, *The Charlottetown Conference* (Ottawa, 1963); and W.M. Whitelaw, *The Quebec Conference* (Ottawa, 1966). Ramsay Cook has edited and written an introduction to *Confederation* (Toronto, 1967), a collection of interpretative essays on the subject. A recent collection is Ged Martin, ed., *The Causes of Canadian Confederation* (Fredericton, 1990). A good primary source is P.B. Waite, ed., *The Confederation Debates in the Province of Canada, 1865* (Toronto, 1963). A lively interchange among historians Phillip Buckner, P.B. Waite, and William B. Baker under the title "The Maritimes and Confederation: A Reassessment" appeared in the *Canadian Historical Review* 71 (1990): 1–45.

Confederation can also be studied through biographies of the protagonists; relevant biographies include D.G. Creighton, *John A. Macdonald*, vol. 1, *The Young Politician* (Toronto, 1952); J.M.S. Careless, *Brown of the Globe*, vol. 2, *Statesman of Confederation, 1860–1880* (Toronto, 1963); Brian Young, *George-Étienne Cartier: Montreal Bourgeois* (Kingston and Montreal, 1981); O.D. Skelton, *Life and Times of Sir Alexander Tilloch Galt*, rev. ed. (Toronto, 1966); and J.M. Beck, *Joseph Howe*, vol. 2, *The Briton Becomes Canadian, 1848–1873* (Kingston and Montreal, 1983). Important biographical sketches can be found in the volumes of the *Dictionary of Canadian Biography* devoted to the late nineteenth century.

On the Maritime provinces and Confederation in 1867, see Kenneth Pryke, *Nova Scotia and Confederation, 1864–1871* (Toronto, 1979); W.S. MacNutt, *New Brunswick: A History, 1784–1867* (Toronto, 1962); F.W.P. Bolger, *Prince Edward Island and Confederation, 1863–1873* (Charlottetown, 1964); H.B. Mayo, "Newfoundland and Confederation in the Eighteen-Sixties," *Canadian Historical Review* 29 (1948): 125–42. On Quebec, see J.-C. Bonenfant, *La Naissance de la Confédération* (Montréal, 1969); and Marcel Bellavance, *Le Clergé québécois et la Confédération canadienne de 1867* (Sillery, Québec, 1992). On Ontario, see D. Swainson, *Ontario and Confederation* (Ottawa, 1967).

On the American and British influence on Confederation, consult Robin Winks, *Canada and the United States: The Civil War Years* (Montreal, 1960); John A. Williams, "Canada and the Civil War," in *Heard Round the World: The Impact Abroad of the Civil War*, edited by H. Hyman (New York, 1969); C.P. Stacey, *Canada and the British Army, 1841–1871*, rev. ed. (Toronto, 1963) and Ged Martin, "An Imperial Idea and Its Friends: Canadian Confederation and the British," in *Studies in British Imperial History: Essays in Honour of A.P. Thornton*, edited by G. Martel (New York, 1985), 49–94.

Time Line: 1864–1867

1864 —Political deadlock in the Canadas and the formation of the Great Coalition to work toward British North American federation.

—Canadian and Maritime delegates discuss a possible plan for union at the Charlottetown Conference, in September.

—The terms of British North American federation are agreed upon at the Quebec Conference, in October.

1865 —The Canadian legislature approves the Quebec Resolutions, but only a narrow majority of the French Canadian members endorse them.

—Premier Leonard Tilley is defeated by anti-Confederationists in New Brunswick's election.

—The Americans announce the termination of the Reciprocity Agreement, effective in 1866.

1866 —A Fenian invasion of New Brunswick is threatened, and the Fenians make raids on the Canadas.

—Leonard Tilley's pro-Confederation party is successful in a second election in New Brunswick.

1867 —The British North America Act is passed, and the Dominion of Canada is created by the colonies of New Brunswick, Nova Scotia, Canada East, and Canada West.

—Canada's population is 3.5 million. John A. Macdonald becomes Canada's first Prime Minister.

Index

427

435

437

441

To the Owner of this Book:

We are interested in your reaction to *Origins: Canadian History to Confederation*, 2nd ed., by Francis, Jones, and Smith. With your comments, we can improve this book in future editions. Please help us by completing this questionnaire.

1. What was your reason for using this book?
   — university course
   — college course
   — continuing education course
   — personal interest
   — other (specify)

2. If you used this text for a program, what was the name of that program?

3. Which school do you attend?

4. Approximately how much of the book did you use?
   — 1/4   — 1/2   —3/4   — all

5. Which chapters or sections were ommitted from your course?

6. What is the best aspect of this book?

7. Is there anything that should be added?

8. Please add any comments or suggestions.

(fold here)

tape shut